This first-class commentary reveals admirable clarity of expression. Allan Ha is very reliable and he faces difficulties i them helpfully. His comments on the l―――― ―――――― ―――― are particularly good and he is very sensitive to features like assonance and alliteration. In fact, his illuminating comments may stimulate some readers to learn Hebrew, although this is not necessary for understanding his book. His commitment to *Isaiah's* unity of authorship and its majestic and moving testimony to Christ is shown as he traces the development of its great themes through its pages.

Dr Geoffrey Grogan

Professor Harman's commentary on the Book of Isaiah is outstanding. What I mean by that is that he has been able to do the work of a first class exegete, yet make it understandable to a wide audience. It is difficult to rub both sides of that exegetical coin, yet Professor Harman succeeds admirably. As I train my theological students in the prophets of the Bible and in the prophecy of Isaiah, in particular, I will send them to this book immediately.

Prof. John D. Currid
Carl McMurray Professor of Old Testament
Reformed Theological Seminary, Jackson

With Allan Harman's 'Isaiah' before me, I know what the saying means that 'even a cat can look at the queen'! His work has made me wish wholeheartedly that I could start all over again. The detailed interpretative work is superb, and Harman's defence of the unity of Isaiah is robust (to say the least), and, in my view, unanswerable. I thrill to a commentator whose prime aim is to understand and explain the Hebrew Text, not just to distil the opinions of others. Thank God for this book – and its author!

Alec Motyer

Other books in this series

ISAIAH

A COVENANT TO BE KEPT
FOR THE SAKE OF THE CHURCH

'Allan Harman's 'Isaiah' has made me wish wholeheartedly that I could start all over again. The detailed interpretative work is superb.'
Alec Motyer

ALLAN HARMAN

CHRISTIAN FOCUS

To the students
of the Presbyterian Theological College, Melbourne
1975-2001
with whom I studied the prophecy of Isaiah

Copyright © Allan M. Harman 2005

ISBN 1-84550-053-9

Published in 2005
by
Christian Focus Publications, Geanies House,
Fearn, Ross-shire, IV20 1TW, Scotland.

www.christianfocus.com

Cover design by Alister Macinnes

Printed and bound by
CPD, Wales

Contents

Part 2: Historical Transition (36:1–39:8)

Part 3: The Book of Comfort (40:1–66:24)

Abbreviations

ANE	*The Ancient Near East,* 2 vols., ed. J. B. Pritchard (Princeton: Princeton University Press, 1973).
AV	Authorised (King James) Version
BASOR	*Bulletin of the American Schools of Oriental Research*
IBHS	*An Introduction to Biblical Hebrew Syntax,* Bruce K. Waltke and M. O'Connor (Winona Lake: Eisenbrauns, 1990).
CHAL	*A Concise Hebrew and Aramaic Lexicon of the Old Testament* (Grand Rapids: Eerdmans, 1988).
DCH	*Dictionary of Classical Hebrew,* ed. David J. A. Clines (Sheffield: Sheffield Academic Press, 1993-).
DOTT	*Documents from Old Testament Times,* ed. D. W. Thomas (Edinburgh: Thomas Nelson, 1958).
ESV	English Standard Version
GKC	*Gesenius' Hebrew Grammar,* 2nd ed., Gesenius, Kautsch, Cowley, eds. (Oxford: Clarendon Press, 1966).
1QIsa[a]	A complete manuscript of the book of Isaiah found among the Dead Sea Scrolls.
1QIsa[b]	An incomplete, and poorly preserved, manuscript of the book of Isaiah found among the Dead Sea Scrolls.
JB	Jerusalem Bible
JBL	*Journal of Biblical Literature*
JETS	*Journal of the Evangelical Theological Society*
LXX	The Septuagint, the oldest and most important Greek translation of the OT made in Egypt about 250 BC.
mg.	margin
ms(s)	manuscript(s)
MT	Massoretic Text, the Hebrew text of the Old Testament that became recognised as authoritative after the fall of Jerusalem in 70 AD.
NASB	New American Standard Bible
NBD	*New Bible Dictionary,* ed. J.D. Douglas (London: Inter-Varsity, 1962).
NEB	New English Bible
NIDOTTE	*New International Dictionary of Old Testament Theology and Exegesis,* ed. Willem A. VanGemeren, 5 vols. (Grand Rapids: Zondervan, 1997).
NIV	New International Version
NKJV	New King James Version
NRSV	New Revised Standard Version
part.	participle
REB	Revised English Bible

RSV	Revised Standard Version
RTR	*Reformed Theological Review*
SJT	*Scottish Journal of Theology*
TB	*Tyndale Bulletin*
TWOT	*Theological Wordbook of the Old Testament*
VT	*Vetus Testamentum*
WTJ	*Westminster Theological Journal*

Note: When referring to passages in the Old Testament in which the covenant name of God occurs (*yhwh*), the form 'LORD' is used. This is in accordance with the practice of English versions, the form 'Lord' being reserved for the translation of words other than *yhwh*.

Glossary

bulla An impression stamped on a piece of soft clay (and then hardened) used to seal documents.

Dead Sea Scrolls About 800 scrolls containing all or part of Old Testament books discovered at or near Qumran, on the north-western side of the Dead Sea.

fixed pair The term 'fixed pair' refers to words that regularly occur in parallel expressions in Hebrew, e.g. head/skull, earth/dust, mouth/lip.

hapax legomenon A word occurring only once. (pl. *hapax legomena*)

inclusio A literary device by which a repeated theme both introduces and concludes a passage, so marking it as a separate section.

Qere A Massoretic marginal note to the Hebrew text meaning 'that which is to be read' (in place of 'that which is written', the Ketiv).

stela An upright stone monument bearing an inscription.

targum An Aramaic translation or paraphrase of some part of the Old Testament. They were oral at first but were later written. The earliest examples (from Qumran) are from the second century BC.

theophany A visible appearance of God.

trisagion The threefold declaration of God's holiness ('holy, holy, holy').

The Period of Isaiah

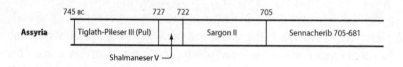

Assyria

745 BC	727	722	705	
Tiglath-Pileser III (Pul)		Sargon II	Sennacherib 705-681

Shalmaneser V

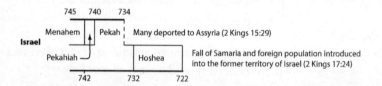

Israel

745   740   734

Menahem | Pekah | Many deported to Assyria (2 Kings 15:29)

Pekahiah

Hoshea | Fall of Samaria and foreign population introduced into the former territory of Israel (2 Kings 17:24)

742   732   722

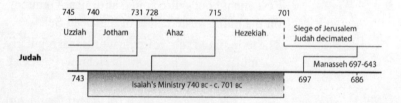

Judah

745 740   731 728   715   701

Uzziah | Jotham | Ahaz | Hezekiah | Siege of Jerusalem Judah decimated

Manasseh 697-643

743   Isaiah's Ministry 740 BC - c. 701 BC   697   686

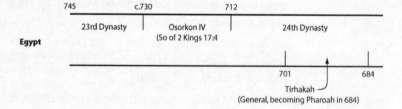

Egypt

745   c.730   712

23rd Dynasty | Osorkon IV (So of 2 Kings 17:4 | 24th Dynasty

701   684

Tirhakah
(General, becoming Pharoah in 684)

Foreword

This is the third major Old Testament book on which I have been privileged to comment, all of which have been published by Christian Focus Publications (*Psalms* in 1998 and *Deuteronomy* in 2001). As with my previous books I acknowledge my indebtedness to many previous writers whom I have read over the years, and whose views have now become part of my own thinking and are indistinguishable from it.

As is the case with my other commentaries I have considered it my main aim as a commentator to set out the meaning of the Hebrew text for modern readers. I do not think a commentator's role is simply to give a distillation of the views of previous commentators. Hence, while I have had many commentaries near at hand as I have written, yet I have found it more beneficial at the early stages of writing to refer much more to Hebrew lexicons and dictionaries such as the *Theological Wordbook of the Old Testament* and the *New International Dictionary of Old Testament Theology and Exegesis*. Hebrew grammars such as *Gesenius-Kautzsch-Cowley* and the magisterial *Introduction to Biblical Hebrew Syntax* by Waltke and O'Connor have been indispensable. At a later stage of writing I have referred to other secondary literature on Isaiah, both books and journal articles, and some of these are documented in footnotes.

Two other commentators on Old and New Testament books respectively have clearly taken a similar approach to my own. The late Dr. Allan MacRae, when writing on Isaiah 40:1–58:8, said this:

> Most commentaries tend to repeat one another's mistakes, and they often jump to conclusions based on the presuppositions of their writers. There is no great profit in playing one off against another. Some commentaries contain useful discussions of linguistic points; others present helpful devotional material. It is rare for one to attempt that comparative study of Scriptural passages that forms a vital part of the approach to this study.[1]

A similar approach has also been taken in regard to writing New Testament commentaries by Dr. Leon Morris. He has described his own method as follows:

> When it comes to the actual writing of the commentary, I find it best to

---

[1] Allan A. MacRae, *The Gospel of Isaiah* (Moody Press, 1977), p. 188.

work through either the whole book or a section of it writing furiously but without making any reference to other commentaries nor for that matter articles or general works. This gets onto paper what the book means for me and it means that the final shape of the book is my own, not a pale adaptation of some other writer who has impressed me. It may be that some other writers are more strong-minded than I, but I find that if in this first stage I refer to other writers I tend insensibly to be influenced by what they say. So at this stage I write out of my own head, with the comforting assurance that this draft is invariably headed for the waste paper basket anyway.[2]

I have chosen, therefore, to try and deal with the difficulties in the translation and interpretation of Isaiah. Progress in solving these problems depends upon the on-going work of commenting on the text. Too often modern commentaries have become a discussion between commentators, rather than an exposition of the text. It is also true that the task of explaining and expounding the Scriptures must be a constant commitment for the church. We have to wrestle with the texts before us (and many difficult passages occur in Isaiah), and depending upon the aid of the Holy Spirit, we have to attempt to set out our understanding of the passages with which we are dealing. A corollary of this is that exegesis is the task of the whole church, not just those who are professionally trained for biblical study.

Each day as I began work on Isaiah I prayed for the illumination of the Holy Spirit. It is surprising how few books on hermeneutics have a section devoted to the ministry of the Spirit, but in coming to Holy Scripture we must recognise that we need spiritual enlightenment ourselves if we are to open up the Scriptures for others. After prayer, I read the appropriate passage in Hebrew, and also listened to it on tape. Often I heard things that my eye had missed when reading it. Aural reception of the text enables one to listen to features like alliteration and assonance and also to hear interconnections within the passage. Then I started to comment on the section, trying to ensure that I covered every verse. While I had hoped to spend more space on wider issues such as literary structure, I came to the conclusion that the greatest usefulness of this book would be if I could explore the Hebrew text and attempt to set out my understanding of its meaning.

---

[2] This quotation is taken from Dr. Leon Morris' discussion, 'On Writing a Commentary', *The New Testament Student at Work*, vol. 2, John H. Skilton, ed., p. 179.

Two friends—Bernard Secombe and Gregory Goswell—have helped by reading the manuscript and it is the better for their queries and suggestions. Another friend, David Assender, has helped with the diagram and map. My wife Mairi has either read the whole manuscript or listened to me reading it as we worked through Isaiah in our evening devotions. Without her help and encouragement completion of the book would have taken much longer.

Allan M. Harman

Suggestions for Further Reading

G. W. Grogan, 'Isaiah' , *Expositors' Bible Commentary* (Zondervan, 1986), Vol. 6, pp. 1-354.

H. C. Leupold, *Exposition of Isaiah*, 2 vols. in one (Evangelical Press, 1977).

Allan A. McRae, *The Gospel of Isaiah* (Moody Press, 1977).

J. A. Motyer, *Isaiah: An Introduction and Commentary* (Tyndale OT Commentaries: Inter-Varsity Press, 1999).

J. A. Motyer, *The Prophecy of Isaiah* (Inter-Varsity Press, 1993).

John N. Oswalt, *The Book of Isaiah: Chapters 1–39*; *The Book of Isaiah: Chapters 40–66* (Eerdmans, 1986, 1996).

August Pieper, *Isaiah II, An Exposition of Isaiah 40-66* (Milwaukee: Northwestern Publishing House, 1979).

Thomas, Derek, *God Delivers: Isaiah Simply Explained* (Welwyn Commentary Series, Evangelical Press, 1998).

Barry Webb, *The Message of Isaiah* (The Message of the Bible Series, Inter-Varsity Press, 1996).

Herbert M. Wolf, *Interpreting Isaiah: The Suffering and Glory of the Messiah* (Zondervan, 1985).

E. J. Young, *The Book of Isaiah*, 3 vols. (NICOT, Eerdmans, 1972).

Ronald F. Youngblood, *The Book of Isaiah: An Introductory Commentary*, 2nd ed. (Baker Book House, 1993).

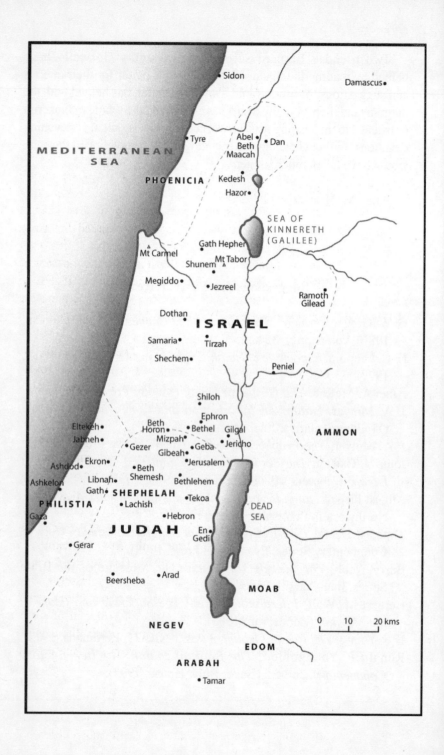

Introduction

1. Isaiah and His Ministry

1.1 Isaiah the Prophet

The name Isaiah (Heb. *y^{e}sha 'yâhû*) means 'the LORD is salvation', and his name symbolises his message.[1] He was the son of *Amoz* (not to be confused with *Amos* the prophet, as the spelling of the two names differs). The medieval Jewish commentator Kimchi claimed that Amoz was the brother of Amaziah, the father of Uzziah. If this is true, then Isaiah was of the royal line, and this would fit in with the fact that he had access to the king. It is clear from his prophecy itself that he came from a family of some rank, as we can infer from his close relationship with the king (7:1-17) as well as his close intimacy with the priest (8:2).

Isaiah was married with at least two sons. The first one, Shear-yashub, had a name whose word order suggests that it meant '[only] a remnant shall return' (7:3), and the name of the other, Maher-shalal-hash-baz, means 'hasting to the spoil, hurrying to the prey' (8:2, 3). While the first son had a name that gave a glimmer of hope for the nation in mention of a remnant, yet it pointed to the coming disaster. The name of the second son referred to Assyria's lust for conquest. These names, as also his own, embodied Isaiah's message to Judah and Jerusalem.

The dates of his birth and death are unknown. He commenced his ministry in 740/739 BC, the year that king Uzziah died (Isa. 6:1). He was a spokesman for the LORD at the time of the Assyrian campaign in 701 BC, and notes Sennacherib's death in 681 BC (Isa. 37:38). Though Jewish tradition claims he was sawn asunder during Manasseh's reign (cf. Heb. 11:37), no reliable evidence is available to corroborate this. Manasseh became co-regent in 696 BC (and sole ruler in 686 BC). Apart from Isaiah's reference to Sennacherib's death, there is no mention in the biblical text of continuing ministry by Isaiah after 701 BC.

---

[1] The first part of the name can hardly be regarded as meaning 'Yah saves', as the verbal form of this root does not occur in the Qal stem in Hebrew.

1.2 Isaiah and His Fellow Eighth Century BC Prophets

A cluster of prophets operated in Israel and Judah in the eighth century BC: Jonah, Hosea, Amos, Isaiah and Micah. There are several reasons why the eighth century was important for both kingdoms. The kingdom of Judah had very significant kings in that century, including Joash, Uzziah, Ahaz, and Hezekiah. In the north there was a succession of short reigns and the only major king was Jeroboam II. In both kingdoms there was great stability because of the long reigns of Jeroboam II (793–753 BC) and Uzziah (792–740 BC). Probably in the case of Uzziah there must have been regencies at each end of his reign, so that he was sole ruler for no more than seventeen years (767–750 BC).[2] The biblical text calls Uzziah both Azariah ('Yah has helped') and Uzziah ('Yah is my strength'). Possibly the former was his throne name and the latter his personal name.

Little information about the achievements of either Jeroboam II (Israel) or Uzziah (Judah) is given. Clearly there was a long period of peace between the two kingdoms, if not a formal treaty arrangement. Israel and Judah came to a peak of prosperity and influence during the reigns of these kings. Most of the territory held by Solomon was again under combined Israelite/Judahite control. 2 Kings 14:25 notes that Jeroboam II restored the boundaries of Israel from Lebo Hamath to the Dead Sea, as Jonah, son of Amittai, had prophesied. The book of 2 Kings gives little information regarding Uzziah, except for the statement that he rebuilt Elath and restored it to Judah (2 Kings 14:22), which meant in effect control over Edom. However, 2 Chronicles 26:1-22 spells out in some detail the reign of Uzziah, including his attack on the Philistines and the building of new Jewish settlements in their territory (2 Chron. 26:6-7). He was a great farmer ('he loved the soil', 2 Chron. 26:10) and he pushed settlements down into the Negev area. The fact that Uzziah made the Ammonites subject to him (2 Chron. 26:8) has often been questioned. But we know from Assyrian sources that a leader of the coalition of Syrian-Palestinian states against Tiglath-Pileser III of Assyria was led by an 'Az-ri-a-u' of 'Ia-u-d-a', who has often been identified with Azariah/Uzziah of Judah.[3] What this statement of 2 Chronicles 26:8 does tell us is not only of the growing

---

[2]This is according to the calculations of E. R. Thiele, *The Mysterious Numbers of the Hebrew Kings* (The Paternoster Press, 1951), pp. 93-97.

[3]See D. J. Wiseman in *DOTT*, pp. 54-57.

power of Judah, but the serious weakening of Israel that was to lead to her demise in 722 BC. This is revealed by the fact that previously Ammon had been under the control of *Israel*, not Judah.

With control re-established over the trade routes, wealth began to accumulate, and this was reflected in the personal possession of the people and their luxurious homes (cf. for example passages such as Amos 6:1-7; Isa. 3:18-23). Clearly the narrative in 2 Kings and 2 Chronicles does not fully detail the prosperity in the two kingdoms, nor on the other hand the basic discontent in society. The scope of the military expeditions suggests wealth for army supplies, but the main knowledge of the period comes from the prophets of the mid-eighth century – Hosea, Micah, Amos and Isaiah.

Economic class levels became very clearly marked in both countries. This is shown by the varied housing that has been unearthed at Tirzah (the capital of Israel before the building of Samaria by Omri) and the references in the prophets to economic, social and moral conditions. Isaiah's catalogue of female finery in Isaiah 3:18-26 points to a high level of income among the upper classes and also a very sophisticated society. Other passages in the early chapters of Isaiah also point in the same direction (see 1:23; 5:8; 10:1-3). While Isaiah was a city dweller, Micah lived in the country and he describes how the wealthier classes took advantage of the poorer classes and maltreated them (Mic. 3:1-3). The situation in the north was similar, as rich owners of vineyards had found ways of appropriating vineyards, like Naboth's, without breaking the law (see Amos 2:6-8).

Assyrian domination was signified by the rise of Tiglath-Pileser III. The impact of Assyria on Israel/Judah and all the other nations of the Near East was to be very great. Jonah was sent to Nineveh, the capital of Assyria, with a message of judgment from the LORD. The temporary repentance of Assyria may have delayed Assyrian conquest of Israel until much later in the century when Samaria fell in 722 BC.

Israel/Judah faced severe external attacks during the eighth century. First, there was the Syro-Ephraimitic War of 734 BC. Rezin of Aram and Pekah of Israel attempted to force Judah into a coalition to oppose Tiglath-Pileser of Assyria. The aim was to depose Ahaz and to put Tabeel in his place (Isa. 7:6). Ahaz responded to the crisis by sending messengers to Tiglath-Pileser announcing that he was his servant and vassal (*'avd^{e}kâ ûvin^{e}kâ 'ânî*, 2 Kings 16:7), and showing this by taking the silver and gold from the Temple and from the treasuries in the palace and sending them to Tiglath-Pileser (2 Kings 16:8). The result was that Tiglath-Pileser invaded Aram, capturing Damascus, deporting people, and killing Rezin (2 Kings 16:9). Likewise Assyria attacked Israel, taking Gilead and Galilee, and deporting many of the inhabitants (2 Kings 15:29).

The second major crisis was the siege and subsequent fall of Samaria in 722 BC. Pekah was assassinated by Hoshea in 732 BC (2 Kings 15:30), who, after the death of Tiglath-Pileser in 727 BC, withheld his tribute money and turned to Egypt for help. The new Assyrian king, Shalmaneser V, attacked Israel and finally after a three-year siege Samaria fell to Shalmaneser's successor, Sargon II, in 722 BC (2 Kings 17:3-5; 18:9-11). This was the final act in the history of the northern kingdom of Israel. People were imported and settled in the former Israelite territory, replacing those taken away into captivity (2 Kings 17:24).

The third military episode was the Assyrian Crisis of 701 BC. When Sennacherib succeeded his father in 705 BC, several subject peoples, including Judah, revolted. Sennacherib attacked Judah, and when he was at Lachish, Hezekiah sent him tribute money. He continued with his attack, but was repulsed by the direct intervention of God (for the two accounts of the crisis, see 2 Kings 18:13–19:37; Isa. 36–37).

The days of crisis for Israel and Judah brought the prophets to the fore with their messages from the LORD. The people had to listen to proclamation that challenged and rebuked. Many of the prophetic messages of judgment are couched in terms that echo the covenantal curses of Leviticus 26 and Deuteronomy 28. While the prophets denounce the people for their sins, they also hold out the hope of blessing and restoration (cf. Amos 9:11-15; Isa. 9:2-7; Isa. 11:1-16).

Not only did the prophets speak God's word to the people, they wrote it, which is in marked contrast with the earlier prophets, like Elijah and Elisha, who themselves left no *written* records. Two main factors seem to be involved with this change to written messages. First, internationalism was becoming far more important. The Assyrian empire reached its peak in the period of Ashurbanipal (668–626 BC), but that was after a century of expansion of the Assyrian empire under his predecessors. This was also a significant period for the development of international relationships, especially through treaties. These treaties were written and the vassals included the general populace. When a treaty was broken, a royal messenger was sent to declare the impending judgment or application of the covenant curses on the rebellious people. In the biblical text there is one notable incident concerning a royal messenger and that is the account of the Rabshakeh (the name of an office, though treated as a personal name in the biblical accounts) who comes on Sennacherib's orders to bring a message to Hezekiah (2 Kings 18:17–19:19, and the parallel in Isaiah 36–37). When we look at the passage there are difficulties because of the change in persons speaking or being addressed (the second person addressee changes to plural in 2 Kings 18:22; Hezekiah is referred to in the third person while the Rabshakeh is referred to in the first person, verses 24, 25). The best explanation of the difficulties is that an official written decree lies behind the Rabshakeh's oral presentation. This may well have been the pattern: a written document which was then given fuller oral explanation. It is significant that the writing prophets emerge at this very period of Near Eastern history. There was a growing sense of international consciousness, with emphasis on contact between the Great King and subject kings and peoples by means of written and oral proclamation by messengers.

The second significant factor was the growth of popular literacy. The emergence of written prophecy could only take place in the context of general literacy of the people to whom the prophecies were addressed. The Gezer calendar (ninth–tenth century BC) is probably a schoolboy's attempt, or else from someone whose writings skills were not well developed, as the script is awkward. Many seals have been found, and the significant thing is that by the seventh century they only contain the name of the owner, without any pictorial representation. That means that literacy was becoming widespread, and hence writing could be used both to record prophetic speeches and to distribute them among the general population. The fact that Isaiah was a scribe is noted by the Chronicler (2 Chron. 26:22), who also refers his readers to the work of Isaiah for additional information about the deeds of Hezekiah (2 Chron. 32:32).

2. Interpreting Isaiah as Poetry
In approaching the book of Isaiah we are confronted immediately with the fact that the majority of the book is prophecy, written in poetic form. The longest prose sections are the largely historical narratives in 6:1–9:7 and 36:1–39:8. This means that in addition to setting out hermeneutical rules for interpreting prophecy, account must be taken

of the poetry and its features that complicate interpretation.

The poetry in Isaiah shares the same marks that distinguish other poetic sections of the Old Testament from prose. These include non-predictable word order, figurative language, the use of parallelism, the presence of acrostics, unusual and older vocabulary, assonance and alliteration, and imagery in the form of metaphors and similes. Some of these features can also appear in prose, which means that the dividing line cannot be drawn sharply between prose and poetry. The distinction between them is one of degree.[4]

Some additional comment is called for in connection with the features of assonance and alliteration. Though there was growing literacy in Israel/Judah in the eighth century BC, yet for many people the reception of Isaiah's message must have been aural. This means that we have to take special note of the repeated use of assonance and alliteration in Isaiah's prophecies, for these must have been important factors in capturing the attention of hearers. Here are some transliterated examples taken from chapters 24–27:

24:3   *hibbôq tibbôq hâ'ârets v^ehibbôz tibbôz*
        'the earth will be utterly laid waste and utterly plundered'.

24:16   *bog^{e}dîm bâgâdû ûveged bog^{e}dîm bâgâdû*
        'The treacherous betray! With treachery the treacherous betray!

24:17   *pachad vâpachat vâpâch 'âlekâ yôshêv hâ'ârets*
        v^ehâyâh hannâs miqqôl happachad yippôl 'el
        *   happachat*
        v^ehâ'ôleh mittôk happachat yillâkêd bappâch
        'fear, and the pit, and the snare are on you, O inhabitant of the earth. And it shall be that the one who flees from the noise of the fear shall fall into the pit, and he who comes up from the midst of the pit shall be caught in the snare.'

25:6   *Mishtêh sh^{e}mânîm mishtêh sh^{e}mârîm sh^{e}mânîm*
        m^{e}muchâyim sh^{e}mârîm m^{e}zuqqâqîm
        'a feast of rich food, a feast of choice wine, choice food full of marrow, choice wine well refined.'

---

[4]See my commentary on *Psalms* (Fearn: Christian Focus, 1998), pp. 10-13, for a brief discussion on the nature of Hebrew poetry.

27:7   *hakk^emakkat makkêhû hikkâhû 'im k^ehereg h^arugâv horâg*
        'like the smiting of the one who smote him did he smite him?'

Another major factor that complicates interpretation of Old Testament poetry is the difficulty in distinguishing precise time changes.[5] Unlike most Western languages, which have a tense system built into the verbal structure, Hebrew verbs (and the same applies to other Semitic languages) are concerned rather with aspect. That is, in narrative Hebrew verbs express whether an action is regarded as complete or incomplete. If complete, then an English verb in the past tense may be appropriate, but at times a present or even a future tense will be required by the context. Similarly, if the action is incomplete, normally (but not invariably) an English future tense will be appropriate.

The situation is even more complex in Hebrew poetry for the two verbal conjugations (often designated by the forms *qatal* and *yiqtol*) are used almost interchangeably, and many aspects of use have still to be investigated thoroughly. In general, context must determine how we understand the tenses in a particular section of poetry, and the consequence is that interpretation must often be tentative in so far as time is concerned. One of the best discussions on this problem is that by Peter Craigie, who wrote:

> . . . it is evident that there can be no simple rule of thumb with respect to the appropriate English tense which may be indicated by the forms of the Hebrew verb. In practice, the context is the principal guide to determining the most appropriate translation, but difficulties arise precisely because context, in nonhistorical poetic texts . . . may leave room for considerable ambiguity and uncertainty.[6]

3. Interpreting Isaiah as Prophecy
In coming to the book of Isaiah we are approaching one of the major prophetical books of the Bible. A cursory reading of the text should alert us to the fact that its style is quite different from the historical books like Joshua or 2 Samuel, and some basic principles need to be

---

[5]On the wider questions of time dimensions in prophetic literature, see the discussion by John P. Milton, *Prophecy Interpreted : Essays in Old Testament Interpretation* (London: Geoffrey Chapman, 1974), pp. 77-108.

[6]Peter Craigie, *Psalms 1-50* (Waco: Word, 1983), p. 111.

kept in mind as the interpretative task is undertaken.[7]

Old Testament prophecy is something far different from history written beforehand. There is a complexity about it that puts it in a different category altogether. At times it contains what appears to be straight-forward messages, but intermingled are many that puzzle, and our interpretation has to be provisional. Exactly the same will apply to our interpretation of the book of Revelation. Prophecy was meant to speak first to the generation who originally received it. It was directed to a precise setting in biblical history that is often alluded to in the prophetic word. However, in reference to the future the descriptions often lack precision, as exemplified in the phrases 'in that day' or 'in those days'.

Prophecy is also difficult to interpret because much of its language cannot be understood by a word for word translation into another language. That is partly because it is given principally in poetic form (see the preceding discussion on 'Interpreting Isaiah as Poetry'), but also because it includes symbolism that needs identification before any sure conclusions can be drawn as to its meaning. The problem is highlighted by reference to passages such as Isaiah 7:18 where the LORD is pictured whistling to the flies and bees, or Isaiah 27:1 with reference to the judgment to come on Leviathan, 'the gliding serpent', or to the identification of the 'destroyer/traitor' in Isaiah 31:1. Biblical prophecy may puzzle us, but it also puzzled those who transmitted it, for they enquired and searched diligently regarding the nature and timing of the sufferings of Christ and the subsequent glory (1 Pet. 1:10-11).

This also means that prophecy was intended by God to be a combination of what is plain intermingled with messages that are ambiguous or multifaceted. The children of God need encouragement regarding the future, but do not need to know with absolute precision everything that is going to take place. There is an important place for faith in the believer's life, with a forward view to future demonstrations of God's grace and power. The general pattern is clear; the precise

---

[7]For fuller discussion of principles of prophetic interpretation, readers should consult Douglas Stuart's concise contribution in Gordon Fee and Douglas Stuart, *Reading the Bible for All Its Worth* (Zondervan, 1993), pp. 172-86; Walter Kaiser Jr., 'What About the Future? The Meaning of Prophecy', in Walter C. Kaiser Jr. and Moisés Silva, *An Introduction to Biblical Hermeneutics: The Search for Meaning* (Zondervan, 1994), pp. 139-58.

outworking is not revealed.

The revelation of God in the Old Testament is progressive, prospective, and preparatory. That is, not all of God's message for mankind was revealed at first, but progressively over a long period of time. Moreover, at each stage of revelation indications are given that greater disclosures of God's will are to come. It also becomes clear with the prophets that all that has happened up to their day is preparatory for the fuller appearance of God's grace and power in new covenant days. This approach means, of course, that the Old and New Testaments are taken as parts of the unified revelation of God, and that the believing community is basically the same in both.[8]

4. The Structure and Unity of the Book of Isaiah[9]

While the book of Isaiah has often been regarded by critical scholarship as a composition of at least three major sections (chapters 1–39, 40–55, 56–66), the last thirty years has seen a major change in emphasis. This is partly because of the influence of Brevard Child's 'canonical criticism' that seeks to emphasise the final form in which a biblical book has come down to us. Thus R. E. Clements can claim that though editorial stages in the formation of the book of Isaiah can be discerned, yet 'all these considerations are sufficient to indicate that the overall structure of the book shows signs of editorial planning and that, at some stage in its growth, attempts were made to read and interpret the book as a whole'.[10] Similarly W. L. Holladay writes: 'Yet beyond all our awareness of the *contrasts* between what comes before chapter

---

[8]For discussion of this point, consult the comments of John L. Mackay in his revised and expanded volume on *Haggai, Zechariah, Malachi* in this same series (*Focus on the Bible*: Fearn, 2003), pp. 349-54.

[9]For much fuller discussions on the unity of Isaiah, recent introductions and commentaries should be consulted such as: W. S. LaSor, D. A. Hubbard, and F. W. Bush, *Old Testament Survey: The Message, Form, and Background of the Old Testament*, 2nd ed. (Eerdmans, 1996), pp. 281-88; R. B. Dillard and Tremper Longman III, *An Introduction to the Old Testament* (Zondervan, 1994), pp. 268-83; John N. Oswalt, *The Book of Isaiah Chapters 1-39* (NICOT: Eerdmans, 1986), pp. 17-28. See also the recent survey on the subject by Gregory R. Goswell, *'My eyes have seen the King': Kingship, Human and Divine, in the Book of Isaiah with Special Reference to Isaiah Chapters 36-39*, Ph.D. thesis, The University of Sydney, 2001, pp. 1-32.

[10]R. E. Clements, 'The Unity of the Book of Isaiah', *Interpretation* 36 (1982), p. 121.

40 and what comes in and after it, contrasts of authorship and of life situation, there is also a curious *unity* which we can perceive'.[11]

This unity in the book of Isaiah extends to language and themes. It has often been pointed out that virtually all the major themes occur in summary form in the opening chapter, and are developed in greater detail as the book progresses. Phrases like 'the holy one of Israel' occur throughout, while themes such as divine kingship and the creator/ redeemer recur with great frequency. Even when Isaiah has the exilic situation especially in view in chapters 40 onward, the standpoint from which he writes is still Palestine in the eighth century BC.[12] References to trees, for example, are those that are typical of Palestine, not Babylon.[13] Moreover, linguistic evidence points to a pre-exilic date for chapters 40–66, a section so often dated by critical scholarship as coming from the post-exilic period.[14] Isaiah is able to address the two basic questions that the exile will raise: 'Is Israel's God *truly* God (as compared with the Babylonian ones)?', and 'Will God forgive the sin of his people and resume fellowship with them?'

The opening and closing of the prophecy are also critical markers of a unified structure for the whole book. In chapter 1 sinful and rebellious Jerusalem is introduced. Her condition is described as a sickness that affects the whole body. While a call to repentance, with the assurance of acceptance with God, goes out, yet it is only much later in the book that the servant of the LORD is depicted as the one who can heal her condition (for discussion on the repetition of language in chapter 53 that first occurs in chap. 1, see the commentary on 53:4). The opening of the book has its counterbalance the concluding pictures of a New Creation (65:17-18) that results in a New Jerusalem (66:20-24). The message, then, of the book of Isaiah relates to the way in which God is going to purify his people through judgment and

---

[11]W. L. Holladay, *Isaiah: Scroll of a Prophetic Heritage* (Eerdmans, 1978), p. 40.

[12]J. Barton Payne discussed this in detail in 'Eighth Century Israelitish Background of Isaiah 40–66', *WTJ* 29 (1966-67), pp. 179-90; 30 (1967-68), pp. 50-58, 185-203.

[13]Robert L. Alden, 'Isaiah and Wood', in John H. Skilton ed., *The Law and the Prophets: Old Testament Studies Prepared in Honor of Oswald Thompson Allis* (Presbyterian and Reformed Publishing Co., 1974), pp. 377-87.

[14]Mark F. Rooker, 'Dating Isaiah 40–66: What Does the Linguistic Evidence Say?' *WTJ* 58 (1996), pp. 303-12.

restore them into a close covenant relationship with himself. Jerusalem's character will be so changed that she will be in the centre of God's kingdom that will embrace Jews and Gentiles in the one fold.

Various parts of the book of Isaiah are marked off by particular groupings of associated messages (such as the messages against the nations in chapters 13–23, or the historical interlude in chapters 36–39). All through the book there is the interplay of historical and eschatological themes, so that an outline of the book can be set out as follows:[15]

1–12	History and Eschatology
13–23	History
24–27	Eschatology
28–33	History
34–35	Eschatology
36–39	History
40–55	Eschatology
56–66	History and Eschatology

While the exile and beyond is the focus of chapters 40–66, yet the exile is also prominent in the earlier parts of the prophecy. Isaiah and his contemporaries were familiar with the idea of exile. Amos announced God's message: 'Therefore I will send you into exile beyond Damascus,' says the LORD, whose name is God Almighty' (Amos 5:27), while in Hosea God's plan for Israel is stated in these terms: 'Therefore I am now going to allure her; I will lead her into the desert and speak tenderly to her' (Hos. 2:14).

Isaiah's reference to ruined cities and the people being taken far away is important both in itself and for the fact that it comes in his inaugural vision (6:11-12). In the previous chapter he anticipates the exile as he proclaims a series of 'woe' oracles. The LORD's declaration is: 'Therefore my people will go into exile for lack of understanding' (5:13). Redemption from exile is also a common theme in the first main section of the prophecy (chaps. 1–12), as it also is in the writings of Isaiah's contemporaries. In chapter 11 he mentions how God is to do something a second time (11:11), when Israel and Judah will be re-united (11:13) following the new exodus (11:16). Similar statements

---

[15]I am following the scheme set out by W. J. Dumbrell, 'The Purpose of the Book of Isaiah,' *TB* 36 (1985), p. 123.

were made by Isaiah's contemporary Amos (see especially 9:9-15). Another contemporary, Micah, also spoke of exile in Babylon and redemption from there: 'Writhe in agony, O Daughter of Zion, like a woman in labour, for now you must leave the city to camp in the open field. You will go to Babylon; there you will be rescued. There the LORD will redeem you out of the hand of your enemies' (Mic. 4:10, NIV).

When the exile is spoken about by Isaiah it is not only Assyria that is named but also Babylon. This is so particularly in chapter 39 in reference to the Babylonian envoys who come to visit Hezekiah (39:1-3). The question that Isaiah asks of the king is not, 'Where did they come from?', but, 'Where are they coming from (*yâvô'û*)?' The way the question is phrased may suggest a succession of 'comings' from Babylon. Isaiah's response to Hezekiah's statement regarding the extent of the visit is to warn of the future event when not only the treasures of the king's palace but also the king's sons will be carried away to Babylon (39:5-7). Isaiah looks even beyond Assyria and Babylon to the Medo-Persian empire, for in 13:17 he refers to the Medes being stirred up against Babylon, while in 21:9 he looks further ahead still to the fall of Babylon.

Little evidence for the writing of a prophetic book such as Isaiah exists. Clearly literacy was widespread, as has already been pointed out, and on occasions in the book of Isaiah the prophet himself is instructed to write (8:1; 30:8). Moreover, from references in the historical books it is clear that Isaiah was one of those recording the history of Judah. He wrote of Uzziah's actions (2 Chron. 26:22) and also of Hezekiah's acts and good deeds (2 Chron. 32:32). No extant evidence tells of how the entire book we know as the prophecy of Isaiah was finally compiled. Sections of it may have existed separately, but in the final composition there is unity and purpose. Within individual sections there is evidence of careful planning and structure. For example, chapters 7–11 contain parallel messages to Judah and Israel, while chapter 6 forms a prologue to the section, and chapter 12 an epilogue. The pattern in this section is:[16]

---

[16]This is based on J. A. Motyer, 'Context and Content in the Interpretation of Isaiah 7:14', *TB* 21 (1970), pp. 118-25.

1. Prologue 6:1-13

	Judah	Israel
2. The Moment of Decision	7:1-17	9:8–10:4
3. The Judgment	7:18–8:8	10:5-15
4. The Remnant	8:9-22	10:16-34
5. The Glorious Hope	9:1-7	11:1-16

6. The Epilogue 12:1-6

Another section is found in the last twenty-seven chapters consisting of three parts, each of which concentrates on a key figure, and each rounded off with a refrain. This division was noted long ago in E. W. Hengstenberg's *Christology* where he commented in this way:

> The fact . . . it is divided into *three sections or books*, is, in the first instance, indicated by circumstances that at the close of chap. xlviii. and chap. lvii., the same thought recurs in the same words: 'There is no peace, saith the Lord, unto the wicked;' and that same thought, viz., the exclusion of the wicked from the promised salvation, is found also a third time at the close of the whole, although there in another form.[17]

The three sections are as follows:

Chapters 40–48
Central Figure: Cyrus
Refrain: 'There is no peace', says the LORD, 'for the wicked' (48:22).

Chapters 49–57
Central Figure: The Servant of the Lord
Refrain: 'There is no peace', says my God, 'for the wicked' (57:21).

Chapters 58–66
Central Figure: The Spirit-Filled Messiah
Refrain: An announcement is made regarding the lack of peace: 'All mankind will come and bow down before me', says the LORD. 'And they will go out and look upon the dead bodies of those who rebelled against me; their worm will not die, nor will their fire be quenched, and they will be loathsome to all mankind' (66:23-24).

It is impossible to set out the process by which the varied prophetic messages that Isaiah delivered were finally integrated in inscripturated form as we now have them. Presumably his messages were remembered, but also committed to writing. Either Isaiah himself or some other person inspired by the Holy Spirit brought them together in the form they have come to us. Perhaps the recording in Holy Scripture of Jesus' words and deeds by the disciples parallels what happened in the formation of the book of Isaiah. The structure of the whole book can be set out in this way:

Part 1: The Book of Judgment (1:1–35:10)

A. Introduction: Judah Rebuked—The Covenant Broken (1:1-31)
1. Title (1:1)
2. Thoughtlessness (1:2-9)
3. Formalism (1:10-20)
4. Judgment and Salvation (1:21-31)

B. Future Glory for Judah and Jerusalem (2:1–4:6)
1. The Glory of the Eschatological Days (2:1-5)
2. Jerusalem's Future Exaltation (2:6–4:1)
3. Jerusalem's Eventual Purification (4:2-6)

C. Judah's National Sins (5:1-30)
1. The Parable of the Vineyard (5:1-7)
2. Six Woes (5:8-23)
3. The Assyrian Invaders (5:24-30)

D. The Book of Immanuel (6:1–12:6)
1. Isaiah's Vision (6:1-7)
2. Isaiah's Commission (6:8-13)
3. God's Word to Judah (7:1–9:7)
4. God's Word to Israel (9:10–11:16)
5. The Epilogue (12:1-6)

---

[17]E. W. Hengstenberg, *Christology of the Old Testament* (McLean, Virginia: McDonald Publishing Company, reprint n.d.), vol. 1, p. 507. He attributes the observation to a Roman Catholic priest, Fr. Rückert.

E. Burdens against the Gentile Nations (13:1–23:18)

F. World Judgment and Israel's Redemption (24:1–27:13)

G. A Cycle of Prophetic Warnings (28:1–33:24)

H. Additional Promises of Judgment and Blessing (34:1–35:10)

Part 2: Historical Transition (36:1–39:8)

A. The Assyrian Siege of Jerusalem (36:1–37:38)

B. Hezekiah's Sickness and Recovery (38:1-22)

C. The Prediction of the Babylonian Exile (39:1-8)

Part 3: The Book of Comfort (40:1–66:24)

A. Israel's Restoration and Return (40:1–48:22)

B. The Messianic Salvation (49:1–57:21)
  1. The Second Servant Song (49:1-7)
  2. The Restoration of Israel (49:8–50:3)
  3. The Third Servant Song (50:4-11)
  4. The Joy of Restoration (51:1-16)
  5. Jerusalem's Preparation for the Returned Exiles (51:17–52:12)
  6. The Fourth Servant Song (52:13–53:12)
  7. Glorious Zion (54:1-17)
  8. The Gracious Invitation (55:1-13)
  9. Incorporation of Others in God's Redemption (56:1-8)
  10. Adulterous Israel (56:9–57:13)
  11. Comfort for the Contrite (57:14-21)

C. The Ultimate Salvation (58:1–66:24)
  1. The Marks of God's People (58:1-14)
  2. Redemption for Penitent Israel (59:1-21)
  3. The City of the LORD (60:1-22)
  4. The Fifth Servant Song (61:1-9)
  5. The Saviour Comes! (61:10–62:12)
  6. The Day of Vengeance (63:1-6)
  7. God the Father and Redeemer (63:7–64:12)
  8. A Patient and Compassionate God (65:1-16)
  9. The New Heaven and the New Earth (65:17-25)
  10. Distinguishing True and False Worshippers (65:1-24)
  11. Zion Triumphant (66:1-24)

5. The Significance of the Book of Isaiah

The prophecy of Isaiah marks a highpoint in prophetic ministry in the Old Testament. It is clear that the development of the prophetic office went hand in hand with the institution of kingship in Israel. The prophets were guardians of the theocracy,[18] and they maintained the principle that the LORD was the king, and Israel was committed to exclusive reliance on him. They were covenant enforcement messengers, as they proclaimed the blessings and curses set out in the law (cf. Lev. 26 and Deut. 28). Those ministering from the time of Samuel to the middle of the eighth century BC did so by oral communication, and their message to the nation was one of repentance and conversion.

---

[18]The English word 'theocracy' is borrowed from the Greek *theokratia*, 'government by God', a word probably coined by the Jewish historian Josephus (born around AD 37).

With Isaiah and his contemporaries two changes took place. On the one hand, they not only spoke but their messages were committed to writing. On the other hand, the content of their messages changed too, for they said that God was not only going to act as he did previously, as at the Exodus, but that he was going to do something far greater. They knew that, 'not repair, but regeneration of the present lies in the womb of the future'.[19]

The doctrinal teaching is striking, doubly so because it is couched in such passionate language. Form and content are inextricably interconnected. Often, though, as is typical of the prophets in general, the argument is not always in strict logical order or sequence. Rather the argument centres around major themes that are looked at from different angles. Reference is made to the same basic truths time and time again. Isaiah's prophecies are unique in that they cover greater scope than any of the other Old Testament prophecies. His vision is the entire progress of God's kingdom that will culminate in a new heavens and a new earth in which a new humanity will dwell. Nature itself will be transfigured, when 'the creation itself will be set free from its bondage to decay and obtain the freedom of the glory of the children of God' (Rom. 8:21, NIV).[20] All in all, 'Isaiah sums up biblical theology in a better way than does any other single book of the Bible.'[21]

History and eschatology are intermingled throughout the book but appear in paired format especially in the opening and closing sections (chapters 1–12 and 56–66). The Holy One of Israel will purify his people through judgment and bring them into a renewed experience of the covenant relationship. The glory of the LORD will fill the whole of creation, for 'the fulness of the earth is [nothing but] his glory' (Isa. 6:3). Even Israel/Judah in exile must know that their God is indeed the creator/redeemer and in him 'all the offspring of Israel shall be justified and shall glory' (Isa. 45:25). The closest parallels to Isaiah's prophecies

---

[19]Geerhardus Vos, *Biblical Theology: Old and New Testaments* (Banner of Truth Trust, 1974), p. 189.

[20]For recent discussions on theology of Isaiah, see John N. Oswalt, *The Book of Isaiah Chapters 1–39*, pp. 31-44; John N. Oswalt, 'Isaiah, Theology of', *NIDOTTE*, 4, pp. 725-32; Thomas Constable, 'A Theology of Isaiah' in Roy B. Zuck, *A Biblical Theology of the Old Testament* (Moody Press, 1991), pp. 305-40; Paul R. House, *Old Testament Theology* (InterVarsity, 1998), pp. 272-98.

[21]John N. Oswalt, 'Isaiah, Theology of,' *NIDOTTE*, 4, p. 732.

in the Bible are undoubtedly parts of the Pauline epistles, and Romans in particular.

> In both there is the same deep impression of the infinite majesty and absolute sovereignty of Jehovah, the same intense conviction of the awfulness of the divine justice and the inexorable nature of its claims, the same overwhelming sense of the insignificance, the unworthiness, the helplessness of sinful man, the same insistence upon the exclusive activity of God in the work of salvation, the same prominence on the idea of faith, the same abounding trust in the marvelous, condescending grace of God, the same unlimited and illimitable faith in the world-embracing scope of the divine purpose.[22]

The number of quotations from and allusions to Isaiah that appear in the New Testament is striking.[23] Approximately one-third of the New Testament is made up of direct quotations or indirect allusions to the Old Testament,[24] and of the Old Testament books the Psalms and Isaiah are those drawn upon most often. About twenty times Isaiah is cited by name, and these quotations come from twelve different chapters spread throughout the book. In consecutive verses in John 12, Isaiah 6:10 and 53:1 are quoted with application to Jesus, for, as John comments, 'he saw his [Jesus'] glory and spoke about him' (John 12:41). Of Isaiah 53, all but one verse is quoted in the New Testament.

This use of the book of Isaiah draws attention to the continuity of biblical revelation between Old and New Testaments. Jesus' own public ministry began with a sermon on Isaiah 61 in which he made the

---

[22]Geerhardus Vos, 'Some Doctrinal Features of the Early Prophecies of Isaiah', in Richard Gaffin, Jr., ed., *Redemptive History and Biblical Interpretation: The Shorter Writings of Geerhardus Vos* (Presbyterian and Reformed Publishing Co., 1980), p. 287. Vos goes on to suggest that if the line of continuity is traced back from Calvin to Augustine, and from Augustine to Paul, then another step can be taken into the old dispensation and to recognise that the line commences with Isaiah. Walter Kaiser Jr., *Towards an Old Testament Theology* (Zondervan, 1978), p. 212, similarly draws the parallel between Isaiah and Paul, saying that chapters 40–66 'are as close to being a systematic statement of OT theology as is the book of Romans in the NT'.

[23]Convenient listing of Old Testament quotations in the New Testament, and allusions and verbal parallels, occurs in *The Greek New Testament*, 4th rev. ed. (Stuttgart: Deutsche Bibelgesellschaft, 1994), pp. 887-901.

[24]For details, see Andrew E. Hill, *Baker's Handbook of Bible Lists* (Baker Book House, 1981), pp. 102-04.

declaration: 'Today this Scripture has been fulfilled in your hearing' (Luke 4:21). Clearly he set the interpretative model for exegesis of the Old Testament by the teaching he gave to his disciples, as he instructed them about everything written concerning him in the Law of Moses, the Prophets, and the Psalms (Luke 24:44). This teaching was that given in his ministry prior to his death, and as the disciples were enabled by the work of the Holy Spirit to remember what was said (John 14:26), they preached and taught accordingly.

Not surprisingly a book like Isaiah features prominently in the apostolic writings of the New Testament Scriptures. It constitutes one of the 'building blocks' utilised by the apostles as they drew upon the Old Testament and integrated its teaching with the newer revelation given by Jesus. Nowhere is this more evident than in the book of Revelation. Out of 348 allusions in it to the Old Testament, the largest number from any book is 79 from Isaiah.[25] With heavy dependence on Isaiah, John depicts the two great cities, Babylon and Jerusalem. Babylon will fall, but the city of God, the New Jerusalem, stands, and in so doing marks out the consummation of history. What Isaiah had prophesied so long before will reach fulfilment. Those from all nations and tongues will come to the eternal city that God calls 'my holy mountain Jerusalem', and there they will see the Lord's glory (Isa. 66:18-20). Reading and using the prophecy of Isaiah should direct the vision of God's people to the one city that will remain. All others will vanish, for the heavenly Jerusalem is not to be created from any earthly city. Rather, it will be part of the 'new things' that God does, and this will be marked by the fact that 'the holy city, new Jerusalem' will come *down* from the new heavens (Rev. 21:2). The believing church must wait expectantly for that dwelling place, and sing:

> How lovely is that city,
> The home of God's elect!
> How beautiful the country,
> That eager hearts expect!
> Jesus, in mercy bring us
> to that eternal shore;
> Where Father, Son and Spirit
> are worshipped evermore.
>
> Bernard of Cluny, 12th century.

Part I

The Book of Judgment
(1:1–35:10)

A. Introduction: Judah Rebuked –
The Covenant Broken (1:1-31)

1. Title (1:1)

The whole of chapter 1 is a prologue to the entire book, with many of the distinctive themes developed later appearing here in embryonic form. It is balanced by the final chapter 66, which forms an epilogue to Isaiah's prophecies. These chapters have in common twenty-eight Hebrew terms, and they also share the same images. The pictures of sinful Jerusalem in chapter 1 are followed by a reference to a new Jerusalem that will be called 'the City of Righteousness' (1:6). This theme is expanded in the epilogue with the call to rejoice over Jerusalem (66:10, 14) and the promise of an ingathering from the nations that will come to the holy mountain in Jerusalem (66:20).

The opening verse appears to be the title of the whole book, for though there are later headings (for examples, see 2:1; 13:1) there is no other passage that notes Isaiah's ancestry or the reigns in which he worked. He was the son of Amoz, who is not to be confused with the prophet Amos, as the spelling is different. Isaiah 'saw' (Heb. *châzâh*), that is, he received supernatural revelation, and the book purports to be the vision (Heb. *châzôn*, from the same root as the verb) that he was given. It concerns Judah and Jerusalem, the main areas of Isaiah's ministry, though the book does contain messages concerning the northern kingdom of Israel (see the use of the term 'Israel' immediately in verse 3). No date is given, but the devastation noted in verse 8 may be when Assyria had denuded territory around Jerusalem and was threatening the city itself (see 2 Kings 18:13-16 and 19:25, 26). Later, in what appears to be an account of Isaiah's call (chapter 6), it is noted that the call came in the year in which Uzziah died. That puts the earliest date of his work at 740/39 BC, and while Hezekiah died in 687/86 BC Isaiah may not have prophesied down to that date. Clearly he knew the circumstances about Uzziah's reign, because it is recorded in 2 Chronicles 26:22 that 'the rest of the acts of Uzziah from beginning to end, are recorded by the prophet Isaiah son of Amoz'. Isaiah's ministry, however, covered over forty years or more in a momentous period for Judah (see the commentary on later chapters such as 7:1-17 and 36:1–39:8).

2. Thoughtlessness (1:2-9)

In the Ancient Near East, treaties or covenants were frequently made between countries. Covenants of this type also appear in the Old Testament, along with bonds between individuals, and bonds between God and his people Israel. All of these are designated by the Hebrew word for covenant (*b^{e}rit*). In the prophetic books of the Old Testament there are various passages that resemble a court scene, in which God challenges his people because of their breach of his covenant stipulations (see Jer. 2:9-19; Mic. 6:1-8). This passage also displays the pattern of a covenantal lawsuit judgment. There is much similarity between it and Deuteronomy 32, and perhaps it is even modelled on it. There are three parties involved:

Judge	—	The LORD
Defendant	—	Israel
Witnesses	—	Inanimate nature

2 Appeal is made to the heavens and earth to act as witnesses to the charge that is being presented (cf. the same invitation in Deut. 32:1; Jer. 2:12), for indeed the covenant God has spoken. The defendant is the nation, likened here to children whom the LORD has reared (cf. Exod. 4:22-23; Hos. 11:1-4). Instead of responding in love the children spurned the LORD and were covenant rebels. The verb used here for 'rebel' (Heb. *pâsha'*) is one of the technical terms used in the Old Testament for covenant violation.

3 The utter thoughtlessness of the people is contrasted with the ox and the donkey that know their masters. On the other hand, God's people, who should have known their LORD, remain ignorant of him. Lack of understanding will later be given as one of the basic reasons why exile was the fate of the people (see Isa. 5:13).

4 God's people are addressed using the Hebrew term (*gôy*) that is normally reserved for the Gentile nations. The appeal is prefaced by the particle *hôy*, 'woe', a word that is only used in prophetic books and most commonly to introduce an oracle of doom. Four terms are used to characterise the nation, depicting it as burdened by its sin and perverse in all its ways. The name by which God is designated is 'the Holy One of Israel', a name that is almost distinctive to Isaiah (26 times, with only 6 occurrences elsewhere). A trilogy of verbs is used to emphasise the severing of the bond between the LORD and his people.

They have forsaken, spurned and turned their backs on him. 'To forsake' (*'âzav*) is one of the most common Hebrew verbs denoting a breach of the covenant (over 100 times), and it is linked here with synonymous verbs 'to spurn' (*nâ'ats*) and 'to turn the back' (*zûr*). The third verb is rarer than the others, but it does occur in Ezekiel 14:5 denoting, as here, alienation from God. All the terms point to a people who with deliberation have turned from the LORD.

5-6 Isaiah now begins to describe in detail the nation's sinful state. The opening question seems to refer to judgments already sent to convince them of their guilt, but yet there was no change in their attitude. They persisted in their rebellion and so are like a person who is desperately and totally sick—head, heart, soles of the feet. There is no indication whether the wounds are from illness or from injuries received in battle. Everywhere in the body there are the signs of wounds that are incurable, and no medication has been applied to them. There is a striking similarity here with Isaiah 53, where the afflictions of the servant of the LORD are described in terms that echo this passage. Apart from a general similarity the following verbal connections are notable, though they are obscured in most English translations:

Isaiah 1	**Isaiah 53**
smitten (verse 5)	smitten (verse 4)
sick (verse 5)	sicknesses (verse 4)
bruises (verse 6)	bruised (verse 5)

The LORD lays on the servant the guilt and iniquity of the people (53:6).[1]

7 Possibly this is a reference to the Assyrian invasion and the stripping bare of the country. Certainly the description is of invasion by a foreign army, and the resulting devastation. The word used for 'strangers' is from the same verb already appearing in verse 4 (NIV 'they turned their back'; the verb *zûr* basically has the idea of alienation or estrangement). There does not seem to be any real difference in meaning between the word here and the more common Hebrew word for 'stranger' (*nokrî*). The point is that Israel is subject now to foreign domination, having been 'overthrown' (all the six other occurrences of this word are applied to Sodom and Gomorrah; see also the mention

---

[1] Two further verbal connections with Isaiah 53 occur in verse 11. See comment on that verse.

of these cities in verse 9). Instead of the land supporting the people of Israel, it is providing crops as food for foreigners.

8 The description of Jerusalem is now 'daughter of Zion' (Heb. *bat tsîyyôn*). Various explanations have been given of this expression. 'Daughter' is used in a similar way with other cities or countries (cf. 'daughter of Tyre' [Ps. 45:12]; 'daughter of Babylon' [Ps. 137:8]; 'daughter of Edom' [Lam. 4:21]), and so the expression is best regarded as a personification of Zion/Jerusalem. The city represents the whole nation, and the phrase serves to emphasise the father/daughter relationship between God and the city he had chosen (see Pss. 2:6 and 132:13-14). A remnant remains, but it is likened to a booth in a field, like a hut in a field of melons, like a besieged city. All of these comparisons speak of the precarious position of what is left of the city and nation. The 'booth' (Heb. *sukkâh*) denotes a temporary shelter, such as those built for 'the feast of booths' (see Lev. 23:34). A 'hut in field of melons' describes a temporary outdoor shelter. It may even have been a hammock to provide shelter from wild animals for those guarding crops at night. Jerusalem is indeed besieged, and not in a position to defend herself, but the fact that she is not totally destroyed is a hint of mercy that becomes explicit in the following verse.

9 The mercy element lies in the fact that the survival of a few is due to the intervention of the LORD of hosts. He had insured that not all the nation perished. Isaiah comes back repeatedly to the idea of a remnant who are not obliterated by God's judgment (see examples in 4:3; 6:11-13; 46:3). This is the first of sixty-two occurrences of the title 'LORD of hosts' in Isaiah. While 'LORD' (Heb. *yhwh*) may be a genitive ('LORD of ...'), it is also possible that the words 'LORD' and 'hosts' stand in apposition. That is, they stand side by side, and the translation will then be, 'the LORD, the all-powerful king', or, 'the LORD, the mighty warrior'.[2] It is clear that 'LORD of hosts' became a special exalted title for God at the close of the period of the judges (see its use in 1 Sam. 1:3). It also points to his universal kingship (see its use in Isa. 6:5 and Ps. 84:3). Unless God had shown mercy the people would have been like Sodom and Gomorrah, the cities that perished under his judgment. This verse is quoted by Paul in Romans 9:29 in a context in which he is dealing with how God has made known his glory to vessels of mercy. Unless this 'holy seed' (see Isa. 6:13) had been preserved, the nation

---

[2]See the discussion by John Hartley in *TWOT* II, pp. 750-51.

would have resembled Sodom and Gomorrah both as to degeneracy and also merited judgment.

3. Formalism (1:10-20)

These verses spell out what God requires of his worshippers. The many offerings they bring are insufficient without accompanying heart sincerity. While the people think they are worshipping the LORD, yet he will not accept their meaningless sacrifices.

10 The similarity of Jerusalem to these ancient cities is continued. The call to hear the word of the LORD goes out as if the people in Isaiah's day are actually the infamous Sodom and Gomorrah. A word of warning and judgment is directed to them that they are called to heed.

11 Multiplicity of sacrifices did not avail with God. This is the same message that Isaiah's eighth century BC contemporary, Amos, brought to the northern kingdom before its fall. He even presented them with a command to come to Bethel and Gilgal with their sacrifices and sin (Amos 4:4-5)! It is not that God removes the demand for sacrifice on the part of the people, as the following verses make clear. Even if they bring the best of animals they will not be acceptable, because outward formality is an attempt to disguise their sinful lives and lack of heart religion. Two more words in this verse are picked up again in Isaiah 53. The LORD has had more than enough (Heb. *sâva'*) of their sacrifices, whereas the servant of the LORD will be well satisfied with his own sacrificial offering (53:11). While God is here *displeased* (Heb. *lô' châfâtstî*, 'I have no pleasure') with the offerings of Israel, in the fourth servant song the LORD *has pleasure* in bringing his chosen one through his vicarious suffering and death (53:10).

12 The rejection of their sacrificial activities extends even to their presence in the temple courts. Because their lives are totally inconsistent with their pretence of worship, they are merely trampling in those courts. The Hebrew verb 'to trample' (*râmas*) is normally used of acts of judgment whereby oppressors come and trample on the land and its crops. Here it signifies a presence in the temple courts that is without sincerity or acceptance.

13 The divine command now is that no more futile offerings are to be presented. Even incense is an 'abomination' (Heb. *tô'êvâh*), a word that is used repeatedly in the Old Testament to describe heathen worship practices (see Deut. 18:9; 1 Kings 14:24; 2 Kings 16:3; 2

Chron. 33:2). Israel's religious practices are no better in God's sight than those of the idolatrous Gentiles. Special times of worship—new moon, Sabbath, and special holiday seasons—are no longer pleasing to the LORD. He declares that he is unable to endure such wickedness and the communal gatherings that marked out the close of the harvest festivals.

14 New moons and appointed assemblies have become hateful to the LORD. The first of these was a celebration on the first day of the month, while appointed assemblies embraced a wide range of special feasts, including passover, feast of weeks, and tabernacles (see Exod. 23:14-17). Instead of being a pleasure they are a burden to the LORD, and instead of being a joy he is utterly tired by them. The continuing denunciation of the worship being practised emphasises how abhorrent it is to the LORD. What should have been a joy to him has become something totally unacceptable as the people persist in their hypocritical presentation of prescribed worship.

15a-c The formality of prayer is practised, but God refuses either to take notice of their actions or to listen to their words. They are no better in this regard than Gentiles, who think that their many words will compel attention by God (see Jesus' words in the Sermon on the Mount, Matt. 6:7). The idea that God, when dealing in wrath with his people, does not listen to their prayers is developed later in this book (see 8:17; 45:15; and 59:2).

15d-17 The real character of the people is spelt out, with the instruction to amend their sinful ways. They are guilty of murder, living unrighteous lives, and taking advantage of the oppressed. In particular they are accused of dealing falsely with the widows and orphans, the most underprivileged group in their society. The only way in which they can put things right with God is to be cleansed and purified. They must desist from doing wrong, learn how to administer just judgment, and defend the cause of the oppressed. Not only does Isaiah say this, but God's word came later through Jeremiah with similar denunciation (see Jer. 22:17). Both Isaiah and Jeremiah are building upon Deuteronomy 28. If blessing is to come to the people, there has to be repentance and the resolution to act with appropriate righteousness in their dealings with others. The same care and protection of widows and orphans is commanded in the New Testament (Jas. 1:27).

18 God appeals to his people to come and enter into a legal disputation with him. The call is softened by the addition of a particle (Heb. *nâ'*) that adds a touch of gentle entreaty. Most English versions bring this out by the addition of the word 'now'; 'Come *now*' (AV, RSV, NKJV, NIV). The verb 'to reason' is a legal term that appears in covenant lawsuit passages such as this one (cf. its use in Mic. 6:2). It does not just mean entering into a discussion. Rather, it conveys the idea 'let us argue our case in court', and thus is virtually equivalent to the word 'contend' (Heb. *rîv*). The lives of the people are stained by their sins, which have been mentioned in the preceding verses. However, what is 'scarlet' and 'crimson' can be changed to 'snow' and 'wool'. This indicates the radical nature of God's forgiveness (cf. Ps. 51:7 for the same use of 'snow' as an indication of how complete is God's forgiveness), provided that true repentance is shown, as the following verse indicates.

19-20 The connection between these verses and the preceding one is clear in the Hebrew text, though concealed somewhat in English translations. Four times the word 'if' (Heb. *'im*) occurs:

> *If your sins are as scarlet . . .*
> *If they are red as crimson . . .*
> *If you are willing and obedient . . .*
> *If you resist and rebel . . .*

Providing the people have a heart to obey they will listen and do what God requires. Then they will find abundant provision for their needs, eating the good things of the land. 'Good things' or 'goodness' can be used to designate the blessings bestowed under a covenant relationship.[3] However, if they persist in their rebellion they themselves will be devoured by the sword. There is a play on the double use of the word 'eat': either they eat the good things, or else they themselves will be eaten. The verse closes with the declaration that the mouth of the LORD has spoken, a repetition with slight variation from what was said in verse 2, so forming an *inclusio*.

---

[3] See in particular A. R. Millard, 'For He is Good', *TB*, 1966, pp. 115-17, and the literature which he cites. For fuller discussion of the covenant significance of the Hebrew words for 'good' and 'goodness', see P. Kalluveettil, *Declaration and Covenant: A Comprehensive Review of Covenant Formulae from the Old Testament and the Ancient Near East* (Rome: Biblical Institute Press, 1982), pp.42-47.

4. Judgment and Salvation (1:21-31)

The marriage metaphor appears here for the first time in Isaiah, as Jerusalem is said to have proved false to the LORD and has become a harlot. There is hope for her, however, for God indicates that she can again become a faithful city, a city of righteousness. A sad description is given of moral degradation that emphasises all that has been already said. The outcome of the issue in relation to God's grace may be seen as Paul expressed it of Antioch in Pisidia in Acts 13:46: 'seeing you thrust it [the word of God] from you and judge yourselves unworthy of eternal life'.

21 The opening word of the verse is a particle (Heb. *'êkâh*) that is used in rhetorical questions to express horror and amazement (cf. its frequent use in the book of Lamentations and especially as the first word of that book). The contrast between past and present is stated in absolute terms – a faithful bride has become a prostitute, a city in which justice reigned has become one characterised by murder. Jerusalem, of course, is used as a synonym for Judah.

22 The refining process is drawn upon to describe the change in the city. Dross was skimmed off in refining so as to leave the silver. Here the imagery is of a precious metal that has become something that is worthless. Another analogy is taken from viticulture, for the choicest wine has become something quite different since water has been added to it. These illustrations reinforce the dramatic change that has happened to Jerusalem.

23 The leaders of the people come in for severe condemnation. Princes become rebels and their love of money shows itself in the way they ally themselves with thieves, and obtain more gain by taking bribes. Perversion of justice was a characteristic of Jerusalem in this period, as Isaiah, Amos and Micah all record (Mic. 3:9-11; 6:8; Amos 5:12). They are accused, however, of more than false justice. When abuses in society involved widows and orphans these leaders failed to take appropriate action and defend their cause (cf. the positive command in verse 17). Two synonymous expressions are used to express legal action – 'to judge' (Heb. *shâfat*) and 'lawsuit' (Heb. *rîv*).

24 This verse is a turning point, as the introductory 'therefore' indicates. A solemn declaration is made by 'the Lord, the LORD of hosts, the mighty one of Israel'. The combination of titles draws attention to the character of the sovereign judge who is going to intervene on Jerusalem's behalf. 'LORD of hosts', already occurring in verse 9, is a title with military overtones, for 'hosts' (Heb. $ts^e v\hat{a}'\hat{o}t$) can refer to armies or to the heavenly hosts. Here it is preceded by another word for 'lord' (Heb. *'âdôn*) and followed by 'mighty one of Israel'. This last title goes back to Genesis 49:24 when Jacob used the expression 'mighty one of Jacob' in invoking a blessing on his son Joseph. There does not seem to be any difference in meaning between 'mighty one of Jacob' and 'mighty one of Israel'. Israel's enemies are God's enemies, and he declares that he will find comfort from their oppression and vindicate himself. This takes place in a preliminary way as God intervenes to set the record straight in human history, but the final vindication will only come on the day of God's vengeance (see Isa. 63:1-6).

25-26 Both these verses begin in Hebrew with the same verb: 'and I will turn'. In the first case God pledges that he will inflict judgment on his own people and carry out a refining process upon them. While the expression 'to turn the hand' against someone can be used in a positive way, here it clearly refers to judgment. The mention of 'dross' in verse 22 is picked up, and God declares that he will remove his people's dross. The parallel expression simply reinforces this idea: 'I will remove all your alloy', using a rare word that is roughly equivalent to 'dross'. In the second case 'I will turn' relates to restoration of justice in the land so that judges and counsellors will again be in evidence, as in the best days of the past. 'As at the first' and 'as at the beginning' are indeterminate expressions that should not be pressed to mean any specific period in the past. Following judgment, Jerusalem 'the faithful city' that has become a harlot (verse 21) will become 'the city of righteousness' (cf. Zech. 8:3 for another description of the restored Jerusalem as 'the city of truth').

27-28 These verses present a contrast that is going to be given attention throughout the book. There is a division within Israel between those truly committed to the LORD and the unbelieving part of the nation. This division will be dealt with in greater detail near the end of the book (see comments on 65:8-16). The godly are called 'Zion'//'her penitent ones'. The latter expression is another form of the verb 'turn' already used in both verses 25 and 26. It describes those who 'turn' to God in repentance and faith. The verb 'redeem' (Heb. *pâdâh*) only occurs four times in Isaiah, whereas another verb 'to redeem' (Heb. *gâ'al*) occurs fourteen times (all within chapters 41–63). There does not seem to be any real distinction in meaning between these verbs. The one used here is particularly associated with the references to the exodus from Egypt in the books of Exodus and Deuteronomy. That the redemption is going to be 'in justice' and 'in righteousness' highlights the LORD's role in Zion's restoration. He will display his justice as he victoriously brings the nation back to the land and back to himself. The impenitent are called 'rebels', 'sinners', and 'those who forsake the LORD'. For them there is no redemption but rather destruction. This teaching is a reiteration of the message of Psalm 1:6: 'The LORD knows the way of the righteous, but the way of the wicked will perish.'

29 The final verses of chapter 1 (verses 29-31) draw attention to both the idolatrous practices of the people and the punishment that awaits them. Isaiah resumes the condemnatory tone before returning in the following chapter to note future blessing. The reference to 'sacred oaks' is one of a number of references to a special tree that cannot be identified with certainty. From the references to it can be gleaned the fact that it was a tree associated with idolatry (cf. Gen. 35:4 where mention is made of Jacob burying idols under it) and under its branches idolatry was practised (Ezek. 6:13; Hos. 4:13). Three times in this book Isaiah mentions special gardens set aside for idolatrous worship (see in addition to this verse 65:3 and 66:17). Ultimately all those who practise worship in connection with these oaks and gardens will find that they reap shame and disgrace.

30 The imagery of lack of water to sustain life is used to depict judgment (cf. again Ps. 1:6). The oak will perish and the garden will dry up. Without the vivifying benefits of water the vegetation will perish. So it will be with those who do not repent and turn to the LORD.

31 The metaphor changes to the use of fire as a symbol of judgment. The word for 'mighty man' is exceptionally rare (see its only other occurrence in Amos 2:9), and though there has been considerable discussion about its precise meaning, the essential thrust of the verse is admirably clear. The mighty man will become chaff and his work a spark, a deadly combination that will result in unquenchable fire. The verb 'to burn' (Heb. *bâʿar*) is commonly used in the Old Testament to speak of God's judgment. Not only will rebellious Gentile nations be visited with fire, but unrepentant Judah will also be subjected to divine judgment. On that day 'sinners of Israel'[4] will be terrified and they

---

[4] Though Isaiah ministered to the southern kingdom of Judah, it is remarkable how many times the term 'Israel' occurs in reference to Judah. The God of

will ask the questions: 'Who of us can dwell with consuming fire? Who of us can dwell with everlasting burning' (Isa. 33:14)?

B. Future Glory for Judah and Jerusalem (2:1–4:6)

1. The Glory of the Eschatological Days (2:1-5)
Several features of this opening of a new section of the prophecy are noteworthy.

1. Verses 2-5 also appear, with some variation, in Micah 4:1-3. There is no way of knowing whether one prophet is dependent on the other. Seeing that there is also a similarity with Joel 3:9-11 it may be that there was a common prophetic tradition from which each of the three prophets drew.

2. The use of the phrase 'last [or, latter] days' marks this passage out as one dealing with the end times. This is one of the phrases used in the Old Testament to designate the eschatological days and it carries with it the note of the ending of an epoch.[5]

3. The message of redemption follows the long indictment contained in chapter 1, just as the further message of redemption in 4:2-6 follows the indictment in chapter 3. These oracles of salvation need to be considered together, for one complements the other.

1 A new title marks off this section, and there is no commencement of a further one until 13:1. Again Isaiah, the son of Amoz, sees (Heb. *châzah*) the word of the LORD concerning Judah and Jerusalem. He is the recipient of supernatural revelation that has relevance for the nation of Judah and specifically for its capital city, Jerusalem.

2 The message is that in the 'latter days' Jerusalem will be elevated above all the other mountains. Even though its height is not the greatest, spiritually it will tower over all the other mountains. The mountain on which God's temple is situated will be the chief mountain and to it the nations will 'stream'. Though the noun for 'river' (Heb. *nâhâr)* occurs frequently in the Old Testament, the verb (Heb. *nâhar)* only occurs four times, all in a figurative sense.[6] The picture is of a confluence of

---

Judah is 'the Holy One of Israel', and Hezekiah can offer prayer to 'the God of Israel' (37:16).

[5] There is an important discussion of these phrases in Geerhardus Vos, *The Pauline Eschatology* (Eerdmans, 1972), pp. 1-7.

[6] The occurrences are Isaiah 2:2; Micah 4:1; Jeremiah 31:12 and 51:44. *CHAL* omits Jeremiah 31:12, which appears to be a simple oversight.

nations entering into the restored Jerusalem.

3 Clearly there is no implication that every nation will be represented in this pilgrimage. 'All the nations' of the previous verse is now replaced by 'many nations' (cf. the use of 'all Israel' in Rom. 11:26). Many nations will not only go themselves but they will encourage others as well to go with them to Jerusalem, called here 'the hill of the LORD' and 'the house of the God of Jacob'. The imagery of the pilgrimage feasts under the Mosaic law is used to depict a vast gathering at God's earthly dwelling place. Not only will it be a place of worship, but it will also become a place of instruction. All assembled there will be taught to walk in the LORD's ways/paths, and from Zion/Jerusalem his word will proceed. Our Lord indicated to the woman of Samaria that salvation is from the Jews (John 4:22), and the proclamation of repentance and forgiveness of sins in his name began from Jerusalem (Luke 24:47).

4 The eschatological time being described will also be marked by righteous judgment and by the absence of war. The LORD himself will be the judge and his rule will be marked by weapons of war being changed into farming implements and by the absence of training in warfare. When the Prince of Peace (Isa. 9:6) reigns over all the nations, conflict and tensions between them will be a thing of the past and universal peace will prevail. Though the United Nations takes this verse as its motto, its inability to produce world peace simply points to the need for a supernatural work that will result in war being forever abolished.

5 Isaiah's description of this pilgrimage to Jerusalem ends in a different way from Micah's (cf. this verse with Mic. 4:4-5). While Micah paints a picture of idyllic existence, with everyone having their own vine and fig tree, Isaiah ends with a word of encouragement to his own people. His desire is that they will walk in the light of the LORD. Here 'light' cannot mean anything other than the instruction that proceeds from Jerusalem, as mentioned in verse 3. He includes himself as belonging to the nation which must walk according to revealed knowledge. 'Light' is used in Psalm 18:28-29 of military victory (cf. also Ps. 27:1) and so here it may also refer to the day of God's final victory and the resultant worldwide peace.

2. Jerusalem's Future Exaltation (2:6–4:1)

a. The City of Mammon (2:6-9)

While there are difficulties in translation in this section, the main thrust of it is clear. It presents the contrast between the future city of God and the existing one. Clearly the present inhabitants of Zion are not living according to God's law, nor are they following in his ways. While they do have idols, yet their greatest idolatry is the worship of wealth. A word is directed to the LORD, followed by a description of Jerusalem, and finally a request that no forgiveness be granted to it.

6 God is said to have abandoned his people, the house of Jacob. The verb 'abandon' (Heb. *nâtash*) is used of allowing land to lie fallow, but it also means 'reject', including God's rejection of his people (for examples, see Judg. 6:13; 1 Sam. 12:22; 2 Kings 21:14; Ps. 94:14; Jer. 23:33, 39). They were rejected in the sense that God allowed them to fall prey to their own follies and consequently come under foreign religious influences. The Hebrew text says: 'They fill from the east, and divinations (or, diviners) like Philistines, and with the children of strangers they clasp hands'. Filling from the east seems to refer to the introduction of religious ideas or even diviners from the east, such as Ahaz's introduction of the altar from Damascus (2 Kings 16:10-16). Probably too his sun-dial had a connection with worship of the heavenly bodies (2 Kings 20:11). Western influence came from the Philistines, who practised the kind of divination proscribed in Deuteronomy 18:9-14. To clasp the hands seems to be an idiomatic way of saying they struck bargains with foreigners, with whom they should not have entered in alliances.[7]

7-8 Three times in these verses the same expression occurs: 'Their land is filled ....' Twice it is followed by the words 'and there is no end to their treasures' (or, on the second occasion, 'chariots'). The picture shows an abundance of wealth in Jerusalem. There is plenty of silver and gold, while horses and chariots abound. In the law of the king (Deut. 17:14-17) he was forbidden to accumulate large sums of gold and silver and to acquire many horses. Breach of these instructions

---

[7] I take the Hebrew verb here (*sâfaq*) to mean clasping the hands, though it is hard to be certain of its meaning because it only occurs three times in the Old Testament (1 Kings 20:10; Job 27:23; Isa. 2:6). It is possible that we are dealing with homonyms, one of which means 'to clap' or 'clasp the hands', and the other 'to suffice'.

would become a sign that the people were no longer trusting in the LORD but in their own power. Later Isaiah warns of relying on horses or chariots instead of looking to the LORD (Isa. 31:1). The ultimate result will be a turning away to trust in idols of human construction. The word for 'idols' (Heb. *'elîlîm*) sounds very like the word for 'God' (Heb. *'elôhîm*). Isaiah's claim is that the people have substituted one for the other, and they are now bowing down in worship to things that are simply human creations, the fashioning of fingers and hands. Not only is this happening on a national scale, but each person is turning to his own individual idol (Heb. 'his hands', 'his fingers').

9 A day of reckoning is coming when all will be humbled. The Hebrew text expresses the comprehensiveness of this humiliation by using two different words for 'man' (Heb. *'âdâm* and *'îsh*). A translation like 'mankind will be brought low, everyone will be humbled' (REB) fits the context well.[8] The interpretation of the final clause in the verse has shown tremendous variation. While literally the translation of the clause is 'and do not forgive them', that does not necessarily mean that Isaiah is praying that God's forgiveness will never be granted to them. Such would be inconsistent with so much else in this prophecy which shows the prophet expecting pardoning mercy to be shown to the sinful nation. In Hebrew this type of negative imperative 'Do not forgive' can be 'used to express the conviction that something cannot or should not happen'.[9] Here it probably means that Isaiah is saying in effect that forgiveness, without repentance on the part of the nation, is unthinkable.

b. The Day of the LORD (2:10-22)

Isaiah leads on from the description of the sinful city to the impending day of the LORD. The concept of the day of the LORD was evidently known prior to the middle of the eighth century BC. That is why the prophets of that period are able to refer to it while at the same time disabusing their hearers and readers of their false understanding of what that day would involve. There was a perception on the part of many that this day would be a day of light, not darkness (see Amos 5:18). Isaiah warns that in that day sinners will flee into the rocks for protection. Three times in this passage the warning is given (verses

---

[8] The REB translators, though, arbitrarily omit the final clause of this verse: 'and do not forgive them'.

[9] *GKC* §109e.

10, 19, 21), and the refrain comes to climactic expression in verse 21.

10 Rocks were a traditional place of shelter in the Old Testament period (cf. Judg. 6:1-2; 1 Sam. 13:6), but when the LORD appears in judgment they will not provide the shelter that people seek. None will be able to hide from 'the dread of the LORD' (Heb. *pachad yhwh*). This phrase, along with the similar 'the dread of God' (Heb. *pachad 'elôhîm*), are terms describing the terror that God's presence causes. The parallel phrase here, 'the glory of his majesty', reinforces the idea that when God's glorious presence is revealed, men will try and hide themselves in the rocks to avert his judgment. The language used is typical of biblical descriptions of the coming of judgment, such as Jesus' words on his way to crucifixion: 'Then they will say to the mountains, "Fall on us!" and to the hills, "Cover us!"' (Lk. 23:30; cf. also the words of Rev. 6:15-17).

11 For the first time in the prophecy Isaiah speaks about this manifestation of God taking place 'in that day' (a phrase appearing forty times in Isaiah, six of which are in chaps. 2–4). This phrase is linked with 'in the last days' (see comment on verse 2) as an expression of the great and final manifestation of God's glory. Another word (Heb. *levad*, 'alone') also appears here for the first time in the phrase 'the LORD alone'. It is used repeatedly in this book to designate the uniqueness of the God of Israel, or the fact that he is the only one to be exalted (see verse 17 for a repetition of words from this verse). When this manifestation of his glory takes place, then human pride and arrogance will be unable to stand before it.

12-16 These verses form a single unit as they spell out to whom this special message is directed. Its opening words speak of a day that belongs to the LORD (Heb. *yôm layhwh*) and that has special relevance for all the proud and lofty ones. Those for whom it is destined are introduced by the same Hebrew preposition (*'al*). It occurs ten times in these verses along with the word for 'all of' (Heb. *kol*). Most English versions smooth out the translation by sometimes omitting the preposition. The NASB comes closest to replicating the Hebrew usage. First, there is a general statement that the day of the LORD is intended for all the proud and lofty and for all who exalt themselves. Then specific examples follow of things of which those in Isaiah's day stood in awe or in which they trusted – the cedars of Lebanon and the oaks of Bashan, the tall mountains and high hills, high towers and fortified walls, trading ships and desirable vessels. Both Lebanon and Bashan (a territory on the east of the Sea of Galilee noted for its lush pastures and tall trees) were admired for their fine products, while majestic hills caused awe to the viewers. Trading ships (lit. 'ships of Tarshish') and stately vessels were large ships such as the ones used by Solomon (1 Kings 10:22) and the Phoenicians (Isa. 23:1, 14) to ferry their products from remote countries. In the coming judgment day none of these things will be grounds for boasting, for human pride and human achievement will be humbled before the LORD of Hosts. The thought of these verses has been taken up in the words of a hymn:

> Pride of man and earthly glory,
>   Sword and crown betray his trust;
> What with care and toil he buildeth,
>   Tower and temple, fall to dust.
>   But God's power,
>   Hour by hour,
>   Is my temple and my tower.
>
>   Joachim Neander (1650–80),
>   *'All my hope on God is founded'*

17-18 The whole of verse 17 repeats what has already been said in verse 11, though with some small modifications in the first part. This verse is a powerful reinforcement of the message that the LORD is going to be exalted whereas human pride will be brought to nothing before him. Verse 18 adds to the message by declaring that the idols they have made will pass away. The word for 'idols' picks up the word already used in verse 8 (see comment), which will be used again by Isaiah in 2:20; 10:10-11; 19:1 and 31:7. The creations of men's hands (*'elîlîm*) will vanish, but the living God (*'elôhîm*) will remain.

19 The message of verse 10 is taken up with some slight variations, and with the addition of the phrase 'when he rises *to terrify* the earth'. Though several English versions have 'shake' instead of 'terrify' (NASB, NKJV, NIV), yet the verb is clearly the latter (Heb. *'ârats*). Here it occurs, as it does so frequently, in association with synonyms from one of the roots meaning 'fear' (either Heb. *yârê'*, *pâchad*, or *châtat*; see Deut. 1:29; 7:21; 20:3; 31:6; Josh. 1:9; Ps. 89:7; Isa. 2:21; 8:12). The LORD's coming will cause the whole earth to fear, and the only escape from fear is to fear him.

20-22 When the day of the LORD comes people will realise that there is no safety in their gold or silver idols. Each one has made his own object of worship (the same individualising as in verse 8) which he unceremoniously tosses away in effort to escape. No longer will he trust in them, for he realises their utter futility (Isaiah returns repeatedly to the theme of idols in passages such as 30:22; 31:7; 40:19-20; 41:7, 22-24; 44:9-20; 46:5-7). They will be prepared to abandon them to dark places like those in which moles and bats live. The idea that these creatures are repulsive may be meant to signify that the idols are now in an appropriate location. The idols are just as repulsive as the inhabitants of dark dens. This verse is probably the basis for Cowper's words:

> The dearest idol I have known,
>> Whate'er that idol be,
> Help me to tear it from Thy throne,
>> And worship only Thee.
>
> William Cowper (1731-1800),
> *'O for a closer walk with God'*

For the third time in this section the refrain occurs relating to hiding before the glory of the LORD. There are some alterations in the wording to the first part, but the second part is identical to verse 19. This is clearly done for the sake of emphasis. The changes do not affect the meaning, as they reinforce the concept that the LORD's glory will cause men to flee from it, finding whatever shelter is available to them. There is, however, a climax to the refrain on its third occurrence. In addition to the reference to hiding, there comes a direct command: 'Give up on man.' The word 'give up' will be used later in this prophecy to describe the rejection of the servant, on whom men give up (Isa. 53:3). The appended reason for 'giving up on man' is that he is simply a creature into whose nostrils God has breathed (Gen. 2:7). The final question is a very idiomatic Hebrew phrase which highlights the inability of man or his self-made idols to stand before the glory of the LORD: 'Of what account is he?' (RSV, NIV, NKJV), or, 'For why should he be esteemed?' (NASB) The thrice repeated refrain (verses 10, 19, and 21) leads to the climactic question that crystallises the folly of attempting to trust in anyone but God.

c. The Coming Social Change (3:1-12)

The last verse of the previous chapter is the basis for this section. The day is coming when the land will be destitute of food and water, and all the leaders of the land will have vanished. 'Mere children' will be in charge (verse 4), and a man will be rushed into a position of leadership (verse 6). Judgment is expressed specifically against Jerusalem and Judah. The catalogue of sins emphasises the degeneracy of all ranks and classes, as the very foundations of society are giving way. The background is the covenant relationship, and in the following section the more formal covenant lawsuit pattern emerges again. Instead of days of blessing that the people are expecting, there will be days in which calamity will be the outcome for them, with the removal of both things and people on which the nation and its capital depended.

1-3 There is a special solemnity in the way this section commences. The opening words ('for behold ...') draw attention to the message that is coming from 'the Lord, the LORD of hosts'. The cluster of titles emphasises the majesty of Judah's God as he confronts his erring people. The threat is that he will remove everything on which the people lean for support. Two synonymous adjectives from the same root are used to convey the idea that all kinds of things on which the people lean will be removed (Heb. *mash'ên* and *mash'ênâh*). All 'supply and support' will vanish. To emphasise the coming devastation it is declared that 'all supplies of bread and all supplies of water' will be taken away. The word in this clause for 'supplies' (Heb. *mish'ân*) comes from the same root as the previous words.[10] The repeated use of the idea of 'supplies' highlights the impending famine. Verses 2 and 3 depict a country bereft of its leaders, both legitimate and illegitimate. National leaders ('hero and warrior, judge and prophet') will be taken away, while local officials ('the elder, the captain of fifty and man of rank') will also disappear. Skilled craftsmen will be absent, while even those who claimed to be in touch with the world of spirits ('soothsayer', 'clever enchanter') will be removed. Many times Israel failed to observe the regulations of Deuteronomy 18:9-13 regarding setting aside occult practices. Perhaps in times of great tension people turned to them if they thought that the LORD was failing to come to their aid. However, faith in such practitioners is misplaced, and they too will no longer be available.

---

[10] I have discussed the Hebrew verb *shâ'an* in *NIDOTTE*, vol. 4, pp. 202-04.

4-5 Social upheaval will follow the removal of the leaders in society. The young, who would not normally be given roles of leadership, will be set in positions of authority by the LORD. Incompetent government will be the outcome, but this in turn will be followed by anarchy. There will be a breakdown in ordered society, so that individuals will strive one against another. Neither age nor social rank will protect from oppression. Bad government (verse 4) will give way to the absence of government (verse 5). The verb used for 'oppress' (Heb. *niggas*) recalls the situation when the Israelites were oppressed in Egypt (see Exod. 5:6, 10). Now the oppression will be from those within the nation itself.

6 Inequalities will still exist in society, as some will have respectable cloaks, while others will lack them. The latter will seize those having cloaks and set them in leadership positions. Normally no force was involved in the appointment of rulers, but now reluctant people are dragged into office. The appointment, however, is not to rule over a glorious city but simply to exercise authority over a heap of ruins. From verse 8 it is clear that this is a reference to the devastated Jerusalem.

7 The time when this will take place is said to be 'in that day' (cf. the use of this phrase already in 2:11, 17, 20), making the description part of the eschatological events. The man seized by others will cry out that he does not want to be a 'healer'. This word is mainly used of binding up of wounds (see its use in 1:6, and later in 61:1), and this is an acceptable way to translate it here. Sick Jerusalem has already been described (1:5-6), and now the reluctant leader acknowledges that he cannot heal her wounds. Having neither food nor clothing he does not want to be thrust into leadership.

8 The future of Jerusalem and Judah is dark. The language used of them brings to mind the picture of a man staggering and finally falling down dead. The verb 'to fall' (Heb. *nâfal*), in a quarter of its occurrences, is connected with death. Those in Isaiah's day had to be under no delusions regarding the ultimate fate of their city and country. In 586 BC Judah was sacked, the kingdom came to an end, and the nation devastated. The words and deeds of the people are against the LORD, and they constitute acts of rebellion. The Hebrew text says that they rebel against 'his glory'. 'Glory' is used elsewhere of God's glorious presence (cf. Exod. 33:22) and ultimately it became almost a synonym for God (see Jer. 2:11; Ps. 106:20 'their glory' = 'their God';

1 Sam. 4:21-22, *Ichabod*, 'no glory').

9 The people blatantly sin. Their very countenance gives them away, and instead of trying to keep quiet about their evil words and actions they actually want to proclaim them just like the men of Sodom did (Gen. 19:4-9, and see also the earlier reference to Sodom in Isa. 1:10). Coming judgment is declared using a regular formula employed by the prophets: 'Woe to . . .' (Heb. *'ôy l*^e). As in this verse, many of these 'woe' sayings are followed by a motivating clause introduced by 'for' (Heb. *kî*). Here the motive is that their sins are going to come to full measure when judgment overtakes them. The word for 'disaster' (Heb. *râ'âh*), as in Amos 3:6, does not denote the moral quality of evil but indicates some event(s) of a disastrous kind.

10 A distinction in the population is made, so that a separate message is appropriate for the righteous. Much later in his prophecy Isaiah will distinguish between two Israels, one the nation as a whole and the other the righteous within it (see in particular 49:3-5). But there is a message of encouragement for the believing community. Whereas the sins of the rebels will rebound upon them, the righteous will enjoy the fruit of their labour. The Hebrew text says 'that [it will be] good', and the use of this word 'good', which often stands for the promised covenant blessings, may well be intentional (see the comment on 1:20 and footnote).

11 The message of verse 9 is repeated with some alterations. The comparison is:

Verse 9   Woe to them (lit. 'their soul'), for they render to them-
          selves disaster.
Verse 11 Woe to the wicked—disaster—for they will be rendered
          what their hands have done.

The alternate form of the message simply reinforces the point that the people who have rebelled against the LORD will receive their just reward. They will reap what they have sown.

12 Twice in this verse the Hebrew word 'my people' (*'ammî*) occurs. Most translations take the first one as the object of the verb 'oppress', 'Youths oppress my people', while taking the second one as a vocative: 'O my people, those who guide you lead you astray'. It is much better to take 'my people' in both occurrences as a vocative, and this also obviates another problem. The word often translated as 'children' (NASB) or 'youths' (NIV) is singular, not plural. It is easier grammatically to take it as the object of a verb rather than as a subject.[11] There is an additional problem relating to the meaning of this word. It could come from either of two roots in Hebrew, though on balance it seems to be from the root that indicates 'children'. There is a final difficulty in that the verse ends with the clause 'and the way of your paths they swallow'. Here the verb 'to swallow' is used in the sense of 'obliterate'. The translation of the whole verse is then:

> O my people, your oppressors are children,
> and women rule over you.
> O my people, your guides lead you astray,
> and they swallow the way of your paths.

Isaiah, in continuing to present the Lord's message, identifies himself with his own people. Such interplay between the Lord's word and that of his messengers is quite common. Isaiah's message is that the immature young men (see verse 4) and the women who rule over them are really leading them astray. In mentioning the women, cases like that of Jezebel (1 Kings 18:4; 21:1-15) or Athaliah (2 Kings 11:1) could well be in mind.

d. The Courtroom Scene (3:13-15)

The charge against Judah and Jerusalem first mentioned in chapter 1 is now put in more formal style. God has taken his place in court to bring charges against Jerusalem and Judah for covenant violation. He enters his brief against the elders and the government officials, and the charge is this: 'They have crushed the poor and taken from them in order to enrich themselves.' This charge of social injustice takes the place of what might have been expected — a more God-centred charge against his glory (cf. verse 8), but the seriousness of social injustice in God's sight is highlighted many times in this book.

13 God takes his stand to judge peoples (Heb. *'ammîm*). Some versions like NIV make this singular, 'the people'. Others such as RSV follow the Greek and Latin versions in translating 'his people'. But a reference to God as the universal judge is quite appropriate in

---

[11] There are numerous cases in the Hebrew of the Old Testament where plurals of persons (especially when the participle is used) are followed by the singular in the predicate. See *GKC* §145 L.

the context. He sets himself to enter into legal dispute with nations, and particularly with Judah whom he calls 'my people' in verse 15. The occurrence of this legal type of language in several of the prophets suggests that they employed covenant terminology as they confronted errant Israel and Judah (for other examples see Jer. 2:5-19; Hos. 4:1-3; Mic. 6:1-8). As here, these lawsuits inevitably lead on to condemnation of the people.

14 The opening clause is synonymous with the opening of the previous verse, but then the next clause is expanded by designating precisely those coming under divine judgment along with the nature of their offences. The elders and leaders of the people have failed to keep God's vineyard, i.e. the covenant nation. This figure of speech is going to be expanded in chapter 5. The main charge against the leaders is that they have oppressed the poor. The language is strong. They have forcibly taken from the poor and transferred the wealth and goods to their own homes. The word for 'spoil' or 'plunder' is rare (it only occurs here, in Lev. 5:23 and in Ezek. 18:7, 12, 16; 33:15), but the verb from which it comes (*gâzal*) has the idea of taking away by force.

15 The charge against the leaders is furthered by using two very strong verbs that relate to crushing to pieces. That is what has been happening with the poor. Those with power have utilised their positions to extract everything they can from them. However, what is taking place is observed by the sovereign Lord, the LORD of hosts.

e. Sins of the Women (3:16–4:1)

The women of Judah come in for special attention with the focus being on their outward attire and particularly their possession of expensive jewellery. This is one of the most detailed listings from the Ancient Near East of the type of attire worn by wealthy women. It contains many words that only occur here in the Old Testament, though the overall meaning is not in doubt. All the items seem to be superfluous to everyday life, while some may have been amulets and lucky pieces. It is also possible that some of the items were connected with idolatrous worship, but present knowledge does not enable a definite connection to be proved. The New Testament contains similar warnings concerning outward embellishment and the need to possess inward spiritual adornment before the Lord (see 1 Pet. 3:3-6).

16-17 The addressees of the LORD's message are 'the daughters of Zion'. This title for the women indicates their important standing, but likewise the necessity of judgment upon them. In spite of their attachment to Zion they display attitudes of boastfulness and pride. Their public appearance is all for show, and their very gait is for display. It may well have been that ornaments around the ankles made walking difficult, and hence they had to take short steps. Part of the judgment will be to give them an outward sign of mourning by removing their hair. In place of their braided locks there will be scabs and baldness.

18-23 The catalogue listed in these verses depicts a luxurious life, with abundant wealth to purchase all these items. Some, such as the crescent-shaped necklaces, may well have had religious significance as part of the worship of the moon god. Others may have been things that appealed to their senses and that they wanted because of their intrinsic beauty. The list does three things. First of all it shows the extravagances to which the women were going, and possibly also the men, for there is some evidence that jewellery was worn by them as well. Clearly not all this jewellery and clothing were worn at the same time, but it represents a society with ample wealth and a desire for material possessions. Secondly, not only the 'crescent necklaces' (NIV) were regarded as magical charms but probably many of the items were amulets to ward off evil spirits. The passage demonstrates, then, with very concrete illustrations, the departure of the people from true commitment to the LORD. Thirdly, the list makes the judgment even more explicit. These were the things that the LORD is going to snatch away from them.

24 When the day of judgment comes there will be a substitution of the things of beauty with things that depict judgment and death— rottenness, rope, baldness, sackcloth, branding. These terms may well have had portending significance, being associated with the leading away of captives into exile. Certainly ropes and branding were often linked with captivity. The only phrase that is difficult in this verse is the last one. It commences with the Hebrew word *kî*. This can be the conjunction 'for', but if that is the case the phrase is incomplete: 'for instead of beauty . . . .' One solution is to take the first word of verse 25 as part of the phrase: 'for instead of beauty, your men'. This, however, is rather forced and still does not yield very good sense. One Hebrew manuscript has 'instead of beauty, shame' (which the RSV follows), but this looks like an attempt to solve a problem by inserting another word. The third and best explanation is that *kî* here is not the conjunction but a noun meaning 'burn' or 'brand' (from a Hebrew verb *kâvah*). This branding could either be a mark to distinguish a captive, or a self-inflicted wound proclaiming profound sorrow.

25-26 In the future there will be judgment. Among other things this will take the form of invasion and destruction by a foreign army. This was one of the threats contained in the covenant curses (see Lev. 26:23-32; Deut. 28:25-26, 49-53). The gates of Zion are personified (see a similar personification in Ps. 24:7, 9) and are said to be in lamentation. Invasion by a foreign army and the exile of most of the people will mean that Zion will be destitute of people and the only appropriate course of action will be to sit on the ground and mourn.

4:1 The final verse in this section commences with the refrain 'in that day', a phrase that reminds repeatedly of the finality of the impending judgment. The picture here is one of the effects of war in that men will be killed, so leaving women as widows or without the possibility of marriage and children. To be unmarried or without children was a 'reproach' (see Gen. 30:22-24; Isa. 54:1). Seven women will all try to grab hold of one man as a marriage partner, even promising to provide their own food and clothing. What they want is their reproach to be removed and to have children called by their husband's name.

3. Jerusalem's Eventual Purification (4:2-6)

Another part of the events 'in that day' will be the cleansing of Jerusalem. There will be a new experience of the LORD's presence manifested in a way similar to that experienced at the time Israel came out of Egypt. Fire and cloud will again symbolise God's immediate presence with his people. This passage complements 2:2-5, which is a song of redemption following the indictment of Judah and Jerusalem in chapter 1. The song here is also a fitting prelude to the indictment of chapter 5.

2 Mention is made of the branch of the LORD being beautiful. The same word for branch (Heb. *tsemach*) is later used as a royal title in Jeremiah 23:5; 33:15 and Zechariah 3:8; 6:12. Many therefore take the title 'branch' here to have messianic significance, but all the later references identify the title with an individual, which is not done here. Jeremiah goes even further and links the title with the Davidic family. But that is not so in Isaiah 4:2. We have to pay attention to the parallelism with 'the fruit of the land' and that suggests that 'branch' here is just another way of describing the future bounty of agriculture in the land, especially as 'branch' is used elsewhere of vegetation (cf. Gen. 19:25;

Ps. 65:10; Ezek. 16:7). A new pride will replace the old pride that is destroyed (see 2:11, 19). This pride will be in the vegetation that will mark the new fruitfulness of the land. In Psalm 72:16 the abundant crops are pictured as growing even to the tops of the mountains. Those rejoicing in this radical change are said to be 'the survivors in Israel'. The doctrine of the remnant has already been introduced by Isaiah (1:9) and will be further developed later (10:20-22; 11:11, 16; 46:3).

3 One distinctive feature of the remnant will be that they will be separated, or set apart for God. This characteristic stands in marked contrast to the present condition of the people stated in chapter 1. Present unholiness will be replaced by holiness, and this will be a universal mark of all recorded as living in the purified Jerusalem.

4 The day of the LORD is going to be marked by a process of purification. 'Filth' and 'bloodstains' are terms used to symbolise the guilt and iniquity of the people. The description of the garments of the high priest Joshua as 'filthy' in Zechariah 3:3 not only denote stained garments but guilt (the Hebrew word is a synonym from the same root as the one used here in Isa. 4). The purification is said to be done by washing or 'by a spirit of judgment and a spirit of fire'. Fire symbolises both judgment (Gen. 19:24; Ezek. 10:2) and cleansing (Num. 31:21-24; Mal. 3:2-3).

5-6 The exodus experience of a pillar of fire and a pillar of cloud will be repeated. Just as Israel had the LORD's protection when they came out of Egypt, so will a renewed and cleansed Israel/Zion. The word for 'canopy' or 'covering' (Heb. *chuppâh*) is only used three times in the Old Testament (Isa. 4:5; Joel 2:16; Ps. 19:5), but it has come into modern usage as the term to describe the canopy over a couple during the Jewish marriage service. The conjunction here with the terms 'shelter', 'shade', 'refuge' and 'hiding place' make it plain that the idea is of a protective canopy that will provide shade and a shield to Mount Zion. The use of the verb 'create' (Heb. *bârâ'*) is significant because it is reserved for when God is the subject. The great creator will act in his sovereignty to protect Zion and all the remnant who gather there.

C. Judah's National Sins (5:1-30)

1. The Parable of the Vineyard (5:1-7)

The song takes up a theme already mentioned in 1:8, where the daughter of Zion is said to be like a shelter in a vineyard. The parable has many affinities with Deuteronomy 32. Both of these passages are songs, and in them the covenant lawsuit pattern is exemplified. The major difference, though, is that this song is directed to the beloved land, and not to the people. The house of Israel and the men of Judah (verse 7) are depicted under the idea of the vineyard which the LORD laid out with great care. Elsewhere in Isaiah we get the same picture (27:2-6), while Psalm 80:8-16 develops the idea with the description of a little shoot having been taken from Egypt and growing into a large vine. Verses 1-7 are broken into three sections by the use of the same phrase in Hebrew (v^e '*attâh*, 'and now') at the commencement of verses 3 and 5. This phrase is often used to denote a new stage in an argument, but with the same subject in view. The language and imagery of this passage are taken up by Jesus in his parabolic ministry. He taught the parable of the landowner who hires labourers for his vineyard (Matt. 20:1-16), and also the parable of the tenants (Matt. 21:33-44; parallels in Mark 12:1-11 and Luke 20:9-18). These passages are based on this description of Israel as the LORD's vineyard, and they contain a powerful message based on a familiar, though not well understood, Old Testament background. Clearly the scribes and chief priests grasped that the parable of the vineyard was directed at them (Luke 20:19).

1 Isaiah sings a song about his loved one (the LORD) and his vineyard (Israel). There is a particle of entreaty after the verb (Heb. *nâ'*) that softens the expression. It is as if the prophet says to his people, 'Please let me sing a song about my beloved.' Two different but cognate words are used for 'beloved' (Heb. *y^edîdî* and *dôdî*), both words of tenderness and love. The location of the vineyard is said to be 'in a horn, a son of oil', or, 'in a horn of a son of oil'. This seems to be the only use in the Old Testament of the word 'horn' (Heb. *qeren*) to denote a projecting crag, and the Targum translates it as 'high mountain'. 'Son of' is a Hebrew idiom to denote the condition of something or someone, like 'sons of rebellion' (*b^enê merî*, 17:25 [Heb.]) or 'son of death' – 'one who deserves death' (*ben mâvet*, 1 Sam. 20:31). Here 'son of oil' denotes a hillside that is fertile and productive of [olive] oil.

2 The picture is of the careful planting of a special vineyard that could be expected to produce excellent grapes, but it only brings forth sour ones. The owner of the vineyard takes unusual care to dig the ground in this special location and clear it of stones before planting the special vine. The word for vine is an unusual one (*sôrêq*) that is related to other words like that in Zechariah 1:8 (*sâroq*) which designates the colour of the horses. Probably here it is used of a special type of grape with a particular colour and also to symbolise the fact that Israel is a special people in God's sight (Exod. 19:5). A tower was built and a winepress dug, and then the owner waited expectantly for the crop to mature. What it produced was something that stank and was viewed with abhorrence by God. Jeremiah takes up this same theme, using the identical word for 'vineyard', but goes on to say that Israel was an alien vine that could not alter her nature (Jer. 2:21-22).

3-4 The LORD turns attention to Jerusalem/Judah and directs questions to her. The movement in the argument is marked by the first use of 'and now' (*vᵉ'attâh*) as the opening words. Let the people be the judge to settle the case between him and his vineyard. Could the LORD have done anything more to encourage the production of good grapes? Can any explanation be given why his expectant waiting only leads to frustration when rotten grapes are the fruit? Verse 4b is virtually the same as verse 2c, with the verb changed to first person singular.

5 The beginning of the third and final stage of the argument is marked by the second occurrence of 'and now' (*vᵉ'attâh*) as the opening words of the verse. The LORD declares his mind and reveals his dire plan for his vineyard. This could be an indication of what is already happening or what is going to happen because the Hebrew text uses a participle (*'oseh*, 'making') that carries in itself no indication as to time. However, the context suggests that future judgment is in view, and therefore it should be translated as 'what *I am going to do* with my vineyard'.[12] The lovingly created vineyard will now suffer destruction, its hedges and walls will be broken down, allowing wild beasts to wander over it at will.

6 God is going to cause the vineyard to become a desolation. There will be no more hoeing of the land or pruning of vines. Instead it will bring forth 'briers and thorns'. This is a fixed expression that Isaiah

---

[12] On the grammatical point in question, see Waltke and O'Connor, *IBHS*, p. 627, where they say that the participle usually 'denotes the full range of ideas connoted by English "I am going to ...," namely certainly, often with immanency'.

uses five more times (7:23, 24, 25; 9:18; 27:4) to symbolise the utter change that is to come over the land. The covenant curses included devastation of the land (Lev. 26:32-35; Deut. 28:38-42), and now that devastation is imminent. Another covenant curse was absence of rain (Deut. 28:23-24; see also verse 12 where rain is mentioned as one of the blessings to be given to obedient Israel). As a sign of disfavour God is going to issue a command as he is the one who controls all the forces. As one of the psalmists expresses it:

> I know the Lord is high in state,
> above all gods our God is great;
> the Lord performs what He decrees,
> in heaven and earth, in depths and seas.
> He makes the moisture to ascend
> in clouds from earth's remotest end;
> the lightnings flash at his command;
> He holds the cyclone in His hand.
>
> Psalm 135:3-7; *Trinity Hymnal*

7 The song ends with Isaiah giving its interpretation. The LORD of hosts is the vineyard's owner, while the people of Judah are said to be his delight. The second part of the verse tells how the LORD's expectation of his people was deeply disappointed. A play on words makes the declaration even more forceful.

> And he looked for justice (*mishpât*),
>   and behold, bloodshed (*mispâch*);[13]
> [he looked] for righteousness (*ts^e dâqâh*),
>   and behold, cries for help (*ts^e 'âqâh*).

The conclusion of the song is pivotal. No matter how privileged Judah and Jerusalem are, this will not be security against divine punishment.

---

[13] This Hebrew word only occurs here in the Old Testament. It clearly denotes something as the opposite of 'justice', and as an alternative to 'bloodshed' it has been suggested that it may mean 'a breach of law' (see *DCH* 5, p. 505). This would also fit the context, and not take away at all from the force of the condemnation.

2. Six Woes (5:8-23)

Following the parable of the vineyard Isaiah pronounces a series of six 'woe oracles'. The Hebrew word 'woe' (*hôy*) is used fifty-one times, always by the prophets. Over forty of these instances are in passages where warnings are being given, such as here. These oracles constitute a catalogue that names some examples of the 'rotten grapes'. The oracles provide a picture of society in Isaiah's day, to which he gives expression in the following chapter when he confesses that he lives among a people of unclean lips (6:5). Three of these oracles are followed by passages that announce coming judgment, including exile (verses 9-10; 13-15; 24-25).

a. Insatiable greed (5:8-10)

8 The first 'woe' is proclaimed on greedy landowners, who try to add more property to what they already possess both in the town and in the country. This statement points to the fact that property was being alienated from the original owners contrary to God's intention for the land (Lev. 25:23). It was his, and the land could only be obtained by inheritance. However, kings and other prominent people managed to circumvent this, and accumulated large tracts of land (see the reference in 2 Chron. 26:10 to Uzziah's estates).[29] In this verse the suggestion is that one man gets so much property that he no longer has near neighbours, but seems to dwell all by himself.

9-10 To Isaiah the Lord announces the judgment he is sending. The first aspect of it will be desolation for the fine houses. It is typical of Isaiah to commence speaking about a matter and then return to it on more than one occasion. Here what is implied is exile for the people, so that the houses are empty. This is made explicit in verse 13, while later in the chapter he adds further details concerning the military invasion that will be God's instrument for their removal (verses 26-30). The second aspect of the judgment is that the vineyards and fields will not produce anything like their normal crops. A ten-acre vineyard (lit. 'ten yokes', the area of land that ten yoke of oxen could plough in a day) will only produce a minuscule amount (Heb. *bath*, approximately 22 litres). The result of planting a homer of seed is that the return will

---

[14] I have discussed some aspects of the land in *Deuteronomy: The Commands of a Covenant God* (Fearn: Christian Focus Publications, 2001), pp. 15-24, and with particular relevance to Isaiah 5 on pp. 20-22.

only be one ephah, i.e. one tenth of the amount actually sown. The paucity of returns from both vineyard and farm will be signs of God's displeasure with his people (see Deut. 28:38-39 for the relevant covenant curse).

b. Disregard of the Works and Words of the LORD (5:11-17)

11-12 Isaiah depicts a life of revelry that confirms what his fellow-eighth century BC prophet, Amos, also describes (see Amos 4:1-3; 6:6-7). There are those who indulge in their drinking from an early hour of the morning, and by late at night they are indeed inflamed by the drink they have consumed. At their banquets they have varied musical instruments to aid in their drunken celebrations. The tragedy of the situation is spelt out in verse 12b. When it comes to spiritual understanding these people are utterly insensitive to the LORD's actions, and to the things he has done. 'Deeds of the LORD' probably includes all the great actions of God in the past (e.g. the Exodus events) when he displayed his power for the benefit of Israel, but may well include other evidences of his power in the lifetime of Isaiah's audience. Spiritual awareness is dulled by the preoccupation of the people with their own life of dissipation.

13 The consequences for the people are now proclaimed. The link between their actions and the punishment of exile is made clear by the introductory particle: 'therefore' (Heb. *lākēn*). Their lifestyle will bring exile as their disobedience to the LORD invokes the due punishment. The coming exile (already hinted in 3:24-26) is made explicit. The reason is expressly said to be lack of knowledge, i.e. lack of knowledge of the LORD and his works. This is the confirmation of what was said at the very commencement of the book: 'but Israel does not know, my people do not understand' (1:3). When invasion and exile occur, the nobility will perish in hunger, while the general populace will perish for lack of water. The distinction between the nobles and the masses appears to be merely poetic.

14 The link with the preceding verse is made by the opening word 'therefore', continuing the consequences of covenant disobedience. Sheol is personified as longing for the death of both nobility and masses. She increases her appetite and opens her mouth wide so that she can swallow all the disobedient revellers. A similar expression is used in Habakkuk 2:5, where Sheol enlarges her desire and is never satisfied.

15-16 The coming day of judgment will see men humbled and the

LORD exalted. In typical poetic fashion Isaiah uses parallel expressions to describe the humiliation. Man/mankind (Heb. *'ādām* and *'îsh*) will be brought low/humbled. It is possible that the second phrase in Hebrew is meant to individualise the general opening one: '*People* shall be brought down, *each man* humbled' (NKJV). The contrast is that the LORD of hosts will be exalted in that day by a manifestation of his justice and holiness. Definitive judgment will proclaim that the LORD is acting according to his own character and it will be a demonstration of his own perfection. Paul expresses a similar thought when he says that the Lord Jesus will come 'to be glorified in his saints and to be admired among all those who believe' (2 Thess. 1:10).

17 The desolation of the land is once more in view. Sheep will be able to graze over areas that previously were inhabited. Possessions of the rich will now be broken down and the land will revert to be feeding grounds for the lambs. This theme has already been presented in verses 9 and 10, and it reappears at the conclusion of chapter 7. Highly valuable vineyards will become a place of briers and thorns, and cultivated ground will become a place where cattle and sheep roam (7:23-25).

c. Defiance of the LORD (5:18-19)

18 The next 'woe' oracle concerns those who are so attached to sin and wickedness that seemingly they drag them along with cords, as if dragging a cart behind them. In Hosea 11:4 the same word for 'cords' occurs, but there it is God who says that he draws his people with 'cords of a man ... with bands of love'.

19 The arrogance of the people is shown by the sarcasm they employ. They place a challenge before God. They want him to expedite his work so they can see it. They want his counsel or plan to be implemented speedily so that they may know it. The title they use for God, 'the Holy One of Israel', is a distinctive part of Isaiah's presentation of God's character (see comment on 1:4), and it appears again in verse 24. There may be a connection between this verse and Isaiah's naming of his son with the symbolic title 'Maher-Shalal-Hash-Baz' ('Hurrying to the spoil, hasting to the prey', Isa. 8:1). Two of the elements in that name ('hurrying' and 'hasting') occur in the first two verbs in this verse. It may be that Isaiah's naming of his son in these terms was to reinforce the point that the people were going to get God's response to their sin quicker than they expected. Later in this chapter he tells them that God is going to bring foreign troops 'swiftly and speedily' (verse 26).

d. Absence of Clear Moral Distinctions (5:20)

20 The fourth 'woe' concerns the ability of the people to make good moral decisions. When it comes to 'good', 'light' and 'sweet', they simply reverse the concepts and call them 'evil', 'darkness' and 'bitter' respectively. The reference to 'light' may have a connection to what Isaiah's contemporary Amos said about the people's misapprehension concerning the day of the LORD: 'Why do you long for the day of the LORD? That day will be darkness, not light' (Amos 5:18). The whole point of the complaint against the people is that their perversity shows in their utter distortion of all moral values, or the ways of God.

e. Spiritual and political pride (5:21)

21 Another sign of how the covenant people had departed from the LORD is their arrogant self-reliance instead of looking to God for guidance. 'Wise' and 'clever' are virtually synonymous. Two other Old Testament passages throw light on this, one earlier than Isaiah and one later. Proverbs 3:5-7 has as its kernel the words: 'Do not be wise in your own eyes; fear the LORD and depart from evil' (NKJV). Jeremiah 9:23-24 has as its kernel the words: 'Let not the wise man glory in his wisdom, let not the mighty man glory in his might, nor let the rich man glory in his riches; but let him that glories glory in this, that he understands and knows me' (NKJV). Commitment to God involves effort to understand his character, his ways and his incomparable wisdom, and to reject even the thinking that opposes him. It was (and is) so easy and haughty to imagine self-sufficiency of understanding. The ancient Irish prayer is the right antidote:

> Be Thou my wisdom, Thou my true Word;
> I ever with Thee, Thou with me, Lord.

> 8th cent. poem translated
> by Mary Bryne 1880–1931

f. Denial of Justice (5:22-23)

22-23 The sixth 'woe' links together heavy drinking with perversion of justice. Mixing of drinks appears to have been a regular custom (see Prov. 23:30). This should not be understood as analogous to modern cocktails, for until the Arabs in the middle ages discovered distillation there were no strongly alcoholic drinks. Probably what took place in ancient Israel was the addition of spices to beer and wine. The same people (probably magistrates and elders) who indulge in these drinking sessions also indulge in bribery to get the guilty acquitted, while they prevent the innocent from receiving justice. The law prohibited taking bribes (see Exod. 23:8; Deut. 16:19), and only those who abstain from such practices can stand in God's sight (see 2 Chron. 19:7; Ps. 15:5; Isa. 33:15). This prohibition is a reflection of God's own practice, for he shows no partiality, nor does he accept bribes (Deut. 10:17). Refusal of bribes was foundational for justice, and clearly this 'woe' highlights the situation in Isaiah's day when abuse produced unjust outcomes in court cases.

3. The Assyrian Invaders (5:24-30)

The final section of this part of Isaiah's prophecy gives the consequences of the sinful state of the nation before God. This is made clear by the introductory 'therefore' at the start of both verses 24 and 25 (the Heb. is slightly different, but there is no appreciable alteration in meaning). The first of five occurrences of the refrain ('yet for all this, his anger is not turned away, his hand is still upraised') appears in verse 25 (the other occurrences are 9:12; 9:17; 9:21; 10:4).

24 Since the people have turned to their own way, God announces that judgment is coming upon them. Fire is used as the symbol of judgment. Just as dry straw or dry grass is consumed by the flames, so God's judgment will consume them. The roots of the plants decay, and the flowers are blown away. Rejection of their covenant God and despising of his words will have inevitable consequences for the nation. The Holy One of Israel will not be inactive as he sees his people rebelling against him.

25 Whereas the people seem to have expected continued favour by the LORD, in reality his attitude is one of anger. His indignation burns against them and with his powerful hand he strikes them in judgment. This act of judgment is regarded as if it is a theophany (a visible appearance of God), so that even the mountains shake before his presence (cf. what happened at Sinai as recorded in Exodus 19:18, and Elijah's experience there in 1 Kings 19:11; see also the comments on Isa. 64:1). Judgment brings death and corpses are spread in the streets. All this does not satisfy, for without repentance the threat of the uplifted hand must remain against them.

26 The idea of the coming invasion is introduced, though nowhere in this context is mention made explicitly of the Assyrians. It is not until 7:17 that Isaiah names the coming invader. This is in keeping with his practice of introducing a concept, and then developing it in stages. In planning judgment against his people God is able to beckon as his agents even far off Gentile nations. Just as armies in that period used banners on poles to signify who they were or to call for assistance, so God is said to summon his messengers of wrath. The idea of whistling is going to reappear in 7:18 where the LORD whistles for the flies of Egypt and the bees of Assyria. There is no refusal of this summons, for the nations come speedily at his command.

27 Contrary to normal experience, the soldiers of the invading army will not have anything out of place to hinder them – not a belt untied, nor a loose sandal strap. They don't even need sleep, and none of them becomes weary or stumbles. Both of these ideas reappear at the end of Isaiah 40, where it is said that God strengthens the young men who grow tired and stumble (40:29-31).[15] The invaders will be endowed with superhuman strength in order to fulfil a divine commission of wrath.

28 When one looks on their weaponry it is all ready for the ensuing battle. Bows are armed with sharp arrows and poised for the attack. Even their horses are able to perform miraculously, for they can cross broken ground or rocks as if their hooves were shod with flint. In the ancient world there was no practice of shoeing horses with metal so they could not be used in rough conditions. The speed of the attack makes the wheels of the chariots sound like an approaching whirlwind.

29-30 The noise of the invaders sounds like lions roaring over their prey. They seize their victims and carry them off, and no one is able to prevent it. The picture is of total annihilation, with the inhabitants of the land forcibly removed. Later Isaiah will use other similes and metaphors to describe the invading Assyrians (bees and flies, 7:18-19; a razor, 7:20; floods, 8:7). The timing of this 'darkness and distress' (cf. the use of the same words in 8:22) is put into the period already described as 'that day' (see the earlier uses of this expression in 2:11;

---

[15] There is a slight variation between Isaiah 5 and Isaiah 40 in the word used for 'weary'. 5:27 uses the Hebrew word *'âyêf,* which is most probably just a by-form for *yâ'êf* that occurs in 40:29. The consonants are the same and the sound is very similar.

3:18; 4:1, 2). The metaphor of growling over prey is mixed now with the simile of the sound of crashing waves. All the imagery simply reinforces the point that inexpressible disaster is about to overtake the nation. It will be as if the brightness of the midday sun will be changed into darkness by the presence of heavy clouds.

This description of impending judgment forms an important prelude to the call of Isaiah in the following chapter. The people are rebellious children (1:2) who have despised their God, 'the Holy One of Israel' (5:19). Isaiah's account of his own call leads into announcements of terrible judgment, and with a specification that is lacking in the first five chapters. The foe is clearly identified as Assyria (7:17), and time frames start to be given more specifically (7:7-9; 7:16-17).

D. The Book of Immanuel (6:1–12:6)

1. Isaiah's Vision (6:1-7)
Chapters 6–12 of this prophecy form a coherent section in themselves, though with reference to what precedes and follows. Chapter 6 is prologue, while the song of praise in chapter 12 forms the epilogue. The message is first to Judah (7:1–9:7) and then to Israel (9:8–11:16), parallel passages that spell out both the impending divine judgment and the blessing that will ultimately come through a Davidic prince. The existing hostility between northern and southern kingdoms will come to an end when Israel and Judah are re-gathered as 'one nation in the land ... and they will never again be two nations or be divided into two kingdoms' (Ezek. 37:22).[1]

The opening words of the whole prophecy (1:1) give the name of the prophet (Isaiah), his ancestry (son of Amoz), the period of his ministry (in the days of Uzziah, Jotham, Ahaz, and Hezekiah), and the scope of his ministry (concerning Judah and Jerusalem). No mention is made of the call of the LORD to him to enter into his prophetic service. In chapter 6 Isaiah gives his own account of the way in which he was called to the service of the living God and how he was given a message from him. This chapter appears to record the initial call of Isaiah to the prophetic ministry. Three reasons suggest this. First, nowhere else does Isaiah mention the subject of his call, and after setting out his introductory message in the opening chapters he now asserts the

[16]In dealing with chapters 6–12 I am following the seminal discussion by J. A. Motyer, 'Context and Interpretation of Isaiah 7:14', op. cit., pp. 118-25.

authority that he has as the bearer of this divine message. Hence it seems that this chapter is deliberately placed here as the account of how he was called to exercise the ministry of a prophet. Secondly, verse 5 points to it as an initial experience of cleansing that is being described, rather than some later account of further cleansing. It is this cleansing that brings Isaiah into a new and vital relationship with God. Thirdly, verses 8-13 deal with commissioning for service, and again the tone of the passage implies the initial call to prophetic proclamation. This is viewed not just as being of a specific and limited nature but of a continuing character that is to be maintained until the land is brought to ultimate desolation under the judgment of God.

1 The account of the vision opens with a reference that sets Isaiah's ministry within a particular time frame. It was in the year of King Uzziah's death (approximately 739 BC) that Isaiah was confronted with this vision of God in his glory and impelled into his service. It is consistent with all that we know of Isaiah's ministry to consider that his work really began in this final year of Uzziah's life. Clearly Isaiah knew of the circumstances about Uzziah's reign because it is stated in 2 Chronicles 26:22 that 'the rest of the acts of Uzziah from beginning to end, are recorded by the prophet Isaiah son of Amoz'.

The mention of King Uzziah in verse 1 stands in marked contrast with the reference to another king in verse 5. Uzziah (also called Azariah in the historical narratives, cf. 2 Kings 15:1-7) permitted the people to continue to offer sacrifices and to burn incense at the high places. For his sin he was afflicted with leprosy (or some serious skin disease) and had to live apart till the day he died (see the fullest account of the sin and its punishment in 2 Chron. 26:16-21). It was in the year that the sinful King Uzziah died that Isaiah saw another king, *the real one.* He says that he saw '*the* King, the LORD Almighty'.

The reference to seeing could be either a real sighting of the LORD, or else a visionary experience. Most probably it was the latter, for Isaiah has already spoken in the opening of the book of it being a vision that he saw concerning Judah and Jerusalem. There are also aspects in the following narrative that suggest that it was not a physical experience. His eyes were fixed on the LORD, high and lifted up, seated on a throne. It would seem from John 12:39-41 that it was a vision of Christ that Isaiah saw. John quotes words from Isaiah as he summarises the ministry of Jesus, and immediately following the quotation from Isaiah 6:10 he says: 'Isaiah said this because he saw Jesus' glory and spoke about him' (NIV). The Greek only has the phrase 'his glory', but in the context it is clear that Jesus is in view. The reference to the Lord being high and lifted may serve to support this interpretation, as these words along with a further word describing high exaltation are used of the servant of the LORD in Isaiah 52:13. Isaiah saw the Lord clothed in a robe that seemed to fill the whole temple.

2 Heavenly messengers are attending the Lord, ready to do his service. The word used for them (Heb. *s^erâfîm*) only occurs elsewhere of the fiery serpents in Numbers 21:6, 8 and Deuteronomy 8:15. Elsewhere Isaiah calls them 'flying serpents' (Isa. 14:29; 30:6). Here the word *s^erâfîm* represents heavenly beings, seemingly with human-like bodies, but with each one having six wings (the Hebrew expression is a distributive one). They used two wings to fly, and the others to cover their faces and their feet. Even heavenly creatures could not look upon the holiness of the exalted LORD.

3 Just like the creatures in Revelation 4:6-8 the seraphim sing of the holiness of God. In Revelation the creatures are depicted as never stopping singing: 'Holy, holy, holy is the Lord God Almighty, who was, and is, and is to come.' In Isaiah the seraphim say: 'Holy, holy, holy is the LORD of hosts; the whole earth is full of his glory.' The Hebrew word for holiness probably comes from a Semitic root that means 'to cut off' or 'separate'. Thus it denotes first the fact that God is the transcendent God who stands apart from all others and from the whole of creation (Isa. 40:25). Secondly, it speaks of the ethical purity of God, and in this sense he is the only one who can be called 'holy', but it also comes to be used of the standard of purity that God requires of his creatures. It is fanciful to try and press the *trisagion* (threefold declaration of holiness) to imply reference to a triune God. The seraphim join together in an antiphonal song of praise to the holy God. They call out one to another, attributing holiness to the LORD Almighty, using the phrase 'the LORD of hosts' (see the earlier comment on this phrase in 1:9). The word 'hosts' can be used of armies or countless angelic beings, or even of all of creation. It is probable that it is in the last sense that it is used here, especially as the seraphim designate that all of creation is filled with his glory. The word 'glory' speaks of the manifestation of God's being and character.

4 The effect of the singing is to shake the very doorposts and foundations of the temple. So majestic and powerful is it that the very building shakes as the song reverberates through it. Moreover, the temple is filled with smoke. It is possible that this smoke comes from the altar referred to in verse 6, and if so would simply reinforce the fact that it was a vision of the sanctuary. However, it is probably better to take it as a reference to a theophany. A comparison with Psalm 18:6-8 helps to shed light upon it. There David recalls how he cried to God and God heard him from his temple. Then smoke came from his nostrils and consuming fire from his mouth. Both passages may well be describing theophanic revelation of God's wrath against sin. The holy one of Israel cannot bear to look upon sin. This would also help to explain the cry of despair that follows in the next verse.

5 The reaction from the prophet is to cry out, 'Woe is me; I am ruined.' The introductory word 'woe' (Heb. *'ôy*) is one of a group of particles that introduce woe oracles in the prophets. It is normally followed, as here, by a clause introduced by 'for' (Heb. *kî*), giving the explanation for the cry. Isaiah realises by his vision and by the song of the seraphim that he is undone. He cannot take part in what is being sung because his lips are unclean, as are those of his fellow-countrymen. The order of words in Hebrew emphasises the consciousness of sin that overwhelmed him (lit. 'a man of unclean lips am I, and in the midst of a people of unclean lips I am dwelling'). He has already graphically set out the sin of his people in chapter 1 in particular, where he said that from the soles of their feet to the top of their heads there was no health in them (Isa. 1:6). The vision of the holy God and the angelic chorus reinforces how separate the prophet and his people are from the transcendent LORD. His description of the sight of the true king is again an emphatic expression (lit. 'the king, the LORD of hosts, my eyes have seen'). He has glimpsed the glory of the great King.

6 One of the seraphim now takes on a different role, an agent of cleansing. The seraph flies towards the prophet with a coal taken with tongs from the altar. There has been no mention of sacrifice but the words here imply it, as do the spoken words of the seraph that accompany the cleansing. The burning coal is clearly a means of cleansing and purifying the unclean lips of which the prophet has just complained. It is striking how with both Isaiah and Jeremiah touching of their lips immediately precedes their commissioning (cf. Jer. 1:6-10). This was a symbolic gesture of the need for purification by a holy God before his servants can go and declare his word.

7 Along with the action there was also a declaration of cleansing:

'Behold, this has touched your lips and your guilt is taken away and your sin atoned for'. The word 'behold' (Heb. *hinnêh*) frequently introduces something new or unexpected, especially in direct speech, and, as here, the subject is almost invariably God. It must be presumed that an offering has been made, and atonement effected. The principle of 'no forgiveness without the shedding of blood' is preserved even in this declaration. A guilty prophet needed purification if he was to be a suitable messenger of God's will for his people.

2. Isaiah's Commission (6:8-13)

8 The divine purpose in all this now appears, for a question is asked by the LORD, who speaks for the first time in the whole vision: 'Whom shall I send? And who will go for us?' The second part of the question contains a striking use of the plural, 'Who will go for *us*?' Just as God speaks in Genesis 1:26 saying, 'Let *us* make man in our image', so here there is an apparent indication of plurality in the Godhead. Some have suggested that the plural refers to God and the seraphim, and though the context might seem to support such a view, it is out of keeping with the rest of biblical revelation. Nowhere is God depicted as deliberating with his creatures in relation to his purposes.

To the question there comes a ready response from Isaiah, and no words are wasted, for in Hebrew his answer comprises just two words which mean, 'Behold me, send me.' The English rendering captures the spirit of the reply, 'Here am I. Send me!' What he has seen and heard earlier, and what has disturbed him greatly, now compels him to offer himself for the work of his God. He had been cleansed from his sin by God's grace, and now offers himself willingly for service. The case of Peter in Luke 5:8-11 is analogous to that of Isaiah here.

9 God's directive now comes to the prophet, first of all in reference to what he is to say to the people, and then as a command to the prophet himself in relation to his task. This commission is a difficult one. From the outset Isaiah knows that his mission is one of hardening and of judgment. He may well have remembered that Moses had to endure a similar experience, for he had to testify against the children of Israel (Deut. 29:2-4). Much later the experience of Isaiah is that of our Lord himself (John 12:36b-41).

The main task of the Hebrew prophet was to declare God's word to his contemporaries, and so Isaiah is directed to go and proclaim God's message to '*this people*'. The object of his ministry must surely

have been Judah in particular; but because of the way in which Isaiah
elsewhere speaks to the northern kingdom of Israel, even within this
book of Immanuel (see especially 9:8–10:4; 10:20–12:6), it is possible
that his message was to the whole nation collectively. In the context
here the emphasis has already fallen on the people of unclean lips
among whom Isaiah was dwelling. The rebellious children whom the
LORD had brought up do not merit the appellation '*my people*' but only
the more disdainful '*this people*'. God is set against these rebels, and
the prophet is to bring them his rebuke.

The content of the message is couched in terms that appear to be
proverbial, as similar expressions occur in several ancient languages.
Stress is placed on the spiritual insensitivity of those to whom the
message of the prophet comes. They will go on both seeing and hearing,
and yet those experiences will not bring them understanding or
knowledge. A judicial blindness and deafness will come with the
proclamation, and this hardening is the intended result of Isaiah's
mission.

10 The same idea is brought out in this verse, given in the form of
a command to Isaiah. His task is expressed as making callous the
heart of the people, so that they will be even more insensitive to the
word of the LORD. Their ears are to be made heavier, so that hearing
is more difficult. With reference to their eyes Isaiah is told to besmear
them so that they cannot be opened. No mention is made here of the
people's sins, or of the withholding by God of his grace. Rather,
emphasis falls on the mission of the prophet and the ultimate effect
that this is going to produce.

The second part of the verse expresses the consequence for the
people if they are able to see and hear with spiritual insight. True sight
will be theirs, and their ears will enable them to hear and grasp the
message being brought to them. '*With* their hearts' (following the
reading contained in many Hebrew manuscripts, including the Dead
Sea Scrolls' manuscript 1QIsa[a], and also the Syriac and Vulgate) they
will be able to appreciate the significance of the preaching, and in
turning to the LORD will find their wounds healed. Frequently in the
Old Testament sin is presented as a sickness that needs healing (see
Pss. 41:4; 147:3). Rather than referring to a turning back to God, the
verb 'turn' may well be part of a regular Hebrew idiom which this
verb has in the sense of 'doing something again'. If so, it places stress
on the fact that God, who had healed his people repeatedly before,

can do so yet again. That emphasis is important because the element of hope in the midst of judgment will be held out to the people at the end of verse 13, as well as later in this book of Immanuel.

The words of verses 9 and 10 appear several times in the New Testament. They are quoted by Jesus in Matthew 13:14-15 in reference to his teaching in parables and the effect that this teaching had upon his hearers. The form of the quotation is identical to that found in the LXX, and differs from the Hebrew text in that the imperatives have been altered to become merely declarative statements. The parallel passages in the Synoptic Gospels (Mk. 4:12; Lk. 8:10) contain part of the quotation, with a further change in Mark in that the Aramaic Targum rendering of the last verb is given as 'be forgiven' and not 'be healed'. In John 12:39-40 the words of Isaiah 6:10 are employed by John in an adapted form to show that the unbelief of the people in relation to Jesus' ministry is something that was foretold by Isaiah and which is attributable to the sovereign will of God. This is made clear by the reference to the action of God in blinding their eyes, lest they turn and Christ heal them. The final quotation of this same passage from Isaiah comes at the end of the book of Acts. When the Jews in Rome did not believe, Paul quoted Isaiah 6:10 and announced the priority of the Gentile mission (Acts 28:25-28). The quotation follows exactly the LXX version. The use of these words in all these New Testament passages carries a uniform interpretation, which is precisely in accord with the sense of the words in the context in Isaiah 6. One divinely ordained aspect of the ministry of Isaiah is that the deaf become deafer and the blind blinder still, though he can also offer gracious invitations to come and find abundant blessing with the LORD (cf. Isa. 55:1-5). The same paradox can be seen in the ministry of both our Lord and the apostle Paul. Sinners who refuse to listen to gracious gospel invitations find that their hearts are hardened, just as Pharaoh's was (Exod. 9:12; 10:20, 27; 11:10; 14:8). Turning to find healing from the LORD can only come through the gracious and sovereign intervention of God.

11 Having heard the commission given to him by the LORD, and understood the effect that his ministry will produce, Isaiah now asks a question, 'How long, Lord?' It is difficult to be sure precisely what Isaiah meant by this question. It could be that he was asking how long was his own ministry going to continue. On the other hand his question may have been enquiring how long the hardening of the hearts of the people would be. Possibly there is no need to distinguish sharply between these two, as they are co-terminous.

12 The LORD's answer is unmistakable. The cities will be devastated, and emptied of occupants, so the houses will be deserted, and the fields, hitherto so carefully tended, are to be desolate. Even more pointedly the judgment entailed in the prophet's mission is brought home to the people with the warning of impending exile. God is going to remove the inhabitants of the land to a far-off place. The God who had given them the land had been provoked to plan their deportation and exile to a far country. Later Isaiah spells out more closely how this is to take place. In the following chapter he specifies for the first time that the instrument to accomplish it in respect to the northern kingdom will be the king of Assyria (7:17), and then he details the desolation of the land, especially in reference to the cultivated farmlands (7:21-25). The agent in God's hand to accomplish his purpose of judgment is again stated in 8:7 to be the king of Assyria. Here in chapter 6 the exile is introduced to specify the time limit that is to apply to the prophet's ministry.

13 The element of hope at the end of verse 10 is amplified here. There are difficulties in translating this verse, but these do not obscure the essential elements in Isaiah's message. One difficulty is the sense in which the verb 'laid waste' is used. In the form used here it can mean 'to burn', 'to kindle a fire', 'to consume', or 'to exterminate'. Certainly 'laid waste' captures the general idea sufficiently well. Another difficulty is to determine whether the land, or just the tenth part, is to be subjected to the desolation. Most probably it is the tenth, i.e. the remnant, that is described as undergoing further judgment. The translation and interpretation of the verse is further complicated by the use of a rare word ('cut down') and another in an unusual sense ('stump'). In spite of these problems it is clear that Isaiah is depicting a remnant that will be preserved from destruction during the coming devastation, and even though this remnant undergoes further judgment, hope for the future still remains. Just as with trees such as the terebinth and the oak, which when cut down to a stump will sprout again, so the remnant will yet bring forth life, and produce seed which is holy (for a symbolical presentation of the teaching of this verse, see Ezekiel 5:1-4, and for the idea of the holy seed, compare the use of the expression 'godly seed' in Malachi 2:15).

When the question 'How long?' was asked at the beginning of

verse 11 it might have seemed that only judgment could be in view for the future. But now there is a glimmer of hope. Amidst the mass of the nation that is to perish as a result of the visitation of God's judgments, there is a remnant of devout servants of the LORD. In the following chapters Isaiah develops this theme of the remnant, even calling his own son Shear-jashub, which means '[only] a remnant will return' (7:3), and then depicting the return of this remnant to the Holy One of Israel (10:21). Beyond the impending doom for the nation there is a flicker of hope.

3. God's Word to Judah (7:1–9:7)

a. The Moment of Decision (7:1-16)
For the first time in the book, Isaiah appears as the practical statesman, thus fulfilling the role he is to assume throughout the remainder of his life. He has just related the vision of the heavenly king on his throne, but he has yet to learn how God's kingdom on earth is to be realised. The promise of an enduring Davidic kingdom in 2 Samuel 7:8-16 was clearly much in the mind of true believers in Israel (cf. Pss. 89 and 132). This was in spite of the many disappointments in the history of David's family and of the twelve tribes. The enduring nature of the Davidic covenant and the continuing presence of a descendant on the throne of Judah are the central issues in this section. This passage, especially the Immanuel prophecy in verses 14-17, has been the focus of intense discussion since early Christian centuries. There are important issues regarding translation that must be settled before the whole passage can be explained. There are also problems in that the use of singular and plural forms interchanges suddenly in the Hebrew text, and this of course is concealed by the use of the ambiguous English 'you' in translations.[17]

i. Danger from Assyria and the Impending Invasion from Syria and Israel (7:1-2)
1 The narrative places the events in the reign of Ahaz, who at the age of twenty succeeded his father Jotham in 735 BC. Even before Jotham died, Syria and Israel had begun to wage war against the southern

---

[17]Of the massive literature I single out three key articles that have helped form my own opinion. These should be consulted by those wanting to pursue further study, as should the literature to which they refer. They are: G. J.

kingdom of Judah (cf. 2 Kings 15:37). Egypt and Assyria were the major powers in the Near East at this period, and the smaller nations were often caught between them. Hence there were attempts to form alliances to try and keep the major powers at bay, and one such attempt forms the background to Isaiah 7. For a broader account of this struggle between the conjoint forces of Syria and Israel in the north and Judah in the south we have to turn to 2 Kings 16 and 2 Chronicles 28. It would appear that Ahaz had already been captured and then released, and the huge amount of spoil mentioned in 2 Chronicles 28:5-8 had been taken. Now a further episode in this war is mentioned, when the confederate states of Syria and Israel come up against Jerusalem itself.

The text specifies the kings involved. Rezin was the heathen king of Syria, reigning from Damascus. Pekah was the ruthless ruler of the ten northern tribes (Israel), reigning from Samaria. He was not of the royal line but usurped the throne when he led a conspiracy against Pekahiah and killed him in Samaria (2 Kings 15:25-27). It would seem that these two kings had attempted to persuade Ahaz to join them in opposing Assyria but had failed. Now they come up against Jerusalem and try to conquer it. The verb is in the singular (lit. 'he went up'), which may indicate that Rezin was the prime mover in this plan, and that Pekah was subordinate, or it may be a Hebrew grammatical usage (not without parallels) in which a single verbal form is used with a compound subject. Both Isaiah 7:1 and 2 Kings 16:5 record that the attack was unsuccessful. There are slight verbal differences in the accounts (e.g. in Isa. 7:1 the verb 'was not able' is singular, whereas in 2 Kings 16:5 it is plural, as is the reading from the Dead Sea Scrolls manuscript 1QIsa[a]).

2 Word is brought to the royal household regarding this new danger that is at hand. The reference to 'the house of David' draws attention to the fact that Ahaz was a successor to the throne of David, yet so different from David in character. This reinforces the whole threatening tone of the subsequent account, including the imposition of the sign to the house of David (verses 13-14). The fear of the king and the people as a whole is graphically described with the comparison with trees of the forest swaying before the wind.

Wenham, 'B[E]TULAH 'A Girl of Marriageable Age', *VT* 22 (1972), pp. 326-48; J. A. Motyer, 'Context and Content in the Interpretation of Isaiah 7:14,' op. cit.; M. R. Adamthwaite, 'Isaiah 7:16: Key to the Immanuel Prophecy', *RTR* 59, 2 (August, 2000), pp. 65-83.

ii. The LORD's Message to Ahaz (7:3-9)

3 The LORD's word now directs Isaiah to go out and meet with Ahaz at the conduit of the upper pool, and with him is also to go his son Shear-jashub. Two things are noteworthy about this meeting. One is that the names of Isaiah and his son are of particular importance, as in themselves they carry a message for the king. Isaiah means 'the LORD is salvation', while Shear-jashub means 'a remnant will return'. Ahaz is being reminded in a very pointed way that his only safety lies in the LORD and his might, while receiving also an indication that some of the captives of Judah will yet return. This may refer to the return of the captives taken to Samaria mentioned in 2 Chronicles 28:8-15, or perhaps with greater relevance to the ultimate return of the remnant to the mighty God that Isaiah speaks of later (Isa. 10:21). Secondly, the place of meeting is important, because it is clear that Ahaz is expecting the attack upon Jerusalem and is making sure that the water supply is secure. The exact location of this spot is uncertain, but most probably it was south-west of Jerusalem and perhaps the same water supply as mentioned in 8:6. What is significant is that at the same spot the next king of Judah, Hezekiah, was to be put to the test about thirty-five years later (see Isa. 36:2).

4 The LORD's word to him is plain: 'Take heed, be quiet, do not fear, and do not let your heart be faint because of these two smouldering stumps of firebrands, at the fierce anger of Rezin and Syria and the son of Remaliah.' Disdain for Pekah is shown by the fact that his name is not mentioned—he is simply 'the son of Remaliah'. To a king who was so fearful of the ensuing conflict comes a message that directs him to stay quiet, and have his confidence placed in the LORD and his promises. The assurance is given that Pekah and Rezin are just like smouldering ends of a fire on the point of being extinguished. There is no need to fear their heat, for they shall soon be snuffed out!

5-6 The plan of these kings against Judah is described, with their decision to attack Judah, bring it into submission, and appoint the king of their choosing over her. They wanted to tear it apart and divide it among themselves. The use of the Hebrew verb 'tear apart' (Heb. *qûts*) is a vital clue to the interpretation as it reappears in verse 16. The name 'Tabeel' may be Aramaic, and in the Nimrud archives a land of Tabeel is mentioned.[18] Alternately, it may be a reference to a

---

[18]See W. F. Albright, 'The Son of Tabe'el', *BASOR* 140 (1955), pp. 34-35.

son of the royal household born to a princess whose home was in Tabeel.[19] Whatever the origin of such a king, he was clearly intended to be a puppet doing the bidding of his masters, Rezin and Pekah.

7 With solemn emphasis the declaration of God concerning this plotting is given: 'It shall not stand, and it shall not come to pass.' Although God's hand was behind the attacks upon Judah (see 2 Kings 15:37 and 2 Chron. 28:5), yet the king is told that the plotting of his northern neighbours will not succeed.

8-9 Moreover, as far as the northern kingdom is concerned (called here as elsewhere by the name of the most prominent tribe, Ephraim) it is going to disappear within sixty-five years. This was indeed fulfilled very soon in the invasion by Tiglath-Pileser of Assyria, and then in the capture of Samaria and the deportation of the ten northern tribes (2 Kings 17:6).

Concerning the expressions dealing with Damascus, Samaria, Rezin and the son of Remaliah, two points need to be made. First, these expressions imply that despite the seeming probability of a successful attack on Jerusalem, that is not going to happen, and so they are not going to have Jerusalem as their capital. The capital of Syria is still going to be Damascus, and that of Israel Samaria. Secondly, the implication is that there is nothing gained by putting faith in alliances and confederacies, and this is a salutary caution to Ahaz. There is also a threat in these words for Ahaz. Just as Israel, trusting in the alliance with Syria, will find that it results in her extinction, so will Judah's appeal for help to Assyria result in her own downfall. What then is the final word to Ahaz from the LORD? 'If you do not believe, surely you will not be established.' There is a play on words here in the Hebrew text that is hard to bring out adequately in English translation. The words translated 'believe' and 'be established' come from the same root in Hebrew. We may find such a play on words strange, but often in the Old Testament in the most solemn circumstances this type of usage appears, and doubtless added force to the saying. In trying to bring out the Hebrew usage John Bright has translated it, 'If you do not stand firm—i.e., in trust—you will not be stood firm—i.e., in your position.'[20] George Adam Smith attempted to convey the play on words

---

[19]The MT gives his name as *Tâv'al*, whereas the LXX, the Syriac and the Vulgate have *Tâv'êl*, which is the form of a man's name used in Ezra 4:7. The change in the form of the word from 'God is good' to 'good for nothing' may be deliberate in Isaiah 7:6.

by using a term from the north of England so that the rendering can be: 'If you do not have faith, you cannot have staith.'[21] Some modern English versions have managed to capture the play on words (cf. NIV: 'If you do not stand firm in your faith, you will not stand at all'). The challenge is not just to Ahaz to put his trust in the promises of the LORD, for the verbs in verse 9b are plural. If the house of David fails to show faith then the alliance with Assyria and the destruction of the kingdom of Judah will be the inevitable result.

iii. The Sign of Immanuel (7:10-16)

10 Often in both Testaments God's spokesmen are identified with God himself. The LORD speaks again to Ahaz, presumably at the same place. Sometimes the prophet speaks as if he were the LORD, but here the LORD speaks as if he were the prophet. What tender love God showed to the rebellious king in continuing to speak with him!

11 Ahaz is instructed to ask for a sign (Heb. *'ôt*). This word can describe two different kinds of signs. The first kind is those that are intended to persuade a person in the immediate present to perform a specified action. A good example occurs in Exodus 4:8 in relation to the signs given to Moses by God, which were intended to produce a certain result. But the word translated 'sign' can also be used to designate a future confirmation. It follows a series of events and confirms that they were of God's doing. Good examples are the promise that Israel will worship God at Sinai (Exod. 3:12), or the promise that the cultivation interrupted by Sennacherib's invasion is going to be resumed (Isa. 37:30). In verse 11 the sign is of the first type, and Ahaz is told to ask for anything, making his request as high as the heavens, or going down as deep as Sheol, the under-world. The older interpretation of the Hebrew word *she'âlâh* is that it is an emphatic imperative of the verb *shâ'al*, 'to ask', but grammatically it seems preferable to follow the Aramaic Targum, and the Greek translations of Symmachus and Theodotion, and take it as the word 'Sheol' with the ending indicating direction towards a place. Perhaps by suggesting a sign high in the heavens the idea is of an eclipse or some other conspicuous feature involving the heavenly bodies. The thought of a

---

[20]John Bright, *The Authority of the Old Testament* (Baker Book House, 1975), p. 221.

[21]G. A. Smith, *The Book of Isaiah*, vol. 1, The Expositor's Bible (Hodder & Stoughton, 1897), p. 106.

sign from the underworld or afterlife recalls the incident concerning the appearance of Samuel to Saul (1 Sam. 28:5-25). It is striking that at this stage Ahaz is told to ask this sign of 'the LORD your God'. Even to the king who had already so hardened his heart, God is still prepared to acknowledge that he is his God. There was still something of a relationship between the two, for Ahaz had not yet openly denied the God of his fathers (as he was afterwards to do).

12 The king gives his answer and in so doing reveals his unbelief and shows that the seemingly pious answer is but hypocrisy. Ahaz appears to echo words taken from Deuteronomy 6:16, words which our Lord used to rebut the tempter (Matt. 4:7). Clearly Ahaz would not have tempted God by asking for a sign, because God had just offered him one! To have accepted the offer would not have been putting God to the test. The king rejects the offer because he would have had to believe the sign if it was given. His outright refusal is given a religious cloak to try and hide his real motives. Behind the refusal lies the plan that Ahaz seems already to have made. He will not seek consolation in God's promises for he has decided to call for Assyria's help, which he soon does (2 Kings 16:7). Even as Isaiah had been told (6:9-13), his preaching results in hardening of hearts, including that of the king.

13 Now the prophet speaks, for though the subject of the verb in Hebrew is simply 'he', it is clear from the rest of the verse that Isaiah is the speaker. The word is addressed not just to the king but to the whole of the royal family, 'the house of David', as the use of the following plurals show ('Listen' [you pl.]; 'for you'; 'you weary'; 'to you'). The expression might have been deliberately chosen in order to contrast the false piety of Ahaz with the true piety of David. The accusation against them is that not only have they resisted men like Isaiah to the point of weariness, but they have gone much further and wearied Isaiah's God. God is the one who declares himself to be slow to anger and of tender mercy, but now he is wearied by the actions of the Davidic dynasty.

14-16 Judgment is pronounced upon this unbelief, but as so often in God's dealings, judgment is tempered with redemptive blessing. The divine word commences with 'therefore' (Heb. *lākēn*), a common introductory word for a punitive message. The disdained sign shall nevertheless be given, a sign of God's own choosing, and it is for the whole house of David ('the LORD will give *you* [pl.] a sign'). Here we come to the wonderful Immanuel prophecy concerning the sign from God. 'Sign' is now used in the second sense mentioned above, for the birth of the child will be too late to prompt Ahaz to adopt the stance of a true believer. A virgin is going to conceive and give birth to a son whom she will call Immanuel (Heb. *'immânû 'êl*, 'with us, God'). The name 'Immanuel' is part of a threatening message, and those lacking in faith could not take any comfort from it. In the context it applies only to those whose trust is in the LORD.

This prophecy has given rise to a vast volume of literature that seeks to deal with the many problems that are raised. It should always be remembered that there is often an element of obscurity in the prophetic word, i.e. the prophets were not just writing history beforehand. In this case the enigmatic nature of it may have been part of the judgment inflicted upon Ahaz.

To those who deny predictive prophecy in the Old Testament the words of verse 14 are thought to be a reference to the birth of a child to Isaiah's wife, or to some other contemporary mother. This view is up against considerable difficulties within the passage itself, some of which will be noted below. Also many of those who hold this view have difficulties with verses 15-17, and often have recourse to the idea that these verses (or parts of them) were the clumsy additions of a later editor. It is always precarious to fall back upon the idea of a redactor or editor to help solve exegetical difficulties, for even if there was an editor one must presume that the piece of writing he completed made sense to himself.

Hezekiah has been suggested as the Immanuel child, but, apart from any other considerations, chronology rules this out because on the most probable dating Hezekiah would have been born several years before this prophecy was given. He was twenty-five years of age when he acceded to the throne (2 Kings 18:2) and hence his year of birth would have been 740 BC.

Among those who take the view that the prophet is here predicting a sign that was to find its ultimate fulfilment in the birth of Jesus there is considerable diversity of interpretation. Several of the major viewpoints are set out briefly, before the preferred one is given fuller exegetical treatment.

First, there are those who believe that verse 14 is predicting an event of the distant future. To use Machen's words: 'I see a wonderful child, the prophet on this interpretation would say, a wonderful child whose birth shall bring salvation to his people; and before such a period of time shall elapse as would lie between the conception of the child in his mother's womb and his coming to years of discretion, the land of Israel and of Syria shall be forsaken.'[22] On this view the prophet is speaking of an extraordinary event in the future when Immanuel will be born, and the time span of his infancy is made the time measure of the judgment upon Syria and Israel. There are variants of this position especially relating to verse 15. Leupold,[23] for example, feels that a contemporary child is inexorably demanded by the passage, but then goes on to suggest that the fulfilment of a prediction could often be postponed, and in this case the appearance of the child Immanuel did not take place until much later. Such a view seems to raise more problems than it solves, and there is nothing in the text to suggest any idea of delayed fulfilment.

Another variant is that of Calvin, who, while allowing that verses 14-15 are speaking of the messianic child, holds that a different child is in view in verse 16. Thus consecutive verses would be regarded as dealing with two children, the Messiah in verse 15 and then possibly Shear-jashub in verse 16. This child was present at the interview. However, the text itself does not suggest a different subject is in view in verse 16.

A further variant position adopted by many evangelical commentators is that the Immanuel prophecy must be considered as having a dual fulfilment. Those who adhere to this viewpoint direct attention to verse 16, and insist that a contemporary child must be in view in order to provide the sign for Ahaz. Thus a young woman in Judah will become a mother in the usual way, and, as a sign of faith, will call her child Immanuel. However, the prophecy is also said to have a further meaning in that it finds its ultimate fulfilment in the coming and birth of our Saviour, the Lord Jesus.[24]

Of these various interpretations the first is to be given the

---

[22]J. G. Machen, *The Virgin Birth of Christ* (Marshall, Morgan & Scott, 1930), p. 292.

[23]H. C. Leupold, *Exposition of Isaiah* vol. 1 (Evangelical Press, 1977), pp. 157-60.

[24]For this viewpoint, see among older commentators J. A. Alexander, *Commentary on the Prophecies of Isaiah* (Edinburgh: T. & T. Clark, 1873), vol. 1, pp. 169-170; and, among more recent ones, G. Grogan, 'Isaiah', *EBC* 6 (Grand Rapids: Zondervan, 1986), p. 64.

preference. Supporting reasons are as follows:

1. While the introductory word 'behold' (Heb. *hinnêh*) may not always in Isaiah designate future time as Delitszch claimed,[25] yet it is often employed in the Old Testament to announce a birth of unusual importance (Gen. 16:11; Judg. 13:5, 7). A cognate word (*hl*) has been found in Ugaritic and this demonstrative particle appears to have been regularly employed to announce an important birth. Isaiah seems to have used this customary introductory word as it suited his purpose and draws attention to the statement that follows. Thus the introduction prepares the way for the momentous announcement.

2. The word 'maiden' (Heb. *'almah*) without any qualification can hardly refer to the prophet's wife or to any other woman long married. In the Old Testament *'almah* generally means 'maiden' or 'damsel', and in some instances it is either stated or implied that the reference is to a virgin. It can be affirmed emphatically that the word is never used of a married woman.

3. The sign will have to be something more than a normal birth, which could hardly constitute the type of sign indicated by verse 14. The birth of a child to a virgin clearly will fulfil the requirements of the context, and thus we are precluded from thinking of the birth of any child in Isaiah's own day.

4. The proximity of this passage to the one in Isaiah 9:6-7 (see the later discussion on these verses) and the closeness of meaning between them, suggests that the child spoken of here as being born of a virgin is one who is truly divine, and therefore this also militates against the interpretations that do not give this prophecy a future reference.

5. Such a viewpoint is in full accord with the evidence from the New Testament in connection with the birth of Jesus. Matthew records that the angel spoke to Joseph and told him not to be afraid to take Mary as his wife, and that she would bear a son, Jesus, who would save his people from their sins. To this Matthew adds the comment: 'Now all this took place that what was spoken by the Lord through the prophet might be fulfilled, saying, "Behold, the virgin shall be with child, and shall bear a son, and they shall call his name Immanuel;" which translated means, "God is with us" ' (Matt. 1:22-23, NASB). By itself this New Testament use of the passage may not exclude

---

[25]His comment can be found in C. F. Keil and F. Delitszch, *Commentary on the Old Testament*, vol. VII (Grand Rapids: Eerdmans reprint, n.d.), p. 216.

other interpretations, but certainly in conjunction with other evidence from the Old Testament it strengthens the impression that the reference in Isaiah 7:14 is only to find fulfilment in the birth of our Lord. It is possible that the words just quoted are not a comment of Matthew but form an integral part of the angel's announcement. If so, then this would be even stronger confirmation of the interpretation as it constitutes part of the divine message communicated to Joseph by the angel.

To adopt this particular interpretation is not to ignore the difficulties it involves. Two of these may be mentioned. First, there is the problem of how an event of the far-distant future could be a sign for the house of David. This sign is clearly intended to be a judgment upon him and to much of its import he was probably blind. However, the vision of this future event was present, and the prophet speaks as if the fulfilment is there and then taking place. Ahaz will not be alive to see the fulfilment of the prophecy, but he has the prophetic description as his sign. Secondly, there is the problem of how the infancy of the promised child can be related to the contemporary events as verses 15-16 may seem to demand. These verses are the key to the whole passage, and a revised translation of them leads to a satisfying explanation that excludes the need to think of a different child in verses 15-16 as compared with verse 14.

The key lies in the translation of the verse 16b.[26] The crucial word is the verb often translated as 'abhor' or 'dread'. This is the same Hebrew verb (*qûts*) that has been used in verse 6, though traditionally it has been taken to be another Hebrew verb meaning 'to feel disgust'. But it is far better to take it in the sense in which it has already been used in verse 6 and to accept the following translation:

> For before the boy will refuse the evil and choose the good, the land that you [*Ahaz*] are tearing apart [*by your unbelieving policies*] will be forsaken of her two kings.

This translation deals with some difficulties that have wrongly influenced the traditional understanding.

1. 'The land' is correctly treated as singular, namely, the land of promise (Israel), rather than the two lands of Israel and Aram (Syria).

---

[26]I am here following the interpretation proposed by M. R. Adamthwaite, op. cit., pp. 77-81.

2. The expression 'you are tearing apart' points to the disastrous policies of Ahaz that are in the process of 'tearing apart' his own land. Though the king has posed as so godly (see comment on verse 12), yet in reality his apostasy is going to result in the ending of the line of Davidic kings at the time of the exile. From this point onwards all is downhill as far as Judah is concerned.

3. This fits in with the reference that immediately follows, to the division of the land into Israel and Judah following Solomon's death ('a time unlike any since Ephraim turned from Judah').

4. It views the child in verse 15 to be the same as the child mentioned in the Immanuel prophecy in verse 14. This verse simply asserts that before that child comes to maturity (irrespective of whether it means physical or moral maturity) the disaster for Israel will have taken place, and exile will be the result. It becomes clear that Assyria will be one agent in the process (verse 17), while later in the prophecy Babylon becomes the ultimate agent for the downfall of Judah and Jerusalem.

5. It gives a coherent interpretation of 7:1-17. Any interpretation involving the conception and subsequent birth of Immanuel in Ahaz's time would be a fulfilment far too late to produce any alteration in his mind. The change from the offer of a sign from 'the LORD your God' (verse 11) to the sovereign imposition of one (verse 14) marks the threatening nature of the message and points to Immanuel's involvement with a far distant time. Immanuel is to eat 'butter and honey' (verse 15), which is food of a desolated country (verses 21-23), and his coming confirms an act and state of judgment. Ahaz has the choice of trust in God's promises or entrance into an alliance with the king of Assyria. He makes his decision to seek tributary status for Judah under Assyria (see 2 Kings 16:7-8), and so the fate of Judah and the Davidic dynasty is sealed. The element of hope already indicated at the end of chapter 6 is confirmed by the promise of Immanuel, and slowly throughout the book the promise will be amplified until it coheres with the figure of the servant of the LORD.

b. *The Assyrian Invasion (7:17–8:8)*

i. *Impending Doom (7:17-25)*
From the assurances concerning the ultimate coming of Immanuel the message now reverts to the immediate future when God is going to intervene in the affairs of Judah by bringing the Assyrians as his agent of destruction. This oscillation between the far-distant future and the

more immediate days is typical of prophetic style.

17 The fact that it is the Assyrians who are coming is now made plain for the first time. Back in chapter 5:26-30 the prophet has depicted the unnamed army coming in response to the LORD's whistle to seize its prey and to carry it off. Now the coming king is named explicitly, as well as the fact that it is God who brings this opponent against them. The split in the kingdom after Solomon's death was both a judgment of God on his people and a result of human sin. Ephraim (using the name of one of the prominent tribes to indicate all the northern tribes) had broken away from Judah. All later Old Testament writers regard this as a calamity for Israel, but even that experience will pale into insignificance before the coming of the Assyrian and Egyptian aggressors.

18-19 The phrase 'in that day' is used both of the immediate future and of the final eschatological days. It is used here of the expected Assyrian invasion, which this and the next chapter describe in considerable detail. In 5:26 God was said to be raising his ensign as a signal for his chosen instruments of judgment to come. Here he is said to be whistling for the flies from Egypt and the bees of Assyria. Egypt is clearly regarded as the minor irritant, and therefore the stress hereafter falls on Assyria, though both nations are brought together again in 52:4. The idea of the bee is used elsewhere in the Old Testament (cf. Deut. 1:44) to depict a vicious enemy. There are well-documented cases in the ancient world of bees responding to whistling, though the details of how it was done are lost. The picture is of a massive invasion that is going to reach every corner of the land. Even the most inaccessible ravine and every bush and waterhole are to know the presence of the invading bees.

20 In this and the following verse the phrase 'in that day' recurs (see comment on verse 18). In that dramatic day of God's visitation, he will bring a hired razor from beyond the River (i.e. the Euphrates) to sweep through the land in judgment. The reference to a hired razor is almost certainly an allusion to the fact that Ahaz had already made his momentous decision in regard to his immediate danger. Instead of giving heed to the LORD's message (see verses 7-9) he had already sent word to Tiglath-Pileser, King of Assyria, saying: 'I am your servant and your son.' This was the language of a covenant vassal to a superior. Ahaz went even further in that he took silver and gold from the temple treasuries and sent them as a gift to Tiglath-Pileser (2 Kings 16:7-8).

The irony of the situation is that God will use as his instrument of judgment the very razor that Ahaz had hired with that gift.

21-22 This picture presents the situation after the Assyrians invade the land, and the way in which, because of lack of people to care for the land, it degenerates to wilderness. The Assyrian invasion will completely denude the land. A few people are going to remain (cf. 6:13), and a man will be left with just a remnant of his former herd, and so will be kept alive by the produce of his young cow and two goats. All the inhabitants left in the land (with the implication that there will be comparatively few) will manage to survive on milk products and also honey. They will only be left with famine fare (cf. verse 15).

23-24 These verses depict the reversal of cultivated land to its natural state. Where there had previously been vineyards planted at great cost, briers and thorns will grow, because there are not enough people left to continue the various agricultural activities. Instead of coming there to cultivate the vines and to gather the fruit, men will come out with bows and arrows to hunt for wild animals. Alternately the idea may be that they will need to be armed for their own safety if they come into those areas.

25 Whereas the people had previously gone out with their hoes to cultivate the hillsides, now they will not go there because the hillsides have been taken over again by wild vegetation. All that they can do is to send out the cattle and sheep and let them roam through those areas. Palestine, intended as a new garden of Eden, will revert to being a desolate land.

ii. The Message for the People (8:1-4)

This chapter opens with the proclamation concerning another birth, this time one in the near future. Just as Isaiah's other son (Shear-jashub) had a symbolic name, so also the second son will bear a name that has relevance to the immediate situation.

1 The prophet is instructed by the LORD to take a large scroll and write 'concerning Maher-shalal-hash-baz'. The reference to a man's pen may mean that the letters were to be large and easily read. The name is clearly intended to be that of another son to Isaiah and his wife, though that is not immediately spelt out. It is only in verse 3, after the birth of the child, that it becomes plain that this is to be his name. It is a symbolic one, meaning something like 'speedy spoil, hasty prey', or 'Quick pickings, easy prey' (J. B. Phillips). It has as its reference point the coming of the Assyrians, and therefore speaks of the way in which they will come quickly and hasten after the prey.

2 The LORD gives a further pledge concerning this by having the writing confirmed by the witnesses, Uriah the priest and Zechariah the son of Jeberechiah. Uriah is mentioned in 2 Kings 18:10-16 as the priest who was willing to obey Ahaz's instructions regarding the building of an altar after the pattern of the one that Ahaz had seen in Damascus, and of offering sacrifices upon it. Zechariah may well have been the father-in-law of Ahaz (2 Kings 17:2; 2 Chron. 29:1), possibly the same person who is named as being a Levite of the family of Asaph (2 Chron. 29:13). These witnesses will not only note the prophecy but also its fulfilment. Moreover, the birth of *this* child will be soon, and he will be a living witness to the word of the LORD.

3-4 The reference to the prophetess need not imply that Isaiah's wife was acting in the capacity of a prophetess. It may be no more than simply the feminine form of the Hebrew noun 'prophet', and thus a designation of the prophet's wife. She conceives and bears a son and then the prophet is instructed to call him 'Maher-shalal-hash-baz'. The significance of this name is then explained. Before the young child is old enough to say 'Mummy' and 'Daddy', the Assyrians will have looted Damascus and Samaria of their riches. This is the explicit announcement of their impending doom. This was fulfilled in reference to Damascus in 732 BC and in relation to Samaria in 722 BC.

iii. Coming Judgment Reiterated (8:5-8)

5-6 A further message from the LORD gives more information concerning the coming devastation. There is a double explanation. The people are despising God's provision for them and they also have an approving attitude to Rezin and Pekah, rejoicing over their expected capture of Jerusalem. This seems to suggest that Ahaz lacked popular support, as the people esteemed Rezin and Pekah more highly than him. God's kingdom is being despised, and even if the little stream that fed the waters of Siloam is increased to the size of the Jordan, yet it will not be esteemed any more highly (cf. Namaan's words in 2 Kings 5:10-12: 'Are not Abanah and Pharpar, the rivers of Damascus, better than all the waters of Israel?'). Clearly there are people rejoicing in the prospect of the coming of these two foreign kings. The reference to Pekah, though, is very derogatory, still calling him only 'the son of Remaliah'.

7 The people who are despising the softly flowing waters of Siloam will soon find that other water is coming. There is to be a mighty flood from Assyria, described here as if the River Euphrates broke its banks. It will not be an accidental event, but one in which the LORD's hand is clearly displayed. It is he who is going to bring the king of Assyria in all his glory to fulfil his sovereign purposes against both Judah and Israel. In Ahaz's arranging for the 'help' of Assyria, he had set the seal of destruction not only on Samaria, but on Jerusalem too (cf. 7:17). Judah is to become a victim as well.

8 The whole land will be flooded, as the mighty waters sweep through Judah, yet there is some prospect of escape held out as the flood will reach up to the neck. This may imply that there will be some who will escape destruction, for God has set limits upon the coming invasion, and later Isaiah is to hold out hope to the people (cf. 10:24-27). But the real hope of deliverance lay in the connection they had with Immanuel. The land (i.e. Israel) is Immanuel's land and cannot be appropriated by someone else.

c. The Remnant (8:9-22)

i. The Assurance (8:9-10)
9 The call of God goes out to the Gentile nations, especially to Assyria as the oppressor. Three times the nations are told that they will be shattered (the imperatives are virtually equivalent to future perfects), in order to stress God's sovereign intervention on behalf of his people. All their strategies will be overthrown. Though the armies gird themselves for battle, yet God will deal with them and shatter them.

10 Even though the enemy nations consult together (probably a reference back to the united strategy of Syria and Israel, cf. 7:1), their plans will never come to fruition. They may speak together and devise their strategy but it will not stand. The phrase used here for 'it will not stand' is identical to that which the LORD has already used in his message to Ahaz (7:7). It may also be an echo of Samuel's words to Saul when he told him that his kingdom would not stand (1 Sam. 13:14). The reason is then given at the end of the verse. Two translations are possible. Either, it can be rendered 'for God is with us', or else it can be taken as the personal name 'Immanuel'. As the name 'Immanuel' has just occurred in verse 8, there is some presumption in favour of taking it here in the same way. The only difficulty is that for the English reader the force of the name in the context is not as apparent as it would have been for the original Hebrew readers or listeners. Perhaps in English we need to add explanatory words: 'because of Immanuel (i.e. God is with us).' God's plans will not be thwarted. Contrariwise, the plans of the nations will be overthrown because the people are assured, 'God is with us.'

ii. The True Israel (8:11-15)

Encouragement is held out to the people of Judah as the prophet speaks God's words regarding the devices of the enemy nations, and of the need to make the LORD himself the object of their fear.

11 Again the LORD ministers his word to the prophet Isaiah, and this time it is said that it is 'with a strong hand'. This phrase implies the emphasis that the LORD places on the course of action that he is setting before his people. The instruction is put in a negative way, for Isaiah is told not to go in the way of the people. That is to say, his own attitude has to be markedly different from the average person in Judah who is living in fear of the impending invasion. The hearts of the people are being moved just like the trees of the forest that are shaken by the wind (see 7:2).

12 The reference to a 'conspiracy' is probably to what the people were calling the attitude of Isaiah and those who sided with him, who wanted to depend upon the LORD for their deliverance. The people as a whole, however, viewed that as a conspiracy or treason. Isaiah is not to take heed to their name calling, nor to be afraid of the threats that they might make. We do not read of actual threats against Isaiah's life, but it may well be that just as in the case of Jeremiah his life was, at times, threatened by those opposing him.

13 The one they are to fear is the LORD himself, 'the LORD of hosts.' He is the holy one of whom the seraphim had sung in Isaiah's inaugural vision (6:2-3). The use of this phrase appears to be deliberate in order to emphasise the power of God, who is able to marshal his hosts in support of his people. There is also emphasis on the phrase because of its position at the very beginning of the sentence: 'The LORD of hosts, *him* you shall treat as holy.' The object of their fear is not some foreign king, but the living God. The people are called on to change their total thought patterns in the present situation and to treat as holy him who is indeed 'the holy one of Israel'.

14 The opening phrase gives the encouragement that the people are needing. For his people, God will be a sanctuary. The Hebrew word for 'sanctuary' (*miqdâsh*) comes from the root 'to be holy' (*qâdash*) and is normally used of the tabernacle and the temple. It is used here, as in Ezekiel 11:16, to refer to a place of refuge. The contrast between the LORD's relationship to his people and to those who despise him is brought into sharp focus in the following words. To both Israel in the north and Judah in the south the LORD will be a stone of stumbling and a rock of offence. To those who live in Jerusalem he will be a trap and a snare. The words 'a stone of stumbling and a rock of offence' are quoted in 1 Peter 2:8, while in 1 Peter 3:14-15 words are taken from both verses 13 and 14: 'And do not be afraid of their threats, nor be troubled. But sanctify the Lord God in your hearts.' It is striking that Peter identifies the Lord of hosts with Christ, a further confirmation of the identification with him of the exalted Lord of Isaiah 6:1 (see comment).

15 The section closes with a strong warning. Many of the disbelievers will stumble and fall, and the snare will catch them. Just as Isaiah has been warned in his commissioning (6:11-13), so now he is reminded that his preaching ministry will show little fruit. Instead, a majority of the people will experience that the LORD is indeed set for the rising and falling of many in Israel.

iii. The Remnant (8:16-22)

This section has its own difficulties, mainly because there seems to be a change of speaker between verses 16 and 17, and again between verses 18 and 19. In the passage the idea is developed of an Israel within Israel, disciples of the LORD and 'children' of Isaiah, who are to be signs for Israel as a whole. It has been suggested that there is a time gap between this section and the one before, but this question can only be decided on the basis of contextual considerations. There is no reason why it should not follow on immediately from what precedes.

16 It appears to be the LORD who is speaking in this verse, and the fact that the imperatives are singular is further confirmation of this view. The message is addressed to Isaiah. There does not seem to be any individual whom the prophet would address in these terms. The LORD calls for a binding of the testimony he has given, and a sealing of the law to his 'disciples'. This is a new term for the believing remnant in Israel, and it may also suggest that the circle of the prophet's activity is in the future to be concentrated on this smaller group.

17 The prophet speaks in response, as he recognises that at present the LORD is hiding his face from the nation. In contrast, the prophet has hope and expectation in the LORD. Both the Hebrew verbs used in this verse suggest waiting with eager longing and expectation. The first verb, as in Isaiah 64:4 [MT verse 3], denotes earnest expectation and hope, while the second one occurs in other passages such as Isaiah 26:8 and Lamentations 3:25 in which the true believers are encouraged to trust in the LORD even in the midst of divine judgment.

18 The group who will seal the testimony and preserve the law of the LORD are the prophet and his spiritual children. Some commentators have taken the children to be Isaiah's own sons, Shear-jashub and Maher-shalal-hash-baz, but the immediate context here suggests a wider application of the word. The true disciples form the remnant who will hold to the testimony of the LORD, and also preserve it for future use. Words from the previous verse, 'I will put my trust in him', and the words from this verse, 'Here am I and the children whom God has given me', are used in Hebrews 2:13 in reference to Christ and his people. The small group linked with the prophet is regarded as typical of the church gathered around Christ.

19-20 In times of crisis in Israel the people often reverted to forbidden practices, and we see that in these verses. The people are engaging in the practices forbidden in Deuteronomy 18:9-13, and they are seeking from the dead messages for the present. Consulting mediums and wizards was among the Canaanite practices that were declared abhorrent to the LORD. The people in general clearly thought that they should seek a word from the dead that was relevant for the immediate situation. But messages for the present only come from the word of the LORD. The testimony and law already spoken of (verse 16) are to be the source of revelation concerning God's will. While it is true that 'torah' can be instruction, the Mosaic law was regarded as the primary source of instruction and the foundation of moral life. Those who pretended to speak the word of the LORD from sources other than this have not even a glimmer of light about them.

21-22[27] Those who continue to despise God's word will wander in darkness and despair. The contrast between the two groups in Judah

---

[27]In the printed Hebrew texts 9:1 of the English translation is verse 23 of chapter 8.

is made very plain. Whereas the one group rest their confidence in their God and walk in his light, the majority in the land will experience nothing but darkness. They will go through the land and suffer from hunger because of the famine conditions that are going to exist. Then many people will reach the point of being so enraged that they will curse both their king and their God. All that they will see around them will be darkness and trouble. The final phrase of verse 22, 'they will be driven into darkness', seems to point towards the captivity in Babylon as the culmination of their unbelief.

iv. The Glorious Hope (9:1-7)

Having described the gloom over the land, Isaiah now directs attention to the coming glory in the person of the promised Davidic king. A day is ahead for the people when a great light will shine and a special child will be born.

1 The expression in this verse seems rather elliptical, and it is probable that we should insert words like 'no more' before 'gloom': 'There will be no more gloom for those who were in distress' (NIV). The reference to Zebulun and the land of Naphtali is important, because being in the north they were to be among the first areas of the land to experience the onslaught of the Assyrians. However, the significant point is that they are to be the first parts of the land to see the messianic glory. It was from Galilee of the Gentiles that Jesus came. Matthew in his Gospel quotes verses 1-2 in reference to the ministry of Jesus when he came to reside in Capernaum (Matt. 4:13-16).

2 The same area that had experienced such darkness (described here by the parallel phrases 'walking in darkness'='dwelling in the land of the shadow of death', cf. Ps. 23:4, 'the valley of the shadow of death') will ultimately be radiated by glorious light. The word 'light' stands for all the blessings that the Messiah will bring.

3 The nation is described as being radically changed. The word used for 'nation' here is the Hebrew word *gôy*, which is normally reserved for the Gentile nations, though there are some other Old Testament examples where it is used of Israel (cf. Gen. 12:2; 18:18; Exod. 19:6; Isa. 1:4). The nation will be enlarged compared with its size on the return from exile, and its joy will be increased. Some versions like the AV translate the first two clauses of this verse as 'Thou hast multiplied the nation and *not* increased the joy'. In the context the positive note of joy is demanded. Hence, it is best to read the Hebrew

word *lô'* not as the negative but as the preposition and suffix, 'to it':
'You have enlarged the nation and increased the joy to it.' Two
metaphors are used to describe the joy. There will be more joy than
harvesters have on the successful completion of the harvest, and a
group of soldiers have when dividing the spoil after a great victory.

4 This and the next two verses all begin in the Hebrew text with
the word *kî*, 'for', so that three explanations are provided for the joy
of the people, culminating in the birth of the special child in verse 6.
This can be set out as follows:

> You [the LORD] have multiplied the nation and increased its joy . . .
>> *For* you have broken the yoke of his burden . . .
>> *For* every warrior's sandal will . . . be used for burning . . .
>> *For* to us a child is born . . . .

The messianic day will be marked by the lifting of burdens, and the
work of Jesus will be far greater than that of Gideon in the past (Judg.
6–8). The bondage is probably not physical servitude but the oppressive
burden of sin which is to be lifted by the messianic proclamation of
good news. When Jesus began his preaching ministry in the synagogue
at Nazareth he declared that he was fulfilling the task described later
by Isaiah (61:1-3) of setting at liberty those who were oppressed (Luke
4:18-19).

5 Another explanatory clause follows. A further feature of the
theocratic rule that will cause great joy will be the coming of peace.
This is not necessarily peace between nations but peace between God
and men. The angels announce this at the birth of Jesus, as they sing,
'Glory to God in the highest, and on earth peace, good will toward
men' (Luke 2:14). Jesus himself proclaims his special peace to his
disciples (John 14:27), and the apostle Paul declares that Jesus who
himself is our peace, has broken down the middle wall of partition
through the blood of his cross (Eph. 2:14-18). Here Isaiah says that
that day will be like abolition of war, when all the implements of battle
are destroyed by being thrown into the fire.

6 The final reason for the joy is the greatest of all. Isaiah tells of
the birth of a special child who will come from the Davidic line. The
language used here and in the following verse is based on the covenant
made with David (cf. 2 Samuel 7). The child born will be destined for
rule, as the government will rest on his shoulders. His names are to be

indicative of the character he has and the work he will do. It is best to take it that there are four names given, as in Hebrew they have a common grammatical form. These names are, 'wonderful counsellor', 'mighty God', 'everlasting father' and 'prince of peace'.

The first word, 'wonderful,' is most significant, as in Hebrew it comes from a root that is almost exclusively used of the things that only God can do. Immediately Hebrew readers saw the word or auditors heard the word *pele'*, it would alert them to the fact that something is being described that is beyond human capability. Therefore when it is linked with 'counsellor' the meaning is that the child will be a divine counsellor, who will instruct with the wisdom that comes only from God.

The second phrase, 'mighty God', confirms the implication of the first phrase, and especially when one compares the use of this phrase in 10:21 ('a remnant will return, the remnant of Jacob, *to the mighty God*'), the impression is clearly given that deity is being ascribed to the child. Though he will be 'born of the seed of David according to the flesh' (Rom. 1:3), yet he will be God himself 'who is over all, the eternally blessed God' (Rom. 9:5).

He will also be 'father of eternity'. The reference to 'father' should not be taken to mean that the messianic king will be the first person of the Trinity in his human appearance. Rather the emphasis is on the character he bears, and the manner in which he cares for his children with fatherlike compassion and tenderness. For all eternity he will deal with his children as a loving father.

Finally, the Messiah will be 'prince of peace'. The Hebrew word 'peace' (*shâlôm*) means much more than our English word, which points to the absence of warfare and strife. The Hebrew word designates prosperity as well as tranquillity. Many of the other prophets in the Old Testament speak about the messianic period as a period of peace.

Taken together the terms speak of the child as one who will instruct with wisdom which is divine, who will act in power as the mighty God, who will love and care for his children eternally, and whose coming will bring lasting peace and blessing.

7 The messianic child is someone far different from other children, even those born into David's family. The child called 'Immanuel' (7:14) is going to 'sit on the throne of David and over his kingdom ... from that time forward, even forever'. His kingdom will be an everlasting one, and the government he exercises and the peace he brings will know no end. The Hebrew word for 'government' (*misrâh*) comes from the word 'prince' (*sâr*), and the indication is that it will be a Davidic prince who will be the messianic ruler. The final clause in the verse shows how all this will come about. It will come only because the zeal of the LORD of hosts will accomplish it (cf. Zech. 8:2). No human agency can achieve this result. It will depend solely on the power of a sovereign God. He brings about the peace and then the child will rule over the peaceful kingdom.

4. God's Word to Israel (9:8–11:16)

Attention switches principally to the northern kingdom of Israel. Isaiah presents a similar picture for this kingdom as he has done for the southern one of Judah.

a. The Moment of Decision (9:8–10:4)

The depiction of the crisis confronting Israel is set out in four paragraphs – foreign invasion, defeat in battle, anarchy, and captivity. They are marked out in the text itself by the repetition of the refrain, 'For all this his anger is not turned away, but his hand is stretched out still' (9:12, 17, 21; 10:4). This refrain has already occurred in 5:25.

i. Foreign Invasion (9:8-12)

8 God now sends a word, i.e. proclaims his message through his servant the prophet Isaiah, against Israel. In the parallelism of the verse Israel is called 'Jacob', using the older name that was changed after the incident at Peniel (Gen. 32:22-32).

9-10 With a good measure of bravado the people of Israel face the future. In their pride and arrogance they make boastful statements of how they will restore everything. Not only will they rebuild, but the replacements will be even better than the original ones. They will replace bricks with hewn stones, and sycamore with cedar. Isaiah's contemporary Amos denounces the stone mansions built by the wicked (Amos 5:11), while cedar from Lebanon was reckoned as the most valuable wood and was used in the temple (1 Kings 6:15). Judgments of God will not affect the sinful heart of the people, as they set out to plan their future with grandiose ideas.

11 The commencement of the verse needs some words to carry over the thought pattern from what has preceded. Probably the words from the beginning of verse 9 are to be understood as applying here too: 'All the people will know....' What the people will also know is that the enemies of Rezin are under the LORD's direction. The reference seems to be to the Assyrians whom the LORD was spurring on to do his bidding. As often in the prophets the message shows that God is not only controlling the destiny of Israel and Judah but of the surrounding nations as well. He is the God who controls all of human history.

12 The Syrians and the Philistines will both be used to inflict punishment on Israel. The scene described is a pincer movement, with attacks from two sides. This may well have developed between the time of the fall of Damascus in 732 BC and the capture of Samaria in 722 BC. There is no hope held out to Israel, which will be swallowed up by its attackers. The first time the refrain occurs is at the end of this verse. The first part of it emphasises the anger of God that is still directed towards Israel, while the second part is not an indication of mercy but a threat of even further judgment from the LORD's hand. This refrain should have acted as a warning of the storm near at hand.

ii. Defeat in Battle (9:13-17)

13 On the part of the people no repentance is to be seen. The word rendered 'turn' (Heb. *shûv*) is often used in covenantal contexts in the sense of turning in repentance to God. Even under the smiting hand of the LORD there is no change in their attitudes. The true approach from the people should have been to seek the LORD, but that is conspicuously absent from their lives. Whereas Jeremiah uses the verb 'to turn' forty-eight times in the sense of 'repentance', Isaiah only uses it ten times. This may point to the fact that the die is cast for Israel, and judgment is inevitable. The hearts of the people have been made heavy and there will be no turning to the LORD (see Isa. 6:10: 'otherwise they might ... turn [*shûv*] and be healed').[28]

14-15 These verses point to a dramatic climax which is coming in the history of Israel, when it will lose its leaders in one decisive day. The Hebrew word translated 'cut off' (Heb. *kârat*) may well be very significant, for it echoes the threat of Genesis 17:14 against the unfaithful covenant servants. The reference is probably to the end of

---

[28]For excellent discussions on the theological use of the Hebrew word *shûv*, see those by Victor Hamilton in *TWOT* 2, pp. 909-10, and by J. A. Thompson/Elmer Martens in *NIDOTTE* 4, pp. 55-59.

the northern kingdom (see 2 Kings 17:1-6) when Hoshea the last king is imprisoned by the Assyrians. 'Palm-branch and bulrush' seem to relate to the most prominent and least prominent in the land. Hence the idea is that all will be affected by the LORD's judgment at that time, from the least to the greatest. Verse 15 is a parenthesis that explains that 'the head' already referred to means the elder and the honourable people, while 'the tail' is the false prophets who tell lies. God's judgment is to be set against the leaders in both the civic and religious affairs of Israel. The same terms head/tail and palm-branch/bulrush are used in Isaiah 19:15 of the leaders in Egypt.

16 Both teachers and those taught are in the same category. The one group instructs falsely, while those who are their students accept the teaching and are led to destruction. Judgment begins with leaders (cf. Jas. 3:1), but followers share in it. Both groups should have been guided by God's law, but together they set it aside to their own ruin.

17 Even the classes in society that normally merited God's special attention will come under the same judgment. Young men, orphans and widows were afforded special protection and care, but when they become ungodly and evildoers they cannot be excused from the general judgment. The word used here for 'ungodly' (Heb. *chânêf*) occurs most frequently in the book of Job where it describes those who are perverse and arrogant. Not only does Isaiah use it to describe Israel, but later he will use it to warn that God is bringing judgment by means of an ungodly nation (10:6). Everyone in the land is regarded as speaking what is folly in God's eyes, and once again the refrain rings out its peal of judgment.

iii. Anarchy (9:18-21)

18-19 A different figure is used in reference to the sin in the land. It is depicted as if it is a fire that consumes. Just as a fire starts in the 'briers and thorns' (the same pair of words as in 5:6, and 7:23-25), and then gets hold of the forests, with the smoke rising into the sky, so sin having started in a small way now consumes the land. But another fire is coming, the fire of God's anger, which is going to sweep through the land and bring complete devastation. It is possible to view this reference in verse 19 to God's anger as being expressed in the self-inflicted judgments of the people, especially in the light of the coming reference to civil anarchy. There is a marked contrast between the days of peace when stained battle clothes will be fuel for the fire (9:5) and the coming judgment when the people themselves will be reckoned as fuel for the fire.

20 The picture of fire is set aside, to be replaced by the imagery of a hungry man desperately seeking some food. He snatches whatever is within his reach. It is said that he will even eat the flesh of his own arm, i.e. attacking the very thing that is to be his defence. No one would think of doing that. The NIV takes a different line in assuming a reference to cannibalism, when a man will even eat some of his own family. The difference comes through alternative interpretations of one Hebrew word ($z^ero\,'\hat{o}$). If the Massoretic vocalisation is maintained, it is 'his arm'. If the vocalisation is changed to $zar\,'\hat{o}$ it means 'his seed' i.e. his family. In the context the first interpretation is to be preferred, as the expression seems to be metaphorical.

21 Sin will so destroy the society in Israel that even the brotherly tribes of Ephraim and Manasseh will turn on each other. The tribes that were intended to be a model for the others, and whom other tribes would mention in prayer ('May God make you as Ephraim and as Manasseh!' Gen. 48:20), will themselves degenerate to indulging in intertribal war. Their hostility against the south will be such, though, that they will co-operate in their antagonism against Judah. It is only in the future messianic day that the long-standing rivalry between Ephraim and Judah will be abolished (11:13). Once more the sad refrain sounds its solemn note as the section closes.

iv. Captivity (10:1-4)

1-2 This may be one of the series of woes that began in chapter 5 and that culminates in 10:5-19. It directs attention to the rulers in the land who instead of acting with uprightness and integrity set out laws that oppress the poor and needy. The words translated by the NIV as 'unjust' (Heb. *'âven*) and 'oppressive' (Heb. *'âmâl*) occur together elsewhere in the Old Testament (see Ps. 90:10). 'Oppressive' is often applied to unpleasant factors of work and toil, always with negative overtones. Again, as in 9:17, reference is made to the most needy in the society being the very people who are suffering from injustice. The needy, the poor, the widows, and the fatherless have no one to defend them, and therefore are worthy of extra protection from society as a whole. Instead they are the victims of injustice.

3 However, a day is coming when wrongs will be avenged. By means of three questions the LORD challenges the people. What is their response going to be when God brings a nation from afar to visit them? To whom then will they be able to look for assistance? When that day comes, where can they store up their ill-found wealth? The day of visitation will see God's punishment meted out to them.

4 Two possibilities are open regarding their future. Either they will be taken captive by the Assyrians, or else they will be killed in battle. The historical account of the fall of the northern kingdom speaks of how 'the LORD rejected all the descendants of Israel, afflicted them, and delivered them into the hand of the plunderers, until he had cast them from his sight' (2 Kings 17:20). Once more the refrain reinforces the coming expression of the LORD's anger.

b. The Assyrian Invasion (10:5-19)

5 The description of the coming invasion commences with an expression of woe against the very instrument that God is using. Assyria is the chosen rod of God's anger and the staff of his indignation, but that fact is not going to exclude Assyria itself from the same judgment of the LORD. God is able to use heathen nations to carry out his purposes against Israel and Judah, yet he holds those nations in his hand as well, and they are to be held responsible for their own sins. Divine sovereignty does not exclude blame for sinful actions, as Peter proclaimed to the crowd listening to him in Jerusalem on the day of Pentecost ('This man was handed over to you by God's set purpose, ... but you ... put him to death', Acts 2:23).

6 The divine 'I' here ('*I* send ... *I* command') reminds us of how God is sovereignly sending his chosen instrument on a mission of invasion and destruction. The reference to an ungodly nation recalls the use of the same Hebrew word in 9:17 (*chânêf*). It speaks of hypocrisy and deceitful living. A commission has been given to Assyria to seize the spoil, to take the prey, and to tread the people down like dust in the streets. The mention of spoil and prey points the reader immediately to the naming of Isaiah's second son (8:1-4). Maher-shalal-hash-baz received his name to show how quickly and ruthlessly the Assyrian army will descend on the land, and with what rapacity it will take the riches away. In this verse the words *shalal* ('loot') and *baz* ('plunder') occur, both preceded by cognate verbs, a feature that often occurs in Hebrew but which is avoided in English. A literal translation is that Assyria is coming 'to loot the loot and to plunder the plunder'.

7 The thinking of the Assyrians about their actions is false. They know something about their role as the agent of the living God (cf. 2 Kings 18:25, 'The LORD said to me, "Go up against this land, and destroy it" '), but yet in their pride and lust they wish to carry out their attacks not only on Israel and Judah but on many nations. Imperialistic pride is dominating their thinking.

8-9 In his pride the king of Assyria is able to look on his past conflicts and consider that Calno, Hamath, and Samaria will fall to him like Carchemish, Arpad, and Damascus have already done. The fate of these cities should serve as object lessons to Israel. Carchemish, a fort guarding a crossing of the Euphrates River north-east of Aleppo, fell to the Assyrians in 717 BC, while Arpad, to the north-west of Aleppo, was captured by the Assyrians in 754 BC and totally destroyed in 740 BC. Damascus was subjected to repeated attacks by the Assyrians, culminating in Isaiah's time in the spoiling of the city (see 8:4) and the carrying away of many of its inhabitants (2 Kings 16:9). The fact that Samaria is mentioned in this way suggests that the prophecy comes in the period prior to the fall of Samaria in 722 BC. The list of places follows a geographical order from north-east to south-west, moving from Carchemish on the Euphrates down to Samaria. Over all the captured provinces the king had set his officers as puppet-kings.

10-11 The thought of the Assyrian king progresses to the idea that he has not only conquered nations but conquered their gods as well. He has taken nations with far more outward religious symbols than Jerusalem and Samaria. These kingdoms are regarded as having belonged to their idols (using the Heb. word *'ᵉlîl* which in its plural form *'ᵉlîlîm* sounds very like the usual Heb. word for God, *'ᵉlôhîm*; see comment on 2:8). In his way of thinking, if he had managed to conquer those nations, why should he not do so to Jerusalem and her idols as well? The fact that Samaria is named as having been taken does not stand against the view that the prophecy is prior to the final fall of the city in 722 BC. Samaria fell several times before its final demise.

12 The Assyrian king makes his proud boasts without taking into account what is the mind of the LORD. His intention is to use Assyria as the rod of his anger, and then to visit that proud and haughty nation as well. However, the pre-condition for that is that the LORD will first finish off his work against Mount Zion and Jerusalem. The threatened judgment comes against the covenant people, followed thereafter by visitation upon the very means that God is using in that judgment. The attitude and actions of Assyria will not ultimately go unpunished.

13-14 The boasting of the king of Assyria is now given by the prophet, with the king referring to himself nine times in these two verses. This is in keeping with the Assyrian records themselves, and both biblical text and external records show how confident the Assyrians were in their own power. One king, Adad-Nirari, made this claim: 'Building by Adad-Nirari the great king, the mighty king, king of the world, king of Assyria, the king whom Ashur, king of the gods of the Upper World, chose while still in his youth and granted him an unrivalled princeship.'[29] The kings acted in their own wisdom and with the power that was available to them. They even arbitrarily moved international boundaries (see 2 Kings 17:24). Not only that, but the riches of people were picked up as if they were eggs in a bird's nest. The thieving mentality of the Assyrians is brought out by these words. They clearly despoiled the conquered territory as well as insisting on vast amounts of tribute that conquered kings and countries had to pay them. When listing their military achievements, the Assyrian kings note the tribute they collected.[30] Verse 14 ends with another expression of proud boasting. Not a single bird moved its wing, or gave even a cheep, while this theft was in process.

15 The futility of this boasting is brought out by the prophet's words. An axe cannot boast of itself over against the one who wields it, nor a saw over against the one who saws with it. A rod or a club cannot turn on anyone who lifts it up. So Assyria should realise that, though an instrument in the LORD's hand, she should not boast of her own might.

16 Against Assyria the LORD will move in his own way, by sending leanness or wasting. This seems to refer to some disease that will afflict the well-fed and proud Assyrians, such as that recorded in 2 Kings 19:35 when Sennacherib's troops were besieging Jerusalem. The LORD is going to kindle a fire, and the Hebrew uses three words to describe this. They are all from the same root, and give an onomatopoeic ring to the proclamation (Heb. *yêqad y^eqod kîqôd 'êsh*). The arrogant imperial power will be humbled before the fire of the LORD.

17-18 The LORD is referred to in an unusual way as 'the Light of Israel'. The messianic era has already been described as one bringing

---

[29]*DOTT*, p. 51. There are numerous other examples in this selection of Assyrian documents, pp. 46-75.

[30]For examples, see *DOTT*, pp. 48, 51, 52, 55, 56.

light even to Gentile areas of Palestine (9:2), but here the thought is not of bringing light but causing fire to break out. It is linked with the idea of God's holiness that is a flame which destroys with judgment fire. This will take place with decisiveness, 'in one day.' As in 9:14 ('palm branch and bulrush'), it seems as if all of society from the greatest ('the glory of the forest') and the humblest ('his thorns and his briers') are being described by the use of just two expressions. The section ends by reverting to the idea of a wasting disease afflicting the proud warriors (cf. verse 16). Their boasting will not save them on that day.

19 The ultimate outcome for Assyria will be that her warriors will be so few in number that even a little lad will be able to count them. Just as some trees survive a forest fire, so some will survive the desolation that the LORD will bring, but the might and power of Assyria will be forever broken.

c. The Remnant (10:20-34)

20 The concept of the remnant is once more presented. The first reference to it was in 1:9 ('unless the LORD had left us some survivors'), while the message that Isaiah received in his inaugural commissioning contained the thought of the preservation of 'a holy seed' (6:13). In the next verse there is going to appear an allusion to the name of Isaiah's first son. In that future day, which has been described already, a remnant from Israel and from the house of Jacob will truly depend on 'the Holy One of Israel'. The constant recurrence of this phrase as a descriptive title of the LORD demonstrates how pervasive the concept of God's holiness is for Isaiah. The people will rest upon him for safety, and never again on the Assyrians. This appears to be an allusion to Ahaz' trust in Assyrian help (2 Kings 16:8, 9, and Isa. 7:20). He averted his immediate danger but brought greater problems for both Israel and Judah.

21 A remnant is going to be converted, and the use of the word 'remnant' (Heb. sh^e 'ar) recalls the name of Isaiah's older son in 7:3, Shear-jashub, '[only] a remnant will return.' The expression draws attention both to the fact that it will only be a small number who survive, and to the truth that it will be a conversion experience for them. The remnant of Jacob will come back to 'the mighty God' (cf. the use of this term as one of the names of the messianic king, Isa. 9:6) in penitence and faith.

22 There is a reference here to the promise to Abraham of a large family. It was to be as great as the sand on the seashore (Gen. 22:17). However, it is not said that the whole nation is going to return, but only a remnant. The thought of an Israel within Israel developed in the Old Testament itself, and comes to fullest expression in the New Testament. Abraham is the father of all those who believe (Rom. 4:16; Gal. 3:7), while the true Jew is not one who only outwardly bears the mark in his body, but one who inwardly has circumcision of the heart (Rom. 2:28-29). Paul quotes this passage in Romans 9:27-28 and goes on to argue that there is an election chosen by grace. The last part of the verse is best taken as indicating that the destruction in the land is by God's decree, but yet it is done in righteousness. The Assyrian invasion is within God's decretive will, and yet it will manifest his righteous dealings with his people as he punishes them for their sins.

23 The thought of the last part of the previous verse is continued in the idea that the LORD will carry out his plan to bring destruction upon the land. The word 'land' is ambiguous in Hebrew for it can mean both 'land' and 'earth'. Here the reference is to the land of Palestine, rather than to the whole earth, as that is the subject in the immediate context. The compound title given to God ('the Lord, the LORD of hosts') gives all the greater solemnity to the message of judgment.

24 Re-assurance now comes at least for Judah ('my people who dwell in Zion'), for Assyria is going to be smitten. The LORD recalls his love in times past for his people. Assyria is going to act towards them just as Egypt had been the oppressor at an earlier time. The Hebrew text says it will be 'in the way of Egypt', but the word 'way' is regularly used in the Old Testament to mean 'manner' or 'custom'. Assyria's rod and staff are going to be lifted up against them (cf. the use of rod and staff in 9:4 and 10:5), but Judah is not to fear. Isaiah has already encouraged the people to be fearless (cf. 7:4; 8:12,13), and later in the book there are various sections that commence with the same words, 'Do not fear' (cf. 41:10, 14; 43:1; 44:2).

25 This is a difficult verse to translate and to interpret. The opening of the verse is literally: 'For still a trifle, a little [time].'[31] Following verse 24, which gives assurance of impending relief from the Assyrians,

---

[31]The Hebrew expression here (m^e '*at miz'âr*) only occurs four times in the Old Testament, all in Isaiah. Here and in 29:17 it refers to a very short period of time, while in 16:14 and 24:6 it refers to a small number. The word *miz'âr* may be a phonetic variant of the root *tsâ'ar* which has a similar meaning.

it suggests that God's anger will soon be over. In a short time, the anger of the LORD will bring Assyria to an end, and the destruction will be complete.

26 God is going to raise some other power to act as a scourge against Assyria. Comparison is made with the events recorded in Judges 7:24-25, and especially to what took place at the rock of Oreb when Oreb (the name in Hebrew means 'raven'), one of the Midianite leaders, was killed. Just as previous invaders such as the Midianites had been overcome, so the LORD will disperse the Assyrians. The last part of the verse alludes to what happened at the time of the Exodus when Moses stretched out his rod over the Red Sea (Exod. 14:26-28). The same phrase 'in the way of Egypt' is used as in verse 24. As Egypt had been smitten, so will another rod be lifted up over Assyria.

27 The Assyrian threat is not going to last, for the assurance is given that the yoke will be removed. Mention of the yoke of Assyria carries on quite naturally from reference to the oppression in Egypt. While the main thrust of the verse is clear, the final phrase is difficult. Why should the yoke be removed because of the oil? Various explanations have been given, but none as yet seems entirely satisfactory. The most common one is that the oil is probably a reference to a fat animal, that is able to toss off its yoke. So Israel, like such an animal, will be able to cast off its burden.

Verses 28-34 picture an Assyrian threat that is to be brought to nothing. Assyrians are coming from the north to within a few miles of Jerusalem. This is done to inspire fear, and then the picture switches to a typical judgment scene of forest giants toppling (verses 33-34).

28-32 This is not the real route that the Assyrians took when they did attack Jerusalem. They actually came from Lachish in the south-west (see 36:2). The dreaded foe is coming nearer and nearer to Jerusalem, with the last ten or twenty miles of his approach depicted. Most of the places, except for Gallim and Laish, can be identified, and they are all in a north-south line. The description fits in with the thought of the advancing army. At the pass of Michmash the baggage has to be attended to or even stored. At night the soldiers have to find lodging at Geba, while Jeremiah's home town is addressed as 'poor Anathoth'. There is wordplay here as 'poor' and 'Anathoth' are similar in sound in Hebrew (*ᵃniyyâh* and *ᵃnâtôt*). News of the advancing army causes people in Madmenah and Gebim to flee. At Nob (possibly the modern Mt. Scopus overlooking Jerusalem) he shakes his fist at

Jerusalem, but that is as far as the dreaded attacker will come. He will have to be satisfied with a look at Jerusalem, and with the gesture of impotence as he shakes his fist.

33-34 The mighty power of Assyria, that inspired such terror, is nothing before the might of 'the Lord, the LORD of hosts'. He will lop off the branches as if he is a woodcutter wielding his sharp axe. This is a favourite metaphor of Isaiah when he is speaking about judgment (cf. 2:12-13; 6:13; 10:18-19). The reference to Lebanon does not seem to have any special significance in connection with the Assyrian invasion, but simply because mention of it fits in with the metaphor of large trees.

d. The Glorious Hope (11:1-16)

Just as the message for Judah ended on the encouraging note of a divine child (9:1-7), so here too with the message to Israel there is a vision of a glorious day coming. We should also note the contrast regarding trees between this chapter and the preceding one. In 10:33-34 the trees of the forest are fallen, but here a tree is felled but it still has life in it (cf. 6:13 where it is Judah). In this passage the idea of a tree is used of David's house. There is no allusion back to Immanuel (7:14) or to the royal child (9:6-7), but the three passages form a unity in their presentation of a remarkable birth. For those in Isaiah's own day, there is no clear identification of this figure, but as the Old Testament period progressed, further teaching aroused expectation concerning the one who would come to bring consolation to Israel (Lk. 2:25).

1-2 From the descendants of Jesse (David's father, 1 Sam. 16:10-13) there is to come one who is referred to by two descriptive words, 'rod' and 'branch'. These are both technical terms used here in parallelism. Both are said to go forth from the root or line of Jesse, thus describing a key descendant of David in whom the promises of 2 Samuel 7 will be fulfilled. However, it is not by royal birth alone that such an individual would be fitted for office. Rather, God's Spirit is necessary to fit him for the tasks which will be committed to him. In contrast to some others in the Old Testament who were endowed with the Spirit for special tasks (e.g. Bezaleel and his helpers in building the tabernacle, Exod. 35:30-35), the Spirit of the LORD will take up his abode upon him (cf. Matt. 3:16-17, 'And he saw the Spirit of God descending like a dove and alighting upon him. And suddenly a voice came from heaven, saying, "This is my beloved Son, in whom I am well pleased" '). The threefold gifts with which he will be endowed are wisdom and understanding for government, counsel and might for war, and knowledge and fear of the LORD for spiritual leadership. No king in Israel or Judah ever had all these gifts. It is only in the perfect ruler to come that these manifold endowments will find embodiment.

3-5 These verses set out the way in which he will carry out these offices as guide, guardian, and example. Central to his whole character is the fact that the fear of the LORD will be his delight. His whole life will be lived under the control of the divine will that commissions him to act. There will be no impulsive judgments based on immediate sight or quick hearing of cases. Moreover, his rule will be characterised by utter righteousness, denoted here by a cluster of words depicting how impartial his judgments will be ('righteousness' [twice], 'equity', and 'faithfulness'). How far removed he is from human rulers is spelt out in verse 4b, for he will have divine power at his disposal, while verse 5 regards the attributes of righteousness and faithfulness as his distinctive dress.

6-9 The vision is now directed to the ultimate realisation of the messianic kingdom. The picture of the transformation of nature given here has much in common with the later pictures in chapters 65 and 66 of this book. All the imagery of verses 6-8 suggest an idyllic situation in which there is no disharmony in nature, and animals that now (and probably from creation itself) are enemies, will be able to co-exist in complete peace. Moreover, the relationship between little children and the animal world will be one in which there is no cause for alarm or hurt. The little child shall lead the animals (verse 6), and even babies will be able to play with notoriously dangerous reptiles (verse 8). In verse 9 the speaker is the LORD, or else the prophet has again become the direct mouthpiece of the LORD's words. The reference to 'my holy mountain' is certainly the hill of Zion or Jerusalem, but the latter part of the verse takes the vision much further to encompass the whole earth. Isaiah 65:25 draws on verses 6, 7, and 9, while Habakkuk 2:14 uses the second part of verse 9 in a similar way to the meaning here. This whole section is speaking of great transformations that lie ahead at the coming of the ultimate messianic age.

10 The day of the coming king is described as a day of salvation. He will be both the offspring of Jesse (verse 1) and the root of Jesse (verse 10), descriptions that are brought together in the book of

Revelation. Jesus declares: 'I am the root and offspring of David, the bright morning star' (Rev. 22:16). The word for banner (Heb. *nês*) is used of a standard for gathering troops together for battle, but it also used by the prophets as they describe a return to Zion (Isa. 49:22; 62:10). Here, however, Isaiah personifies the banner as being the messianic ruler himself, and he is the one who will be sought after by the Gentile nations. He is the one who will be lifted up, and then will draw all kinds of men to himself (Jn. 12:32; cf. Jn. 3:14; Phil. 2:9-11). An ingathering of the Gentiles is part of the end-time phenomena that Old Testament eschatology sets out.

11 The theme of the exodus is still present, for the reference to 'the second time' alludes back to the first experience of the LORD's power when he redeemed his people from slavery in Egypt. The name of Isaiah's first son, Shear-jashub ('a remnant shall return'), was a prophecy to the people of the eventual return of a small number. Isaiah now says that the LORD will in his sovereign way obtain for himself the remnant in Assyria, Egypt, Pathros, Cush (Ethiopia), Elam, Shinar, Hamath, and the islands of the sea. Over the years there had been a scattering of Jewish people throughout the Near East, for captives taken in war were often sold off to other nations. Here, as later in Isaiah 40–55 in particular, this ingathering of the remnant is but part of the greater work of salvation in bringing many of the believing sons and daughters of Abraham into the kingdom (cf. 45:22-25; 49:22-26; 51:1-6).

12-14 In the last days, the LORD will set up the Messiah as a banner, and Jew and Gentile will both be brought together from the four corners of the earth. The outcasts of Israel and the dispersed of Judah will join with Gentiles in being drawn to that banner. It is this vision that inspired the hymn writer to say:

> Let Zion's time of favour come;
> O bring the tribes of Israel home;
> And let our wondering eyes behold
> Gentiles and Jews in Jesus' fold.

> William Shrubsole, 1759–1829,
> 'Arm of the Lord awake, awake'

That day will also see something more than just a reconciliation of Jew and Gentile in the kingdom of God. It will also involve a reconciliation between the divided kingdoms of Israel and Judah. The old animosities will be gone, and no longer will the jealousy of Ephraim against Judah mar relationships. It was this jealousy that contributed greatly to the division of the kingdom in the first place. It will disappear, and Judah will not harass Ephraim in any way. The two will be united in their relationships towards their old enemies. On the Mediterranean coast they will overrun the Philistines. Towards the east and south they will plunder their old enemies of Edom, Moab, and Ammon.

15-16 The coming deliverance is likened to another exodus from Egypt. God will utterly destroy (the word used also for the destruction of the Canaanites) the 'tongue' (i.e the gulf) of the Red Sea, just as he did when he brought the children of Israel across it long before. Over the [Euphrates] River,[32] God will shake his fist. Then the river will be divided into seven little streams so that people can go across dryshod. The final verse of the chapter carries on this theme by pointing out that just as God provided a highway for his people out of Egypt, so he will do it again. From Assyria there will be a highway for the returning remnant. This thought, of a greater exodus with a highway for the people, is developed much further in later sections of this book of Isaiah (cf. 35:1-10; 48:20-21; 51:9-11; 52:11-12).

5. The Epilogue (12:1-6)

Very fittingly the book of Immanuel, and indeed the whole of the first twelve chapters of this prophecy, concludes with a song of praise. In the biblical doctrine of salvation praise forms an important response on the part of the believing community (cf. the Song of Moses, the Song of Deborah, the Song of Hannah, the Magnificat, the Benedictus, and the songs in the book of Revelation).

There are allusions in chapter 11 to the Exodus in verses 11 ('the second time'), verse 15 ('dry up the Egyptian Sea') and verse 16 ('highway ... as it was for Israel when they came up from Egypt'). Now in chapter 12 there are allusions to the Song of Moses: verse 2b, 'The LORD, the LORD, is my strength and my song; he has become my salvation', parallels Exodus 15:2a: 'The LORD is my strength and my song; he has become my salvation', while verse 5a, 'Sing to the LORD for he has done glorious things', parallels Miriam's response in Exodus 15:21a: 'Sing to the LORD for he is highly exalted.' The unusual

---

[32]The word used here in Hebrew, *nâhâr*, is often used of the Euphrates without the accompanying designation *pᵉrât*, 'the Euphrates'.

combination of divine names in verse 2 (*yah yhwh*, cf. Exod. 3:14, 15), only occurs elsewhere in Isaiah 26:4. The shortened form of the divine name, Yah, occurs mainly in poetry, in the expression *hallelû-yah*, and as a terminal element in names such as Elijah (Hebrew *'ēlîyâhû*, 'my God is Yah').

The hymn falls into two strophes, clearly marked by the occurrence of the words, 'And in that day you will say' (verses 1, 4).[33] There is no more mention of the wrath of God hanging over his people (cf. the fourfold refrain in 9:12, 17, 21; 10:4) but of anger turned away and of salvation provided (verses 1, 2, 3). Then the final part of the song turns the wonderful deeds of the LORD into a missionary hymn.

a. A Psalm of Praise (12:1-3)

1 A spontaneous outpouring of praise is to flow from the heart of each of the LORD's redeemed (the verbs in verses 1-2 are singular). The verb used for praise (*yâdâh*) is a common one to express proclamation of what God has done. It often carries the idea of making a public confession of the great and wonderful things achieved by his sovereign power (cf. Pss. 89:5; 105:1; 106:1, 145:10). The object of the confession is to announce that the anger that had been manifested against God's people is now turned away. There is no longer any estrangement between the LORD and his people. As a result, there are many expressions of God's mercy displayed towards his children, and he comforts them with his grace. The theme of comfort for those still in exile will receive much greater attention later in this prophecy, when Isaiah 40 opens with the words, 'comfort, comfort my people, says the LORD your God.'

2 This theme of comfort is brought into sharper focus as the singer explains what has happened, with attention being drawn solely to the great saviour of Israel. The opening word, 'behold' (Heb. *hinnêh*), emphasises the significance of the announcement being made: 'the LORD is salvation.' The symbolic name of Isaiah (*yᵉsha'yâhû*, 'God is my salvation') has proved true, and deliverance has come from him. Hence the singer can say that he continually trusts in the LORD and he has no fear. Salvation brings with it as a consequence the absence of fear of God's wrath. Whoever abides in love, abides in God, and there is no fear in love because we can have boldness in the day of judgment (1 John 4:16-18). The singer then completes the idea by using words

---

[33]In verse 1 'you' is singular; in verses 3-4 it is plural.

taken from the Song of Moses in Exodus 15:2. The only significant change is the presence of the additional divine name (*yhwh*) to the form *Yah* that occurs in Exodus. Combinations of divine names are not unusual in the Old Testament, though this one may be deliberately used to emphasise that the salvation has been wrought by the gracious covenant God.

3 Just as God had put an end to all fear, so also he had put an end to all want. Because water was such an important and necessary part of life in the Near East, it is used to represent the blessings of salvation. God is the source of 'living water' (Jer. 2:13), and the invitation is to come and drink of the waters of salvation (Isa. 55:1). In the New Testament our Lord uses the same analogy (John 4:10-15; 7:37).

b. The Missionary Vision of the Redeemed (12:4-6)

The experience of salvation now prompts the redeemed to have God's deeds made known even to the Gentiles. Similar expressions of praise and missionary vision can be found for example in Psalms 67, 96 and 98. The closest parallel to the hymnic portions of Isaiah such as this are to be found in the Psalter.

4 The opening phrase is repeated from verse 1 (except that the pronoun is now second personal plural), and then follows the ascription of praise to the LORD. The phrase, 'call upon his name', is ambiguous in Hebrew. The verb translated 'call' (*qârâ'*) can also mean 'proclaim'. Here, because of what follows, it is best to take it in the second sense, and therefore the opening of the verse will be: 'Praise the LORD, proclaim his name.' Luther always translated this phrase into German as: 'Prediget seinen Namen' ('Preach his name'). Declaration is to be made among the nations of the righteous deeds of the LORD. The word used here for 'deeds' is often used of the LORD's renowned and righteous deeds as contrasted with the wicked actions of men. His name is set on high (Heb. *nisgav*, the same word is used in Isa. 2:11, 17), as it will also be in the ultimate day of his salvation.

5 The opening phrase can be rendered in two ways. The normal English rendering is 'Sing to the LORD', as in many other places in the Old Testament. The difference is that in those places there is a preposition 'to' preceding God's name (*layhwh*). Here there is no preposition, so it is quite possible that 'the LORD' is the object of the verb, and hence we can render, 'Sing *of* the LORD.' The LORD had manifested himself in great acts of mercy towards his people, and even the nations surrounding Israel were not unaware of what he had done (cf. Deut. 4:6-8). Even the Gentile nations had seen the righteousness of the LORD and his salvation (Ps. 98:2-3).

6 As the song comes to its climax, the note of exultant joy increases with the use of two different verbs ('cry out' and 'shout'). The LORD's people are able to sing of the fact that he is in their midst. The declaration is made that the holy one of Israel (one of Isaiah's favourite designations of God) is a great God and he dwells in power amongst his people. It is fitting that the Book of Immanuel should end on such a note. The concentration throughout it has been on the character and work of God, and now the epilogue closes on that note. The great God – redeemer, saviour, provider – is the focal point for his people.

E. The Burdens against the Gentile Nations (13:1–23:18)
Several things need to be said about this section, since it is similar to passages in other prophets.

1. Prophecies against the nations are an integral part not only of Isaiah but also of Amos 1:1–2:3, Jeremiah 46–51, and Ezekiel 25–32. These passages testify to the fact that the prophets' vision encompassed the known world. Isaiah lists all the nations that are presented in these other prophecies with the exception of Ammon.[1]

2. There is no evidence that these prophecies were ever proclaimed to the nations to whom they are addressed. They were primarily intended for the people of Israel/Judah, and they carry important teaching not only about the attitude of God to foreign nations but also regarding God's attitude to his own people. In the speeches against Babylon (14:1-4), Philistia (14:32), Moab (16:1-5), Damascus (16:6), Ethiopia (18:7), Egypt (19:16-25), Jerusalem (22:20-25), and Tyre (23:18) there is express mention of God's gracious intentions concerning his own chosen people. Hence 'burdens against the nations' may not be the most suitable title for these passages as they were intended for Israel/Judah and contain both direct and indirect assurances of divine mercy.

3. Here in Isaiah the section begins with a heading: 'The burden of Babylon which Isaiah the son of Amoz saw' (13:1). This is the third heading up to this point in the book. That in 1:1 was the heading for the

---

[1]For a chart listing the messages against the foreign nations, see Lamar Cooper, Sr., *Ezekiel* (NAC: Broadman & Holman, 1994), p. 244.

whole book, while 2:1 serves to introduce a series of prophecies against Judah and Jerusalem. It is noteworthy that the burden against Babylon follows immediately after the song in 12:1-6, in which the people encourage one another to make known among all nations what God has done for them.

4. The section contains distinctly Isaianic characteristics. There are many parallels between Isaiah 13–14 and other sections in chapters 1–39. These expressions are not found in other Old Testament prophets.

5. The oracles are pre-exilic since later prophets make use of them. For example, Jeremiah in chapters 50–51 refers to Isaiah's oracles. This is particularly true of Jeremiah 50:16 and 40, which are very close to Isaiah 13:14-22.

6. The theological standpoint of these oracles is that God is sovereign over all nations, and he uses them to fulfil his will and purpose. Accordingly, they have a message for the people of God, which destroys the delusion of thinking that they are immune from divine judgment. If God pronounces such judgment against the Gentile world, how much greater will be the judgment upon his own people who rebel against him?

7. There is chronological order in Isaiah's oracles, shown by the fact that all the dates given in Isaiah are in sequential order (see 6:1; 7:1; 14:28; 20:1; 36:1). The oracles as a group come from Hezekiah's reign. While there is no discernible geographical grouping, there does seem to be significance in the order.[2] The listing of the nations is placed in groups of five:

First List	Second List
Babylon (13:1–14:27)	Wilderness of the Sea (21:1-10)
Philistia (14:28-32)	Dumah (21:11-12)
Moab (15:1–16:14)	Arabia (21:13-16)
Damascus (17:1–18:7)	Valley of Vision (22:1-25)
Egypt (19:1-25)	Tyre (23:1-18)

Both lists commence with the mighty world power of Babylon, while the second one ends with the great commercial power of the time. The first five are the major political powers, with a general

---

[2]One of the best discussions on the order of the oracles is by G. C. Douglas, *Isaiah One and His Book One* (London: James Nisbet, 1895), pp. 88-89, 99-116, 163-72.

correspondence between the order here and the periods of subservience shown by Israel to foreign powers during the period of the judges.[3] The second five differ from the first in that the first four names are symbolical ones ('Wilderness of the Sea', 'Dumah', 'Arabia', and 'Valley of Vision'). There seems to be some order in these. Babylon again is given a dominant position, followed by reference to those in the patriarchal line who were not immediate ancestors of the people of Israel, namely, Edom and Ishmael. That the reckoning could sometimes be backwards is clear from the words of Leviticus 26:42: 'then I will remember my covenant with Jacob and my covenant with Isaac, and my covenant with Abraham.' Then comes a message for Jerusalem, followed by the prediction of the fall of Tyre.

8. Throughout these oracles the thought of hope is present. Amidst all the storm of nations in tumult, Zion stands firm (14:32). The pronounced judgment on the nations is also a reminder to Israel to trust only in the LORD.[4] It is, therefore, a continuation of the message already set out in chapters 1–12 that the people have to set aside trust in alliances with foreign powers and trust only in the living God.

1. Against Babylon (13:1–14:23)

a. The Title (13:1)
1 The first of the messages does not only begin with the phrase that appears ten times ('a burden of ...') but also with the words 'which Isaiah, the son of Amoz, saw.' This links this section of the prophecy with the longer opening title in 1:1. These ten messages to the nations in Isaiah are all called 'a burden' (Heb. *massâ*'). The occurrences of this Hebrew word, with the exceptions of Proverbs 30:1 and 31:1, all appear in threatening speeches in the prophets. Even from pre-Christian times there was a difference of opinion on whether this word came from the oft-occurring Hebrew word 'to carry' or 'to lift up' (*nâsâ*'), or from a hypothetical root meaning 'to utter', 'to prophesy.'

---

[3]This point is embodied in the discussion of the burdens by G. C. Douglas, ibid., pp. 106-09.

[4]For expansion of this idea see S. Erlandsson, *The Burden of Babylon* (Lund: Geerup, 1970), pp. 65-66.

[5]I am following here the arguments presented by E. W. Hengstenberg for preferring 'burden' to 'oracle'. See his comments on Zechariah 9:1 in his *Christology of the Old Testament*, vol. 2, op. cit., pp. 1017-20.

Preference is to be given to the first explanation,[5] for the messages are not merely speeches but are all condemnatory in tone. There are severe proclamations of judgment, and 'burden' should be retained to convey that concept. This particular one is against 'Babylon', which from this context (see 14:24-27) and elsewhere must have incorporated Assyria. For example, Darius is called 'the king of Assyria' (Ezra 6:22) while Cyrus is called 'the king of Babylon' (Ezra 5:13). 'Babylon' ultimately became the symbol for the world powers hostile to God (see 1 Pet. 5:13; Rev. 14:8; 16:19; 17:1-18:24).

b. Approaching Judgment (13:2-8)

2-3 God calls for his armies to assemble against Babylon. The idiom, 'to lift up a banner', has already been used in 5:26 and 11:10, 12. It is associated here with calling by the voice and beckoning with the hand to the gathering troops. They are designated as God's consecrated ones, his mighty warriors. Their task is to be his messengers of wrath (cf. the phrase 'the rod of my anger' in 10:5). He commands with divine authority and those who respond are those who rejoice in his exaltation. They will come and be able to enter into the very gates of mighty kingdoms such as Babylon.

4 The gathering is already taking place, and the sound of it can be heard. There is uproar among the nations as they assemble together as a great multitude to carry out the LORD's bidding. The purpose is plainly declared. It is the LORD of hosts who is gathering his army together for war. The word used for 'army' (Heb. *tsevâ'*) is the singular of the word for 'hosts' (Heb. *ts^{e}vâ'ôt*). The mighty warrior God, who has all the 'hosts' at his command, is preparing his troops for battle.

5 It is not just the nearby nations who are taking part in this encounter, but those 'from distant lands, from the ends of the heavens'. There does not seem to be any difference between the expressions 'ends of the earth' and 'ends of the heavens'. They both depict the remoteness of the places from which the army will come. The fact that it involves people who are unknown adds to the terribleness of the judgment. Babylon and all her territories will suffer under the divine judgment.

6 The heathen nations have to lament their own destruction. Babylon is to wail because the day of the LORD comes ever closer. When that day comes it will be like destruction from the Almighty (Heb. *k^{e}shod mishshaddai*). The Hebrew shows a play on words, with 'destruction' and 'the Almighty' being similar in sound in Hebrew. It is also possible that both come from the same Hebrew root (*shâdad*, 'to destroy'), which would add even greater force to the wordplay.

7-8 Impending disaster will cause all strength and courage to fade away. Hands will be limp and hearts will fail because of fear. The people will be captive to their own emotions, with terror controlling them as it seizes them in its grip. They will be in pain similar to a woman in childbirth (cf. the use of childbirth imagery in 26:17; Jer. 4:31; 6:24), and with faces flushed with anticipation of the coming destruction they will look from one to another. This is a highly poetical description of Babylon's fall and the reaction of its inhabitants. The mighty Babylon is forewarned that her doom is sealed.

c. Apocalyptic Judgment (13:9-16)

9 Any false expectation regarding the nature of the day of the LORD is set aside. Israel, Judah, and the foreign nations have to realise that God's wrath is going to be manifested with great severity. The mounting description of the coming day ('cruel, with fury and burning anger' [NASB]) reinforces the idea of its destructive nature. The result of it will be devastation for the earth, with its inhabitants being destroyed from it (not 'with it' as the NIV translates).

10 Apocalyptic imagery is used to describe the cosmic changes that will be evident on the day of the LORD. Sun, moon, and stars will be darkened. This feature is a typical characteristic in prophetic descriptions of divine judgment (see Amos 5:18, 20; Joel 2:10, 31; 3:15; Ezek. 32:7-8; Rev. 6:12-13). The symbolic nature of Babylon as the embodiment of all godlessness is part of the vision here, for what is to happen to the actual Babylon is a precursor of the ultimate destruction of all who oppose God and his kingdom (see the description of the fall of Babylon the great, the city of wickedness in Revelation 18).

11 Punishment is coming on the whole world. The Hebrew word for 'world' (*têvêl*) is used in several different ways, but in this context its common meaning of 'inhabited world' is intended. The judgment on Babylon is only part of God's purpose, for he is going to extend it to the whole inhabited world. A visitation in judgment is going to reach all sinners, and the arrogance and pride of sinful man will be destroyed.

12 Just as war reduces the male population, so in the day of the LORD the destruction will obliterate the men. The comparison of the remnant that will be left is with pure gold, or the gold coming from

Ophir in southern Arabia that was noted for its high quality. Hebrew poetic usage appears in the assonance between the first and last words of the verse: 'I will *make man rarer* . . . than the gold of *Ophir*' (Heb. *'ôqîr* . . . *'ôfîr*).

13 Cosmic disturbances are going to occur just as they did when God appeared at Sinai (see Exod. 19:16-18; 20:18). Storms, thunder and earthquakes were often features associated with God's self-revelation (cf. 1 Sam. 12:18; 1 Kings 19:11-12). The second half of the verse reaffirms what has been said already in verse 9 concerning God's anger, using the same words ('fury and burning anger').

14 The Babylonian empire was made up of many different people groups. In the day of the LORD there will be a scattering, and like a wild animal fleeing from her pursuers, or like sheep bereft of a shepherd, people will return to their own native parts. The kingdom will be shattered and what has been a unified nation will be so no more. Dispersion of the population will be a consequence of the destruction of the might of Babylon.

15-16 Anyone fleeing will be exposed to the danger of being caught and killed. The sword will carry out its deadly mission. Invading armies often slaughtered women and children, making sure by this action that there were no future warriors to trouble them. Houses will be robbed of anything that is useful or valuable, while women will be 'ravished'. This word only occurs four times in the Old Testament, and in each case the Massoretes added a marginal note to read instead the verb 'sleep with' (Heb. *shākav*). Clearly the word 'to ravish' (Heb. *shāgal*) was too obscene a word for them, and therefore they altered it to the more neutral 'sleep with'. The curse on Babylon in Psalm 137:8-9 has verse 16 as its background. The psalmist prays for what has already been proclaimed concerning Babylon.

d. The Medes (13:17-22)

17-18 The final verses of chapter 13 consist of a declaration concerning God's use of the Medes in overthrowing Babylon. The Medes were from an area south-west of the Caspian Sea and they were conquered by Cyrus in 550 BC. Both Isaiah and also Jeremiah 51:11, 28 foretell the fall of Babylon to the Medes. When it was captured Darius, the

---

[6]This comment means that I am equating Cyrus and Darius the Mede. Though various other identifications have been suggested, this appears to

new ruler, was called 'Darius the Mede' (Dan. 5:31; 11:1).[6] Isaiah introduces the Medes using one of his favourite expressions, one that is normally used to designate important announcements (Heb. *hin^eni*, 'behold I ...'). The reference to gold and silver suggests that the lust for blood transcends love of money, so that there is no possibility of the Babylonians saving their lives through payment of ransom. Not only will the young men be killed, but even the children will be massacred, thereby excluding any hope for Babylon in the future.

19 Babylon occupied an important place in the Near East, and its hanging gardens, built by Nebuchadnezzar for Amytis, his Median wife, as a reminder of her homeland, were one of the seven wonders of the ancient world. It was pre-eminent among the nations for a century, 'a jewel of the kingdoms.' It was the pride of the Chaldeans from southern Babylonia who led the Neo-Babylonian kingdom from 612 to 539 BC. Nebuchadnezzar could boast about it: 'Is this not Babylon the great, which I myself have built as a royal residence by the might of my power and for the glory of my majesty?' (Dan. 4:30). There is a marked contrast between this description of Babylon in the first part of verse 19 and the way her overthrow is depicted in the second part. This is the heart of Isaiah's message regarding her. She will be supernaturally overthrown, just like Sodom and Gomorrah. These cities have already been cited as a warning for Judah in Isaiah's first message (see 1:9-10).

20 The ultimate disgrace for Babylon is that she will be so devastated that no one will inhabit her territory ever again. Not even the Arabs will pitch a tent there. The Hebrew word for Arab used here (*^aravi*) also occurs in Jeremiah 3:2, where it denotes a person who sits waiting in the wilderness. It appears, therefore, that it is used here in the sense of a 'nomad'. So far from having stable settlement, Babylon will not even have occasional visits from Bedouin tribes. In 539 BC the Persians under Cyrus captured the city and, though some of it was spared, it was finally destroyed by Xerxes in 439 BC, and has not been inhabited since.

21-22 No longer will shepherds tend their flocks around Babylon.

---

be the best. For support of this view, see D. J. Wiseman, 'Some Historical Problems in the Book of Daniel', *Notes on Some Problems in the Book of Daniel* (Tyndale Press, 1970), pp. 9-16; J. M. Bulman, 'The Identification of Darius the Mede', *WTJ* 35 (1973), pp. 247-67; Joyce Baldwin, *Daniel* (Tyndale Series, Inter-Varsity Press, 1978), pp. 26-28, 126-28.

Instead it will become the place inhabited by various wild birds and animals, and the houses, strongholds, and palaces will be occupied by these animals. It is hard to be certain about their precise identification. One word (Heb. *s^e'îrîm*) has been taken to mean 'demons' on the basis of its use in Leviticus 17:7 and 2 Chronicles 11:15. This is unlikely as all the other names used in these verses refer to animals or birds, and probably it simply means 'a long-haired goat'. There is an interesting alteration at the beginning of verse 22. The hyenas are said to howl in 'his palaces' (*'alm^{e}nôtâv*). There is no known Hebrew word *'almân*, but there is a word *'armôn*, that is used twenty-two times in the Old Testament, eleven of which are in Amos. One possible explanation is that there is a play on words, as *'almânâh* (pl. *'almânôt*), which means 'widow', occurs over fifty times, while *'almôn*, 'widowhood', is used in Isaiah 47:9 of Babylon.[7]

e. Comfort for Israel (14:1–2)

In the midst of declarations concerning the downfall of Babylon, Isaiah brings reassurance to the people of God. This is an indication that the burdens against the nations were primarily intended for God's own chosen people.

1 The opening word in Hebrew is a particle (*kî*) that provides an important link with the preceding section.[8] It marks the contrast between the judgment on Babylon and the compassion to be shown to Israel. The translation can either be '*for* the LORD shows compassion', or, '*when* the LORD shows compassion'. Babylon falls so that Israel may rise again. Love for his own people impels the LORD to indicate that his favour continues to rest on Israel. His relationship with Israel is still one of choice.[9] Restoration to the land will be accompanied by Gentile 'strangers' coming into association with the house of Jacob. The stranger (Heb. *gêr*) had some rights in Israel but did not belong to the covenant

---

[7]No fully satisfactory explanation has been given of this particular Hebrew word. The problems are that the word is otherwise unknown and that the suffix is third-person singular ('his'), whereas the subject is masculine plural ('hyenas'). Babylon is feminine in Heb., but the reference may be to the king of Babylon and then the masculine singular suffix would be appropriate.

[8]Many English translations, including RSV and NIV, leave out this word.

[9]I prefer to understand this as indicating continuing choice of Israel, rather than thinking of it as denoting another choice. There is no suggestion in the context that a 'new' covenant is in view.

community. In the future the strangers will become the head, while Israel will become the tail (Deut. 28:43-44).

2 Gentile nations will take 'them' (the united strangers and house of Israel) and settle them 'in their place' (Canaan), or as it is also called here, 'the LORD's land'. Moreover, there is going to be a complete reversal in roles. Those who oppressed Israel in exile will themselves be taken captive and become servants, as Israel takes possession of them. The use of the word 'oppressors' recalls the bondage of Israel in Egypt when they were oppressed and in slavery. When the new exodus takes place Israel will be the ruler. This theme is going to be developed much more fully later in the prophecy (see, for example, comments on 42:18–43:13).

f. The Humiliation of Babylon and her King (14:3-23)

Just as the former exodus was followed by a song of the redeemed (Exod. 15:1-18), so will be the second exodus. The song is called here in Hebrew a *mâshâl*, a word that not only denotes a short pithy saying like many in the book of Proverbs, but also something longer like a parable. Three times prophets are told to lift up a *mâshâl* (Isaiah in this passage, Micah [Mic. 2:4] and Habakkuk [Hab. 2:6]), just as the term is employed of the object lessons used by Balaam (Num. 23:7; 24:3, 15, 20, 21, 23). The intention is to force the hearer or reader to make a judgment about himself,[10] so this suggests that the essential thrust of the burdens against the nations was really against Israel/ Judah.

3-4a The poetic parable is to be taken up against the king of Babylon when the LORD redeems his people from their captivity. The language is couched in terms that immediately recall the captivity in Egypt. The LORD will *give rest* (cf. the use of this verb in Deut. 12:10; 25:19) from

---

[10]See the discussion on the term *mâshâl* by A. S. Herbert in *SJT* 7(1955), pp. 180-96.

[11] 'Another way in which the blessings of the land are described is to speak of *rest* in the land (Heb. *menuchah* 3:20; 12:9; Heb. *heniach* 12:10; 25:19). The reference in 25:19 is important because it links together the gifts of rest and of the land. In the section dealing with covenant curses expulsion from the land is described as lack of rest (28:65). This *rest* meant the end to life as refugees, so that Israel could look forward to enjoying a sedentary pattern of life. It also meant security from their enemies. It was to be life in the full enjoyment of God's blessings, along with the absence of war and conflict.

their *hard labour* (cf. the identical expression in Exod. 1:14 *bis*; 6:9).[11] Even the rare word 'turmoil' (Heb. *rogez*) recalls the use of a related adjective (*raggâz*) in Deuteronomy 28:65 to describe the condition of the rebellious nation in exile. Part of the punishment is to be that God will give them 'a troubled heart'. Now the promise is of deliverance from the second captivity with its suffering, turmoil, and harsh slavery. Comfort is later given by Isaiah when he announces that Israel's labour is over (Isa. 40:1-2). The message is directed to the proud king of Babylon who will not ascend to heaven but rather descend to the grave (see especially verses 12-15).

4b The song commences with two rhetorical questions: 'How has [the] oppressor ceased?' 'How has [his] fury ceased?' The word 'how' (Heb. *'êk*) often introduces a question or exclamatory statement of horror or amazement. The word 'oppressor' picks up on use of this word in verse 2, while 'ceased' translates the double usage of the Hebrew verb 'to stop working' (*shâvat*; cf. the noun *shabbât*, 'sabbath'). The word 'fury' is a word unknown anywhere else in Hebrew literature. To accept a commonly suggested alteration (*marhêvâh* instead of *madhêvâh*) does not help as it too is unknown. The parallelism of the verse requires a word to balance the use of 'oppressor', and 'fury' is quite acceptable.

5-6 Babylon ruled with harshness and unrelenting anger against her enemies. She brought nations into submission by her military might. Twice in verse 6 mention is made of how she struck down other peoples, treading upon them in anger, and persecuting[12] them without cessation.

'In Psalm 95 God encourages his people not to be like the wilderness generation, and the closing verse of the Psalm (verse 11) speaks of his oath that his people would not enter into his rest (Heb. *menuchati*). The reference appears to be to Numbers 14:23, 30 or to Deuteronomy 1:34, 35, except that instead of *land* the psalm uses *rest*. Clearly rest and the promised land were equated. The epistle to the Hebrews draws upon this psalm in a unit dealing with believers entering into the eschatological rest (3:7–4:13). Just as rest awaited the church in the wilderness, so rest yet awaits New Testament believers. In this section of Hebrews rest is identical with "the heavenly country" sought by believers, "the lasting city which is to come" (Heb. 13:14; cf. Heb. 11:16)' (Allan M. Harman, *Deuteronomy*, op. cit., pp. 19-20).

[12]The MT vocalises the word as a passive ('persecuted', or 'deemed to be persecuted') but I think it best to follow the Targum and vocalise it as an active participle ('persecuting').

But the might of Babylon cannot stand against the Lord who will intervene to render her impotent, this being symbolised by reference to the broken staff and sceptre.

7-8 Nature is personified as being brought into peace and responding to this by singing. Whereas Babylon and Assyria had taken so much pine and cedar timber from Lebanon, the day will come when no timber cutter will be at work there. Babylon's fall will put an end to her trade in precious woods.

9-10 The 'death' of Babylon is going to provoke a welcome from other prominent leaders who have already died. The description of the way in which the departed will welcome Babylon is phrased according to normal practice. The spirits rise to greet her, and kings get up from their thrones. The departed have a blunt message for Babylon – 'Even you have been made weak as we, you have become like us' (NASB). The might of Babylon will be no more for she will be reduced to the same state as other former empires and rulers.

11 The pomp and revelry of Babylon will finish when she is abased in the grave, for it will open its mouth and swallow up nobles (see 5:14). During normal decomposition of bodies maggots and worms are active, and so the description is given of Babylon having a bed composed of maggots and a bed cover of worms. The point is that proud Babylon will be utterly debased, so that even abhorrent insects will feed on her dead body. Instead of pride there will be corruption such as that undergone by a corpse.

12 For a long time there has been a Christian interpretation of this verse as a description of the fall of Satan. This probably goes back to the Vulgate translation of 'morning star' as 'Lucifer' ('bearer of light'). However, the words refer to the king of Babylon, who in his immense pride exalted himself as though he were a god. There may well be use of the imagery of Mesopotamian star gods to make the point that the king was elevating himself to divine status. This 'god' will however be humbled to the dust, and his former glory as he ruled over nations will have gone for ever. Babylon also becomes a representative figure in the Bible, appearing in the eschatological visions in the book of Revelation (see especially Rev. 18:1-24).

13-14 The proud king made boastful claims. All these centred around his supposed ability to make himself like 'the high God' (Heb. *'elyôn*). This term for God occurs thirty-one times in the Old Testament, mainly in the Psalms. It was clearly an early term for God (see its use in connection with Melchisedek in Genesis 14:18, 19, 20, 22). All the associated vocabulary here emphasises the aspect of pride: 'I will ascend' (twice), 'I will raise my throne', 'I will sit enthroned', 'I will make myself like 'Elyôn'. At the end of verse 13 there is a reference to Zaphon ('the utmost heights of *the sacred mountain*', NIV; 'on the farthest sides *of the north*', NKJV). Zaphon was a mountain in northern Syria that the Canaanites believed was the dwelling place of Baal, and it was also considered a meeting place for the gods. The Babylonian king regarded himself as exalted above all 'the stars of God' (verse 13), probably in this way referring to other monarchs.

15 Any claims by the king to be divine will be destroyed when death takes him to the grave. The Hebrew word $sh^e{'}\hat{o}l$ is used as in verse 11. While this word has a range of meanings, here in this passage it has as synonyms 'pit' (Heb. $b\hat{o}r$) in verses 15 and 19, and 'grave' (Heb. $qever$) in verse 19. Clearly it is used here of the place of burial.[13] No matter how exalted the king thinks he is, he will be brought to the grave just as all other men.

16-17 When this happens onlookers will be amazed. The contrast between the claims and the reality will cause them to question whether this was indeed the man who shook the world. Kingdoms trembled before him, cities were overcome, captives were taken away to Babylon and detained there. Deportation of people from captured nations was a regular element of both Assyrian and Babylonian foreign policy, as it ensured there was less chance of rebellion if leading figures in a population were deported (see the account in 2 Kings 24:14-16 of the events after the fall of Jerusalem in 586 BC).

18-20a Normal practice was for kings to be buried with full honour, each one having his own tomb (called here 'his house'). However, the threat for the king of Babylon is that his body will not be respected in this way. The contrast between normal practice (verse 18) and the fate awaiting the king is emphasised at the start of verse 19: 'But *you* are cast out....' When the ultimate destruction comes to Babylon the scene will be like a battlefield with even the king's body covered with other corpses. His body will find no burial place, a thing of utter disgrace for anyone, let alone a king. In his death he will have to take responsibility for what happens, because he is the one in the last analysis who has

---

[13]For an excellent brief treatment of the word $sh^e{'}\hat{o}l$, see the article by R. L. Harris in *TWOT*, 2, pp. 892-93.

destroyed his own land and killed his own people (verse 20a).

20b-21 To have no more descendants (verse 20b) was a disgrace in the Near East (see, for example, Psalms 41:5; 109:13). A man's children were his memorial, and if they were cut off then there would be no more mention of them. Though the Babylonian royal line may have seemed so powerful, yet the sons are to be destroyed as the sins of their fathers come to culmination in this divine judgment. The end of the dynasty is at hand, for the sons will not be there to inherit the kingdom or oversee the building of cities.

22 This is the only verse in Isaiah in which the expression 'says the Lord' (Heb. n^e'um yhwh) occurs twice. The expression is overwhelmingly a prophetic one to introduce a message of divine origin and authority, occurring 360 times in the Old Testament. All but twenty of these occurrences are in the books of Isaiah (23x), Amos (21x), Jeremiah (167x), Ezekiel (83x), and Zechariah (20x). The word n^e'um is a noun, not a verb, and should strictly be translated 'an utterance', 'a [divine] word'. The Lord's declaration is a further threat against Babylon. A remnant has been promised to Israel (see 6:13; 10:20-22; 11:11, 16) but not for Babylon. Her name and remnant will be cut off. The parallel expression, 'offspring and posterity' (NKJV), is a rare combination only found here and in Genesis 21:23 and Job 18:19. As the Hebrew expression contains alliteration (v^enîn vâneked) a good English equivalent is 'kith and kin'.[14]

23 This verse reinforces what was said in 13:20-22 of the coming desolation in store for Babylon. She will be known for her swamplands, not her wonderful buildings. Destruction is to be her fate, when the Lord sweeps her with a broom. The words 'sweep' and 'broom' are from the same Hebrew root, and this is their sole occurrence in Hebrew literature. The context and the translations in the early versions give us the clue to their meaning. Just as the threat started with 'says the Lord' in the previous verse, so now it ends with 'the Lord of hosts'.

2. Against Assyria (14:24-27)

Isaiah now takes up the Lord's declarations concerning Babylon's predecessor, Assyria, which in his own day was the greatest threat to Israel and Judah. The northern kingdom fell to Assyria in 722 BC, while towards the end of Isaiah's ministry Judah and Jerusalem were faced

---

[14]This is the translation of Victor Hamilton, *The Book of Genesis: Chapters 18-50* (NICOT, Eerdmans, 1995), p. 86.

with the threat of annihilation at the hands of Sennacherib (king of Assyria 705–681 BC) and his forces (see chapters 36–39). While directed to Assyria, this message contains hope for Judah (see verse 25).

24 Following the declaration of the LORD of hosts at the end of the previous verse, the prophecy against Assyria starts with reference to an oath by the LORD. Though uncommon in the earlier chapters of Isaiah (in addition to this verse, see 19:18) solemn oaths feature more strongly in the later chapters (see 45:3; 48:1; 54:9; 62:8; 65:16). They serve to emphasise the solemnity of divine declarations. Though this one starts with a negative in Hebrew (*'im-lô'*, lit. 'if not'), clearly in the context modern versions are justified in translating it as 'surely'. In translation the form of the declaration appears to have two parallel sentences: 'As I have planned, so it will be; as I have purposed, so it will stand.' This disguises the fact that the aspect of the verbs is different ('it will be', Heb. *hâyâtâh*, a prophetic perfect; 'it will stand', Heb. imperfect *tâqûm*). The change of aspect is probably to indicate that the threat to Assyria is surely coming soon, while that to Babylon is in the more distant future. The idiom is the same as in 7:7 (though the verbs are used in reverse order), but the message is different. In 7:7 it is human plans that will not stand, while here it is the divine purpose that will be fulfilled.

25 God is going to intervene on behalf of his land (Canaan) and his people (Israel/Judah). The mighty Assyria is going to be humbled, and its power broken. The combination of 'yoke/burden' has already been used in 9:4 and 10:27. Clearly this is a pairing in Hebrew to depict harsh servitude such as was meted out to Israel by Midian (Judg. 6:1-6), or imposed upon her earlier by Egypt. Assyria stands in this line of oppressors, but its hold on God's people is going to be broken.

26-27 The destiny of nations is in the LORD's hand, and that hand is still stretched out. This recalls the use of the same idiom in the recurring refrain relating to judgment in 9:12, 17, 21. All the nations are under his authority and he can use them to fulfil his purpose. By human standards Assyria is a mighty power, but that power will be unable to stand against God's will. The rhetorical question that ends the prophecy, 'And who can turn it back?' speaks of the inevitability of the coming judgment.

3. The Burden against Philistia (14:28-32)

The second burden relates to 'all you Philistines'. The Philistines occupied a group of city states on the southern Mediterranean coast of Palestine (the name 'Palestine' is just an anglicised corruption of 'Philistine'). They had no all-encompassing government, and so it is appropriate that Isaiah addresses this burden simply to 'all you Philistines'. The language used is cryptic, illustrating yet again that intentional obscurity of declaration is a common feature of prophecy. For Judah the most important message is contained in verse 32, a reassurance that Zion is God's choice and his creation.

28 For the second time Isaiah dates a prophecy by relating it to the death of a king. In 6:1 his inaugural vision is said to have come in the year of Uzziah's death. Now the death of Uzziah's son, Ahaz, in 716/ 715 BC gives the relevant date. It is possible to understand that the message came while Ahaz was still alive, so that comparison with what is recorded in 2 Chronicles 28:18 may be relevant (see also the reference to the Philistines in 9:12).

29 The important question facing any expositor is the identification of the 'rod' mentioned in this verse. Many suggestions have been made, including Tiglath-Pileser III or Shamaneser V (both kings of Assyria), but they do not seem to fit. The crucial factor relates to who is the ruler ('rod') that struck the Philistines but then himself was broken. The only one that seems to fit is David (or the Davidic dynasty). It was David who finally triumphed over the Philistines (see 1 Sam. 17:50; 18:25-30; 23:1-5; 2 Sam. 5:17-25; 8:1). But in the period of Ahaz, the pro-Assyrian king (see Isa. 7:1-17 read in the light of 2 Kings 16:1-20), the sovereign independence of Judah came to an end as Judah became a vassal of Assyria. However, the complete power of this 'snake' was not altogether broken, and from its root will still come a viper that is able to sting the Philistines. Perhaps they made overtures to Judah under Ahaz or the new king Hezekiah, only to find that the seeming broken rod was still able to create great harm for them. The concepts of 'rod' and 'snake' are borrowed from Exodus 4:2-3 and 7:10-12.

30 Having made clear that more trouble is in store for the Philistines, the message goes on to contrast the position of Judah and Philistia. The most humble in Judah will be secure, while the very root of the Philistines will be destroyed so that there will be no 'remnant' (NIV, 'your survivors'). The opening expression 'the first born of the poor' is without parallel in the Old Testament. Perhaps it means that even the firstborn of the poor, who normally would not own pastures, will do so. It may be another allusion back to the bondage of Israel in Egypt (Exod. 4:22). The Philistines are last mentioned in the Bible in the early post-exilic period (Zech. 9:6).

31 The message is directed to the gates and cities of the Philistines. They are to become utterly dispirited in the face of Assyrian attack. This is a brief summary of the invading army (cf. the longer description already given in 5:26-30). As it moves around 'the fertile crescent' and makes its approach from the north the troops will create a dust storm that looks like a cloud. The last clause is awkward to translate. Literally it means 'there is no lone one in his appointed place' (or possibly, 'time'; see NKJV). In a context dealing with an invading army the suggestion that this refers to the absence of any stragglers is certainly plausible.

32 There is an implied overture to Judah behind the opening question in this verse. Perhaps under the guise of coming to bring a message of consolation on the death of Ahaz, the Philistine representatives raised the matter of a possible coalition to stand against Assyria. The language implies a Gentile nation made the approach (Heb. text uses *gôy*). The answer is that Judah's welfare is with the LORD alone, for he has chosen Zion and there his people will find refuge (see Ps. 132:13-15). Diplomacy will never save; only finding refuge under the wings of the LORD will provide safety (for the idiom see Ruth 2:12; Pss. 17:8; 36:7; 57:1; 61:4; 91:4).

4. The Burden against Moab (15:1–16:14)

Moab features prominently in the writings of the prophets (in addition to Isa. 15:1–16:14 and 25:10, see Amos 2:1-3; Jer. 48:1-47; Ezek. 25:8-11; Zeph. 2:8-11). At times both Moab and Edom seem to be used as symbolic of all of God's enemies (for Edom see Isa. 34:5-17). The Edomites were descendants of Esau, while the Moabites (and the Ammonites) were descendants of Abraham's nephew Lot (see Gen. 19:36-38). The Israelites had obeyed the divine direction to leave both of these groups alone as they moved around the east of the Dead Sea to arrive in Canaan (Deut. 2:1-23). However, the Moabites did not leave Israel and Judah alone, and there was repeated conflict over the centuries, and when the exile took place the Moabites moved into

many of the vacant areas (Jer. 48:20-42; 49:1-2). The amount of
geographical information here is greater than anywhere else in Isaiah
(but cf. 10:28-34), and many of the places mentioned cannot be
accurately located. The most important extra-biblical record concerning
the Moabites is the so-called Moabite stone (ninth century BC;
discovered in 1868) erected by King Mesha to celebrate his victory
over Israel.[15]

a. Summary (15:1)

1 The burden against Moab commences with a rhyming couplet:

> For in the night Ar of Moab is destroyed; it is undone.
> For in the night Kir of Moab is destroyed; it is undone.

The introductory 'for' is an important feature of this burden, as it
appears eight times in this chapter (verses 1 2x; 5 2x; 6 2x; 8; 9). NIV
omits them all in translation, while NKJV uses 'because' for the first
two in this verse and then 'for' in the remaining six. Ar and Kir were
probably major Moabite settlements, though precise identification has
not yet been made. Mention of the night seems to indicate the sudden
and unexpected nature of the destruction. Calling them 'undone' recalls
Isaiah's use of the same word to describe himself when he saw the
LORD in his glory (6:5).

b. Moab's Grief (15:2-4)

2-4 Most of the places mentioned in these verses can be identified.
Dibon, situated four miles north of the Arnon River, was taken at the
time of the Exodus (Num. 21:30), given to the tribes of Reuben and
Gad (Num. 32:2-3), and later built up by the Gadites (Num. 32:34). It
was at Dibon that the pillar containing king Mesha's inscription was
found in 1868. Nebo may be mount Nebo (Deut. 34:1), or else situated
in close proximity to it. Heshbon is 18 miles (29 km) east of the northern
tip of the Dead Sea, and after being taken by the Israelites it was
given to Reuben (Num. 32:37), but later lapsed back under Moabite
control. Eleaheh is always mentioned in connection with Heshbon,
and was only a mile (1.6 km) north of it. Medeba is six miles (9.5 km)
south of Heshbon, while Jahaz is just north of the Arnon River. The

---

[15]For the Mesha inscription, see *DOTT*, pp. 195-98.

activities mentioned are typical of Old Testament descriptions of mourning. The people of Dibon go up to their 'house', i.e. their temple, which is also called the sanctuary (16:12). Heads are shaved, beards are cut (verse 2), sackcloth is worn, and bodies are prostrated (verse 3). Voices are lifted up in despairing cries, while the warriors of Moab find their courage wanes away (verse 4).

c. Refugees flee from Moab (15:5-9)

5-9 The geographical references continue, with mention of another eight place names. The location of Eglath Shelishiyah, Luhith, Horonaim, waters of Nimrim, ravine of the poplars, the borders of Moab, and Beer Elim are all unknown. Presumably Zoar is the place at the southern end of the Dead Sea to which Lot fled (Gen. 14:2; 19:23, 30). Dimon, whose waters are full of blood (verse 9), is probably just a deliberate variant of Dibon (verse 2), with a play on the Hebrew word 'blood' (*dâm*). Such word-plays are quite frequent. In Hosea, Beth-el (house of God) is changed to Beth-aven ('house of vanity', Hos. 4:15; 5:8; 10:5), while the change of the name of the river Abanah to Amanah in the majority of Hebrew manuscripts (2 Kings 5:12) displays exactly the same alteration as here in Dibon to Dimon. There is also assonance in the clause: *kî mê dîmôn mâlᵉ 'û dâm*, 'For the waters of Dimon are full of blood.' This makes it doubly notable.

Isaiah expresses his concern for Moab, as her fugitives flee (verse 5). The prophet's spirit finds fuller expression in the lament of Jesus, the great prophet, over Jerusalem (Lk. 13:34-35). Isaiah's grief is caused by the sight of the Moabites weeping and lamenting over their destruction. A variety of expressions is used to convey the depth of their distress. They weep, lament, cry out, and wail. The absence of vegetation may be due to the fact that springs and other sources of water are blocked. They try to carry their accumulated wealth with them, and their grief reaches to the utmost limits of their territory, both to the northernmost point (Eglaim) and to the southernmost (Beer Elim). The waters near Dibon will flow with blood as many Moabites die. Two of Isaiah's contemporaries also use the imagery of the LORD as a lion (Hos. 5:14; Amos 5:18-19). Here the indication is given in verse 9b of the completeness of the judgment. Whether people become refugees or stay in the land there will be no difference in their fate. Death and destruction will be their lot.

d. An Invitation to Moab (16:1-5)

1-2 In the crisis facing Moab she is encouraged to pay tribute to the king in Jerusalem. In 2 Kings 3:4 mention is made of the annual tribute that Mesha of Moab had to pay to king Ahab—100,000 lambs and wool of 100,000 rams. The word for 'lamb' used there (Heb. *kâr*) is a rare one, but the same word appears here in 16:1. The way of safety for Moab is to submit to the rule of the house of David. Though 'Sela' is treated as a proper name in many translations, it is better to render it simply as 'rock' or 'cliff', as in Jeremiah 48:28. It can hardly be Sela, the fortified capital of the Edomites, for this prophecy is directed to Moab, not Edom, unless it means that Moabite refugees in Edom are called on to provide tribute. Jerusalem is personified as 'the daughter of Zion'. The women of Moab are at the southern border of their land ('the fords of Arnon'), utterly helpless like young birds forced to leave their nests. They are trying to get out of their present territory and seek refuge in Edom.

3 Exegesis of verses 3-5 is difficult. A decision has to be made as to who the speakers are, and to whom the appeals are directed. The verbs in verse 3 are also a problem, for the first and second ones in the Massoretic Text (MT) are masculine plural imperatives,[16] while the third and fourth are feminine singular imperatives. A similar shift takes places in verse 4, where a third person plural is followed by a second person feminine singular. There is an abruptness about the Hebrew text and it contains sudden shifts. The identification of 'destroyer' (verse 4a) and 'the oppressor' (verse 4b) is also hard. The best solution to the difficulties is to regard verses 3-5 as continuing the address to Moab. It comes within a 'burden' addressed to Moab, and in verse 4 Moab is called upon to help the refugees from Judah. The alteration in verbal forms is to be taken as a stylistic feature. Appeal is made to the people of Moab to respond to Judah's need. A decision is required like that of a judge (the actual Heb. expression, *'âsû pᵉlîlâh*, is a rare one). Let them provide shade so that the midday becomes like night and the refugees find a hiding place. Moab is asked not to betray them (the Heb. verb is *gâlâh*, 'to uncover', 'reveal').

---

[16]The Massoretic note on the first verb gives a Qᵉrᵉ reading that makes it a feminine singular form (*hâvî'î*), while many of the early versions (LXX, Aramaic Targum, Syriac, and Latin Vulgate) make the second verb feminine singular as well.

4 Various modern versions of this verse use the phrase 'the Moabite refugees', but this translation cannot be sustained. The literal rendering is 'Let my fugitives, Moab, sojourn with you'.[17] The message is the LORD's, and he wants his people to be allowed to have guest rights in Moab, just as Israel allowed foreigners certain privileges. Hence Moab here is to be regarded as a vocative, 'O Moab.' She is commanded to be a hiding place for them in the face of the destroyer ('hiding place' is from the same root as 'hide' in the previous verse). Several expressions denoting malicious enemies are used: 'destroyer', 'oppressor', 'aggressor'. Presumably the attacker is Assyria. However, the latter part of the verse brings re-assurance to Judah. The aggressor's time is limited, and destruction will come to an end.

5 In the midst of the message to Moab comes an assurance of divine grace. God's steadfast love (Heb. *chesed*) is going to establish a throne, and on it will sit one from David's house (Heb. has *'ôhel*, 'tent'; cf. Amos 9:11, *sukkat Dâvîd*, 'David's booth', and the quotation of this verse in Acts 15:16). The earthly throne was a counterpart of the heavenly throne (Isa. 6:1), and Isaiah has already given the message that a divine child will come to sit on David's throne (Isa. 9:7). Just as David himself is said to have ruled in justice and righteousness for all his people (2 Sam. 8:1), so the coming king spoken of here will be a faithful ruler who seeks to dispense justice without any delay. Any Moabite must have puzzled over this message, but, as pointed out earlier (see page 116), the real recipient of these burdens was Judah. This prophecy reinforces the notion of a coming Davidic king whose reign will be a true reflection of God's own kingly rule.

e. Lamentation for Moab (16:6-12)

This section is a lamentation over Moab, whose fall is certain, and whose vain boasting will not save her. Two new geographical names are introduced, Sibmah and Jazer, in addition to three names already occurring in chapter 15. While neither Sibmah nor Jazer can be identified with absolute certainty, both were captured by the Israelites (see Jos. 13:19, 21; and Num. 21.32) but later reverted to Moabite control as confirmed by verse 9 and also Jeremiah 48:32. There is close similarity between Isaiah 16:6-12 and Jeremiah 48:29-39, and

---

[17]The Massoretic punctuation separates 'my fugitives' from the following 'Moab'. Also, the vocalisation is 'my fugitives', not 'fugitives of.'

Jeremiah's phraseology even has echoes of the wider context in Isaiah 15–16. Verses 7-12 consist of three sentences all preceded by 'therefore' (two with *'al-kên* and one with *lâkên*), and most modern versions, except the NASB, fail to show this.

6 The cluster of synonymous terms emphasises Moab's arrogance: 'pride' (*gâ'ôn*, appearing twice in the same verse), 'haughty' (*gê'*), 'boastfulness' (*ga'avâh*), and 'arrogance' (*'evrâh*). Though only a small nation, Moab exalted herself in her own eyes, but what she said was only empty talk, mere bragging. That talk had reached Judah, and so Isaiah says '*we* have heard'.

7-8 The picture is of Moab wailing on account of her own desolation. The MT says that 'Moab wails for Moab', an expression that denotes mutual expression of grief. They groan for the men of Kir Hareset,[18] who are indeed 'stricken'.[19] This appears to be the same 'Kir' as already mentioned in 15:1, and means 'the wall of potsherds'. Invasion often resulted in devastation to crops and vineyards. In Moab the rich areas around Heshbon (see on 15:4) and Sibmah (Jerome said it was 500 paces from Heshbon) wither away, while the vines that stretched from Jazer in the north to the desert in the south and west to the Dead Sea are destroyed.[20]

9-10 The one weeping in these verbs has to be the LORD himself, for he is the one who has caused the cessation in the joy of harvest (see the final clause of verse 10). Four geographical names (Jazer, Sibmah, Heshbon, and Elealeh) are selected as representative of all of Moab. There is no more harvesting or wine-making, both things associated normally with joy on the part of reapers and winemakers. There is stillness over the whole land, for the LORD has brought about this situation. It is his doing. The absence of shouting is marked, and

---

[18]The Heb. has a noun *âshîsh* in a plural masculine construct form, which many take to be the equivalent of the feminine word *âshîshâh* that occurs five times with the meaning of 'raisin cake'. However, in the parallel in Jer. 48:31 'men of' (Heb. *'aneshê*) occurs. I incline to the view noted in *DCH* (vol. 1, p. 413) that *âshîsh* is probably a rare word denoting an adult. Presumably Kir Hareset is the same place as Kir in 15:1, and located a few miles south of the Arnon River, and inland from the Dead Sea.

[19]The word only occurs here in the Old Testament, though two cognate words appear elsewhere.

[20]Psalm 80 uses the imagery of a transplanted vine to depict Israel settling in Canaan, with her western border being 'the sea', i.e. the Mediterranean. Here 'sea' must be the Dead Sea.

these verses repeat the same Hebrew noun for 'shouting' in successive verses (Heb. *hêdâd*). The parallel passage in Jeremiah even uses this same noun three times in the one verse (Jer. 48:33), a fact that English versions find difficulty in translating adequately. God expresses his grief over Moab, as he brings destruction on it (note the repeated 'I' in verses 9-10, and the double use of 'my' in verse 11). The language is strongly anthropomorphic, depicting God weeping along with Jazer, and pouring his tears over Heshbon and Elealeh.

11-12 The third and final sentence in this section also begins with 'therefore'. As God looks over the fate of Moab he is deeply moved with grief. The divine pity is likened to the sorrowful sound of a harp. Kir which was probably the capital of Moab is given a variant title here. While 2 Kings 3:25 and Isaiah 16:7 have 'Kir-Hareset', here in verse 11, as in Jeremiah 48:31, the name is given as 'Kir-Heres'. The LXX gives it as 'the new city', which presupposes that the text the translator was using changed an *r* to a *d*, or else misread one letter as *d*.[21] There is every presumption that the variant names are all used of the same place. The Moabites may well have been very religious, going to their high places to pray, but these prayer sessions are of no avail. There is a wordplay in verse 12a that makes this folly so clear: '[And it shall be] when he presents himself he wearies himself' (Heb. *kî nir'âh kî nil'âh*). Prayer at their sanctuary does not produce any results, as is made clear at the end of verse 12: 'he will not prevail.' Those worshipping at the high place will find no results flow to them. The Moabite God was Chemosh, who was worshipped by some of Solomon's wives (see 1 Kings 11:7).

f. The Fulfilment of Prophecy (16:13-14)
13-14 The final verses in the chapter give further confirmation that this message was indeed one from the LORD. How long before this it had been given is unclear, since the Hebrew word at the end of verse 13 (*mê'az*) can indicate long ago in the distant past, or something only recent. The message has a precision about it. Within the space of three years, just as a hired labourer looks to the end of his contract, so

---

[21] J. A. Thompson, *The Book of Jeremiah* (NICOT, Eerdmans, 1980), p. 711, suggests that the original name may have been Kir-hadeshet ('the new city'). No Hebrew manuscript supports this. A further change of the letter *sin* to *shin* is also needed. This city may be the place *Qrchh* mentioned in Mesha's inscription. See D. W. Thomas, *DOTT*, p. 196.

Moab's glory will come to a certain end. The addition of this message at the conclusion of the burden against Moab is not only to indicate a time frame, but to inculcate urgency in responding to the LORD's denunciation of Moab's pride. The judgment is going to result in the large population of Moab being reduced to a small remnant. No indication is given in the Old Testament of the actual fulfilment, though devastation by the Assyrians in 715/713 BC would certainly meet the description of the coming judgment. A similarly phrased message to this one appears at the end of the burden against Arabia (21:16-17).

5. Against Damascus [Syria] and Ephraim [Israel] (17:1–18:7)

The date of this burden must be from earlier in Isaiah's ministry as it is directed against Damascus, the capital of Syria, and also against Ephraim, one of the largest tribes making up the northern kingdom of Israel. These two nations, Syria and Israel, were in alliance in 734 BC attempting to force Ahaz of Judah to combine with them against Assyria (see comments on 7:1-9). Assyria, under Tiglath-Pileser III, subdued Damascus in 732 BC, while Samaria fell in 722 BC (see 2 Kings 17:1-6). The threat of these two neighbours of Judah when they besieged Jerusalem (see 2 Kings 16:5 and Isa. 7:1) failed in accordance with the LORD's word: 'It will not take place, it will not happen' (Isa. 7:7). Isaiah's message points to the humiliation of Israel in that she is listed in a subservient place to a Gentile nation.

a. Ruin for Damascus/Aram and Ephraim/Israel (17:1-11)

1-2 'Behold', the opening word of the message, draws attention to the significant proclamation concerning Damascus. The capital of Aram (Syria) is going to be devastated, so that all that is left is a pile of ruins of what was an important city (see the comment on 10:9). Right down to the southern border of Aram at the river Arnon (about 14 miles [22 km] east of the Dead Sea) the townships will be deserted. People will be removed, while the animals will be left to graze among the ruins without any fear of being disturbed.

3 Suddenly a message for the northern kingdom of Israel is included. Aram and Israel had been in close alliance against Judah (see comments on 7:1), and now they are linked together in an oracle of doom. Even the nation that retained the distinctive name 'Israel' is not going to be differentiated when it comes to judgment. The strongholds of Israel will be treated in the same way as Damascus, and her glory will not transcend that of Aram. Remnants of both will survive, but they will be but a faint shadow of earlier glory.

4-5 The introduction of Israel into the picture in verse 3 leads on to a more detailed message for her in verses 4-11. The words 'in that day' refer to the day of visitation for Israel when the Assyrians will come in devastating power. The descriptive terms used speak of utter ruin—glory gone, fat replaced by thinness, the land swept clean of food, even the seemingly rich Valley of Rephaim (north-west of Jerusalem; see Jos. 15:8; 18:16; 2 Sam. 5:18, 22; 1 Chron. 11:15; 14:9). 'Gleaning' is used here metaphorically for the extent of judgment upon Israel.

6 The only hope held out to Israel is that a remnant will be spared. This is a message that Isaiah had already declared (6:13), and one of his sons, Shear-jashub ('a remnant will return'), bore a name that indicated the same truth but also injected the note of hope (7:3). The comparison is made to the few olives that remain when a tree is shaken to remove the ripe fruit. Whether the agricultural practice was gleaning fields or harvesting olives the same principle applied—some of the crop would remain. So it will be for Israel. There is evidence that some of the people left in Israel after the fall of Samaria managed to migrate down into Judah. As with verse 3, this verse also ends with the declaration that this is a message of divine origin and authority (see comment on 14:22). Whereas God names himself 'the LORD of hosts' in verse 3, here he is the covenant God of his people, 'the LORD, the God of Israel.'

7-8 Those mentioned in these verses are probably the remnant of Israel. In the day of calamity their eyes will be directed to their Maker, the Holy One of Israel, rather than to the false gods they had worshipped. With their own hands they had made altars, Asherah poles, and incense altars. 2 Chronicles 34:4 notes that these three items were linked to worship of Baal. Judgment will have the effect of teaching the futility of pagan worship, and of the need to look to the real source of help.

9 Reference is made to strong cities. In the context it seems that the cities are those that the Israelites captured when they came into Canaan. Now, however, Israel is virtually equated with the Canaanites and so these same cities in which they have lived are going to be devastated. Fine cities will be left to become places noted only for their wild undergrowth.[22] The pronouncement over them will be just one word: 'desolation'.

10-11 One of the instructions given to the covenant people was not to forget the LORD (Deut. 8:11). Now the accusation comes through Isaiah that this is precisely what they have done. The addressee is feminine singular, doubtless the nation. She has forgotten her saviour, her rock, and her fortress. The use of 'rock' as a metaphor for God echoes Deuteronomy 32, where it is used five times to describe the permanence of God and the safety he affords to those who trust in him (Deut. 32:4, 15, 18, 30, 31). 'Stronghold' is a familiar term for God in the psalms, sometimes appearing along with 'salvation' as here (see, for example, Ps. 27:1). These expressions reinforce the accusation that the nation has departed from their safety with the LORD, and therefore forfeited his saving action on their behalf. Even if Israel at great cost plants precious imported vines, and somehow expedites their growth to maturity, there will be no harvest at all. Impending destruction by the Assyrians is described as if it will be like disease and pain.

b. God's Judgment on the Nations (17:12-14)
12-14 The final section of this particular burden repeats in different language the message of 10:28-34. The section comprising verses 12-14 begins with the Hebrew exclamation *hôy*, which is usually a prophetic term introducing a woe oracle. The object of the message is again Damascus/Assyria, though other nations may be included. Uproar among the nations may cause great fear, but God's sovereign hand is controlling them and at his rebuke (verse 13) they will desist in their attacks against the covenant people. Isaiah has already used the analogy of raging flood waters to depict the Assyrian invasion (8:7-8). Here he mounts up terms to suggest sudden and wild invasion – 'raging seas', 'great waters', 'mighty waters'. Just as God had rebuked the Red Sea (see Ps. 106:9), so will he rebuke the Assyrians and they will flee. The metaphor changes now. Israel's enemies are chaff or tumbleweed (so-called because of its wheel-shaped stem) which will be driven before the wind. A common occurrence in Palestine is now the metaphor that Isaiah uses to describe the sovereign intervention of God to scatter the enemies, both his and those of his people. At evening sudden terror will surprise the enemy, and by morning they are not [in

---

[22]Instead of 'thickets and undergrowth' (NIV), the LXX translators inserted 'Hivites and Amorites'. This fits the context, but there is no support for this among Hebrew manuscripts. Hence, the MT must be allowed to stand.

existence]. Destruction is the allotted portion of those who came to loot and plunder. There is probably a deliberate attempt to describe the actions of Assyria in terms that recall the name of Isaiah's second son, *Maher shalal chash baz*, 'speedy spoil, hasty prey' (see comments on 8:1). The verb for 'plunder' in verse 14 is from the same root as 'baz' in the son's name.

c. The LORD's Message to the Nations (18:1-7)

As the formal opening, 'A burden of ...', is missing, it is best to take this section as constituting a continuation of the oracle against Damascus. It switches attention away from Assyria in the north to the broader issue of the antagonism of the nations in general against Israel. In doing so it prepares the way for the burden against Egypt in chapter 19. Egypt and Cush are linked together in chapter 20 as captives whom Assyria will take away into exile. The focus remains on Jerusalem even in this oracle, for mention is made of gifts that will be brought to 'Mount Zion, the place of the Name of the LORD Almighty' (NIV). The recipients of the message of these burdens is clearly the people of God.

1-2 The opening 'Woe' (again the Heb. *hôy*) is directed to a land of 'winged crickets', which is 'over the rivers of Cush'. These rivers are probably the Upper Nile and its various tributaries. The reference to insects may be to the characteristic presence in Cush of a certain species, or else be figurative language to describe the Cushite army. The Amorite soldiers are likened to bees (Deut. 1:44), as are the Assyrians (Isa. 7:18), while the Egyptians are flies whom the LORD can call to do his bidding (Isa. 7:18). The biblical Cush is not Ethiopia (Abyssinia) but the region south of Egypt known as Nubia. The call is to the Cushites to act as God's messengers. Perhaps the use of messengers from afar reinforces the concept of God's control of all the nations. However, it is unclear to whom the messengers are to go. The people concerned are described as tall (lit. 'drawn out') and smooth-skinned (probably meaning 'clean shaven'), a nation widely feared and one whose language is like garbled speech (Heb. *qav qav*).[23] These terms are too indefinite to enable a precise identification to be made. The reference to messengers going 'by sea' probably

---

[23]There are three Hebrew words that have the same spelling and pronunciation. The others mean 'rule' (Isa. 28:10) and 'a measuring line' (Isa. 34:11).

means the Nile, while 'papyrus boats' recalls the craft in which Moses was placed on the river (Exod. 2:3). While the one in which Moses was placed might have been small, papyrus was used to construct fairly large boats.[24]

3 The substance of the message that the envoys will take is contained in verses 3-6. The nations were a constant threat to Israel's existence, and often banded together with a common aim of destroying her. When the calls to battle are made (raising a banner and blowing a trumpet) it will be widely known among the populations in the region.

4-5 The LORD's declaration to Isaiah is that he himself will take note of what is happening. He will watch from his heavenly dwelling and not intervene, remaining inactive like a farmer observing his growing crops. But then just as the grapes are ripening, the divine harvester will take his pruning knife to the vines. The branches will be cut off and taken away. The message is clear. The LORD will let the nations have their day, but their doom is sealed for he will judge at the appointed time.

6 The description of judgment shifts to the picture of corpses strewn around the countryside. Birds and wild animals will have their fill through all the months of the year. A similar description of impending judgment on Judah and Jerusalem is given by Jeremiah, who likens the bodies of the people to the dismembered pieces of animals when a covenant is made (Jer. 34:18-20; cf. Gen. 15:10-11, that records Abraham's action in cutting up animals and birds, and then driving away the birds of prey). Ezekiel also presents the picture of corpses lying around, with men traversing the countryside in order to bury them (Ezek. 39:12-16).

7 Just as Moab was asked to send gifts to Jerusalem (16:1), so now those to whom this message has gone will bring gifts to the LORD of hosts in Jerusalem. The description of the people is almost identical with that in verse 2. One interesting alteration is that they are now referred to by the term for 'people' that is normally reserved for God's people (Heb. *'am*). The expression 'to bring gifts' (*yôvîlû shây*) is only used twice elsewhere in the Old Testament, both of which describe Gentile kings bringing offerings to the LORD (Pss. 68:29; 76:11). The origin of the word for 'gifts' is unknown (Heb. *shây*), but the context in these three cases is clear. Mount Zion is the destination, for there

---

[24]Oswalt's notes on his translation and his following interpretation are very helpful. See his *The Book of Isaiah: Chapters 1-39*, op. cit., pp. 357-63.

God's name is proclaimed. 2 Chronicles 32:23 records how, after the deliverance of Judah from the attack launched by Sennacherib, the people brought gifts to Jerusalem for the LORD and for Hezekiah. Zephaniah picks up the theme and depicts all God's scattered peoples coming with their offerings to him (Zeph. 3:10).

6. Against Egypt and Cush (19:1–20:6)

Attention now turns to another of the major powers, Egypt. Something more than judgment is to come to her. A spiritual change will occur, with the Egyptians swearing allegiance to the LORD of hosts (19:18). The language has overtones of what is recorded in Exodus of God's judgment on Egypt at the time of Israel's release. The declaration is made that the arch-enemies of Israel, Assyria and Egypt, will one day be united with her and the three nations will be blessed by the LORD (19:25). This burden differs from the earlier ones in that it includes an historical section that refers to an attack by Assyria on the city of Ashdod which rebelled in 713 BC.

a. The LORD's Hands against Egypt (19:1–15)

i. Swift Judgment on Egypt (19:1-4)

1 The burden opens by announcing the coming of the LORD, riding on a swift cloud. He is the mighty one who makes the clouds his chariots (Ps. 104:3), and just as the idols/gods of Egypt were judged previously (Exod. 12:12), so will they be again. The word for 'idols' is the same one that Isaiah has already used several times (see comments on 2:8, 18). This word (*'elîlîm*) may sound like the Hebrew word for God (*'elôhîm*) but it denotes what is empty or valueless. The Egyptians will be in a state of fear, with none of their 'gods' able to offer any comfort or support.

2-3 Civil war will break out in Egypt, as God intervenes to incite man against man, brother against brother, neighbour against neighbour, city against city, kingdom against kingdom. The mention of all these is to give a picture of complete anarchy in the land. God's hand will further be demonstrated in frustrating the Egyptian's plans.[25] They

---

[25]The Hebrew verb for 'bring to nought' is *bâla'*. The difficulty is that there are four distinct Hebrew verbs with identical spelling, and at times there may be some interchange of meaning. Certainly here the meaning that the context requires is something like 'confuse' or 'bring to nought'. See *DCH*, 2, p. 180.

will be demoralised, and try to find comfort by getting advice from the dead or seeking help from mediums or spiritists. While the word for the 'dead' (*'ittîm*) only occurs here, the other two expressions are well-known, and both occur in the passage in Deuteronomy where Israel is forbidden to follow Canaanite customs in seeking a word of guidance (Deut. 18:9-13). Israel did revert to heathen practices in times of crisis (see Isa. 9:13). Here the Egyptians, faced with overwhelming turmoil, turn to their only, but vain, hope.

4 The judgment on Egypt will resemble the manner in which they treated the Israelites so long before. The people who imposed harsh labour (Exod. 1:14) will themselves be subject to a harsh ruler, to a fierce king (Heb. *melek 'az*). The adjective 'fierce' is never used of God and when used of people always depicts them as enemies. This probably is a reference to the king of Assyria, for in typical Isaianic style the cryptic allusion here is later amplified with explicit mention (see 20:4). As in 17:6 the message ends with the confirmation that it is indeed a word from 'the Lord, the LORD of hosts'.

ii. Devastation of Food Supplies and Commerce (19:5-10)

5-7 The River Nile was central to life in Egypt.[26] It provided the water for irrigation of fields. Any diminution in its flow had drastic consequences for the whole country, as the crops necessary to sustain the population could not be produced. Isaiah's message is that the LORD is coming in judgment, and this will mean that there will be no water in the Nile or subsidiary canals, and hence all the crops will fail. The ground will be so dry that it will be swept away by the wind. What were once fertile fields will become a desolation. The succession of words to describe the coming catastrophe simply heightens the picture of total distress – 'dry up', 'become parched' (2x), 'to be dry' (2x), 'to stink', 'to dwindle', 'to rot'. Just as Hebrew has a great range of words for streams and rivers, so it has a correspondingly wide range of words to describe the lack of water.

---

[26]While the normal Hebrew word for Egypt (*mitsrayim*) has been used six times in verses 1-4, in verse 6 a variant form (*mâtsôr*) is used, as in 37:25 and Micah 7:12. Since the dual form of the normal word may refer to the two parts of Egypt (upper and lower) it may be that the use of *mâtsôr* here denotes only Lower Egypt. As the word *mâtsôr* is identical in form with the word 'defence', some have followed the AV in this interpretation. However, the context seems to demand a further reference to Egypt.

8-10 Fish were plentiful in Egypt, as the Israelites recalled when they started grumbling in the wilderness (see Num. 11:5). But cessation of the flow of water naturally results in elimination of the work of fishermen. Hooks and nets will become useless items. Production of cloth will also cease. The Egyptian flax industry was well known, and the fine linen produced from the flax was an important export for the country. Not only did flax require abundant water for its growth, but its production into linen also required much water. It was soaked for several weeks and then dried for up to two years (cf. the account of Rahab hiding the spies under the flax in Joshua 2:6). The disappearance of the flax and linen industries will cause economic chaos, and the workers will feel crushed at heart. Egypt's commercial heart will be devastated, as the wage earners realise that their livelihood is gone.

iii. No Astute Advice in Egypt (19:11-15)

11 Deliverance for Egypt will not come from clever advice of officials or wise men. Zoan, well known to the Israelites because of their Egyptian sojourn (see Ps. 78:12, 43), was situated in the north-east of the Nile Delta. To the Greeks it was known as Tanis. It was a major city (hence listed by Ezekiel among the cities to suffer God's judgment, Ezek. 30:14), and naturally one with many officials and advisers. However, any counsel they give will be useless, even though they had a reputation for great wisdom (1 Kings 4:30). How empty is the claim to wisdom that any of the wise men make, even if the assertion is that they come from a family noted for its wisdom, or an earlier royal line!

12 Just as Isaiah later in his book challenges the people to produce their false gods to predict the future (41:22), so here the challenge is to the wise men of Egypt to predict what the LORD has in store for their land. He has formed his purpose for them, but their 'prophets' are unable to declare it. The opening words of the verse emphasise the taunt: 'Where are they, then ... ?' (Heb. *'ayyâm 'êfô'*).

13 The officials of Zoan are now linked with the leaders at Nof. In Hosea 9:6 this city is called Mof, and it is probably from that form that the Greeks named it Memphis, which modern English translations use. It was south of the apex of the Nile Delta, and continued as an important centre until captured by Alexander the Great in 331 BC. The leaders of the people are designated 'cornerstone', used here as in 1 Samuel 14:38 with the metaphorical sense of leader(s). They had made Egypt stagger, an accusation repeated in verse 14.

14-15 Egypt's distress is of the LORD's making. She will be given a spirit that will make her unable to think aright, like someone with a fit of dizziness. The opening and middle parts of verse 14 have problems. The literal rendering is: 'The LORD has poured into her the spirit of dizziness; they make Egypt stagger in all his work.' Questions arise relating both to the identity of the people who make Egypt stagger and of the person whose work is mentioned. The LXX has smoothed out the difficulties by translating 'The LORD has poured *into them* the spirit of dizziness; they make Egypt stagger *in all her work*' (the NIV follows this).[27] While this reads well, it involves emendation of the text. If the MT is preserved, the verb at the beginning of verse 14b will have to be understood as an impersonal usage (though this is not common with the plural), while the change to masculine ('his work') is stylistic. Certainly in the next verse Egypt is regarded as a masculine word ('that *he* does'). The point is clear from the final part of verse 14 that Egypt will be so disorientated that her condition and behaviour will resemble that of a person hopelessly drunk. The end result spelt out in verse 15 is that there is absolutely nothing that Egypt can do. The totality is emphasised by using the same phrase as already employed in 9:14: 'head or tail, palm branch or reed.'

iv. The Threat from Judah (19:16-17)

16 Four successive sections, all of which start with 'in that day' and which are in prose not poetry, bring the oracle against Egypt towards its close. They depict in eschatological terms the utterly revised situation that is going to come about. Rather than Judah being the oppressed, she is going to cause terror to other nations. With the reversal of fortunes the Egyptians will be like women who fear the coming conflict. The LORD's hand of judgment is upraised, and terrified Egypt waits the impending doom.

17 God's plan involves a special role for Judah. Wherever people hear that name mentioned they will fear. This will be a sign to them that the purposes of the LORD of hosts are being fulfilled. He has planned judgment against them, and the very mention of the name of Judah produces dread.

---

[27]The first emendation is the change of one letter (*bᵉkirbâh* to *bᵉkirbâm*); the second one is slightly greater (*maʿăsêhû* to *maʿăseyhâ*).

v. Conversion of Egyptians (19:18)

18 Religious conversion also features in God's programme for the future. Five cities will speak in unison with Judah, as they talk in Hebrew[28] and pledge themselves by solemn oath to the LORD. It is unclear why one of them is singled out for special mention. The majority of manuscripts of the MT have the name as 'the city of destruction' (*'îr haheres*), while some have 'the city of the sun' (*'îr hashemesh,* i.e., Heliopolis, now a suburb of Cairo). If the Massoretic reading is preserved, the idea may well be that even a city of such a character as this will participate in the unified worship and service of the LORD. The city originally doomed to destruction will be one of those who are in this new alliance with one another and with the LORD Almighty.

vi. Judgment and Mercy on Egypt (19:19-22)

19-20 Instead of a picture of Egypt coming to worship in Jerusalem, Isaiah presents us with the picture of a place of worship being established in Egypt itself. An altar will be erected in the centre of the land, while at its border there will be a pillar dedicated to the LORD. These will be both a sign and a witness to him, signifying that he is indeed the saviour who responds when they cry out to him. Now it is not Israel who is oppressed in Egypt, but the Egyptians themselves. Their cry in distress will be heard and the LORD will send deliverance. Just as he delivered Israel at the time of the Exodus, so will he now deliver Egypt.

21 The conversion of Egypt is depicted in terms of conformity to the worship established under the Sinai covenant. God will make himself known to the Egyptians, and in turn they will know him.[29] The expression 'to make oneself known' is used in the Old Testament of God's self-revelation (cf. Exod. 6:2-3), which was a reminder that such knowledge was beyond human ability to achieve. It required God himself to act. Egypt will follow the pattern set for Israel in serving the LORD (Heb. *ve'āvedû*, 'and they will serve [worship]'), presenting sacrifices and grain offerings. They will also make vows to him that they will keep.

---

[28]This is the closest that the Old Testament gets to giving a name to the language spoken by Israel. It is simply called in Hebrew 'the lip of Canaan'.

[29]It is better to take these expressions as being the two sides of the same experience (God's making himself known, and Egypt's knowing him) rather than taking the action of Egypt as acknowledgment of the LORD.

22 Just as Israel was smitten with plagues in Egypt (Exod. 7:14–11:10) so now the LORD will smite Egypt. However this plague is not to destroy but to encourage repentance on her part. She will turn to him and her cries will be heard, and she will be healed (the verb 'to heal' is used twice to emphasise the result of repentance). Again, the repetition of earlier actions by the LORD will take place showing him to be the healer, just as he had done for Israel long before (Heb. *'ᵃnî yhwh rôfeka*, 'I am the LORD your healer', Exod. 15:26).

vii. A Threefold Unity in Worship (19:23-25)

23 The connection between Assyria and Egypt is described as though a new highway will be created, enabling rapid movement from Assyria to Egypt and vice versa. Both nations will find themselves united in worship.

24-25 But something more will occur. Israel will be united with her arch-enemies Assyria and Egypt in commitment to the LORD and in becoming a blessing to the earth. Abraham had been promised that in his seed the nations of the earth would be blessed (Gen. 12:3), a promise repeated many times in the Old Testament. Psalm 72 speaks of the extent of the rule of the Davidic king ('from sea to sea and from the River [Euphrates] to the ends of the earth', 72:8; cf. Zech. 9:10), and that all nations are going to be blessed in him (Ps. 72:17). Religious conversion in Egypt and Assyria will mean that the trio of Israel, Egypt, and Assyria will be a blessing. God himself will pronounce a blessing on them, using expressions used elsewhere of Israel—'my people', 'my handiwork', 'my inheritance'.

viii. The inevitability of Judgment on God's People (20:1-6)

The message is ostensibly for Egypt and Cush, but the closing words of verse 6 show that the real recipient of the message is God's people. When they see what he does to their enemies they will realise that their only hope is to repent, for how else can they escape?

1-2 Another of Isaiah's messages is set in an historical context. Sargon II of Assyria attacked and captured the Philistine cities in 711 BC, and specifically Ashdod was taken. He did not come in person but sent the man who was the supreme commander of his army (the title given him in the Heb. text is *tartân*). It was in that very period that God spoke through his servant Isaiah. In this case the message is directed to Isaiah himself, who is instructed to carry out symbolic actions. This was a teaching medium that God used with other prophets as well (cf., e.g., Jer. 13:1-11; Ezek. 4:1-16). Isaiah is to remove both clothing and footwear for a period of three years. The Hebrew word for 'naked' (*'ârôm*) can apply to partial nakedness. If that is the case here, then it means that Isaiah is to remove all but his loincloth. Either way, he is set to experience a prolonged period of humiliation and discomfort.

3-4 The purpose of these actions is intended as a sign and portent to Egypt and Cush. There is no significant difference between the Hebrew words 'sign' and 'portent'. The message is that Isaiah's actions have been intended to indicate what is going to happen to the Egyptians and the Cushites. They are all, young and old alike, going to be taken in a shameful way into exile by the Assyrians. The words 'captives' and 'exiles' seem to be synonyms used for variety.

5 Observers of the events are going to be filled with fear when they realise what has happened. If help is expected from Cush and Egypt, then these events will show the folly of trusting in them. They cannot deliver themselves from the Assyrian king; what hope is there for those who depend on them?

6 The designation for those dwelling in Palestine is 'those who dwell [on] this coast'. While technically the Hebrew word *'î* means 'island' it is used here and elsewhere in Isaiah for coastlands (see 11:11; 41:1, 5; 42:10; 49:1; and commentary). People, who in the face of Assyrian threats looked south to Egypt and Cush, will be disappointed. The saviours they hoped would defend them are gone. What now remains for them? No possibility of escape remains, and they must anticipate the same actions towards themselves as Egypt and Cush have experienced.

7. The Burden against the Wilderness of the Sea [Babylon] (21:1-10)
The focus of the burdens is redirected to Babylon (see comments on the whole section prefacing 13:1), though this time a symbolical name is used (as with the next three burdens). While the earlier burden is probably to be dated from around the period 732–722 BC, this one seems to be from a little later (possibly around 710 BC). The great themes of redemption and Israel's comfort feature prominently once again.

i. The Call for Judgment (21:1-5)

1 Though in verse 9 Babylon is mentioned explicitly, here in the opening verse a symbolical name is chosen: 'the desert of the sea.' The word 'sea' (Heb. *yâm*) has been used of the River Nile in 18:2 and 19:5, so it is possible it could be used here of the River Euphrates. However, like the description of Jerusalem in 22:1 ('the valley of vision'), the name is mysterious. In particular, the use of the word 'desert' may have been intended to bring to mind the judgment passed on Israel long ago of wandering in 'the desert', and imply the similar fate coming for Babylon. The judgment for Babylon will consist of an enemy[30] coming from 'the desert', whose approach will provoke terror. The comparison with a whirlwind emphasises both the suddenness and the destructive power of the attack.

2 The vision Isaiah receives is a hard or harsh one, like the one Ahijah had for Jeroboam (1 Kings 14:6). The first part of the message consists of alliterative clauses: 'the plunderer plunders and the destroyer destroys' (Heb. *habôgêd bôgêd v^ahashshôdêd shôdêd*). In the context this seems to be a description of Babylon's character. Elam and Media are commanded to bring an end to all the groaning [she caused]. These words in parentheses are not in the text but something like them is needed in English translation, unless the meaning is that the groaning is *over her*. Mention has already been made of the role of the Medes in Babylon's downfall (see comment on 13:17). Elam was a constant enemy of Babylon, and Josephus says that they were the ancestors of the Persians.[31]

3-4 The prophet's emotions overwhelm him as he considers the impending judgment on Babylon. There is much similarity with the opening of the first burden against Babylon. After the initial declaration concerning the uproar among the nations as they mass in response to the LORD's call, Isaiah indicates that the day of the LORD will come 'as destruction from the Almighty' (Heb. *k^ashod mishshaddai*, 13:6). Then he specifies the emotional response (13:7-8). Here the destruction has been stated (verse 2), and now the effect on Isaiah is described using some of the same language as in 13:6-7. The variety of verbs employed simply reinforces the idea of complete turmoil, while the

---

[30]The Hebrew text simply says 'he (or it) comes': 'As windstorms in the desert sweep on, it comes from the wilderness, from a terrifying land' (NASB). The NIV 'invader' is an interpretative addition.

[31]Josephus, *Antiquities*, 1.6 § 4.

analogy of a woman in travail in both passages (13:8; 21:3) may suggest the necessary anguish that precedes the coming of the new moral order. Isaiah's reaction is paralleled by Daniel's response to the visions he was later given (Dan. 8:27; 10:16-17).

5 The Babylonians, far from being ready for battle, are lounging in idle dissipation. They have spread their carpets and are busy with their eating and drinking. What is needed is alertness in the face of danger. They should 'get up and oil the shields'. Only here and in 2 Samuel 1:21 is the verb 'anoint' used with other than a significance for ritual inauguration. Oiling the leather shields presumably was to make them more flexible or slippery to deflect a glancing blow, though it may also have had some ritual significance.[32] Grammatically the shift from infinitives in Hebrew (participles in English: 'setting', 'spreading', 'eating', 'drinking') to imperatives ('get up', 'anoint') highlights the need for sudden action to assess the coming danger. The account of Babylon's fall in Daniel 5 depicts the festivities in the city as danger surrounded it. When attack was least expected, the Medes and Persians under Cyrus entered the city and took it.

ii. The Impending Danger (21:6-10)

6-7 The LORD's message to Isaiah is to station a lookout on Jerusalem's walls to await word from Babylon. He has to be highly vigilant, reporting any approach of chariots or riders. The introductory word 'for' (Heb. *kî*) suggests that these instructions follow on from the preceding vision of Babylon's destruction. The Sovereign Lord (Heb. *'ªdônây*), ruler over all, including both Babylon and Judah, wants his people to get speedy word when the prophecy concerning Babylon is fulfilled.

8 The opening of this verse has long been a problem, as the MT reads: 'And a lion called out.' Attempts have been made to suggest that the watchman 'called out [with the voice of] a lion', but this is rather forced. Long ago, in 1778, Lowth, the Anglican bishop and biblical scholar, suggested that the reading should be 'lookout', 'watchman', and this is what appears in 1QIsa[a] (*hr'h*). However, as Young notes, this seems too easy a solution to an acute difficulty.[33] Another approach

---

[32]See the comments by John N. Oswalt on this verb in *NIDOTTE* 2, pp. 1123-27.

[33]E. J. Young, *The Book of Isaiah* (Grand Rapids: Eerdmans, 1972), II, p. 71. He says that 'none of the attempted explanations, valiant though they be, really satisfies'.

could be to link it with the word *hâ'aryêh* in 2 Kings 15:25. While that passage is also difficult, the appearance of this word with the article suggests that it may be a title, 'the [chief] warrior.'[34] If this solution is taken it means that 'warrior' and 'lookout' are virtually synonyms here. The response of the watchman is that he has been standing day by day at his watchtower, stationed every night at his guard post.

9 The watchman startles with his cry: 'Look, here comes ....' What has been expected (see verse 7) now comes to pass. A man in a chariot and a pair of horses approach, and the man (Heb. 'and *he* answered and said') cries out, 'Babylon has fallen, has fallen'. Babylon, 'the jewel of the kingdoms' (13:19), has indeed fallen, with the repetition of the verb simply making the statement as emphatic as possible. The expression is echoed in John's description of Babylon's destruction in the book of Revelation (14:8; 18:2). Even the very gods in which the Babylonians relied on lie broken on the ground. The images in which they trusted have been no help at all in the time of trouble (see also 46:1-2 in reference to Babylon's futility of trusting in her gods).

iii. The message for Judah (21:10)
10 Isaiah affirms for his own people that he has been a faithful messenger of the LORD of hosts, the God of Israel. What he has heard, he has spoken. It is with great emotion that he now addresses them: 'O my crushed [people], the son of my [threshing] floor.' The verb 'crush' (Heb. *dûsh*) means to thresh grain, but it can also be used in the sense of exterminating (2 Kings 13:7). As in 28:23-29 Isaiah is using the familiar language of agriculture to make his point. While Israel/Judah is going to endure punishment at the hands of the Babylonians (see 39:5-7), yet Isaiah speaks with tenderness about his own people, knowing that God's purpose for them is good. They might well be compared to a threshing floor, or an afflicted city (54:11-15), but though God will thresh the nations yet this will be to separate the wheat from the chaff. Israel ultimately will be gathered in one by one (27:12-13).

8. The Burden against Edom (21:11-12)
Four times Isaiah brings specific messages concerning Edom (11:14; 21:11-12; 34:1-17; 63:1-6). This one is less condemnatory than the others. A symbolical name is chosen, Dumah. It means 'silence', or

---

[34]See entry under *'aryêh* II in *DCH* I, p. 378.

even 'death' (Pss. 94:17; 115:17). This is a play on the name 'Edom', and it fits well with the threefold occurrence in this short oracle of the idea of night. Two Hebrew manuscripts actually substitute 'Edom' for 'Dumah'. The use of the name Seir makes it plain that the oracle concerns Edom, for Seir is another synonym for it.

11 After the title, there is an abrupt sentence: 'To me [one] calls from Seir.' No identification is given of either the caller or hearer. In the context it is best to understand the prophet Isaiah himself as the one of whom inquiry is made, and he is the 'guard'. This is a different word for 'watchman' than used in the preceding verses, and it is more indicative of a civilian guard than a military one. Either a particular person calls, or else the nation is personified as the speaker. The inquiry is: 'Guard, what of the night? Guard, what of the night?' There is a change in the word for night, but this is of no consequence. While it is possible that the question means 'What about the night?' it is also possible to read it as an inquiry regarding how late it is: 'Guard, what hour of the night is it?'

12 The prophet's answer is a cryptic one: 'Morning has come, and also the night.' This could be an answer regarding the time, or alternately, there could be a contrast between day and night. If the latter is intended, the message would be that while there might be some light with morning, yet the darkness of night is still coming. Edom is not to become complacent regarding the future. The prophet encourages the Edomites to come again (the Heb. verb *shûv* when used with another verb often means to do something again) and ask concerning this matter. Two rare verbs are used in this verse ('come', 'ask'), both much more common in Aramaic than in Hebrew. Perhaps they are used deliberately as part of the diplomatic *lingua franca* of the period to hint that Edom as well as Judah have to deal with major international powers such as Assyria and Babylon in coming days.

9. The Burden against the Arabians (21:13-17)

This burden parallels that against Moab in the first cycle (15:1-16:14), and here the Hebrew word *'aráv* must be given its usual meaning of 'Arabs'.[35] It is the only one that uses a preposition (Heb. *b^a*) in the

---

[35]See E. J. Young, *The Book of Isaiah* II, op. cit., p. 79, fn. 43. In the heading Young uses the word 'Arabians' but in the translation he gives 'Arabia'. The former is the better choice. See confirmation of this in J. A. Motyer, *The Prophecy of Isaiah* (Inter-Varsity Press, 1993), p. 178.

heading. Whereas in all the others there is virtually a grammatical relationship (called a construct) between 'burden' and the name ('the burden of ...'), here it is a burden 'on' or 'against' the Arabians. The use of this general term seems to be intentional, for instead of specifying another national group Isaiah indicates a wide group of people who could apply this burden to themselves. This adds to the threat element. There may be word-play involved as well, for the second occurrence of *ba'erâv* should be revocalised as *bâ'erev*, 'in the evening', which then fits in admirably with the verb 'you lodge [for the night]'.

13-14 In the face of fugitives or wanderers from Kedar (see verses 16-17) the people of Dedan and Tema are providers of water and food. Dedan, in the time of Jeremiah and Ezekiel (Jer. 25:23; 49:8; Ezek. 25:13; 27:15, 20; 38:13), was a flourishing city with its wealth built on trade. Tema, occupied by Nabonidus during his self-imposed exile from Babylon, was an oasis in the Arabian desert. It is also linked with Dedan in Jeremiah 25:23 and 49:7-8. These sites are in north-west Arabia, approximately 250 miles (400 km) from Medina.

15 This verse does not specify who the wanderers are, but in the context the only ones identified are those from Kedar (see next verse). From an unnamed enemy they are fleeing. The people who themselves were armed with bows flee from sword, drawn sword, drawn bow, and from the heat of battle. The repetition four times of 'from' (Heb. lit. 'from before') emphasises the gravity of the attack upon them by a much larger and well-armed enemy. The Assyrians attacked the Arabian tribes in 734 BC, and then again under Sargon II in 725 BC.

16-17 A divine declaration announces Kedar's fate. The word 'Kedar' is used in the Old Testament to denote a wealthy and powerful Bedouin tribe on the Arabian peninsula south-east of Damascus. The name comes from one of Ishmael's sons (Gen. 25:13), and it is coupled with Meshech in Psalm 120:5 as a symbol of barbaric people. Kedar's glory will end within a year, and her military might will be destroyed, so that only a remnant of her fighting force remains. The final words of verse 17 balance the opening ones of verse 16: 'For thus says the LORD .... For the LORD, the God of Israel, has spoken.' Isaiah's message is for his people Judah, but yet he continues to speak of their God as 'the God of Israel'. Though deprived of the name 'Israel', the southern kingdom was still regarded as the direct successor of the original nation Israel.

10. The Burden against the Valley of Vision [Jerusalem] (22:1-25)
This burden, addressed to the Valley of Vision, is clearly a message
for Judah. The references to the Palace of the Forest and the City of
David (verse 8), the Lower/Old Pool (verses 9, 11), the houses of
Jerusalem (verse 10), and the section relating to the Shebna and Eliakim
(verses 15-25) clearly show that Jerusalem is the focus of this message.
Isaiah calls the addressees 'my people' (verse 4), and the feminine
singular suffix is used repeatedly, in keeping with fact that 'Jerusalem'
is feminine in Hebrew. The address to Shebna is distinctive, for
nowhere else in this collection of messages to the nations is an individual
singled out for attention. No explanation is given for the title 'Valley of
Vision', but it may be a sarcastic comment on Judah's lack of vision.[36]
The fact that one of the messages is specifically directed to Jerusalem
reinforces the point made already in the introduction to chapters 13–
23 that these oracles are primarily intended for Judah/Jerusalem.

i. The Threat to Jerusalem (22:1-14)
1 Jerusalem is posed a question. 'What's the matter with you now,
that you have all gone up to the housetops (NASB)?' It is difficult to
attempt a dating of this whole burden. Some parts suggest that it may
refer back to the siege by Sennacherib in 701 BC, while other parts
seemingly point to future devastation for Jerusalem that occurred in
586 BC. This is so because the language of verses 1-4 in particular
parallels the language of 2 Kings, Jeremiah, and Lamentations
concerning the destruction of Jerusalem by Nebuchadnezzar. The
presence of the people on the roof can be explained in various ways,
but it may well be that they were partying there (see verse 13) at a
time when they should have been seeking the LORD.

2-3 The description of the city ties in with comments on the previous
verse. The people are engaged in tremendous revelry so that their city
is regarded as being characterised by noise of uproar. In this respect
Jerusalem is no different from Babylon (see 21:5). The battlefield does
not claim many dead. Rather, many die in captivity, for they flee even
before the opposing forces come near. They do not even take up the
bow and sword, but in trying to escape they find themselves taken
captive. This certainly happened when Zedekiah and his army fled
before the Babylonians (see the historical account in 2 Kings 25:4-7).

---

[36]So John N. Oswalt, *The Book of Isaiah: Chapters 1-39*, op. cit., p. 405.

4 Isaiah himself is deeply moved at this vision of the coming catastrophe. He doesn't want consolation from anyone, for he sheds tears over the destruction of Jerusalem. Again the parallel with Babylon becomes clear, for the same verbal root (Heb. *shâdad*) is employed which was used twice earlier to describe her destruction (13:6; 21:2). The prophet speaks of his own people as 'the daughter of my people', a phrase that should be retained in translation as it is echoed by Jeremiah on several occasions (4:11; 6:26; 8:11, 21, 23; 9:6; 14:17). This may be a deliberate choice by Jeremiah, as he describes his people hastening to ruin. Jeremiah also shed tears over the fate of Judah (Jer. 9:1, 18; 13:17; 14:17).

5 Isaiah conveys the message that covenant curses are going to be fulfilled on Judah/Jerusalem. The use of 'day' seems no different from the longer phrase 'in that day' (verses 8 and 12). The announcement comes with the authority of the Lord, the LORD of hosts, for it is indeed *his* day. It is phrased in rhyming words in Hebrew: *mehûmâh ûmevûkâh ûmevûsâh*; 'tumult and trampling and turbulence'.[37] One of these words (*mehûmâh*) appears in Deuteronomy 7:23 (along with its root verb *hûm*) in the assurance that God will deal with the occupants of Canaan by throwing them into confusion. It appears again in Deuteronomy 28:20 where the curse of panic is part of the threatened ruin for the nation if it is disobedient to the LORD. The second last clause has been a difficulty from ancient times, as the oldest versions indicate. Modern versions are not much help, as they too display great variation. The problem relates to two Hebrew words *meqarqar qir* (with a repetition three times of the combination *qr*). The first of these occurs only here in the Hebrew Bible. Of all the suggestions the best is that the verb comes from a root meaning to bore or dig, while the second word may mean a pit, or else it is a shortened form of the Hebrew word for a spring (*mâqôr*).[38] If this approach is taken the clause fits in well with the references to water storage in verses 9 and 11. The final clause indicates a call to the mountains to provide some help or defence.

6-8a Elam, which previously was called upon to attack Babylon (21:2), is now pictured as attacking Jerusalem with infantry, archers

---

[37]The translation is from O. Kaiser, *Isaiah 13-39: A Commentary* (OT Library, SCM, 1974), p. 137.

[38]See the note on the verse in John D. W. Watts, *Isaiah 1-33* (Word Biblical Commentary, Word, 1985), p. 279, note 5.

and charioteers, a complete army. Kir uncovers the shields ready for battle. Elam was situated north-east of Babylon, and while Kir was probably in the same general area, an exact location cannot be determined. No city of this name is known in extra-biblical sources. Since Elam and Kir appear in parallel it may be that they are to be equated. The valleys will no longer be noted for wonderful crops but for the presence of chariots, as the enemy forces press in on the city gates. Verse 8a simply says 'and he revealed Judah's cover', i.e. the Lord planned this attack on Jerusalem, but instead of it moving the inhabitants to look to him for help, it exacerbated their disregard of the city's Maker (see verse 11).

8b-9 In the following section the emphasis is on Jerusalem's actions in the face of attack: 'You looked ... you saw ... you stored ... you counted ... you tore down ... you built ....' Feverish activity was the hallmark of the people's response to the danger. The first step they took was to look to the weaponry stored in the House of the Forest. This was the building erected by Solomon out of wood from Lebanon (see 1 Kings 7:2), and used to store shields (1 Kings 10:17, 21). They realised that there were many breaches in Jerusalem's walls that posed danger points, and especially the water supply needed protection (cf. Ahaz' inspection of the city's water supplies at the time of the Syro-Phoenician war, 7:3). The water supply for Jerusalem was an ancient problem, and the biblical text refers to the shaft that the Jebusites had (2 Sam. 5:8), the 'upper pool' of Ahaz' time (Isa. 7:3), and the various efforts under Hezekiah to safeguard the water resources especially in the face of siege (2 Chron. 32:2-8, 30). The 'lower pool' mentioned here is presumably to be identified with 'the old pool' in verse 11. Two aqueducts have been uncovered leading from the upper pool. One is relatively short, while the other is the tunnel cut in Hezekiah's time leading down to the lower pool, probably the modern Birket el-Hamra.[39]

10 Steps were taken to alleviate the danger created by having breaches in the walls. Supplies of stone were needed quickly, and hence a calculation was made of the number of houses in the city, presumably in order to decide which could be destroyed in order to provide material for strengthening the city walls.

11 The first part of this verse refers again to the water supply for Jerusalem. A reservoir was created 'between the two walls',

---

[39]See the note and map by John D. W. Watts, ibid., pp. 282-84.

presumably between the wall of David's city and the wall built in the eighth century BC that butted onto it. Amidst all this effort to defend and protect Jerusalem the people failed in the most obvious regard. Physical activity was no substitute for spiritual response in the face of danger. They failed to look to Jerusalem's Maker and Founder. Their attitude was quite different from an Israelite poet, who asked, 'Where does my help come from?' and who provided the answer: 'my help comes from the LORD, the maker of heaven and earth' (Ps. 121:1). The unspiritual response of the people gives credence to the idea that this attack cannot be the one described later of Hezekiah's time, when he received the message from Sennacherib and immediately prayed to God for deliverance (Isa. 37:20).

12-13 God's call to the people is for mourning, and for the actions normally accompanying deep grief. They are to weep and wail, to pull out hair, and to put on the traditional sackcloth. Wearing sackcloth (Heb. *sâq*, from which our English word 'sack' is derived) was not only done when mourning the dead but also in times of national disaster, both in Israel and in other Near Eastern centres such as Damascus (1 Kings 20:31), Moab (Isa. 15:3), Ammon (Jer. 49:3), Tyre (Ezek. 27:31) and Nineveh (Jon. 3:5). The response of the people stands in stark contrast (marked in Heb. with the opening words of verse 13, *vᵉhinnêh*, 'but instead' [NKJV]). They regard the time as one for festivities, preparing meat and wine for their banquets. What they say to one another is: 'Let us eat and drink for tomorrow we die' (cf. Paul's use of these words in 1 Corinthians 15:32). In this respect they were no better than the Babylonians, who similarly feasted when danger was at hand (21:5).

14 The section ends with a dire prediction. This is made all the more solemn by the repeated use of the divine title: 'the LORD of hosts' and 'the Lord, the LORD of hosts', and by the introductory word (Heb. *'im*) which often precedes an oath. It is quite appropriate to translate the opening as 'Surely this iniquity...', or even more explicitly as 'I swear this guilt will not be atoned for....'[40] The way the message came to Isaiah also adds to its solemnity, for Isaiah says that this oath came when the LORD revealed it to his ear (cf. the use of the simple 'he revealed' in verse 8). The idiom is close to the one used of the servant in 50:4 ('he roused my ear to listen'). The judgment is that this

---

[40]This is the translation of John D. W. Watts, ibid., p. 279.

sin will never be expiated. The people who themselves had spoken about death (verse 13), will die in their sins. The language would have recalled to listeners or readers the punishment on Eli's house: 'Therefore I swore to the house of Eli [says the LORD] that the iniquity of Eli's house shall never be expiated by sacrifice or offering for ever' (1 Sam. 3:14).

ii. A Message for Shebna and Eliakim (22:15-25)

Nowhere else in Isaiah's prophecies does he prophesy against an individual. At the end of the oracle against Jerusalem he directs a word of judgment against Shebna, and a prophecy that Eliakim will only enjoy a short-lived time as his successor. The message clearly relates to the historical period of Hezekiah's reign set out in 2 Kings 18–20, 2 Chronicles 29–32, and Isaiah 36–39.[41] The fact that the unusual name 'Shebna' (apparently a foreign word [possibly Aramaic] and without any lineage being noted) appears also in 2 Kings 18:18, 26, 37 and Isaiah 37:2, suggests identification is demanded. If Shebna is not of Aramaic origin, it may be an abbreviation for Shebanyahu, 'return O LORD'. The first part of the message is poetic in form (verses 15-19), while the latter part is in prose (verses 20-25). In the poetic section there are some striking usages of language with repetition and use of similar sounding words from the same root (see comments on verses 16, 17, 18).

15 Isaiah begins the message to Shebna with a typical prophetic introduction: 'Thus says the Lord, the LORD of hosts.' The use of this extended title for God follows on from the usage already in the earlier part of this chapter (see verses 5, 12 and 14). He calls him 'this steward' who is over the house (Heb. *sokên 'al habbayit*), similar to the corresponding expression in Ugaritic (*skn bt melek*). From its use in 2 Chronicles 26:21 in reference to the heir-apparent, Jotham, it probably designates the person next in power to the king. If that is so, it points to a problem in Judah at this period in time. Shebna, a foreigner, is second in charge of the kingdom. The designation 'this steward' may be a disdainful usage (cf. the use of 'this people' in 6:9; 8:11, 12).

16 The verse begins with two questions: 'What to you here?' and 'Who to you here?' The first question is a repetition of verse 1 (except

---

[41]See the summary of the period given by Paul House, *1, 2 Kings* (The New American Commentary: Broadman & Holman, 1995), pp. 352-54.

for the use of *pôh* in place of *'êfô '*). The use of 'to' as an indication of possession is common in biblical Hebrew. The rendering 'What have you here and whom have you here?' (NKJV) brings the meaning out well. The first question relates to his own position, while the second one relates to his family connection. Because of his exalted position Shebna coveted a king's burial place, a sepulchre set high up on the cliff face. Prominent people often prepared their own grave (see regarding Asa in 2 Chronicles 16:14).[42] The indication is given that the grave is 'here', the third time that this adverb is used in the verse. 'Here' must be the tomb or mausoleum that he is preparing.

17 The LORD's message to Shebna is one of judgment. He is to be thrown far away. The Hebrew uses both the verb 'to throw far away' and also a cognate noun meaning 'thrown far away', so that when read there is a striking quadruplication of the syllable *tl* (*m^{e}taltel^{e}kâ taltêlâh*). The translation of the final two words in the verse is problematical. Both words are from the same root (Heb. *'âtâh*), and many English translations regard it as meaning to seize or grasp. That meaning is not well supported, and it may be better to regard it as the verb 'to wrap' or 'cover'. The figurative use of it in Psalms 71:13 and 109:29, 'to cover with shame' or 'cover with scorn', fits better here. Shebna's fate is that he will be thrown away as an object of derision.

18 The idea of being thrown away like a ball continues, and once more there is the repetition of one basic root. Here the root *tsânaf* appears as a finite verb, an infinitive, and a cognate noun (Heb. *tsânôf yitsnâf^{e}kâ ts^{e}nêfâh*). Shebna's fate will be to be thrown away into a country whose boundaries are extensive, and *there* he will die. The contrast between 'here' in verse 1 and 'there' (twice) in this verse is clearly deliberate. He will have no royal burial and his chariots (evidence of his wealth and position) will be there as well. Whatever he may arrogantly think of his present position will be contradicted when he is seen to be a thing of shame and scorn.

19 God's final word to Shebna is the simple message: 'I will throw you out of your office; from your position you will ousted.' The present proud official will lose his high rank. It is hard to say whether this meant complete removal from an office under Hezekiah or simply a demotion, as the use of the word 'scribe', 'secretary', of him in Isaiah

---

[42]The NIV renders 'your grave' and 'your resting place' whereas the MT has 'his grave' and 'his resting place'. However, it is quite common to find a statement in the third person following a question (see *GKC* §144p).

37:2 and 2 Kings 19:2 may point to him continuing in the king's service but in a more humble rank.

20-21 Attention now turns to Shebna's replacement, Eliakim (his name means 'God establishes'). In an unspecified period of time God is going to call Eliakim, whom he designates as 'my servant', and he will be clothed in the insignia of authority that Shebna presently wears. His relationship to Judah and Jerusalem will be like that of a father as he offers them protection. In the Old Testament 'father' is used of authority figures and thus can designate prophet (2 Kings 6:21), priest (Judg. 18:19), and king (1 Sam. 24:11 [Heb. 12]). The term 'father' is here referring to Eliakim's role as governor. By 701 BC Eliakim had replaced Shebna, assuming the role that Shebna had previously held (see the Heb. phrase 'who is over the house' used of Eliakim in 36:3 in contrast to its use in relation to Shebna in 22:15).

22 With allusion to the words of Isaiah 9:7 (Heb. 6), God declares that Eliakim will carry 'the key of David's house', i.e. the symbols of authority given him by the king who is of the Davidic line. Such is that authority that entry into the royal palace will be controlled by him. These words may lie behind Jesus' statement to Peter concerning the keys of the kingdom (Matt. 16:19) and also in a portion of the message in Revelation to the church in Philadelphia (Rev. 3:7).

23-24 Eliakim's role is likened to a peg firmly attached to a wall (see Judges 16:14 where it is used in connection with a loom). Normally the word is used of tent pegs, but here it is clearly a piece of wood inserted into a wall in such a way that it will bear weight upon it. His elevation to such a position will be a thing of great honour for his family, as if they had come to possess royal status. On him will hang all his family's glory, both for contemporary family members and in time to come for their descendants (two very unusual words appear for 'offspring and offshoots' [NIV]). A position such as this had economic implications for the immediate family, from the more insignificant 'vessels' to the most important 'storage jars'.

25 Again there is mention of an event 'in that day'. This has to be a day subsequent to the one mentioned in verse 20. The apparent security afforded by Eliakim's promotion to second-in-command in Judah will come to an end. The peg will give way and its load will fall. Just as the message to Eliakim started with a declaration that it was the LORD's word (verse 15), so it ends with confirmation that the LORD has indeed spoken. Both the historical record in 2 Kings 18–19 and the prose passage in Isaiah 36–37 record that Eliakim went out to meet the Rabshakeh, and following that Hezekiah sent him to carry the news to Isaiah (see later comment on chapters 36–37).[43]

11. The Burden against Tyre (23:1-17)

The final burden is against the powerful port city of Tyre, commonly coupled with its near neighbour Sidon in thought and reference by people in biblical times. Herodotus, the Greek historian, mentions that Tyre dates back at least to 2750 BC, and it was probably the greatest of the Phoenician city states. About the end of the first millennium BC Tyre forged strong links with Israel, and Hiram I was on friendly terms with both David and Solomon (see 1 Kings 5:1). With Solomon he made a formal covenant (1 Kings 5:12) and the preparation of stone and timber for the building of the temple in Jerusalem was a cooperative venture by Solomon's and Hiram's men and the men of Gebal (better known by its more modern names of Byblos or Jebail). Sidon, 25 miles (40 km) to the north of Tyre, was also an important Phoenician city port. It was noted for its shipbuilding, the production of purple dye, and its glassware. Both Tyre and Sidon were attacked many times during their history, and control moved from conqueror to conqueror. A great number of people came from Tyre and Sidon to hear Jesus and to be healed by him. Jesus also used the two cities as an illustration when denouncing the cities in which many of his miracles were performed. If Tyre and Sidon had seen those miracles they would have repented long before (see Matt. 11:21-22). It was at Tyre that Paul landed on his final journey to Jerusalem (Acts 21:1-7).[44]

---

[43]Three sixth century BC seals have the inscription 'belonging to Eliakim, the servant of Joiachin'. This evidence may point to Eliakim continuing in royal service into the reign of Jehoiachin.

[44]While working on the text of the early part of this chapter my wife and I visited Tyre in September 2002. Three main archaeological sites are accessible. Extensive Greek and Roman remains are located on the south side of the old Phoenician island-city. The remains of a crusader cathedral are nearby on the north side. Further inland is a vast site containing the remains of a Roman road (with several arches over it), an extensive necropolis, and the site of an incomplete hippodrome with seating for 20,000 spectators. The main shopping area of modern Tyre is built over the land comprising the old causeway linking the island and the mainland.

1 The burden commences with a call to the ships of Tarshish to mourn the destruction of Tyre. No more will there be lucrative trade between these ports, for Tyre is to be destroyed. Houses will be demolished and the harbour around which Tyre's wealth was built will be no more.[45] This message is received by the men of Tarshish via the *kittim*, which is a biblical term for the inhabitants of Cyprus (see Gen. 10:4).[46]

2-3 The people of both Tyre and Sidon are commanded to be quiet. Tyre was indeed an island until it was captured by the forces of Alexander the Great in 332 BC, after an ingenious plan of building a causeway across to the island and bombarding it with specially built battle machines. The third part of verse 2 is awkward, though not impossible to translate and explain. The NIV footnote gives a translation based on one Dead Sea scroll,[47] but it looks like an emendation to make the text easier. Maintaining the MT with the harder reading still yields a passable translation: 'Be silent, inhabitants of the island and the merchant[s] of Sidon, [for] the seafarer[s] have filled you [with plenty].' Tyre's source of wealth came from the great trade that passed through her port. Grain came from Shihor (probably a synonym for 'the Nile'), and the harvest from the Nile valley was part of the produce that made her a great market place. Trading patterns in the Mediterranean ensured that for centuries Tyre was a vital commercial centre where goods were both bought and exchanged.

4 The variety of translations of this verse is testimony to problems within it. NASB keeps very close to the Hebrew text: 'Be ashamed, O Sidon; for the sea speaks, the stronghold of the sea, saying, "I have neither travailed nor given birth, I have neither brought up young men *nor* reared virgins." ' Sidon, the subsidiary port to Tyre, is counselled to feel shame, for even the [Mediterranean] Sea will be bereft of

---

[45]While the MT consonantal text can be retained, it does make good sense to revocalise and then read, as the NIV does, 'harbour' instead of 'entering'.

[46]The descendants of one of the sons of Javan (Gen. 10:4=1 Chron. 1:7) settled in Cyprus and gave their name to a town called Kition. Some of the remains of Kition have been excavated and can be seen on the eastern side of the present day Larnaca. In Jeremiah 2:10 the term seems to be used more broadly of the Greek islands, while in Daniel 11:30 it refers to western coastlands or possibly to Rome.

[47]'Sidon,/ who cross over the sea,/ your envoys are on the great waters. The grain of Shihor, the harvest of the Nile....'

ships on her waves. The absence of shipping will leave her like a bereaved mother, having neither sons nor daughters to bring up. This is a better explanation than trying to see in the Hebrew word for sea (*yâm*) the name of the Canaanite god of the sea.[48]

5 This verse is linked with what has already been said in verse 3 concerning the harvest from the Nile being the revenue of Tyre. If Tyre is destroyed then the commerce of Egypt will be affected. Just as Tyre is to bewail the changed circumstances, so will Egypt be in similar anguish.

6-7 Far off ports like Tarshish will also feel the ramifications of Tyre's downfall. The exact location of Tarshish cannot be determined. It was clearly a distant place (Isa. 66:19) from which came metals such as silver (Jer. 10:9), iron, tin, and lead (Ezek. 27:12). The suggestion that it is to be equated with Tartessus in Spain (mentioned by Herodotus) is quite plausible, and lacking any more certain identification is to be provisionally accepted. Tyre is described as an arrogant city, given over to pleasure. She is an old city (Heb. *mîmê-qedem*, 'from days of old'), and her foundations or origins (Heb. *qadmâhtâh*) are clearly back in antiquity. Sometime prior to 2000 BC Tyre was established. She was more than just a trading port, for she also colonised Carthage in north Africa (a rival of Rome in the late BC period), and quite possibly places like Tarshish in Spain.

8-9 Tyre is not going to fall through simply human schemes. The question, 'Who planned this?', produces the answer, 'The LORD of hosts planned it.' The city that created colonies and appointed rulers (lit. 'the bestower of crowns') is going to lose her glory. Her merchants are princely in stature, and her traders are respected everywhere. But all her glory is going to vanish because in God's purposes Tyre is going to be destroyed. He will act to remove her wealth (Heb. 'the pride of all beauty') and her widespread renown (Heb. 'honoured ones of the earth'). There is a play on words in that *ts^{e}vâ'ôt* ('hosts') would also be the plural form of the word for beauty (*ts^{e}vî*).

10 There are two major difficulties in translating and interpreting this verse. The imperative 'cross over' that opens the verse is often replaced in modern translations by 'work', or 'till'. While this only involves a change of one letter (Heb. *dalet* for *rêsh*), yet in the oldest Hebrew these two letters were quite distinct. Hence, though the LXX

---

[48]For this explanation, see John N. Oswalt, *The Book of Isaiah: Chapters 1-39*, op. cit., pp. 430-31.

and one manuscript from the Dead Sea community make the change, it looks like a late alteration. Secondly, Tarshish is said to lack something, but the word used (Heb. *mêzach*) only occurs here and in Psalm 109:19 where it refers to a girdle or belt. Two possible emendations have been proposed,[49] but in the face of uniform manuscript tradition these must be set aside. Either *mêzach* means harbour or shipyard,[50] or else it carries over the meaning of belt in the sense of restraint. The latter is probably to be preferred. The meaning will then be that the inhabitants of Tarshish (personified as 'the daughter of Tarshish') are encouraged to go through their city or land like the waters of the Nile, and because of the destruction of Tyre there is no longer any restraint upon them. Previously Tyre had kept them under close control.[51]

11-12a Earlier the expression that God's hand has been stretched out occurs several times (see 9:12, 17, 21: 14:26-27). Just as God's hand was stretched out against Egypt (Exod. 15:12), so will the Phoenician cities be subject to him. Here its use reinforces the teaching that God's sovereign power is being displayed over the Phoenician cities and even over the Mediterranean Sea that the Phoenicians regarded as their fiefdom. An order has been given that the Canaanite fortresses along the coast are to be destroyed. In the Old Testament 'Canaan' can be used of the whole coastal plain of Palestine including as far north as Sidon (see Judg. 1:31). Here it is used in a more restricted sense to denote the Phoenician strongholds around Tyre and Sidon. The message for Sidon is again that she will not escape destruction. There will be no more revelry (cf. the reference to Tyre's revelry in verse 7, using the same Hebrew root as here), for Sidon is reckoned as already crushed. Several times Sidon was captured. The Assyrians under Tiglath-Pileser I captured the Phoenician cities around 1110 BC and extracted tribute from them (including Sidon), while Nebuchadnezzar took it around the same time as the fall of Jerusalem (c. 587 BC).

12b-13 Even if the inhabitants of the Phoenician cities try to flee and gain refuge in Cyprus, there will be no rest for them there. They have to realise that the Assyrians, who had taken Babylon more than once, could easily overcome Phoenicia. Proud Babylon, who boasted,

---

[49]ibid., p. 433.

[50]See the entry in *DCH*, vol. 5, p. 208.

[51]This interpretation can also be found in G. Grogan, *Isaiah (EBC)*, op. cit., vol. 6, p. 148.

'I am, and there is none besides me' (Isa. 47:8, 10), is to become of no account. Similarly Phoenicia is to be devastated. The message is simply that if Babylon could not escape siege and destruction, no more can Tyre and Sidon. We cannot be certain which attack on Babylon is mentioned here. It could be the one by Sargon in 710 BC or the later one by Sennacherib in 689 BC. Lack of precise identification of the attack does not lessen the point. Just as Babylon could be razed, so could the Phoenician cities.

14 This verse forms a conclusion to the message regarding Tyre. The ships of Tarshish (see the same term in 2:16) are personified, and called upon to lament the fact that their stronghold of Tyre is destroyed. It forms a chiastic echo of verse 1 and reinforces the message of its coming destruction. The repetition of the opening phrase at the conclusion is undoubtedly characteristic of certain laments (see David's lament over Saul and Jonathan, 2 Sam. 1:19, 27). Though Nebuchadnezzar captured the mainland part of Tyre in 572 BC, it was not until the time of Alexander the Great that the island part was conquered in 332 BC.

i. The Results of Judgment (23:15-18)

A short section in prose (except for the prostitute's song in verse 16) spells out the future history of Tyre. A seventy-year period is coming when Tyre will be forgotten. At the end of that period Tyre will regain her place, but her character will be unaltered. The prostitute, out to gain wealth for herself, will ply her trade again, but she will not be able to use her profits to her own advantage. Rather, her earnings will be stored up before the LORD, and those living in obedience to him will be the recipients (cf. the passages dealing with the wealth of the nations coming to Israel in 60:5-11 and 61:6).

15-16 Tyre is going to be forgotten for seventy years. This act of forgetting is not a case of voluntary amnesia, but a divine judgment. The seventy years is not linked directly with the message of Jeremiah that Judah is to suffer a seventy year captivity (Jer. 25:8-11; 29:10). However, it may be that this is the first hint of the Babylonian captivity, given not directly to Judah but in a message of judgment upon Tyre. In both cases the seventy years is probably a known idiom of the day descriptive of the definitive nature of the period of judgment. 'The days of one king's life' merely emphasises the completeness of the period in question. At the end of the seventy years Tyre will still be the same in moral character, and Isaiah depicts her singing a prostitute's song (verse 16). This may have been a well-known song inviting the prostitute to resume her trade after the seventy-year interval. In other words, even radical punishment will not effect spiritual change without a work of God's Spirit (see the same principle set out in God's words before and after the flood, Gen. 6:5; 8:21).

17 The end of the seventy years will see Tyre resume her trade. She will be like a prostitute returning to her former ways, always interested in what profits she can gain from her activities. Her old trading patterns will be resumed and she will once more be a force in the commercial world of the Mediterranean. Just as her punishment was from the LORD (see verse 11), so will her restoration be a divine visitation (Heb. 'the LORD will visit Tyre'). The seventy year period spans the years between Sennacherib's campaign in 701 BC, and Tyre's recovery of strength around 630 BC.

18 One radical change will come, however. The profits of her trade will be regarded as 'holy to the LORD'. This phrase is used elsewhere in the Old Testament to denote things set apart from common use and dedicated for God's service (see Lev. 5:15-16; Lev. 27:28; Josh. 6:19). Whereas in Deuteronomy 23:18 it is forbidden that the earnings of a prostitute should be given to the LORD, this case is closer to the provision for the wealth of cities devoted to destruction to be dedicated to him (cf. the case of Jericho, Jos. 6:17-19). The profits of Tyre will not just be placed in the treasury but will be available for 'those who live before the LORD'. This precise phrase only occurs twice elsewhere in the Old Testament (Judg. 20:26; 2 Sam. 7:18) where it denotes worship before the LORD. Here then the thought is that true worshippers will be rewarded with food and gifts purchased with Tyre's wealth, an idea very similar to that already expressed in 18:7 (see comments on that verse).

F. World Judgment and Israel's Redemption (24:1–27:13)

Chapters 24–27 are often called 'Isaiah's apocalypse' or 'the little apocalypse'. However, they do not show the typical characteristics of apocalyptic literature that are seen in either Daniel or Revelation. The distinction between prophecy and apocalyptic is not readily apparent. Often the attempt is made to delimit apocalyptic literature by pointing to a distinguishing 'key', such as the presence of divine intermediaries, the setting in a time of oppression, or the use of unusual imagery (especially animals). This is too narrow a focus to determine what constitutes apocalyptic literature.

The better approach is to say that there is no one characteristic that can serve as a key indicator of this type of literature. Rather, prophecy and apocalyptic share many similar characteristics. Briefly, apocalyptic has some of the characteristics of prophecy but it has them in an intensified manner. It clusters them together, so giving apocalyptic its typical combination of traits (eschatology, dualism, heavenly disclosures, etc.). There is, then, no clear break between prophecy and apocalyptic, because they share some common features. The following diagram sets out the relationship:

> Mainly prose
> Directed to the future
> Presence of dualism
> Revelation by intermediaries
> Animal symbolism
>
> ↘↘↘

Prophecy_____**Apocalyptic**

ↆↆↆ

Mainly poetry
Revelation by God to the prophet
Directed to the contemporary situation
Contains predictive elements

Clearly symbolism takes on a higher profile in apocalyptic than in prophecy. This is true of prophetic actions as well as the symbolic nature of many of the visions. Plants and animals take a much more prominent place, as can be seen in the cases of the beast in Daniel and Revelation. It is not that apocalyptic replaced prophecy, but that it supplemented it.[1]

Just as the Exodus provided many of the concepts to describe God's coming salvation (both the return from exile and the coming of the Messiah), so also the exodus events provided the imagery that was to

---

[1]For an excellent discussion on apocalyptic, see Raymond B. Dillard and Tremper Longman III, *An Introduction to the Old Testament* (Zondervan, 1994), pp. 343–45.

be used both by pre-exilic prophets to some degree and the post-exilic to a greater degree. The earlier use of this imagery formed a natural bridge to the later development of apocalyptic sections in the Old Testament.[2]

Isaiah 24–27 is distinctly eschatological in its orientation. That is to say, it is concerned with the end times, but it does not exhibit the other features of apocalyptic. It is very similar in outlook to chapters 65 and 66, and also bears strong resemblance to Zechariah 9–14.

These chapters form a finale to the burdens against the nations (chapters 13–23), just as chapters 34–35 do to the section comprising chapters 28–33. They gather up the theme of God's control over the destiny of nations and embody it in this eschatological framework. Moreover, they do it in song, for within chapters 24–27 there are four songs (25:1-5; 25:9; 26:1-15; 27:2-5) that bring the section to a close with a climax of praise and adoration. It ends on the note of the scattered exiles returning to worship the LORD in Jerusalem, the holy mountain (27:13).

1. Desolation of Judah (24:1-13)

1-2 The commencement of a new section is noted by the presence of the opening word 'behold'. The message is of impending judgment upon the earth, when the LORD will bring devastation upon it. The same verb 'to lay waste' is used again in verse 3. This is an eschatological scene, as the earth suffers under God's judgment, and the inhabitants are scattered. By his sovereign will God acts against the earth, and there will be no escape for anyone. Six pairs of people are listed, and none of the superiors will have a privileged position over against their inferiors when the LORD's wrath is displayed. All will come under a curse (see verse 6).

3 The LORD's word speaks definitively of the completeness of the coming devastation. The message is delivered with striking assonance: *hibbôq tibbôq hâ'ârets v^ehibbôz tibbôz*, 'the earth will be utterly laid waste and utterly plundered.' The use of the rare verb 'to plunder'

---

[2]See the discussion by R. D. Patterson, 'Wonders in the Heavens and on the Earth: Apocalyptic Imagery in the Old Testament', *JETS* 43/3 (September, 2000), pp. 388-403. Geerhardus Vos commented that the principles of the exodus from Egypt were 'made regulative of all future salvation and bind things past and things to come indissolubly together' (*Biblical Theology*, op. cit., p. 110).

(*bâzaz*) recalls the use of the derived noun *baz* as part of the name of Isaiah's second son (Isa. 8:1), but here the plunder is not just the result of Assyrian attack but a much more widespread plundering of the earth.

4 Alternative language to that in verse 1 is employed to emphasise the coming desolation for the whole world. Again assonance helps to make the point with the use of two different verbs but ones that have two consonants in common: *'âvᵉlâh nâvᵉlâh hâ'ârets*, 'the earth dries up and withers.'[3] The parallel expression is that the world (Heb. *têvel*) languishes and withers. The third colon is awkward, for while another parallel expression is expected, the MT has 'the exalted of the people of the earth languish'. An alternative is to take the word 'heights' (Heb. *mârôm*) in the sense it was used in Isaiah 22:16 as a reference to the heavens or spiritual realms, but then the word 'people' has to be revocalised as the preposition 'with' (*'im*). While the MT expression here is without parallel, it does give a good connection with the people mentioned in the following verse.[4]

5 Apostasy of the people is the fundamental cause of the earth's desolation. Instead of showing obedience to God they have *disobeyed* his laws, *violated* his statutes and *broken* the everlasting covenant. Two of the verbs are linked with covenant breaking (*'âvar*, 'transgress' and *pârar*, 'break'). The third (*châlaf*, 'violate') is not commonly used in this theological way (but see its use in Isaiah 40:31 and commentary). Transgression of divine laws is widespread, alteration to his statutes is characteristic of the people, and covenant breaking is their fundamental sin. While the cause of the pollution is left undefined, the verb 'polluted' is used in passages such as Numbers 35:33 and Psalm 106:38 to describe pollution of the land caused by murder. This may well help to explain the use of the phrase 'eternal covenant' that probably relates to the Noachic covenant (Gen. 9:1-17) rather the Abrahamic or Davidic.

6 Isaiah uses vocabulary in this verse that he does not use elsewhere in his prophecies. The words 'curse' and 'guilty' are common in the Mosaic law but only appear here in Isaiah, while the word 'few' is peculiar to his writing (here and in 10:25, 16:14, 29:17). The idea of

---

[3] J. A. Motyer, *The Prophecy of Isaiah*, op. cit., p. 198, refers to Isaiah's 'deliciously assonantal Hebrew'.

[4] This is Motyer's preference, ibid., p. 198, n. 1, though he admits that the suggested alteration would not be unsuitable in this context.

being burned up is one that he uses several times as descriptive of the all-consuming judgment of God. The consequence of violation of his covenant is going to be judgment appropriate to the crime, and only a remnant will escape.

7-9 The effect of divine judgment will be that normal revelry will be absent. With the destruction of vines the source of wine is destroyed and there will be no occasion for using tambourine or harp in joyful celebration at harvest time. Those who previously joined in joyful song will now moan, and even the beer they still have will be bitter to their taste.[5] The language describes a situation in which desolation prevails and there is cause only for distress. What was characteristic of Judah (see 5:11-13) will be conspicuous by its absence.

10-12 The mention of a ruined city is going to be repeated in 25:2, 26:5, and 27:10. Rather than identify it with Jerusalem or another single city, we should probably regard it as a composite of the cities arrayed against the people of God. Depending on the standpoint from which it is viewed it may be Jerusalem, Tyre or Babylon. It is the city of 'chaos' (Heb. *tohû*), a word from Genesis 1:2 that Isaiah uses repeatedly (11x out of its total use of 21x in the Old Testament). The city is likened to primeval chaos as it sits desolate and in ruins, with its gate utterly destroyed. Its mirth has disappeared, or, as the MT has it, it has gone into exile.

13 The concluding summary to the section notes that this is the condition in which the earth will be left after the judgment. There is no conjunction in the text after 'the earth', so the translation should be: 'So will it be on the earth among the nations....'[6] All that will remain is what can be compared to a few olives left after the harvest, or a few grapes that are left after the fruit is plucked from the vines. Only a remnant will survive. This takes up a theme central to Isaiah's theology, and that has already appeared in passages such as 1:8 and 6:13.[7]

---

[5]The word used for 'beer' (*shêkâr*) may have been the original word for all intoxicating drink. When a specific word for wine was introduced (*yayin*), *shêkâr* may have been retained for all other intoxicating liquor, including drinks made from fruits and grain.

[6]The NKJV takes the first word in the verse (Heb. *kî*) as 'when'. Though possible, this interpretation is not well supported by contextual considerations and it is preferable to retain the translation 'for'.

[7]For a full discussion of the remnant theme in Isaiah, see Gerhard F. Hasel, *The Remnant*, 3rd ed. (Andrews University, 1980), pp. 216-372.

2. The Glory of the Righteous (24:14-23)

14-16a The future is not all gloom, for the godly remnant will sing of the LORD's majesty. The subject of the verb is 'they', but in the context this can only be linked to the remnant concept in the previous section. The rejoicing will know no geographical limits, for those 'from the west' (lit. 'from the sea'), in 'the east' (lit. 'in the light' = 'from the sunrise'), from 'the islands of the sea', and 'from the ends of the earth' will exalt 'the name of the LORD, the God of Israel'. The sound that is heard is a song of praise: 'Glory to the righteous one.' Though the word here for 'glory' (Heb. *ts^{e}vî*) is not commonly used as an attribute of God, it does occur especially in conjunction with the word 'majesty' (Heb. *gâ'ôn*; see verse 14). Also 'righteous one' (Heb. *tsâdîk*) is not often a title for God, yet righteousness is frequently predicated of him. Songs of adoration will arise from all points of the compass to Israel's God, the God of majesty and beauty. Presumably the songs are those mentioned in verses 14-15.

16a-18b There is no specific identification of the 'we' in the earlier part of verse 16, nor of the 'I' or 'me' in the later part. Of the interpretative possibilities the best is that the prophet Isaiah is speaking and that the righteous remnant is the audience. The prophet's complaint is that he wastes away. The double expression 'I am ruined, ruined' (Heb. *râzî lî râzî lî*) reinforces the idea,[8] while the following phrase 'woe to me' (Heb. *'ôy lî*) repeats Isaiah's confession in 6:5. The use of alliteration and assonance in these verses is notable. 'The treacherous betray! With treachery the treacherous betray!' (NIV) is in Hebrew: *bog^{e}dîm bâgâdû ûbeged bog^{e}dîm bâgâdû*. The use of a cognate object in the form of a noun from the same root as the verb is a way of strengthening the verbal idea.[9] Thus the NKJV captures the emphasis: 'The treacherous dealers have dealt treacherously, indeed, the treacherous dealers have dealt very treacherously.' 'The treacherous' are those who deal deceitfully with God, and show no faithfulness to their covenant obligations (cf. the use of the same verb in accusations against disobedient Israel in Jeremiah 3:8, 11, 20; 5:11; Hosea 5:7; 6:7; Malachi 2:11). However, alliteration and assonance

---

[8] The noun *râzî* only occurs here in the Hebrew Bible. It is probably connected with the verb *râzâh* (see Isa. 17:4; Zeph. 2:11) and the cognate noun *râzôn* that Isaiah has already used in 10:16.

[9] For the grammatical point, see J. C. L. Gibson, *Davidson's Introductory Hebrew Grammar – Syntax*, 4th ed. (T. & T. Clark, 1994), pp. 114-15.

also occur in verses 17-18, with Isaiah using very effectively twice each the words 'panic', 'pit' and 'pitfall' (*pachad, pachat,* and *pâch*),[10] and also the verb 'to open' (*pâtach*). The point being made is the inevitability of judgment. Escape from one danger only results in being caught by another (cf. the use of animal imagery to teach the same lesson in Amos 5:19).

18c-19 The continuing description of the impending judgment borrows from the account of Noah's flood to heighten the effect. The floodgates of heaven will be opened (see the same phrase in Genesis 7:11; 8:2) and earthquakes will occur. The wording of verse 19 elaborates on this, doing so by using three parallel phrases that carry on the earthquake analogy. The use three times in the verse of the same Hebrew verbal forms also provides a rhythmical cadence to the announcement.[11] The use of the verb *pârar* in the expression 'to be utterly shaken' (*pôr hitpôr^erâh*) carries on the alliteration and assonance of the previous verse.

20 Egypt was earlier compared to a drunkard (19:14). Now the earth is said to stagger like a drunkard, or (as the metaphor changes) to be like a flimsy hut that sways in the wind. So great is the burden of guilt upon it, that it falls and will never rise again. The judgment will be total and final.

21-23 These verses contain a description of judgment on earthly and heavenly powers that is perhaps unequalled in the whole biblical text. The time factor is deliberately indefinite ('after many days', verse 22), and there is no precise specification of who is encompassed by the description 'the powers in the heavens'. The concentration on 'the earth' (occurring as the final word in each of verses 16-19) is replaced by focus on heavenly powers and heavenly bodies.

21 In the future day of divine reckoning the LORD will visit in judgment both rulers on earth and spiritual powers in the heavens. The verb to visit (*pâqad*) can be used both for visitations of mercy and visitations of judgment. The context makes it plain that the visitation will be judgmental. What is significant is that the judgment will take place in the sphere in which the powers have authority. A literal

---

[10]The English alliteration is taken from D. G. Johnson, *From Chaos to Restoration: An Integrative Reading of Isaiah 24-27*, Sheffield: JSOTSS, 1980, p. 102.

[11]The Hebrew three times uses Hitpolel forms of the verbs, with a preceding infinitive absolute.

translation brings out this point: 'In that day the LORD will punish the host of the height in the height and the kings of the earth on the earth.' The rendering of the NKJV, 'the LORD will punish on high the host of exalted ones, and on the earth the kings of the earth' is thus preferable to the NIV interpretation: 'the LORD will punish the powers in the heavens above and the kings on the earth below.' Terrestrial authorities will be subjected to judgment, as well as extra-terrestrial spiritual powers.

22 The language of taking prisoners into custody is employed to describe the gathering of these powers together pending final judgment. As is typical of Old Testament prophets, Isaiah does not give precise time details. He simply says that 'after many days' punishment will be meted out.

23 The key to this verse is the word 'for' (*kî*). The moon and sun (referred to by the use of poetic words, 'the white one' and 'the hot one') will have their brightness surpassed by the glory of the LORD's reign on Mount Zion. While there is no specific allusion back to Isaiah 2:1-5, yet the theme of the LORD's rule is central to both passages, as well as the manifestation of his glory. Exodus 24:9-11 speaks of the elders of Israel seeing God when they were on Mount Sinai. Isaiah tells of another theophany when, after the fashion of human kingship, the LORD will manifest his glory before his servants, 'his elders' (cf. the presence of the elders in the heavenly scenes in Revelation 11:15-17 and 19:4). The account of the heavenly vision ends with a word of exclamation – 'glory'. Isaiah had already seen God's glory (6:1-5, and note the commentary on that passage with reference to John 12:41), but when sun and moon are no more there will be an even greater manifestation of his majesty.

3. A Hymn of Thanksgiving (25:1-5)

As a response to the picture of judgment and deliverance presented in chapter 24, Isaiah sings a hymn in praise and adoration of God. There is no introductory formula, and many of the expressions in the song are left indefinite. These include the city and the foreigners (verse 2), strong nations (verse 3), and the poor and needy (verse 4). In this respect this song is similar to many of the psalms, in which lack of specific details enables them to be used in a variety of personal circumstances. It serves the same function as the Song of the Sea (Exod. 15:1-19) and may well be a distant echo of it.

1 The song opens with a confession of the relationship that the speaker has to the LORD. He acknowledges him as 'my God'. In the Psalms, at times such a profession is accompanied by the same declaration as here, that the LORD is going to be exalted (cf. Pss. 99:5, 9; 118:28; 145:1). The reason for praise is stated in the following words (given in a literal rendering): 'For you [the LORD] have worked a wonder, counsels from afar, faithfulness [and] faithfulness.' While this is the understanding of the Jewish Massoretes (as shown by the accents), yet grammatically 'a wonder of counsels' is quite possible. 'From afar' is an expression used both of space and time, either distant past or distant future. The context makes it plain that it refers to the distant past, 'from of old.' The last two words (*'eemûnâh* and *'omen*) come from the same Hebrew root (*'âmên*), with the last one occurring only here in the Old Testament. It is quite possible to translate them as 'faithfulness [and more] faithfulness',[12] or, if the second word is an adverb, as 'really reliable'.[13] A suggested translation can be: 'For from of old you have performed [your] wonderful counsels, [that are] completely reliable.' Clearly the point is that God has carried out his plans with utter faithfulness, a point already made in the burdens against Assyria and Tyre (14:24, 26-27; 23:8-9). 'Wonderful counsels' recalls the name of the royal child in 9:6 (though here it is in the plural), with the word 'wonderful' (*pele'*) often denoting divine acts of salvation.

2 No precise identification is given of the city that lies in ruins, or of the stronghold that is no more. It could be Nineveh or Babylon or a city of Moab (see verse 10). The point is that mighty cities can be brought to nothing by the LORD's power. The fact that it will never be rebuilt recalls the curse expressed regarding any rebuilding of Jericho (see Josh. 6:26; 1 Kings 16:34).

3 The eschatological vision of conversion of Gentile nations, expressed already in passages such as 24:15, is presented again. Part of God's plans 'from of old' is that there will be a conversion of those outside the fold of Israel. Jesus spoke of the 'other sheep' he had (John 10:16), and the fact that when he was uplifted (on the cross) he would draw all kinds of men to himself (John 12:32). 'Strong peoples' and 'ruthless nations' will ultimately give honour to God and bow in reverence before him.

4-5 The poor and the needy have already been promised safety

---

[12]So *DCH*, I, p. 318.   [13]See *CHAL*, p. 20.

(see 14:30, 32). Reassurance is given that the LORD will be both a refuge (*mâ'ôz*) and a shelter (*machseh*) for them. There is no great difference in the usage of these words in the Hebrew Bible, as is shown by the fact that the NIV normally translates both as 'refuge', but here and in Job 24:8 *machseh* is translated 'shelter'. Both words are almost exclusively used in the Psalms and the prophetical books to describe the safety that believers find in God. The breath of ruthless enemies will not prevail against them, for there is a wall that shelters them. The desert's heat will not overcome them because of their shelter (cf. the language and ideas of 4:5-6), nor will the noisy uproar of the enemies lead to any success in battle.

4. A Mountain Feast (25:6-8)

Isaiah picks up the theme of the LORD's reign from 24:23. Marking the inauguration of that reign there will be a banquet involving people from all nations. When the Sinai covenant was inaugurated there was such a feast (Exod. 24:9-11), while feasts also marked the commencement of the reigns of Saul (1 Sam. 9:19-24) and David (1 Chron. 12:38-40). The universal scope of the invitees is recorded twice (verses 6 and 7). They meet in festive spirit to celebrate the abolition of death (verse 8). There is musical cadence about these verses, as if Isaiah's ear is attuned to the songs being sung at it.

6 Though the location is simply said to be 'on this mountain' it cannot be understood as anywhere other than Mount Zion (see 24:23). The preparation for the feast is made by the LORD of Hosts himself. The rhythmical flow of the verse is enhanced by assonance, with the word for feast (*mishteh*) being repeated twice, as are the words for 'rich food' (*sh^emânîm*) and 'choice wine' (*sh^emârîm*). Seven times in the verse the Hebrew masculine plural ending *-îm* occurs. There is music in words here, that helps to convey the festive joy of such a meal, with its fine food and aged wine.

7 Leading up to the declaration in the next verse that death is to vanish forever, Isaiah speaks of the fact that the LORD will destroy the funeral coverings, the shrouds that encompass dead bodies.[14] If death is to be destroyed, then there is no need for such coverings.

8 This is the explanation of the preceding verse. The Sovereign

---

[14]The same Hebrew verb (*bâla'*) is used at the commencement of both verses 7 and 8. Its primary meaning is 'to swallow', but from that sense it develops a metaphorical meaning of 'swallow up', 'destroy'.

LORD (*'ᵃdônay yhwh*) will swallow up death for ever and he will wipe away the tears from grieving eyes. The primary reference may be to violent death, i.e. death in war and the tears that go with it, but clearly the broader concept is also embraced. A consequence is that the earth will have its disgrace removed, i.e. the sin-induced shame that the earth and its inhabitants presently experience will be gone. No longer will the earth be a battlefield but instead a dwelling place for the LORD's redeemed. Paul quotes the opening words of this verse in 1 Corinthians 15:54 but in a form that does not agree either with the Hebrew text or the LXX: 'Death is swallowed up in victory.' 'In victory' (Greek *eis nikos*) fits the context in Isaiah 25 and may even reflect an understanding that the Hebrew expression *lânetsach* is a term used to describe success, and hence can denote 'victory'.[15] The familiar phrase, 'for the LORD has spoken', ends the passage, and confirms that the word given is not Isaiah's own but the LORD's.

5. A Second Hymn of Thanksgiving (25:9-12)

In hymn-like language this section sings of how God's people in the day of his power will rejoice in his salvation. Again, the expressions used closely resemble many in the Book of Psalms, another indication of how close prophet and psalmist were in both thought and expression. Verse 9 can stand as a short independent song, but it is better to take verses 9-12 as a complete unit, as intermingling of ideas of salvation and judgment occur.

9 The song opens with carefully balanced phrases. Twice there is a declaration ('this is ...') followed by a statement of trust ('we wait for him ...'). The translation can be set out as follows:

> It will be said on that day:
>> Behold, this is our God;
>>> we wait for him that he might save us.
>> This is the LORD;
>>> we wait for him; let us be glad and rejoice in
>>>> his salvation.

The language is closest to Psalm 25:5: 'For you are the God of my salvation and I wait for you all day long.' The verb 'wait for' (Heb.

---

[15]See the discussion of the Hebrew word *netsach* by C. John Collins in *NIDOTTE*, 3, pp. 139-41.

qâvâh) is a word most frequently used in Isaiah (13x) and the Psalms (10x). The thought here mounts from the declaration that this is 'our God' to the fact that he is the covenant God of Israel, 'the LORD.' Moreover, the declaration regarding him as saviour is expanded to become a statement of joy in his salvation.

10 The contrast 'in that day' will be between the salvation of those waiting for the LORD and the judgment on enemies, symbolised here by the choice of Moab as the representative hostile nation. In chapter 34 Edom will be the representative. The hand of blessing will rest on Mount Zion whereas the judgment on Moab can be likened to straw trampled down by the feet of cattle.

11 There is difference of opinion regarding the subject of the verb 'spread out' in this verse. An old interpretation makes the LORD the one spreading out his hands (cf. NKJV: 'And He will spread out His hands in the midst'). It is better, though, to understand it as a reference to the futile efforts of the Moabites to escape judgment. They will be like swimmers desperately trying to escape extreme danger, but all their efforts will not avail to save them.

12 Just as unavailing as their own efforts will be the use of brute force. High fortified walls will provide no protection in the judgment day, for the LORD is able to bring his enemies down to the very dust. This expression denotes both humiliation and subjection.

6. A Third Hymn of Thanksgiving (26:1-6)

This third hymn focuses on Jerusalem, the strong city. It is the communal language of the LORD's redeemed who will continue to look to him as the eternal Rock in the day of their great deliverance. No indication is given in the Hebrew text of which verses actually comprise the song, but though the whole section (verses 1-19) may well be included, it is more likely that the song is only verses 1-6.

1 The opening verse specifies that this song will be sung 'in Judah'. This is not surprising seeing that there has been repeated reference to Mount Zion and Jerusalem (24:23; 25:6-7, 10). The contrast is very marked, being made with the godless city that has just been said to be destroyed (25:12). Jerusalem is indeed a strong city wherein is salvation, for it is the city of the Great King (Ps. 48:2). The ruin of the one city highlights the glory and the permanence of the other.

2 The language is reminiscent of Psalm 118:19: 'Open to me the gates of righteousness; I will enter and give thanks to the LORD.' Though so well fortified with walls and ramparts, the new Jerusalem will be accessible to all who remain faithful. 'The righteous nation' is not further defined, but doubtless comprises those already described from east and west, even from the most distant places (24:14-16), who give glory to God. Those previously scattered will be gathered as a nation of believers into the strong city. The condensed description here is expanded in Revelation 21:10-27.

3-4 These two verses are linked together by the common theme of trusting in the LORD. To the person who shows unswerving devotion to him the promise is given that the LORD will guard him with perfect peace (lit. 'peace peace').[16] Hence the instruction is given to trust in him for ever, for he is 'Yah, the LORD, the eternal rock'. The combination in the Hebrew text of *yâh yhwh* has already been used in 12:2. The use of the word 'rock' as an metaphor for God goes back at least to the period of Moses (see its use five times in the Song of Moses in reference to Israel's God: Deut. 32:4, 15, 18, 30, 31). It stresses his permanence and the security he provides for those whose trust is in him.

5 God's attitude to the proud is that they will be humbled, even to the dust. 'Those dwelling on high' is simply an expression synonymous with 'the hosts on high' of 24:21. The word for city does not have the article attached to it and is to be taken as a collective noun. Other cities have been brought low, but Jerusalem stands impregnable.

6 The ultimate outcome will be in accordance with God's justice, for he deals graciously with the oppressed and the poor. There is a reversal of positions in that those who are proud in their own eyes will be humbled under the feet of those that they despise. God employs 'what is foolish in the world to shame the wise' and chooses 'what is low and despised in the world, even things that are not, to bring to nothing things that are, so that no human being might boast in the presence of God' (1 Cor. 1:27-29).

7. *Patient Waiting for the LORD (26:7-15)*
This section is marked out by a return to the first person singular ('my soul', verse 9) and the theme of waiting for the LORD to display his

---

[16]The LXX and the Syriac both delete one occurrence of 'peace', but the Hebrew mss. unanimously support the retention of both. Cf. *IBHS* for a note on repetition of singular nouns in biblical Hebrew, pp. 115-16.

righteousness to the inhabitants of the world. There is strong affinity with the language of chapter 14, especially reference to the dead (14:9), the failure to arise (14:21), and destruction (14:23).

7 One of the characteristics of the righteous is that their manner of life is uprightness (Heb. *mêshârîm*), an attribute that the LORD looks on with favour (1 Chron. 29:17). They also know that God is 'the upright one' (Heb. *yâshâr*) to whom they can direct prayer, for he can make the way smooth for them. This idea of preparation of pathways is developed much further in 40:3-4, 42:16, 45:13.

8 The expectant waiting on the LORD is in the knowledge that he has expressed his will for obedience to his judgments. The idea of waiting for him (Heb. *qâvâh*) is picked up from its double use in 25:9. The believing community have confidence in the outworking of God's providence both towards them and towards the wicked. Their desire is for his 'name' and his 'memorial'. The use of these two words in conjunction with one another goes back to God's own use of them in his address to Moses (Exod. 3:15). He had declared his name, 'I am whom I am,' and then indicated that this was to be his name and memorial from generation to generation. In Isaiah's day the believing community is still resting with expectant hope in the God of the exodus.

9 The prophet speaks of the intensity of his own longing for God. The verb used here (*'âvâh*) is synonymous with the one in the previous verse, and its cognate noun (*tâ'^{a}v'âh*, 'desire of soul') also occurs in that verse. The communal confession gives way now to the individual, for Isaiah is one of the believing community who look constantly to the LORD for help and deliverance. The NIV translation 'in the night ... in the morning' rests on a widely accepted emendation (altering Heb. *qerev* to *boqer*). However, the MT should be retained as there is no evidence to support this change.[17] The instruction in God's judgment of which the prophet speaks is probably to be understood as meaning that God's providential dealings were in the minds of the people as they waited for God's impending judgment.

10 A sharp contrast is drawn between the way in which the godly learn and the stubborn rebelliousness of the ungodly. Even when gracious favour is shown to them, and they are surrounded by uprightness, they persist in doing wrong. They have no desire to learn

---

[17]The LXX supports the MT, as it has only *ek nuktos*, '*out of the night*,' as the translation of *ballay^{e}lâh*, 'in the night.'

of righteousness, nor do they have respect for God's majesty. They do not see spiritual reality and respond accordingly.[18]

11 While the language of the verse is cryptic, the general meaning is clear enough. It and the following two verses (and also verse 16) all commence with direct address to the LORD. The expression 'the LORD's hand is high' can have various connotations, but here following reference to God's compassion (verse 10) it is best taken as a manifest demonstration of God's favour that the ungodly fail to recognise. This involves taking the verb 'see' (here *châzâh* instead of *râ'âh* used in the previous verse) as conveying the idea of perception. They see but do not understand (Isa. 6:10). The final clauses of the verse describe the contrast – God's intense zeal for [his own] people and his stored up wrath against his enemies. The idea of God's zeal goes back to the second commandment (Exod. 20:5), and Isaiah uses the concept elsewhere to describe the fervour with which God will fulfil his purposes (9:7; 37:32).

12-14 When the final salvation of God is made manifest, there will be 'peace' for the redeemed. 'Peace' has already been mentioned in verse 3, and clearly it means more than just absence of warfare. It stands for life in its fulness. The redeemed will also readily acknowledge that their 'works' are in reality what God has done for them. Over the course of history many foreign rulers dominated Palestine, but the people will ultimately confess to only one master, the LORD. He has judged these earthly rulers, and they are described as *refâ'îm*, never to arise again. The use of this Hebrew word is significant in this chapter as death and resurrection are in view (see comments on verse 19 in which *refâ'îm* recurs). While it may have some connection with a cognate Ugaritic word, yet its meaning has to be determined by its contextual use in the Old Testament. It appears in parallel with death/dead in Proverbs 2:18, Psalm 88:10, 11, and here in verses 14 and 19. Hence it cannot be thought of as indicating some shadowy semi-existence after death but it is simply a word denoting 'dead ones'.[19] God has destroyed these rulers and even the memory of them has been blotted out.

15 An ingathering of many requires the provision of greater living

---

[18]The negative in 'do not see' is *bal*, a Hebrew poetic negative that is used repetitively seven times in verses 10-18.

[19]See the discussion by R. Laird Harris, *TWOT*, 2, p. 858.

space, and so the land is pictured as enlarged by God (see the previous reference to enlarging the land in 9:3, though a different verb is used). The coming kingdom is not going to be restricted to the narrow confines of the promised land, but is going to extend from it outwards, even to the ends of the earth (Ps. 72:8; Zech. 9:10). All this will result in the greater glory to God as his power and grace is revealed through it.

8. Spiritual Resurrection (26:16-19)

Isaiah speaks a message of reassurance. In contrast to the dead rulers mentioned in verse 14, there is going to be a resurrection of 'your dead', with the pronoun 'your' referring to God. Human ability is again shown to be insufficient. What is needed is divine power, so that even those in the sleep of death can be awakened.

16 There is direct address to the LORD, with mention of a past time(s) when the people had called upon him. While some have argued for this to be understood as the Assyrian invasion, the phrase can well be applied to times like that described in the book of Judges. The NIV rendering 'they *came* to you in their distress' is too general, as the verb used is the one that speaks of visitation (Heb. *pâqad*). The idea here is that in their distress, when they could hardly whisper a prayer, the people sought after God.

17-18 The distress of the people is likened to a woman in childbirth, but the difference is that there is no child to show after all the pain. The same point was made in verse 12. Anything achieved was the LORD's doing. Distress and discipline could not accomplish what Israel was meant to be – a light to the nations (42:6; 49:6). God's saving acts are not brought to pass by human effort but by his power. The final clause in verse 18 is unusual as a literal translation shows: 'and the inhabitants of the world have not fallen.' Among a great variety of meanings the Hebrew verb 'to fall' (*nâfal*) can mean 'to give birth', and its use here prepares the way for its occurrence again at the end of the next verse.[20] The meaning is that the inhabitants of the world have not come to new life through Israel's efforts.

19 This verse is not as clear as many translations would suggest (cf. the NIV, 'But your dead will live; their bodies will rise. You who dwell in the dust, wake up and shout for joy'). While 'your dead' is

---

[20]*DCH*, V , pp. 716, 721 lists Isaiah 26:18 as a passage in which *nâfal* means 'be born', while its use in 26:19 is listed under the meaning 'give birth to, cause to be born'.

certainly correct, 'their bodies' is not, for the MT has 'my corpse(s)'.[21] In the context the speaker has to be the prophet, and the addressee God. The message answers an unexpressed question. If God is going to meet with his redeemed on Mount Zion, what about the saints who have already died? The dead are God's dead, and they are going to live again. The prophet identifies himself with the departed saints and calls them 'my corpses'.[22] The dead are then addressed, being called 'those who dwell in the dust' (cf. the phrase 'the dust of death' in Psalm 22:15 [Heb. 16]). They are summoned to arise with a ringing shout of joy.[23] The remainder of this verse is also difficult. It reads: 'Your dew is the dew of lights (or, 'dew of herbs') and the earth will let fall the $r^e f\hat{a}$ '$\hat{\imath}m$.' While preference is to be given to 'dew of lights', the alternative yields very similar sense.[24] Refreshing dew from heaven will cause the dead to come to life again (cf. the use of 'the dew of Hermon' in Psalm 133:3 to convey the idea of life). The earth is going to give up the $r^e f\hat{a}$ '$\hat{\imath}m$', i.e. the dead, as this word is used as a synonym for 'your dead ones' and 'those who dwell in the dust' (cf. its occurrence in verse 14). The final verb is the Hebrew word 'to fall', used here as in the previous verse in the sense of 'give birth'.[25] The message of the whole verse expands on the statement of 25:8 ('he will swallow up death forever'), and while it is not as explicit as Daniel 12:2 yet the idea of personal resurrection (as distinct from national resurrection as in Ezekiel 37:1-14) is certainly affirmed.

9. God's Judgment on the Gentile Nations (26:20–27:1)
The LORD's judgment is going to come, and until it does the faithful should hide themselves from his wrath. In this respect there is an

---

[21]There is no footnote in the NIV on this verse, but the reading 'their bodies' follows the Syriac translation.

[22]The noun 'corpses' is a collective singular in Hebrew ($n^e v\hat{e}l\hat{a}h$) though the verb is plural ($y^e q\hat{u}m\hat{u}n$).

[23]Both Old and New Testaments refer to death as sleep. See Job 3:13; Psalm 13:3; Jeremiah 51:39; John 11:11; 1 Thessalonians 4:13.

[24]See Young's excellent discussion on this point and the whole verse (*The Book of Isaiah*, vol. II, pp. 225-28).

[25]Added weight is given to the argument in favour of taking the verb $n\hat{a}fal$ as meaning 'to give birth' by the fact that a Hebrew noun derived from it ($n\hat{e}fel$) means 'miscarriage'. In Aramaic the verb $n\hat{a}fal$ can mean 'to miscarry' and the noun $n\hat{a}f\hat{\imath}l$ 'a miscarriage'.

analogy with what God did for Noah, shutting him into the ark (Gen. 7:16), or with God's instructions to the Israelites to remain indoors before the final plague upon Egypt (Exod. 12:22-23).

20 This instruction brings the thought back to the impending judgment (see 24:21-23). The people are told that they are to hide themselves in their rooms, behind shut doors, for a short time until wrath passes over them. No specification is given of what constitutes 'a little while'. There is also imbedded in this instruction a word of encouragement, for the implication is that the prophet's people will survive this expression of God's anger.

21 The LORD is going to come from his dwelling place (cf. 18:4) in order to inflict punishment on those who dwell on the earth, but clearly this excludes those who avail themselves of the invitation to hide in their rooms. Divine compassion is shown to the believing community, but severe judgment is to come upon the unbelieving world. God has a concern for the blood of his saints that has been shed, and both Old and New Testaments indicate that he will avenge that blood (see Deut. 32:43; Rev. 6:9-10; 19:2). Here the blood is said to be revealed, so that there will no longer be any covering over of murders committed.

27:1 While this verse could stand by itself as an independent declaration, yet the theme of judgment continues and there is specific mention of God's judgmental visitation (Heb. *pâqad* in both 26:21 and 27:1). The frightening nature of that judgment is emphasised by the collocation of adjectives to describe the LORD's sword – 'fierce, and great, and powerful.' That sword will kill the great monster Leviathan, described as the gliding and coiling serpent, the monster of the sea. The word 'Leviathan' was used in Canaanite mythology of an associate of the sea-god Yam. It is used five times in the Old Testament (Job 3:8; 41:1 [Heb. 40:25]; Pss. 74:13-14; 104:26; Isa. 27:1) without borrowing all its mythological implications from Canaanite use. In Psalm 74 it depicts Egypt, but here it represents evil powers in general. Isaiah uses it to depict God's ultimate victory over sin, oppression and death, with Leviathan being slain by his sword.

10. A Fourth Hymn of Thanksgiving (27:2-6)

This is another song of the vineyard, but it presents a different picture from Isaiah 5:1-7. In the earlier parable the vineyard was unfruitful, whereas now it is a desirable one because it is fruitful. The language of visitation in judgment (Heb. *pâqad*), used of the LORD in 26:21 and

27:1, is now used of the foes who come to do harm to the vineyard (verse 3).

2-3 The great day of the LORD will provide an occasion for song, and specifically one directed towards his vineyard. The LORD's watchful eye is ever upon it, and he waters it 'continually' (lit. 'for moments'; the plural of the Heb. word *rega* ' is used distributively, 'every moment'). Night and day his care is over his people. Once more encouragement is offered to Israel by this assurance of God's providential care.

4 Later in this prophecy God declares that, while he had anger against his people for a short time, he will show everlasting compassion to them (54:8). This song comes from the period when that anger is altogether passed, and therefore God can say: 'I have no anger [against my vineyard].'[26] In Isaiah 5 the growth of briers and thorns depicts the abandoned state of the vineyard. Here the idea is that even if there were briars and thorns presented like an army in battle array, yet the LORD would go out against them and set them altogether on fire.[27]

5 The great promise for Israel is that the LORD offers himself as a refuge for those who grasp hold of him. This has already been confessed in the thanksgiving hymn in 25:4 (see comment on that verse) and now reasserted. He invites them to come and make peace with him. The Hebrew text has two identical clauses (except for the change in word order from 'Let him make peace with me' to 'Peace let him make with me' which is probably done for the sake of emphasis). The change is best taken as circumstantial: 'unless they take hold of me as refuge, making peace with me. Let them make peace with me.'[28]

6 In the song of the vineyard the LORD condemned the fruit because it was so bad (Isa. 5:4-5). However, the eschatological picture here is that Jacob/Israel will take root and produce fruit that will fill the whole

---

[26]Some have found this statement about the absence of wrath awkward in this context and want to follow the LXX and read 'wall' (*chomâh*), or emend to 'wine' (*chemer*). However, the Hebrew manuscript evidence uniformly supports 'wrath'.

[27]The division of words in verse 4 can either be 'Would that there were briers and thorns in battle', or 'would that I had briers and thorns against me. I would march against them in battle'. It makes no difference which division is accepted. The wish is expressed using a regular Hebrew idiom involving the verb 'give' (*nâtan*), lit. 'Who would give ... ?' Cf. its similar use in passages such as Exodus 16:3, Deuteronomy 5:29, and Jeremiah 9:1.

[28]This is following E. J. Young, *The Book of Isaiah*, II, p. 241, n. 22.

world. What both Moab (16:8) and Israel (26:18) were unable to do, will be the LORD's doing in the day of his power. The opening word of the verse is simply 'the ones coming' (*habbâ'îm*), which may be an elliptical expression for 'in the coming days' or else an exclamation 'the coming days', which counterbalances the expression 'in that day' in verse 2.

11. Redemptive Judgment (27:7-11)

There are many aspects of this section that are puzzling. Translation of it is difficult, especially in verse 7 because there is no precise identification of the subjects and objects of the verbs. Also, verse 8 opens with a Hebrew word that only occurs here, and also switches the gender from the masculine of verse 7 to feminine. Moreover, 'the fortified city' in verse 10 is not named. The variety shown in English translations simply testifies to the difficult and sometimes cryptic Hebrew. The general thrust, however, is that Israel has not been punished as severely as her enemies punished her, and atonement will be provided for her sins.[29]

7 This verse is composed of beautiful rhyming Hebrew, having both alliteration and assonance. Two verbs, 'to smite' and 'to kill', are used three times each, and apart from them there is only the particle in the verse (*'im*, 'or'). The MT has:

> *hakk^{e}makkat makkêhû hikkâhû*
> *'im k^{e}hereg h^{a}rugâv horâg*

A literal translation is: 'like the smiting of the one who smote him did he smite him? Or like the slaughter of his slaughtered ones was he slaughtered?' Three different parties are mentioned by the use of the same pronoun 'he' – the LORD, Israel, and Israel's enemies. A good English translation (with the insertion of identifying words) is:

> Has he [the LORD] struck them [Israel] as he struck those [Israel's enemies] who struck them [Israel]?

---

[29] All the complicated interpretative questions cannot be covered adequately in a commentary of this kind. I present my own basic understanding, and recommend the fine and detailed discussions in E. J. Young, *The Book of Isaiah*, II, pp. 242-49, and John N. Oswalt, *The Book of Isaiah: Chapters 1-39*, pp. 495-99.

Or have they [Israel] been slain as their slayers [Israel's enemies] were slain? (ESV)

The question at issue is whether Israel has been punished as severely as God punished her opponents. The answer is evidently 'No!' She has been visited with punishment that was neither as severe nor as lasting.

8 The opening word (an *hapax legomenon*) is very unusual in form and various suggestions have been made. Many have taken it to mean 'by measure' but more probably it is a verb meaning something like the English 'to shoo sway'.[30] While the verb for 'sending away' can mean divorce, yet later Isaiah argues that there has not been divorce between the LORD and his bride, only temporary separation (Isa. 50:1; 54:5-8). It is true that Jeremiah speaks of divorce, but it is that of the northern tribes, not Judah (Jer. 3:8-10). The 'sending away' or 'exile' here may refer to various occasions when captives were taken, rather than thinking solely of the Babylonian exile. These were occasions when God contended with his people, i.e. he entered into formal condemnation of them according to covenant demands. His action against them was like the hot desert wind. Though real, this punishment meted out to them was of a passing nature like the temporary blowing of the east wind.

9 The result of this expulsion by the LORD's strong breath is that Jacob/Israel's guilt will be reckoned as atoned for. When the LORD punished both Israel and Judah it was because of their disobedience and sin. Judah followed the pattern set by Israel: 'therefore the LORD rejected all the people of Israel; he afflicted them and gave them into the hand of plunderers, until he thrust them from his presence' (NIV, 2 Kings 17:20). Temptation to idolatry and false worship will be removed, with altars smashed, and Asherah poles and incense altars destroyed (cf. the comments on 17:8).

10-11 It is hard to be certain of the identity of 'the fortified city'. If it is Jerusalem, then Judah is the 'people without understanding'.

---

[30]See J. A. Motyer, *The Prophecy of Isaiah*, p. 223. Grammatically the form of the word (Heb. *sa'ss^e'âh*) can express 'rapidly repeated movement, which all languages incline to indicate by a repetition of the sound' (*GKC*, §55f). *GKC* cites the verb 'to chirp' as an example, and it makes good sense to take this unusual word here as indicating rapid speech in shooing Israel away into exile.

However, in the context it is better to assume that the city is the same one already described in 24:10-11 (see the earlier comments). It need not be identified with any known city, but rather represents the evil forces arrayed against the people of God. Its power will ultimately be broken, cattle will graze over the ruins, and its trees useful only for firewood. Whereas Israel is to experience further chastisement before restoration, her enemies are going to be punished without any compassion or gracious favour being shown to them. The once fortified city will be destroyed for ever.

12. The Trumpet Call for Israel's Dispersed (27:12-13)

The section comprising chapters 24–27 ends with a picture of ingathered Israel. From as far afield as Assyria and Egypt the people will come and worship the LORD in the holy mountain, Mount Zion in Jerusalem.

12 The frequent introductory phrase appears again, 'in that day.' Its constant repetition focuses attention on the decisive revelation of God's power and grace that is yet to come. A harvest will ultimately be brought to Jerusalem but first there has to be threshing that will sift the true Israel from among the nations. From the River [Euphrates] in the north-east to the Wadi of Egypt (presumably Wadi el-Arish) in the south, the Israelites will be brought in so that not a single true believer will be missed. The word describing the flowing Euphrates (Heb. *shibbolet*) can mean either a stream of water or an ear of grain. The double meaning is picked up by use of the imagery of gleaning. They will be gathered one by one, individual by individual, so that a complete Israel will be brought home.

13 A trumpet sound will serve as the call to return. The trumpet was used for major cultic festivals, but the prophets repeatedly say that what accompanied the theophany at Sinai (Exod. 19:16, 19; 20:18) will again be heard as the Day of the LORD is ushered in (see in addition to this verse Joel 2:1; Zeph. 1:16; Zech. 9:14). The New Testament also features the trumpet call in connection with Christ's return (Matt. 24:31; 1 Cor. 15:52; 1 Thess. 4:16; Heb. 12:19; cf. also its repeated occurrence in Revelation, 1:10; 4:1; 8:2, 6, 13; 9:14). The dispersed are described in parallel phrases: 'those who were lost (*hâ'ovᵉdîm*) in the land of Assyria and those who were driven out (*hanniddâchîm*) to the land of Egypt' (RSV). As the Hebrew verb *'âvad* can mean either 'to perish' or 'to wander, be lost', the context here virtually demands taking the phrase to mean 'those wandering [in exile] in Assyria'. Both groups will come and worship at Mount Zion. While the biblical phrase 'the mountain of the LORD' refers to Mount Sinai, 'the holy mountain' refers almost exclusively to Zion. Redeemed Israel will bow in adoration before the Redeemer.

G. A Cycle of Prophetic Warnings (28:1–33:24)

Six sermonic warnings are grouped together, each one beginning with the word 'Woe!' (cf. the six woes in chapter 5, and see the comments on 5:8 for the usage of the Hebrew word). One important feature is that there is alternation between threat and promise in this section. Each woe is accompanied by a corresponding promise:

Woe	Promise
28:1-4, 7-13, 19b-22	28:5-6, 14-19a, 23-29
29:1-4, 9-16	29:5-8, 17-24
30:1-17	30:18-24
30:25–31:3	31:4–32:8
32:9-14	32:15-20
33:1-16	33:17-24

The section as a whole depicts the dangers confronting both the northern and the southern kingdoms. Trust in human power is shown to be folly. The only hope for both kingdoms is trust in the LORD as king. Chapters 34 and 35, which serve as an appendix to this section, provide both the ultimate warning and the ultimate promise of divine blessing and restoration.

1. Woe to Samaria and Zion (28:1-29)

a. The Downfall of Samaria (28:1-13)

Very often a break is made after verse 6, but as the theme of drunkenness continues in verse 7 and following, it is best to the take the whole thirteen verses as a unit. The continuing existence of the northern kingdom points to a time just prior to the fall of Samaria in 722 BC.

1 The accusations against Samaria, the wreath and the fading flower, are typical of accusations made elsewhere by Isaiah and his fellow eighth century BC prophets – Hosea and Amos (cf. Isa. 5:11;

Hos. 7:5; Amos 6:6). Samaria was situated on a prominent hill overlooking fertile valleys, with views in every direction. Language that could have been used against its drunken elite is applied to Samaria itself, and the lengthy description helps to produce an impression of worldly luxury and sensuous indulgence. The following verses pick up and repeat phrases from this opening verse.

2 A significant message concerning Samaria is prefaced with the typical 'Behold!' The threat is that God has a powerful and strong nation (Assyria) ready to deliver his judgment on Samaria and the northern kingdom of Israel. Language involving imagery of water has already been used by Isaiah to depict an Assyrian invasion (see 8:7-8). Now the threat is couched in terms of an attack by hail, wind, and rain which is personified as being able to cast Samaria to the ground with its hand.

3-4 The language used of Samaria in verse 1 is taken up and used to describe the ignominious treatment that awaits her. Just as the wreath that a drunkard might put around his head will fall to the ground, so will she be trampled underfoot by the invading army. Also, the fading flower will be plucked just like a ripe fig is taken from the tree and eaten. Because of her sins, Samaria is ripe for judgment.

5-6 The language of the preceding verses can also be used to provide a reassuring message, a promise of blessing. In the coming eschatological day the LORD of hosts will be 'a glorious crown' and 'a beautiful diadem' (an alternative word 'diadem' is used in place of 'wreath' in verse 1). This is specifically promised 'to the remnant of his people', a concept already introduced much earlier in his prophecy by Isaiah (see 4:3; 10:20-22; 11:11, which embodies the same phrase as here in 28:5, 'the remnant of his people'). In peace and war the LORD will, by his Spirit, provide help. To those who administer justice assistance will be provided, while strength will be given to those whose responsibility is to defend the city. The expression in the Hebrew text is that the LORD will strengthen 'those who turn back battle at the gate'. This could mean those who manage to turn invaders away at the city's gate, or, those who turn the invaders back to their own city gate. The important message is that there is still going to be a faithful remnant preserved by God's power.

7-8 While the northern tribes are in view in verses 1-6 (cf. the use of 'Ephraim' in verse 1), there is a switch at this point to the southern kingdom. This is marked by the words 'and also these' at the beginning of verse 7. The people of Judah and Jerusalem might listen with pleasure to prophetic condemnation of the north, yet their behaviour is no different. The national leaders, priests and prophets, are indicted for their drunkenness. Not content with a single mention of it, Isaiah repeats phrases to convey the idea that the drunkenness is constant. Three times the verb 'stagger' (*shâgâh*) occurs, twice 'wander' or 'reel' (*tâ'âh*), once another synonymous verb 'to stagger' (*pûq*). The verb 'to swallow' (*bâla'*) is used to show that instead of swallowing the wine, the drinkers are swallowed up by it! Their over-drinking causes them to vomit, so that there is no place untouched by their filth. The tragedy is compounded by the fact that the prophets and priests are said to be drunk while carrying out their official duties ('seeing visions', 'giving judgment').

9-10 The instruction regarding prophetic teaching that God gave through Moses was that the people had to listen to the prophet (Deut. 18:15). But Isaiah found that the people in his day were questioning his authority to teach, and mocking his message as though it was a word to children. They regard his words as if they are directed to babies who have just been weaned, without recognising that his message is not his but the LORD's (cf. the use of the same Heb. word 'message' or 'report' in 53:1). They even mock him, by re-echoing his words in childish babble (or drunken gibberish): *kî tsav lâtsâv tsav lâtsâv qav lâqâv qav lâqâv z^e 'îr shâm z^e 'îr shâm*. The introductory particle *kî* ('for') simply points the way forward and is equivalent to an elliptical expression like 'for [you say]...' All the nouns in this verse are monosyllables, such as young children would use. Various English translations follow the AV: 'For precept *must be* upon precept, precept upon precept; line upon line, line upon line; here a little, *and* there a little.' Others, like the NEB, don't attempt to translate but give an interpretation: 'A babble of meaningless noises, mere sounds on every side.' Most probably the words are meaningless, and therefore it is best to simply transliterate them.

11-12 God had brought his people into a resting place even as he promised (see Deut. 3:20; 12:9-10; 25:19), so that 'place of rest' and 'promised land' are identical. The judgment awaiting the people in Isaiah's day is that the covenant curse of Deuteronomy 28:49 will be realised, and God will bring on them a people whose language they do not understand. Refusal to listen to the LORD will result in having to listen to foreign lips and strange tongues. Paul quotes the words of verse 11 in 1 Corinthians 14:21 when he is speaking of tongues being a sign to unbelievers. While the two contexts differ, yet words are taken from the address to the childish nation of Israel and applied to the childish church in Corinth. The tongues, argues Paul, have a sign value to unbelievers, while prophecy is for believers (1 Cor. 14:22). In both Isaiah and 1 Corinthians tongues are a sign of the covenantal curse.[1]

13 The end result will be that just as they mimicked Isaiah's words, so will God's word become for them a meaningless jumble of sound. The very words they used, '*tsav lâtsâv tsav lâtsâv qav lâqâv qav lâqâv...*' are quoted back to them as a sign that they will be deprived of understanding of divine revelation. The ultimate outcome will be that they will stumble, be injured, be snared and captured. These last words are virtually a repetition of Isaiah 8:13, with a change of only one of the five verbs.

b. Judgment and Mercy (28:14-22)

While further indication is given of impending judgment, yet Isaiah speaks of a precious cornerstone laid in Zion. All human efforts are as fruitless as someone trying to rest on a short bed, with only a narrow blanket for cover. What is needed is a work of God, 'his strange work' (verse 21), and a demonstration of his divine counsel and magnificent wisdom (verse 29).

14 The opening word 'therefore' provides the link with the preceding passage. As a consequence of previously refusing to listen, Judah's national leaders have another word from God directed to them. They have treated previous messages with mockery; now they are commanded to listen.

15 The claim the leaders make is that they have entered into a covenant with death. The parallel says that they have made a *chozeh* with *she'ôl*, while in verse 18 *chozeh* is replaced by *châzût*. Both are rare nouns, one masculine, the other feminine. There is no known connection between them and the word 'covenant'. Though the two words seem to come from the Hebrew root 'to see' (*châzâh*), in the

---

[1]For elaboration of the theme of tongues as a covenantal sign in both Old and New Testaments, see O. Palmer Robertson, 'Tongues: Sign of Covenantal Curse and Blessing', *WTJ* 38 (1975-76), pp. 43-53, and the commentary on the Corinthian passage in Simon J. Kistemaker, *1 Corinthians* (Baker Book House, 1993), pp. 497-505.

context they mean something like 'covenant' or 'agreement'. No explanation is given of the content of this 'covenant'. It could have involved seeking information from the dead, and hence designate some form of necromancy, or else denote the treaty connections with Egypt that are going to bring death. Somehow they thought that this would protect them, even though they acknowledge that this amounted to trusting in deceit, making falsehood a hiding place. She'ol is often used in the Old Testament to speak of death or the grave.[2]

16 These words form one of the three great statements of faith in the Old Testament (along with Genesis 15:6 and Habakkuk 2:4). They come as a formal declaration of the Sovereign LORD,[3] and may well echo the final address of Joshua when the Mosaic covenant with the LORD was renewed just prior to his death. A large stone was set up near the tabernacle, to serve as a witness against the people (Jos. 24:26-27). Isaiah has already spoken of the LORD as a rock of stumbling (8:14-15), and here the imagery is continued. A precious stone is set as the corner stone, one supporting two main walls. It is also 'a stone of testing'. While this could mean 'a tested stone', in the context it more likely means 'a stone that tests [others]'. This meaning both agrees with Isaiah 8:14-15 and the use made of this verse in Romans 9:33 and 1 Peter 2:4-8. Those who believe will never become eager (i.e. anxious),[4] for they know that the LORD has set this stone, and lack of faith in it will cause stumbling. Both in 8:14 and in 28:16 the LORD is the rock. There is evidence that the Jews before New Testament times took these passages as messianic,[5] and certainly the

---

[2]See the discussion by R. L. Harris, *TWOT*, vol. II, pp. 892-93.

[3]The translation needs to bring out the force of the Hebrew: 'Therefore, thus says the LORD Almighty, it is I who have laid....'

[4]The NIV translation 'will never be dismayed' appears to take the verb not as 'hurry' or 'hasten' but as another verb of the same spelling meaning 'be dismayed'. This is possible, but the other rendering, 'Whoever believes will not be in haste' (ESV), better fits both the context and the wider use of this verb in the Old Testament.

[5]The Targum on Isaiah 28:16 renders it in this way: 'Behold, I set in Zion a king, a mighty king, mighty and terrible, whom I will uphold and strengthen; the prophet says: And the righteous in whom is confidence shall not tremble when affliction comes.' The LXX is probably taking the verse similarly, shown by the addition of the words 'in him': 'he who believes *in him* will not be ashamed.' This is the form in which the words are quoted in Romans 9:33 and 1 Peter 2:6.

early church applied them to Christ as the rock. In both testaments the statement gives encouragement to believers who trust in the Rock, while he is a threat of judgment to those who disbelieve.

17 The Lord promises to set the standards by which human actions are to be judged. These are justice and righteousness. The idea of a building introduced in the previous verse is carried on with mention of measuring and plumb lines. Both vertical and horizontal planes have to be in accordance with the set standards.[6] Thought and language already used in verses 2 and 15 are taken up to describe the collapse of a building that does not measure up to divine standards. Hailstorms will 'sweep away' (an *hapax legomenon*) their refuge, while the flooding waters will sweep over their hiding place. The same verb (*shâtaf*) was used in 8:8 as Isaiah pictured the coming Assyrian invasion as a mighty flood sweeping through Judah.

18-19a Any covenant with death will be useless in the day of testing. It will be 'atoned for' (Heb. *kuppar*), that is, it will be wiped away. Similarly, any agreement with She'ol will not stand, that is, it will not last. Despite the brave protestations of the people that the overwhelming flood will not reach them (see verse 15), what they will find is that it will sweep over them and crush them (the noun *mirmas,* 'trampling', is used, recalling the use of a verbal form of the same root in verse 3). This is not just going to be a passing judgment, but one that returns again and again. They will be caught by it. As they contemplate the future they will be terrified by the prospect.[7]

19b-20 Isaiah's ministry, when understood by his hearers, is not going to comfort them. Instead, it will bring them 'sheer terror' (NIV, a good translation of the MT 'and it will be only terror'). Judah is like

---

[6]The word for measuring line (*qâv*) is the same as the one already used in the nonsense speech quoted in verses 10 and 13. However, there is probably no connection between the two as *qâv* may well have been chosen in those verses simply because it was a monosyllable rhyming with *tsâv*.

[7]George Adam Smith, *The Book of Isaiah I-XXXIX* , op. cit., pp. 160-64, points out the use of this chapter by Oliver Cromwell when he wrote to the Scottish Presbyterians in 1650. He says that 'Cromwell...is the best commentator Isaiah has ever had, and that by an instinct born, not only of the same faith, but of experience in tackling similar sorts of character' (p. 161). While some of Smith's application is tendentious, yet he is correct when he says that 'it is only belief in the God of Isaiah, a true and loving God, omnipotent Ruler of our life, that can bring us peace' (p. 164).

a man trying to sleep on a bed too short for him, and without a wide enough blanket for cover. Two things are probably intended by this analogy. First, it suggests lack of preparation for the coming conflict with Assyria, like someone failing to make proper sleeping arrangements. Secondly, it implies lack of human skill and power to bring comfort and consolation. Just as a short bed and narrow blanket don't satisfy a weary person, so the nation is bankrupt spiritually and politically and without the resources to save herself.

21 Historical incidents are recalled to stress the LORD's might, and hence his ability to do 'his strange work', 'his alien task'. The strangeness is that he is going to use foreign nations to bring judgment upon his own people. The reference to Mount Perazim (near Jerusalem) is to the occasion when David defeated the Philistines and captured their gods (2 Sam. 5:20). The allusion to Gibeon could refer to the continuation of the same incident, for while Gibeon is not mentioned in 2 Samuel 5, it is in the parallel passage in 1 Chronicles 14:16. However, more likely the reference is back to Joshua's victory at Gibeon (Jos. 10:9-15), and, if so, then the hailstorm at that time may well be behind Isaiah's mention of hailstorms in this chapter (see verses 2 and 17).

22 A solemn declaration has come from 'the Lord, the LORD of hosts' to Isaiah. The people have to be instructed to stop boasting lest even heavier punishment is given. Isaiah then repeats his message given back in Ahaz' time (10:22-23) that the destruction determined by God will come upon the whole land (10:23 has 'in the midst of the land'). No part of the promised land is going to be exempt from this visitation.

c. A Wisdom Poem (28:23-29)

A short wisdom poem of two stanzas completes the message of this chapter. It draws analogies with farming methods to make the point that God's judgments are not arbitrary and his chastisements are measured. Each stanza finishes with a verse that extols God's wisdom (verses 26 and 29).

23-26 Isaiah appeals to the people in typical wisdom style (cf. similar calls in passages such as Psalm 78:1 and Proverbs 1:8; 4:1; 4:20; 5:1). Two synonymous verbs are used ('give ear' and 'listen') and two synonymous descriptive terms for the content of his message ('my voice' and 'my word'). In verse 24 two questions are posed, both of which imply a negative response. Does the farmer just go on ploughing and furrowing the soil? Of course not! Similarly in verse 25 two further questions relate to the farmer's practice of sowing. When the ground has been ploughed and levelled, doesn't he then proceed to sow caraway, cumin, and different kinds of wheat and barley? Of course he does! The conclusion drawn in verse 26 is that this farming practice is part of God's intention. He gives instruction and teaches what is right.

27-29 The link between the two parts of this poem is made plain in the MT by the introductory word 'for' (*kî*) at the commencement of verse 27. The parable does not stop at sowing, but goes on to draw lessons from harvesting as well. The threshing of various crops is in accordance with their nature. Caraway does not need a sledge, nor does cumin need a cartwheel. Much lighter instruments such as sticks are used. The end in view is to obtain flour with which to make bread. Each of the preceding processes – ploughing, harrowing, sowing, and grinding (the intermediate process of harvesting is omitted) – leads ultimately to the use of the crop for food. So there is both plan and purpose in God's actions with his people and the surrounding nations. In the context the lesson seems to be that God will not deal in judgment with his people forever. His purposes will be worked out and ultimately there will be good for those who trust in him. The second stanza ends with another statement of God's wisdom. All that has been spoken about in verses 24 to 28 originate with him. His counsel is wonderful (*hiflî' 'êtsâh*; cf. the use of the phrase 'wonderful counsellor' [*pele' yô 'êts*] in 9:6) and he increases wisdom. His actions are the outworking of his decrees (see verse 22), and they manifest wisdom that far transcends human thought.

2. Woe to Jerusalem (29:1-14)

The focus turns again to Jerusalem, called here by the symbolic name 'Ariel' (cf. the use of the term 'Valley of Vision' in 22:1). Though continuing with religious observances, the city is noted for its formalism – the hearts of the people are far from God (verse 13). While God will use Gentile nations to besiege Jerusalem, yet they will suddenly be devastated as he unleashes a great storm against them.

1 The woe is directed against Ariel. This name sounds and looks like the Hebrew word *hâ 'ªriêl*, 'the altar hearth', in Ezekiel's description of the new temple of God (Ezek. 43:15-16). However, uncertainty about the correct derivation continues, though there is no uncertainty as to it being used in verses 1-2 to designate Jerusalem.[8] This is confirmed by the reference in verses 7-8 to Mount Zion. It may be that the name simply means 'city of God', just as Isaiah later calls it 'the city of the LORD' (60:14).[9] It was there that David 'camped' (a poetic use equivalent to the prose 'dwelt'), and also where the sequence of ritual sacrifice went on year by year.

2 The threat is that the LORD will oppress Jerusalem (NIV is somewhat free in its rendering 'besiege') so that she mourns deeply (the Heb. expression *ta'aniyyâh va'aniyyâh* is a compound used only here and in Lamentations 2:5; lit. 'she will be [in] lamentation and lamentation'). To the LORD, Jerusalem will become 'like Ariel', i.e. like an altar hearth, a place where the sacrifices are consumed.

3 Though he will use other nations, the action against Jerusalem is regarded as God's own work: '*I* will encamp ... *I* will besiege ... *I* will raise siege works.' The city taken by David when he camped there is going to be the object of military attack and siege initiated by the LORD himself. This is going to be part of the humiliation of Judah/Jerusalem commented on by the historian in 2 Kings 17:20.

4 The people who had a covenant with death (28:15, 18) will themselves be brought down even to the grave. In carefully crafted parallel phrases Isaiah tells how they will speak 'from the earth' (2x), 'from the dust' (2x). Two of the words used ('*ôv*, 'medium', and *tsâfaf*, 'to whisper') are connected elsewhere with spiritism, and already occur in 8:19 where Isaiah is discouraging any reversion to Canaanite cultic practices to secure revelation.[10] The general idea is that Judah will no longer speak out arrogantly, but only mutter from the dust of humiliation.

---

[8]Bishop Lowth made this point 200 years ago: 'That Jerusalem is here called by this name is very certain; but the reason of this name, and the meaning of it, applied to Jerusalem, is very obscure and doubtful.' See his *Isaiah: A New Translation, with a Preliminary Dissertation and Notes, Critical, Philological, and Explanatory*, 13th edition, London: Thomas Tegg, 1842, p. 277. For an extensive note on possible explanations, see E. J. Young, *The Book of Isaiah*, vol. II, pp. 304-05, fn. 1.

[9]See the discussion by Ronald Youngblood, "Ariel, 'City of God'", in Abraham I. Katsh and Leon Nemoy eds., *Essays on the Occasion of the Seventieth Anniversary of Dropsie University (1909-1979)* (Philadelphia: Dropsie University, 1979), pp. 457-62.

[10]The verb 'to whisper [as a sorcerer]' is only used by Isaiah; see, in addition to this verse, 8:19; 10:14; 38:14.

5-6 The picture changes abruptly. It is not only Judah who will be punished, but 'suddenly, in an instant', the LORD will crush all Jerusalem's opponents. Their destruction is likened to production of fine dust or chaff after winnowing. There will be a visitation that displays God's power by means of the mighty forces of nature. It is the language of theophany that Isaiah uses to introduce this thought of deliverance for Jerusalem.

7-8 These verses form an *inclusio*, for after the introductory words in the MT ('and it shall be like a dream, a night vision') the subject is introduced—'the hordes of all the nations.' Then after saying that their prey (Ariel/Mount Zion) will escape them just as things in dreams disappear, Isaiah confirms that this is indeed the situation in respect to 'the hordes of all the nations'. A hungry and thirsty man may dream that he is eating and drinking, but when he wakes he is still hungry and thirsty! Jerusalem's enemies are many, as indicated by the fourfold use of the word *hâmôn*, 'a crowd' (especially in reference to armies), in verses 5-8.[11] However, the size of the attacking armies is irrelevant when the LORD of hosts uses his power to dispel their attacks on Mount Zion.

9-10 Judah is stunned and blind! Two pairs of verbs are used in the first part of verse 9, and the second occurrence of the verb is either for emphasis or expresses the consequence. Their own actions produce a spiritual torpor, so that they are both amazed and blind. They reel and stagger like drunkards, yet their drunken condition is spiritual, not physical. Their condition, while self-induced, is the result of God's judgment on them and on their spiritual leaders, the prophets and seers. They have been brought into 'a deep sleep', a word not used to describe normal sleep but a special state induced by God as on Adam (Gen. 2:21) or on Abraham (Gen. 15:12). Prophets and seers may speak but Judah is blind and deaf to their message, even as Isaiah had been told would occur as a result of his ministry (6:9-10). Words from the first part of verse 10 are combined with quotations from Deuteronomy 29:4 and Psalm 69:22-23 in Romans 11:8-10. Threefold testimony from the law, the prophets and the Psalms is invoked by Paul as he describes the judicial blindness that has come upon the Jews.

11-12 A short section in prose is inserted into the flow of the passage to illustrate how spiritual blindness extends to both literate and illiterate

---

[11] See *DCH*, II, p. 569.

alike. Those who can read will claim that Isaiah's series of visions cannot be read because they are sealed (see 8:16).[12] It was normal practice to seal a scroll with a lump of clay (a *bulla*). The illiterate will claim that they cannot be expected to read it because they don't know how to read. All the population, learned and unlearned alike, cannot understand the message that Isaiah brings to them.

13 The words of this verse are well-known because they are quoted by Jesus as he describes the hypocrisy of the Pharisees: 'These people draw near to me with their mouth, and honour me with their lips, but their hearts are far from me. In vain they worship me, teaching as doctrines the commandments of men' (Matt. 15:8-9). Isaiah speaks to the people in a way that draws a contrast between himself and them. He does not call them 'my people' but 'this people'. He represents the faithful true worshippers in Judah; they represent those who are worshipping in name only. It is tempting to think that Isaiah may have in mind the reformation under Hezekiah when there was a popular upsurge of religious life. But the fact that the reformation came 'suddenly' (see 2 Chron. 29:36) may have meant that there were many people who were outwardly conforming to religious life but whose hearts were not changed at all.

14 The concluding verse of this woe oracle tells of the extraordinary work that is going to be accomplished. God is going to display yet again his power on behalf of his people. Just as he manifested his 'wonders' at the time of the exodus, so he is going to do again in the new exodus (for discussion of the word 'wonder' see the commentary on 9:5 and 25:1). Later in the prophecy Isaiah spells out in greater detail the nature of this new exodus (see, for example, 42:8-9; 43:1-7; 43:14-21; 48:12-22). The formal introduction to this declaration ('Therefore, behold I am about to ...') and the thrice repeated reference to 'wonders' ('to show wonderful things to this people, wonder upon wonder') combine to stress that this work is beyond man's achievement. Mere human understanding that does not acknowledge the ways of God disappears in the presence of divine wisdom (cf. Isa. 55:8-9). Paul quotes the second part of the verse in 1 Corinthians 1:19

---

[12]The phrase in the MT to describe the content of the book is *châzût hakkol*. The NIV takes it to mean 'this whole vision', but a comparison with similar wording in Psalm 119:128 suggests that it means 'the vision of all', i.e. all of Isaiah's prophecies. It may thus imply that some of Isaiah's prophecies were already circulating in written form.

when he is describing how the Cross of Christ makes foolish the world's wisdom.

3. Woe to Those Conspiring with Foreign Nations (29:15-24)

Though not specified precisely in the passage, the danger Judah is facing is the making of plans to conclude alliances with other nations instead of trusting in the LORD. They think they can do this without him knowing. It becomes clear in the next oracle (30:1-33) that alliances with Egypt were not out of the question. However, the people are encouraged to wait patiently for God to reveal his power in coming days when his holiness will be acknowledged by all.

15 Woe is proclaimed to those who attempt to devise their own plans and who think they can keep them secret from the LORD. When they plot at night, thinking that no eye can see them, their activities are seen and known by the LORD. They have not taken to heart the teaching of the psalmist that darkness and the light of day are both alike with him (Ps. 139:12). In view of the fact that the next woe specifically mentions Egypt, this one is most probably directed against secret plots to break the vassal status with Assyria and to look for military assistance from Egypt.

16 So perverse are the people (the suffix on the opening word of the verse is second person plural, 'your perversity') that they would even confuse the clay with the potter. A piece of pottery can't say to the potter, 'You didn't make me!' The people think they can dispense with their Maker, when in reality they are his creatures. What is created can't claim ignorance on the part of the creator. Some of the words of this verse are quoted by Paul in Romans 9:20 (along with others from Isa. 45:9) when he is speaking of God's sovereign purposes for Israel.

17 A sudden shift takes place at this point. Instead of continuing to deal with the current situation, Isaiah switches the vision to the future, just as he did in 28:5-8. It almost seems as if a proverbial saying is employed (cf. 32:15): 'In just a short time will Lebanon not be turned into a Carmel, and Carmel reckoned as a forest?' The expression regarding the short time is one that has already occurred in 10:25 (see commentary). What lies in the future is a complete reversal of circumstances, as if the forests of Lebanon become an orchard, and vice versa. Probably the message in part at least relates to the overthrow of Assyria and the ultimate restoration of Israel.

18-19 The present deafness and blindness of the people are not going to continue. The words of the scroll (possibly that containing Isaiah's prophecy) will be apparent to any hearer or reader. This is what Isaiah later says will take place in the restoration of dispersed Israel when the eyes of the blind will be opened and the deaf ears unstopped (35:5). 'The poor' and 'the needy' represent the faithful within the nation as in 11:4, 14:30, 32, and 25:4. Their confidence is in the LORD, the holy one of Israel, and because of that they can again rejoice and shout for joy.

20-21 If Assyria is in view in verses 16-17 then the reference to 'the ruthless one' (Heb. *'ârîts*) here is also to Assyria. The destruction of this ruthless one has already been mentioned in verse 5. The parallel phrase also refers to Assyria, who scoffed at the idea that the God of Israel could deliver his people out of Assyria's grip (cf. the message that the Rabshakeh brought on Sennacherib's behalf to Hezekiah, 36:7, 14-15, 18-20). The local situation in Judah is apparently in view in verses 20c and 21. There are those who lie in wait for opportunities for evil, trapping the defenders when they appear at the city gate seeking justice. Instead of speaking the truth they condemn with a single word and deprive the righteous of justice.

22-24 The final part of the oracle is a word of promise. The end of Jacob/Israel's history will resemble its beginnings. Just as Abraham had his 'exodus' out of Ur of the Chaldees (or possibly from the hands of Pharoah or Abimelech), so will God's people experience redemption out of pagan and idolatrous surroundings when the new exodus takes place. Twice later Isaiah uses a formula involving the verb 'redeem' used here of Abraham (Heb. *pâdâh*) to describe the return to Zion of the exiles (35:10; 51:11). No longer will the exiles feel the shame of their banishment from the promised land. The opening of verse 23 can have several translations, which in turn affect the interpretation. Many translators give it as: 'For when he [or they] see his [their] children....' But it is better to take the reference to Jacob as a collective, and hence equivalent to 'his children'. The translation will be: 'When he, [that is], his children see the work of my hands.'[13] When the restoration takes place there will be renewed appreciation of the Holy One of Jacob/the God of Israel. The people will sanctify him, and stand in awe before him (cf. the use of the same verb 'stand in awe' in 8:12;

---

[13] I borrow the idea from G. C. M. Douglas, *Isaiah One and His Book One*, pp. 254-55, n. 1.

the cognate noun is the word 'ruthless' in verses 5 and 20). The final
verse suggests that while there may still be those among the restored
exiles who stray or who murmur, they will accept the LORD's teaching
and so gain understanding. Restoration will involve a new spirit of
submission to his instruction.

4. Woe to the Rebellious Nation (30:1-33)

The fourth in the series of 'Woes' is directed against Egypt which had
become a source of hope for many in Judah. Without waiting for a
word from the LORD through his servant Isaiah, messengers had been
sent down to try and find refuge there. This was probably around 701
BC. The only hope for the people is to repent and find their rest in the
compassionate God who blesses all who wait on him (verse 18).
Gracious promises are held out to those who cry to him for help, with
the assurance that the power of Assyria will be broken by his power
alone. Military alliances will fail, but the LORD will display his mighty
power when he shakes the Gentile nations as in a sieve (verse 28).

a. The Folly of Trusting in Egypt (30:1-7)

1-2 A formal declaration is made by the LORD. The people of Judah
are like rebellious children, using the language employed in Deuteronomy
21:18, 20 of a rebellious son in a human family. Though they are
rebellious they are still 'children', a point often made by Isaiah. The
sin is one of rebellion against God by despising his covenant and making
one with Egypt. The gravity of the sin is shown by the expressions
'not from me' and 'not of my spirit'. The expression used for covenant
making is 'to pour out a drink offering'. However, in both biblical and
extra-biblical treaties sacrifice was an integral part of covenant making,
and so the act could be a virtual synonym for the common Hebrew
expression 'to cut a covenant'.[14] The end result of their sin is that
they sweep sin upon sin, which probably means that in addition to
making a treaty with Egypt they sin doubly by their act of concealment.
Before sending messengers to Egypt there was no attempt to seek a
word from the LORD. What Judah wanted from Egypt was 'refuge'
and 'shade', two of the words often used to describe God's protection
of his people (see the use of both words in 25:4). Judah is attempting
to find in Pharaoh what she should have continued to find in the LORD.

---

[14]For a discussion on this point, see Paul Kalluveettil, *Declaration and
Covenant*, op. cit., p. 28.

3 Hence, however attractive trust in Pharaoh and Egypt appear, Judah will find that it is false trust to make these alliances, and that they lead only to shame and disgrace. She will be disillusioned by making such pacts, for thcy amount to rejection of the LORD. The NIV fails to translate one word in this verse (*châsût*). It is probably from the verb 'to put trust in' (*châsâh*), and the phrase can be translated as 'and trust in the shelter of Egypt'. The very thing that Judah is doing contradicts the confession made elsewhere, such as in Psalm 91:1-2.

4-5 A meeting takes place at Zoan, in the north-east delta of the Nile. This was the effective capital of Egypt from around 1100 BC until 660 BC. The parallelism in verse 4 demands that Hanes be identified with Zoan (see the mention of Zoan already in 19:11, 13), or else be understood as a term describing the king's palace at Zoan.[15] There is a change in number in the verse that also affects translation and interpretation: 'For though *they* have officials in Zoan, and *his* messengers have arrived....' In the context 'his' has to refer to Pharaoh. So what is described is a meeting of deputies from Judah with the Egyptian officials at the royal palace at Zoan. The outcome of the meeting is utter futility, because Egypt is unable to provide the necessary assistance. The end result will be 'shame', repeating the term already used in verse 3, though adding here 'reproach' in place of 'disgrace'.

6-7 As part of this 'woe' message a short 'burden' (Heb. *massâ'*) is included (see comments on 13:1 for the meaning of this word). It concerns the Negev, the arid desert area south of Beersheba, through which the Judaean messengers went. Though the description, 'a land of hardship and distress,' could apply to the coastal route, it may imply that the deputies from the king had to traverse more inhospitable tracks in order to avoid Assyrians who were holding the normal road south. Through an area with many wild animals and reptiles, the messengers carry the money and gifts that are intended to purchase Egyptian help. But, says Isaiah, repeating the description of Egypt used in the preceding verse, she is 'a people of no use', 'Rahab the Do-Nothing'. Rahab is a poetic name for Egypt (cf. 51:9; Ps. 87:4). There are various explanations of the Hebrew expression 'the Do-Nothing', but all of them have in common the idea of inactivity.[16] Egypt is of no use to Judah.

---

[15] This latter suggestion is that of Kenneth Kitchen, *NBD*, p. 504.
[16] A literal rendering of the Hebrew shows up the various difficulties in this

b. An Unwilling People (30:8-18)

8 As at another critical period (see 8:1) Isaiah is instructed to go and write on a tablet for the people. No indication is given of the message to be written, but it may be the very words just spoken, 'Rahab the Do-Nothing', just as the words 'Maher-shalal-chash-baz' were used on the earlier occasion. Here the expression used indicates that the writing was not in the presence of the people but 'with them', indicating a co-operative effort involving prophet and people as they set up this enduring witness.

9 Whereas a family term was used in verse 1 to describe the character of the people of Judah, now a technical term is used to indicate their covenant unfaithfulness (Heb. *merî*, 'rebellious', from the verb *mârâh*, 'to be rebellious'). While Isaiah only uses the adjective here, and the verb three times (1:20; 50:5; 63:10), Ezekiel makes it a key word as he describes the rebellious nation. Out of fifteen occurrences in Ezekiel, thirteen are in the expression *bêt merî*, 'rebellious house'. The people embody lies, and they are stubborn children who have set their wills against listening to the LORD's instruction.

10-11 The LORD's instruction came mainly from seers and prophets. The word seer (Heb. *ro'eh*) was an early term for a prophet (see 1 Sam. 9:9), while the word here for prophet (Heb. *chozeh*) comes from a verb frequently used of receiving prophetic visions (1:1; 2:1; Amos 1:1). The people don't want what is true. Instead they would rather have fantasies and illusions. They tell the prophets to desist from their action in warning the people and to cease from facing people with the reality of the Holy One of Israel. While the NIV rendering of verse 11a is rather free, it does capture the meaning well: 'Stop confronting us with the Holy One of Israel' (lit. 'Stop from our faces the Holy One of Israel').

12-14 Though the people want no more to do with the LORD, he is not finished with Judah. Through the prophet he makes the solemn declaration that the oppression and deceit that they practise will not

---

verse: 'And Egypt [is] worthless; they provide empty [help]; therefore I call this one (fem.), Rahab they [are] sitting'. This translation assumes that the final word in the verse (*shâvet*) is from the verb *yâshav*, 'to sit', but there are other possibilities. The verb could, for example, be *shâvat*, 'to cease'. Whatever the precise translation, the point is that the arrogant Rahab can offer no help whatsoever.

stand them in good stead. They may think that their practice is a protective wall ensuring their well-being. In reality it will crack and collapse suddenly, depriving them of any supposed protection. So thorough will be the breaking that no fragment of it will be of any use, not even for scraping out the fire or scooping up water from the cistern. Instead of trusting in the LORD they are trusting in their own sinful ways.

15 Now comes a word of consolation and blessing. The declaration is made particularly impressive and solemn by the way in which the LORD is introduced. He is 'the Lord GOD, the holy one of Israel' (Heb. *'ᵃdônay yhwh qᵉdôsh yisrâêl*). This is the only time that Isaiah uses this combination of names to speak of the God of Israel. He is the LORD, the covenant redeemer, and also the one distinguished by his holiness. He reassures his people that there is salvation in repentance and rest, i.e. if they return to him and cease to trust in their own faithless self-reliance. Only if there is confidence in the LORD will there be strength//salvation. The tragedy is that Judah would not go the LORD's way, and so the blunt words at the end of verse 15 describe her rebellion: 'and you were not willing.'

16-18 Judah is trusting in the horses she has procured from Egypt (see 31:1). Her planned means of escape will fail as her enemies overtake her easily. A thousand will flee before one, and when five threaten everyone will go! This is an allusion to the covenant curses in Leviticus 26:8, 36 and Deuteronomy 28:25; 32:30. A solitary outpost is all that will remain. And what hope is there if Judah repents? The answer is given in verse 18. The LORD waits to show compassion to a repentant people. In the MT the double use of 'therefore' in successive clauses draws attention to divine mercy: 'Therefore the LORD waits to be gracious to you, and therefore he exalts himself to show mercy to you' (ESV). The salvation/strength spoken of in verse 15 can only come through the exercise of mercy by a just God. That being so, a blessing is pronounced on all who wait for him. The word used for blessing (*'ashᵉrê*) is the normal one used in Hebrew when human activity is being praised (cf. Ps. 1:1). Isaiah's contemporary Hosea has a similar message concerning repentance and blessing. When the people realise that their horses can't save them, they will acknowledge that their idols are not real gods, and they will find compassion with the LORD (Hos. 14:1-3).

c. Covenant Blessings (30:19-26)

In a prose passage Isaiah describes how the time of trial and affliction
will be superseded by the coming of promised covenant blessings. As
a covenant document, the book of Deuteronomy clearly lies behind
this passage. The period of weeping will give way to a time when the
LORD shows his compassion and heals his people. Jeremiah uses the
same imagery of weeping to depict the exile, so that Rachel is instructed
to dry her tears, for her children will be brought back to her (Jer.
31:15-20).

19 The flow of the text suggests that those who wait for the LORD
are characterised now as the people of Zion (the introductory *kî*, 'for',
makes the connection). The time is coming when they will no longer
weep, for the assurance is given that the LORD will be gracious to
them when they cry to him, and as soon as he hears that cry he will
respond. Indeed, the Hebrew text may even be translated to suggest
that the cry has already been answered: 'He will surely be gracious to
you at the sound of your cry; when he hears, he *has* answered you.'

20-21 While the people may not receive all the temporal blessings
they expect, yet they are promised spiritual blessings. Their food will
be that associated with deprivation (cf. 1 Kings 22:27 = 2 Chronicles
18:26, 'meagre rations of food and water'), but spiritually they are
promised two things. First, no longer will their teacher(s) be hidden
from them,[17] while secondly, they are promised that their eyes will
see him (or, them). The word for 'teacher' could be either singular or
plural, as the form of this verb here does not allow precise
determination. The preceding verb is singular, and therefore it is best
to take it as a reference to God himself. The people who had failed to
accept his teaching in the past will now see and hear him. When they
err, turning to right or left, there will be a voice saying, 'This is the
way; walk in it.' 'Way' conveys the idea of manner of life, and this
instruction ties in with the warning of Deuteronomy 28:14. In the Acts
of the Apostles 'way' is probably a Hebraism used in reference to the
early church (see Acts 9:2; 19:9, 23; 24:14, 22).

22 Repentance will inevitably bring a new attitude toward idols.

---

[17]The verb 'to hide' appearing here (Heb. *kânaf*) is a *hapax legomenon*,
and its meaning can only be ascertained from the context, for even the early
translations of the Old Testament had difficulty. Because of the seeming
connection with the Hebrew word for 'a wing' (*kânâf*), there may be some
idea of sheltering or hiding under the wing.

They had taken much time and money to make, but when a new spirit enters the hearts of the people they will want to be rid of them. 'Go away,' they will say, as if they are casting off a soiled garment. What they had previously reverenced they are going to call unclean (*timmê'tem,* 'you [pl. masc.] will declare unclean'). The plural verb is used whereas in the two preceding verses masculine singular suffixes occur, as also happens with the nouns in this verse. The switch may be deliberate to suggest that the whole community is involved in the destruction of the idols.

23-24 The covenant promise of rain to produce good yields at harvest time was conditional upon obedience (Lev. 26:3-4; Deut. 11:13-15). The implication, then, in this passage, is that the covenant requirements will ultimately be met, so that abundant harvests will come from the sown fields. Cattle will have good grazing areas, while the working animals, the oxen and donkeys, will be able to feed on good fodder.

25-26 In the future lies a day of devastation. Whereas the term 'slaughter' is applied to Judah in Jeremiah 19:6 ('the valley of slaughter'), here it refers to Judah's enemies. The towers could be either offensive or defensive. Because the phrase follows immediately on the thought of the slaughter (of enemies), it is best to take it as a reference to siege towers. Part of the eschatological picture is the vision of pristine Edenic conditions being restored. Streams of water will flow from every hill. The picture of flowing streams is part of the biblical eschatology to convey the idea of the abundance of God's provision for his people (cf. Isa. 35:6-7; Rev. 7:17; 21:6; 22:1). In poetical language Isaiah says that time is coming when the moon will be as bright as the sun, while the sun will be seven times brighter, just like seven full days of sunlight.[18] This description also becomes part of John's language in reference to heaven, where there will be no night (Rev. 21:25; 22:5). Two things are significant about the reference to seven days. First, history culminates in the seventh day, the Sabbath, and we still await the final consummation in the heavenly rest (Heb. 4:8-11). Secondly, the number seven may well be significant, indicating that the sevenfold curse of Leviticus 26:18, 21, 24, 28 is reversed. The reference to binding up and healing reverts to the theme of brokenness

---

[18]The poetical words used for moon (*lᵉvânâh*) and sun (*chammâh*) are a fixed pair that only occurs three times in the Old Testament (Isa. 24:23; 30:26; Song of Sol. 6:10). Their basic meaning is 'white' and 'heat'.

in verses 12-14, but it is not until 61:1 that how this healing ministry will take place is clearly delineated, for it is the servant who is going 'to bind up the broken-hearted'.[19]

d. Redemptive Judgment in the Second Exodus (30:27-33)

The Exodus and events associated with it were in Isaiah's mind (see verse 29, 'as in the night when a [passover] feast is celebrated', and 31:5, 'he will pass over it (*pâsoach*) and rescue it'). The punishment of Assyria will be accompanied by a theophany. Like earlier biblical occasions God's voice will again be associated with fire, cloudburst, and thunder. The mighty warrior God will punish Assyria, and even as Israel rejoiced in song after the Exodus, so once more the sound of festive songs will be heard (verses 29, 32).

27 The introductory word, 'See', marks the transition to a condemnatory message concerning Assyria. The 'name' of God is simply his character, his self-revelation. There are allusions here back to Isaiah's first message concerning the danger from Assyria (5:25-30). In that earlier passage Assyria was the nation that was coming 'from afar'; now it is the LORD who comes 'from afar'. There it was the LORD's anger that burned against his people (5:25); now his anger burns against Assyria. In typically anthropomorphic language God's nostrils, lips and mouth are all utilised to indicate his intense wrath.[20]

28 The connection with earlier statements about Assyria continues. Whereas Assyria was depicted as a mighty river that invaded the land and reached up to the neck (8:8), now it is God's breath (lit. 'spirit') that is the overflowing torrent reaching to the neck. In both passages the language describes imminent danger. God is going to sift the nations, not in order to protect the true Israel (see the same imagery used in Amos 9:9), but in order to destroy (lit. 'a sieve of worthlessness'). The metaphor changes at the end of the verse to the idea of putting bridles on wild horses. The nations are going to be so restrained by God that they are brought to destruction.

29 The imagery of the passover festival is employed to describe the joy of the people when the divine judgment on Assyria takes place.

---

[19]The theme of 'brokenness' connects Isaiah 30:13-14; 30:26; and 61:1, the first two passages using the same word (*shêver*) while 61:1 uses a verbal form from the same root (*nishbar*).

[20]The Hebrew word for 'nose' or 'nostrils' (*'af*) is widely used in the Old Testament as a synonym for 'anger'.

For Judah it will be salvation, and hence songs, similar to those employed at the passover, will come from joyful hearts. On that pilgrimage occasion the tribes went up annually to give thanks to the name of the LORD (Ps. 122:4). They went to Zion, called here 'the LORD's mountain', where they worshipped 'the rock of Israel'. This is an old title for God (see Deut. 32:4, 15, 31, 37) that stresses his permanence and the security he affords to those who trust in him.

30-31 The LORD is going to act again as he did against Egypt. There are several allusions to the record in the book of Exodus of the plagues in Egypt. The mention of 'hail' recalls the times this word is used in Exodus (9:24, 28; 10:5), while the word for 'rod' in verse 32 is the word used of Moses' rod (see Exod. 4:2, 4; 7:9, 17). That rod had no power in itself; it was merely a symbol of God's might. The references to the LORD's hand in Exodus (see, e.g., Exod. 3:20; 7:4) are paralleled by the reference to the LORD's arm (verse 30). There are also clear inter-connections within this whole section, as the reference to God as 'a consuming fire' (verse 30) takes up the expression from verse 27. Moreover, the introductory 'for' in the Hebrew text (*kî*) at the commencement of verses 31 and 33 provides a connecting link with what precedes. The reference to the LORD's majestic voice, along with thunderstorm and hail, is reminiscent of similar descriptions of theophanies in Psalms 18:6-15; 68:7-8; 77:14-20. God's great acts of salvation are pictured alike by psalmist and prophet (cf. this passage in Isaiah with Psalm 97 and Habakkuk 3). Assyria will be shattered with a word from the LORD, even though she was accustomed to smiting others. The second part of verse 31 is a reference to Assyria, not to the LORD. The expression here used regarding Assyria has already been used in 10:24. Hence the translation should be: 'For through the voice of the LORD Assyria, who struck with a rod, will be beaten down.'

32 Just as Moses' rod was a symbol of God's judgment to Pharoah, so will be every occasion the LORD causes his rod to rest on Assyria.[21] Most English versions implicitly adopt an emendation to the Hebrew text when they speak of a punishing rod. This involves the change of one letter in Hebrew (altering *mûsâdâh*, 'appointed', to *mûsârâh*, 'punishment'), but while the letters *d* and *r* may be similar in the later

---

[21]The preposition and suffix is 'upon him' (*'âlâv*), and instead of rendering with most English versions 'on them' (NIV, ESV), it is better to retain 'on him'.

Hebrew script, they were not in the earlier scripts. The translation of
the MT as 'the appointed staff' makes good sense. When God's
purpose of judgment comes on Assyria it will be accompanied by festive
music. The divine warrior will display his victorious arm in battle, and
then, as following the victory at the Red Sea (Exod. 15:1-18), songs of
joy will sound as the people rejoice in God's salvation. This same pattern
is to be repeated at the end of history when the redeemed saints will
rejoice over the final divine victories (Rev. 18:20; 19:1-10).

33 The place of judgment has already been prepared. Topheth
was in the valley of Hinnom to the south of Jerusalem (Jer. 7:31-32)
and it was noted as being the place where children were offered to
Molech, the god of the Ammonites. That has brought forth suggestions
that the Hebrew word 'king' in this verse should be altered to 'Molech'
(this only involves a change in vowels). But the Hebrew manuscripts
are uniform in preserving the reading 'king', and also in noting it with
the definite article: '*the* king', that is, the king of Assyria. The place
Topheth becomes symbolic of God's judgment on sin. The word itself
may come from an Aramaic root meaning a fire-place, which would
be a very appropriate description of the wide and deep pit, ready with
plenty of wood and fire to consume all. In particular it is ready for the
Assyrian king, when God kindles the flame by his breath. The language
of course is poetic, but the message is plain. The fate of Assyria and
her king is settled.

5. Woe to Those Relying on Egypt (31:1–32:20)

The second part of the message concerning Egypt commences at this
point. Just as there are two burdens against Babylon (13:1–14:27 and
21:1-10), so there are two woes relating to those trusting in Egypt's
help. This one recapitulates the essential points of the first part, but
moves to a call for repentance (31:6) and focuses more strongly on
the thought of restoration. The city of Jerusalem will be deserted until
the Spirit of God moves, and then it will become the peaceful home
and place of undisturbed rest for renewed people (32:15-20). As with
the first woe, the real enemy in view is Assyria, while the recipients of
the message are those of Judah and Jerusalem.

a. The Folly of Trusting in Egypt (31:1-3)

1 Constantly the covenant people were tempted to rely on human
means to overcome their enemies. Psalm 20 describes those who trust

in chariots and horses in contrast to those who trust in the name of the LORD (20:7), while the people in communal song declare that they do not trust in bow and sword (Ps. 44:4-8). Isaiah renews his message that Egypt is 'Rahab the Do-Nothing' (30:7), from whom no help can be expected. The only source of help is from the LORD, the holy one of Israel.

2 In effect what the people are doing is challenging the wisdom of God. They have already been rebuked for thinking that the clay can dictate to the potter (29:15-16). Now they are reminded that the wise God can bring disaster. The Hebrew says that 'he brings evil' (*râ'*), but the use of 'evil' is the same as in Amos 3:6: 'When disaster comes to a city, has not the LORD caused it?' God has no need of recalling his words, for they fulfil his purpose, not returning empty (55:11). He will move against evildoers and those who give them assistance.

3 A striking contrast is drawn. On the one hand Isaiah speaks of 'God' and 'spirit'; on the other hand, he speaks of 'men' and 'flesh'. This highlights the folly of Judah. They have looked to a merely human substitute for God, and the Egyptian horses are no replacement for the Spirit of God. Hence the message is that political alliances are simply another form of apostasy from the covenant God. When God stretches out his hand (cf. the use of this idiom in 5:25; 9:12, 17, 21; 10:4) judgment will come on both helper and the one helped. This judgment will be both simultaneous and complete (lit. 'and together all of them will disappear').

b. The Lion and His Prey (31:4-5)
4 The use of imagery of a lion to describe God has already occurred (see 15:9; for its use by Isaiah's contemporaries, see Hosea 5:14 and Amos 1:2; 3:8; 5:18-19). Through the prophet, the LORD makes his declaration concerning impending judgment. The lion is roaring as he looks on his prey, a whole band of shepherds called together against him. 'The shepherds' are the foreign rulers, for in the ancient Near East many rulers were referred to as 'shepherds' who 'pastured' their flocks. Whatever clamour they make will not deflect the lion. The LORD of hosts will come down on Mount Zion and its 'heights'. This word (*giv'âh*) is used in the prophetic books to describe blessings flowing from the hills (see 30:25), or, as here, when imminent judgment is being foretold.

5 On several occasions the Old Testament uses the analogy of a

bird sheltering her young to depict God's providential care of his children (see Deut. 32:11; Pss. 17:8; 61:4; 91:4). Now the promise is given that the LORD of hosts himself will protect Jerusalem. He will not only shield it but he will deliver it, passing over it and causing it to escape. The use of the verb 'to pass over' in the same sense as in Exodus 12:13, 23, 27 suggests an allusion to the experience of Israel in Egypt when the LORD 'passed over' the houses of his people when he brought judgment on Egypt.[22] Jesus used the same analogy of sheltering under wings when he grieved over stubborn Jerusalem, which sinfully willed not to come under the protection he offered (Matt. 23:37).

c. A Gracious Invitation (31:6-7)
6-7 Just as Isaiah's contemporary Hosea had encouraged his fellow Israelites to return to the LORD (Hos. 6:1), so now a fresh call for repentance is given: 'Return to the one you have so deeply revolted against, O children of Israel.' Their sin was covenant disobedience. The verb 'to revolt' (*sûr*) is often used in contexts in which breach of the covenant is in view (see Deut. 9:12, 11:16). The reality of repentance will be shown by the rejection of the idols that the people have sinfully made. The word for idols (*'elîlîm*) sounds like the Hebrew word for 'God' (see comments on 2:8). Imitation gods will have no place in worship when the hearts of the people again turn to the LORD.

d. The Certainty of Assyria's Fall (31:8-9)
8 There is no need to look to Egypt for military help for Assyria is not going to be vanquished by human agency. Twice in the verse it is said that the sword that causes the fall of Assyria is not of human origin. The LORD will put Assyria to flight, and her young men as prisoners-of-war will have to submit to all the pain and indignity of forced labour. The people of Judah, oppressed by Assyria, are given the consolation that the young Assyrian warriors who escape death by the sword will be compelled to undergo oppressive captivity. The fulfilment of the prophecy is set out in 37:36-38 (see commentary).

9 The prediction is made that Assyria's fortress (Heb. *sela'*, 'rock') will fall, for attack upon it will cause the Assyrians to panic. The sight of an uplifted banner, as the signal for attack, will bring the realisation that the fall of their city and kingdom is near. 'Rock' is used in the Old

---

[22]I have discussed the Hebrew verb 'to pass over', along with comment on the Passover festival, in *NIDOTTE*, 4, pp. 1043-46.

Testament as the name of an Amorite fortress (Judg. 1:36) and for a place taken by Amaziah (possibly Nabatean Petra, 2 Kings 14:7). Probably Nineveh is meant, which fell in 612 BC to Nabopolassar, who proceeded to consolidate Babylonian rule before finally defeating the Assyrians at Carchemish in 605 BC. The LORD dwells in Zion, and from there the fire of judgment will reach out to Assyria. This is his solemn declaration (*n^e'um yhwh*).

e. A Changed Judah (32:1-8)

While there is a chapter break at this point, the material in chapters 31 and 32 form a single unit. All of this section is part of the 'woe' expressed against those who look to Egypt for help. As with the other 'woes', threat and promise are blended together in a single message. In 32:1-8 a picture is given of an altered Judah coming into existence, with a righteous king and with society as a whole regenerated.

1 Judah is going to have a just ruler. No mention is made of him being from the line of David, so this passage differs from ones like 9:6-7 and 11:1-3. This is not a messianic reference, but a description of a period in Judah's history when government will be exercised with integrity. The king and senior officials will act in accordance with their calling to office, as they display righteousness/justice in their decisions. The renovation of society is to begin at the top, as the leaders' behaviour is patterned on that of God himself who is exalted by justice and displays his holiness by his righteousness (5:16).

2 In the renewed society everyone will reflect the character of God himself. He has been declared to be a refuge and a shelter from the storm, a shade from the heat (25:4). Each of the LORD's redeemed will provide assistance that resembles what God is to those who trust in him. They will be places of refuge, a blessing just like streams in the desert are or the shadow of a great rock is to the weary traveller in a thirsty land. The only uses of the Hebrew word for 'waterless places' (*tsâyôn*) are in 25:5 and this verse, which provides an interpretative clue. Not only will God himself be a place of shelter, but his people will be also.

3-4 Having given the first result of good government, Isaiah spells out in these verses the second result. The spiritual state of the people is going to change. They have been declared to be blind and deaf (29:9, 18), but in days to come they will see and hear aright, a promise that is going to be repeated in 35:5. Spiritual understanding will be restored to them, and their minds will understand deeply. Those who have been unable to speak easily (presumably about spiritual issues) will find that their tongues are loosed and they speak distinctly. Clarity of thought and speech is to be one of God's gifts.

5 This verse is a bridge between the description of the just reign and the contrast drawn between folly and nobility in verses 6-8. The presence of rare words makes the translation and interpretation difficult, though poetic parallelism assists in understanding the intent of verses 5-8. In the new order there will no longer be confusion between the fool (*nâvâl*) and the noble (*nâdîv*). The assonance helps to emphasise the contrast. The parallel expression uses one word that only occurs here (*kîlay*) and another that only occurs twice (*shôaʻ*). Clearly the first is a synonym for 'fool', and the second is a synonym for 'noble' (it parallels *sârîm*, 'princes', in Job 34:19). The point is that ethical distinctions will be made, and the character of people will be clearly distinguished.

6-7 In a series of parallel phrases Isaiah depicts the true nature of the fool. In thought, speech, and actions he is far removed from godliness. He only speaks folly to others, and he practises ungodliness. Even in address to God he speaks arrogantly (translation should reflect the MT text in verse 6b as it says 'to speak *to* the LORD', not about him, as most English versions suggest). The needy he leaves without relief from hunger and thirst, and he plots maliciously against those who are poor and wretched. The language resembles that of the Book of Proverbs, but in the context here in Isaiah it is the leaders of the nation who are being addressed. There are also links with the preceding messages. The expression 'to practise ungodliness' (*la ʻᵃsôt chonef*) recalls the expression for making alliances used in 30:1 (*la ʻᵃsôt ʻêtsâh*). There is a possible play on words too when Isaiah describes the speech to the LORD as being arrogant (*tôʻa*), for this word sounds very like the word he has used for the staggering of drunken prophets in 28:7 (*tâʻû*).

8 No mention is made in verses 6-7 of punishment of the fools, yet the implication is that they are punished, and that nobility of rank in society will ultimately be matched by nobility of character. Noble actions are planned and by them the leaders in society will be characterised. As part of the new order, perversion of justice will be removed, and leaders will be true leaders, with their actions reflecting their innate nobility. Future government of the nation will see leaders with integrity and their governance will be marked by transparency.

f. A Call to Complacent Women (32:9-20)
Isaiah has already confronted the women of Zion in 3:16-26. He has rebuked them for their pride as they display their wealth in the abundance of jewellery that they wear. Now he warns them of impending judgment that is going to leave Jerusalem deserted until a future day when the Spirit will be poured out and God's people will live in quiet resting places (verse 18). The Hebrew word for 'quiet' is the same word that is used in verse 9 to describe the complacency of the women. Isaiah's contemporary Amos also applies the same word to the condition of those who feel secure in Zion (Amos 6:1).

9 The call goes out to the women to listen to the prophet's word as he directs a special message to them. They feel self-satisfied, and are confident that they are secure. The Hebrew word for 'feel secure' is the verb 'to trust' (*bâtach*). It is used ambivalently in the Old Testament. While it often describes true reliance on the LORD, it also, as here, depicts the false hope of those who have found some substitute for him.

10 Amos has already warned the women that they are going to be taken away into exile (Amos 4:1-3). Isaiah says that they only have a little over a year before devastation is going to come on the land. The Hebrew text specifies the time frame as 'days above [or, more than] a year'. While an unusual expression, it appears to denote a time over one year. This may relate to the coming of Sennacherib and his army in 701 BC. The covenant curse will apply, and the people will have an unproductive harvest (see Deut. 28:38-42). Nothing will be left to reap, and this calamity will cause a feeling of security to be replaced with a sense of fear.

11-13 The opening of verse 11 picks up three of the words already used in verses 9-10: 'complacent', 'shudder' and 'feel secure'. This repetition serves to drive home the perilous condition of the women and the calamity that awaits them. They have to prepare by donning mourning clothes and engaging in rituals, such as beating their breasts, that are associated with death. They will lament over the desolation that is coming, with the land ('the land of my people', as Isaiah calls it) being overgrown with thorns and briers (see the similar imagery in 5:6 and 7:23). The city that gave all the appearance of joy and merriment is in reality one to be pitied, and over which lamentation occurs.

14-15 Amos had already spoken of the destruction of the 'palaces' or 'citadels' of Gentile cities (see Amos 1:4, 7, 10, 12, 14), but also predicted the destruction of the citadels of Jerusalem (Amos 2:5) and of Israel (Amos 6:8). 'The city of revelry' (verse 13) is going to become 'the deserted city'. Jerusalem, the defended city, will become a place where donkeys and other animals can wander (see the description of the land after the Assyrian invasion in 7:21-25). The threat, however, is tempered by a promise. When the Spirit is poured out from on high (presumably the Spirit of God is meant) there will be a reversal of existing conditions. The desert will become like garden-land (Heb. *karmel*) while the garden-land will become like a forest. The thought in general is the same as 29:17, and the last three words in the verse are identical in both passages (except that in 29:17 the article is used before *karmel* ('and *the karmel* will be reckoned as forest'). No indication is given of the time when this catastrophic change will take place, though in the context of this whole section the post-exilic restoration seems to be the setting (cf. 29:17).

16-17 These two verses tie in with the opening of the chapter and the reference to just rule in the land. In verse 16 'justice' is paired with 'righteousness', while 'desert' is paired with 'garden-land'. Justice/ righteousness will take up abode in the land, and as a consequence three visible effects will flow in perpetuity—peace, quietness and security. Two different words are used concerning 'righteousness', both denoting the effect or result of work. NIV and other English translations use 'fruit' for the first one, but this is importing an idea foreign to the context and to the usage of the Hebrew word (*ma'aseh*), which is never used elsewhere in this sense. It is better to translate 'the work of righteousness' and 'the effect of righteousness' (NKJV).

18 Isaiah uses one of his favourite expressions once more, as he speaks in God's name. 'My people', he says, will find secure and peaceful dwelling conditions. The word that was used in verse 9 to describe the complacency of the women occurs here in a positive statement to describe undisturbed rest. On the one hand it denotes undisturbed minds or consciences; on the other, it speaks of rest without the presence of anything to disturb it. This is another way of describing the effects of righteousness when the Spirit of God is poured out. The storms of life will be over, and God's people will be in a haven of rest (Ps. 107:29-30).

19-20 The message of verse 19 seems to break in very suddenly. However, the comparison between objects of judgment and mercy has already occurred, and hence verse 19 is to be taken as a reference to Assyria, while verse 20 relates to Judah/Jerusalem. The city is not that of verses 13-14, but Nineveh. By contrast those who live in the renewed land will have crops planted by streams of water (cf. Ps. 1:3), and their cattle and donkeys will be able to graze freely there. The picture is of abundance for both humans and their animals. The descriptive terms used throughout this chapter regarding the blessings for city and land go beyond anything that happened when the return from exile took place. In the light of other biblical teaching, it is best to link it to the effects of Christ's coming and death, and therefore it is to the new Jerusalem that the eye of faith is directed.

6. Woe to an Unnamed Invader (33:1-16)

The final woe is directed not to Jerusalem but to a traitorous opponent, most probably Assyria. In the midst of words speaking of the destruction of the enemy there are embedded prayers by the prophet directed to the LORD (see verses 2-4 and 20). As with the other woe oracles gracious promises are also interspersed, for the LORD is exalted in Zion (verse 5) and as the saviour of his people he is judge, lawgiver and king (verse 22). There are many verbal connections with previous passages in the prophecy.

a. Denunciation of the Destroyer (33:1)

1 Up to this point in time the unnamed enemy has been both destroyer and a treacherous opponent (the Heb. verb used, *bâgad*, denotes faithless dealing with someone), but Assyria has herself managed to escape destruction or betrayal. However, Isaiah now announces that in the future she will herself be subject to destruction, and the type of faithless conduct she exhibited in the past will be practised against her. There is a rhythmic flow in the Hebrew text, with repetition of different forms of the two verbs 'destroy' (*shâdad*) and 'deal faithlessly' (*bâgad*), each occurring four times, while the letter *d* (Heb. *dalet*) occurs eleven times. The music of the words heightens, rather than hides, the message of doom.

b. Prayer to the Exalted LORD (33:2-6)

2 The language of Isaiah bears a strong resemblance to the petitions in the Psalter. He pleads with God to show favour, for the hope of the people is directed towards him ('we wait for you'). In the MT there is a switch in persons from first person ('we') to third person ('their arm'), while the first person occurs again at the end of the verse ('our salvation'). It may just be a stylistic change that some of the early versions try to smooth out by rendering it as 'our arm' (so the LXX, Targum, and Vulgate), or else an early grammatical feature of which little is known.[23] The plea is that God's arm, i.e. his strength, will be manifested morning by morning for the benefit of his covenant people. The parallel phrase asks for his salvation in time of distress.

3-4 The message already given in 30:27-33 is repeated, though in summary fashion. The LORD's voice is able to shatter even powerful nations like Assyria. When he rises up as the warrior ready for battle, nations flee before him. The destruction of Assyria will mean that spoil will be left behind, and it will be gathered just like the way in which some devouring insects (perhaps locusts) seize upon plants or food. The word for 'spoil' (*shâlâl*) recalls its use in the name of Isaiah's second son (see 8:1).

5 The switch from second person address ('O LORD ... your voice ... you rise up') to third person ('he dwells on high') is not unusual in the book of Psalms (see, e.g., Pss. 7, 16, 18, 23, 25). After speaking directly to God, Isaiah now continues in the third person to speak of his God. The language he uses, especially the combination of the verb 'to dwell' (*shâkan*) and the expression 'on high' (*mârôm*), occurs again in 57:15. Though he is such an exalted God, yet he will stoop to visit Zion so that it will be noted for its justice and righteousness. This is repeating in different words the promise that was made in 1:26-27.

6 A glance at various English versions will show that there are different ways of construing the Hebrew words in this verse. The simplest way is to assume that the subject is 'the LORD' as in the previous verse: 'The LORD will be a sure foundation....' The only hindrance to this interpretation is the final word in the verse, 'his treasure', where 'her treasure' (referring to Zion) could have been expected. However, the MT is confirmed by the major scroll of Isaiah found among the Dead Sea Scrolls (1QIsa[a]). It is not impossible, though, to render the final clause: 'the fear of the LORD, that is his

---

[23]The grammatical form is called *enclitic mem*, which simply means the letter *mem* occurs leaning on the previous letter. Its function is unknown, and later Jewish scholars thought it was the plural suffix 'their'. For discussion on the grammar, see J. C. L. Gibson, *Davidson's Introductory Hebrew Grammar–Syntax*, op. cit., pp. 24-25; *IBHS*, pp. 158-60.

treasure', i.e. the treasure that God stores up for his people. There are eight nouns arranged in pairs: 'the sure foundation of your times'; 'the store of salvation'; 'wisdom[24] and knowledge'; 'the fear of the LORD'. The assurance is given that following times of distress (see verse 2), other times will come in which the LORD will provide salvation for his people, with the catalogue of blessings emphasising the abundance of his gifts.

c. Judgment on the Nations (33:7-12)

The prayer appears to end at verse 6, and it is followed by a declaration of judgment on the nations, principally on Assyria. The introductory 'Behold', as so often in biblical Hebrew, marks the commencement of the new section. Verse 8 points to the negotiations with Sennacherib's officials (see 36:2-22). The judgment on Assyria will also be an exaltation of the LORD himself.

7 Attention is called immediately to the men of Judah, though the subject of the verb 'cry aloud' is uncertain. Since it occurs in parallelism with 'messengers of peace', it is presumably a Hebrew word of similar meaning. Hence, a noun such as 'herald' meets the situation.[25] The three men who go out to confer with the Assyrian field commander (see 36:3, 11, 22) certainly fit the description, though the identification cannot be confirmed. Their weeping bitterly could be reflected in 36:22, which says that they went to report to Hezekiah with torn clothes.

8 A consequence of the political situation is that nobody wants to travel, and hence the highways (a favourite word with Isaiah: see 7:3; 11:16; 19:23; 40:3; 49:11; 59:7; 62:10) are deserted. The reason is that the treaty (Heb. *bᵉrît*) has been broken, cities[26] despised, and no one

---

[24]The word for 'wisdom' appears as *chokmat*, which is really the construct form, 'the wisdom of.' It may be a reversion to an old form of the feminine noun, or a deliberate change to avoid having the sounds *mâh vâ* in successive syllables (for other examples, see Isaiah 35:2 and Ezekiel 26:10).

[25]This is the suggestion of E. J. Young, *The Book of Isaiah*, vol. II, pp. 410-11. See also footnote 13 on p. 410 where he discusses the various suggested derivations of the Hebrew word in question.

[26]The MT has 'cities' ('ârîm), but many commentators and translations emend to 'witnesses' ('ēdîm). While 1QIsa[a] has 'witnesses', this by itself is not strong enough evidence to support the alteration. For discussion of further suggested emendations, see Paul Kalluveettil, *Declaration and Covenant*, op. cit., pp. 30-31.

reckons human life highly. The language reflects the technical terms for breach of treaty, and points to Sennacherib's actions in accepting the tribute he demanded for leaving Jerusalem untouched, but then going back on his word and proceeding to besiege it.

9 The devastation caused by the Assyrian invasion is widespread, and places are mentioned that depict the whole land: north (Lebanon), west (Sharon and Carmel), east (Bashan) and south (the Arabah). With the exception of the Arabah all the other places are noted for their vegetation, but what has happened is that they have all become desert like the Arabah. Invasion has ruined the whole country.

10 The LORD is going to be exalted through his judgments. They will display his sovereignty over men and nature as he visits Assyria with the threatened punishment and Zion with salvation (see the previous descriptions in 29:5 and 31:4-5). The declaration is made using three verbs, with the thrice repeated 'Now'. This use of 'now' is emphatic, and as elsewhere it comes in a passage speaking of the imminent actions of the LORD in judgment and blessing. The first verb 'I will arise' (*qûm*) is common in the Psalms, when God is asked to act for his people or against his enemies. The second verb (*rûm*) is used of God's throne (Isa. 6:1) and of God himself (30:18), while the third one (*nâsâ'*) is applied to the LORD's temple (2:2) and to his throne (6:1).[27]

11-12 Not only does the LORD speak of his own exaltation but he defiantly confronts the enemies with the accusation that all their plotting is useless. There is no substance in what they plan, for it will turn out to be like chaff or straw, while any fire they kindle will turn back on themselves and they will be consumed. They will be completely burnt to lime. Amos 2:1 gives the clue to the meaning for it is said there that Moab burned the bones of the king of Edom to lime, and, as the Targum interprets it, this was so that it could then be used for building purposes. Here the meaning is clearly that the burning was complete, and that the fire raged as if the fuel was dry thornbush.

d. The Promise of a New City (33:13-24)

The final message of the sections containing the 'Woes' is a promise of blessing. While sinners will be punished, the righteous will see the king in his beauty and the renewed Jerusalem, a peaceful city. No one

---

[27]Two of these verbs (*rûm* and *nâsâ'*) are also used in the description of the exaltation of the servant of the LORD in Isaiah 52:13.

can stand before the consuming fire (verse 14), but forgiveness will
come from the LORD (verse 24).

13-14 The LORD speaks through his servant Isaiah, calling on all,
whether near at hand or far away, to listen to what he has done and to
know for themselves his power.[28] The sinners in Zion tremble before
the certainty of coming judgment, and their dismay is mirrored in their
questions: 'Who of us can dwell with the consuming fire? Who of us
can dwell with everlasting burning?' (NIV) The word for 'burning'
(*môqêd*) only occurs here and in Psalm 102:3, but the parallel
'consuming fire' shows that the meaning must be synonymous with it.
There is also a related noun (*môqᵉdâh*) that describes the place where
the burnt offering was kept (Lev. 6:9). The questions appear to be
modelled on those in Psalms 15:1 and 24:3, with the language closest
to Psalm 15:1 since the two verbs there (*gûr*, 'to sojourn', and *shâkan*,
'to dwell') both appear in this context (verses 14 and 16). The solemn
inquiry by the sinners receives an explicit answer, with mention of six
characteristics: righteous walk, upright speech, no extortion, no bribes,
no participation in plotting murder, rejection of planned evil deeds. There
is a general similarity to the answers in Psalm 15:2-3 and Psalm 24:4.
Only those who have these characteristics will escape divine judgment.
The general principle that character determines destiny is reinforced
in the New Testament (Matt. 7:21-23), with James insisting that faith
without works is dead (Jas. 2:14-26). Works are simply the fruits of
godly character.

16 Whoever lives according to the will of God lives in the love of
God, and will know his protective power. He will have his abode in the
safe places ('the heights', 'the fortress of rocks'), and his food and
water will be supplied. There is clear reflection here on what has
already been said about God in verse 5. Just as God is exalted and
dwells on high, so he who trusts in him will also dwell on high. The
believer finds his security in God alone, and is thus free from the anguish
that sinners feel when confronted with divine judgment.

17 The reference to the king has been interpreted by many
commentators to be either the Davidic king or the Messiah. But in the
context the LORD has been spoken of in verse 5 as the exalted one,

---

[28]The manuscript 1QIsa[a] makes both verbs in this verse indicatives instead
of imperatives: 'they hear ... they know', but no other evidence exists for this
alteration.

while in verse 22 the explicit statement occurs that he is 'our king'. Nothing in the passage refers to the Davidic line. Hence it is God himself who is in view, and the verb 'see' can indicate spiritual perception (cf. Job 23:9; Pss. 46:8; 63:2; Isa. 26:11). Nowhere else is the adjective 'beauty' applied to God. The vision will also be of Judah as a land expanded again in size (cf. 26:15) to make up for all the diminution caused by successive invasions.

18-19 At the time the LORD is seen, the people will recall the things that previously caused them terror – the chief Assyrian official, the financial officer in charge of raising revenue, and the officer in charge of the fortifications. These officials represent the detestable features of Assyrian control. A day is coming when arrogant Assyria will no longer hold sway over Judah, and the covenant curse of invasion by a people whose language they did not understand (Deut. 28:49) will be reversed. Hearing the Assyrian language of their captors around all day long was a constant reminder to the people of God's displeasure against them. Now the promise is given to them that they 'will not see [any longer]' the Assyrians nor hear their 'obscure speech, with their strange, incomprehensible tongue' (NIV).[29]

20 The final verses of this last 'woe' oracle form a fitting conclusion to the whole of chapters 28–33. There are certain things that those in Judah are to see, and along with the vision they will have of God himself (verse 17) they will also see a new Jerusalem. This idea is developed more fully in Isaiah chapters 65–66 and ultimately in Revelation 21–22. The alternation of threat and promise ends with the picture of a forgiven people living in an enduring city. Zion/Jerusalem is described by use of the language relating to the tabernacle. She will be the abiding dwelling of God, a new 'tent' that will never need to be moved. This is the city where meeting with God will never end. The language of 'the tent of meeting' borrowed here (Heb. *'ôhel mô'êd*) suggests an appointed meeting, a tryst (to use an old English word in the absence of any good modern equivalent).

21-22 The best news of all is that the LORD himself is going to be 'there' (Heb. *shâm*), that is, in the new Jerusalem. The language is echoed in Ezekiel's name for it, *yhwh shâmmâh*, 'the LORD is there'

---

[29]This is an excellent example of good translation by the NIV. A very literal translation of the verse is: 'a people of deepness of lip from hearing, of a stammering tongue there is no understanding.'

(Ezek. 48:35). He will appear as 'the mighty one' (*'addîr*), an epithet that can be applied both to God and non-divine persons or things. In this very context God is contrasted with the mighty ships (verse 21b). Jeremiah applies the same term to the one who shall rule over restored Israel (Jer. 30:21). He will also be the judge, lawgiver, and king of his people as announced in three identical phrases in verse 22. The occurrence four times in two verses of the divine name, 'the LORD' (*yhwh*), both emphasises the nature of God and ties in with the assertion that 'it is he who will save us'. The saviour is indeed the covenant lord and redeemer of his people, and without him the people would be helpless. Broad rivers and canals will surround Jerusalem, yet no large ships, whether for defence or attack, will sail on them.

23 The idea of shipping is carried further, with Jerusalem of Isaiah's day likened to a ship whose rigging, mast, and sail are not ready for action. Presumably the picture is of Jerusalem unprepared for any battle with Assyria. However, in the future there will be an abundance of goods to be distributed, plentiful spoil to be shared (cf. comment on verse 4 where *shâlâl* has already appeared). Even the physically handicapped will find it easy to pick up and carry off what they want. The introductory word 'then' (*'az*) quite often as here marks a future event (cf. its use in Isa. 35:5; 60:5).

24 At that time further changes will be apparent. Illness will be for ever banished, with no one saying, 'I am sick'. Moreover, all (Heb. *'âm hayyoshêv bâh*, 'the people who live in it') will as a unity experience forgiveness of sin. The use of the expression 'people' seems deliberate in order to stress the collective aspect. Those in the renewed Jerusalem will indeed be God's people, and complete absence of sin will characterise them. The book of Revelation amplifies the description. No mourning, crying or pain will characterise life in the heavenly Jerusalem, and nothing sinful will intrude into the relationship between God and his people (Rev. 21:3-4, 27).

> His gracious hand shall wipe the tears
> from every weeping eye:
> And pains and groans, and griefs and fears,
> and death itself, shall die.　　(Scottish Paraphrase 67:5)

H. Additional Promises of Judgment and Blessing (34:1-35:10)

These chapters stand in a similar relationship to chapters 28–33 as chapters 24–27 do to chapters 13–23. In both cases they form a conclusion and carry the overtones of both judgment and blessing from the preceding chapters. In chapters 24–27 Moab is singled out as an illustration of divine judgment on the nations, while in chapters 34–35 it is Edom who is cited as the object of God's displeasure. Both sections deal with the overthrow of oppressors and Zion's restoration, and there are also linguistic links between them.

Burdens against the Nations
(chapters 13–23)

↘

Judgment (Moab) and Blessing
(chapters 24–27)

'Woe' Oracles against the Nations
(chapters 28–33)

↘

Judgment (Edom) and Blessing
(chapters 34–35)

The language of chapter 34 in particular has many similarities to the rest of the book of Isaiah.[1] Moreover, it seems certain that Jeremiah not only knew and used words from other eighth century BC prophets such as Hosea, Amos, and Micah, but he knew and utilised Isaiah's words as well. This applies specifically to his use of Isaiah 34.[2]

The text of the major Dead Sea Scroll of Isaiah (1QIsa[a]) is very close to the MT, but it does have one surprising feature. There is a gap of three lines between chapters 33 and 34. No fully satisfactory explanation has been given for this feature. To contain the whole of Isaiah on a papyrus scroll must have been difficult, and this gap may be linked to a practice of breaking it into two scrolls at this point.

---

[1]For a discussion of these, see E. J. Young, 'Isaiah 34 and Its Position in the Prophecy,' *WTJ* 27, 2 (May, 1965), pp. 110-14.

[2]ibid., pp. 105-10.

1. World Judgment (34:1-4)

In this section no one nation is singled out for judgment. Rather, the message is one of universal judgment on the nations.

1 Elsewhere in Isaiah the nations are challenged to come and present their case before a divine court (cf. 41:1; 45:20). Here, however, the case is already settled, and the nations are summoned to come and hear the LORD's sentence pronounced. Four terms ('nations', 'peoples', 'earth', and 'world') are used to describe total humanity. As in Psalm 24:1 the fullness of the earth means those who live in it, and likewise 'all that comes out of the world' will also be a reference to humans.

2 The nations are the object of God's wrath, and none of them can exclude themselves from his judgment. Wrath is expressed 'against all the nations', 'against all their host'. In fact, they are dedicated for destruction. The verb used (Heb. *châram*) is employed in Deuteronomy for the destruction of the Canaanites, who were under a 'ban' or 'curse'.[3] Here the 'ban' is said to extend to all nations, a concept stressed by the parallel expression, 'he appointed them for slaughter.'

3-4 While the expression 'the day of the LORD' is not used, Isaiah

---

[3]I have discussed this concept in my commentary, *Deuteronomy: The Commands of a Covenant God*, op. cit., pp. 46-47, 97-98. The following is an extract from my comments on pages 97-98: 'The Hebrew verb *charam* (Hif.) means 'to devote to the ban', or 'to dedicate to destruction', while the noun *cherem* refers to what is 'dedicated to destruction', or 'placed under a curse'.... The application of the principle of the *cherem* has to be seen as foreshadowing the ultimate judgement of God. The banning or cursing was not just a verbal action, but it involved the handing over of someone or something so that they were at the exclusive disposal of God. What was banned belonged henceforth to God alone. Achan was to find out how serious his sin was in keeping back what was *cherem* for his own use (Josh. 7:1-26) and Israel never forgot his sin, as mention in the post-exilic genealogies shows (1 Chron. 2:7 where *Achan* is called *Achar*. The reference is clear however as he is called 'The son of Carmi ... the troubler of Israel, who transgressed in the accursed thing'). The destruction of the Canaanites was an intrusion of God's judgement into Israel's history and it shows the same pattern of separation that will take place when God irrevocably separates believers and unbelievers. The judgements of hell are really the principle of the curse come to full and final manifestation. God had appointed his rule over Israel (the theocracy) as a divinely appointed symbol of the ultimate kingdom of God. Hence in the period of the theocracy there is an intrusion of the ethical pattern that will prevail at the final judgement.'

speaks in eschatological language. He describes cataclysmic events
that will involve all nations. Dead bodies will lie unburied, defiling the
earth by their blood and smell. The stars will dwindle away, and the
sky will disappear just like a scroll being rolled up. The language is
taken up in the New Testament in descriptions of the coming of the
Son of Man in power (cf. Matt. 24:27-30; Rev. 6:12-14).

2. The Destruction of Edom (34:5-15)

Just as Moab is singled out in the appendix to the burdens against the
nations (25:10-12), so here Edom is singled out as an illustration of
nations in revolt against God. The Edomites were the descendants of
Esau, and there is a progressive hostility to them marked out in the Old
Testament until Malachi, the last of the canonical prophets, speaks of
them as 'a people always under the wrath of the LORD' (Mal. 1:4).[4]
The Edomites rejoiced in the destruction of Jerusalem in 586 BC (Lam.
4:21; Ps. 137:7), wanting the city to be razed to the ground.

5-7 Graphic language, borrowed from descriptions of warfare in
the ancient Near East, depicts the slaughter that will eventuate. Edom
will be put to the sword as the curse is inflicted on her (in verse 5 the
noun *chêrem*, not the verb as in verse 3, is used). The sword of
vengeance will descend on Edom and there will be a great sacrifice.
The same type of language is used in Jeremiah 46:10; 50:27; and Ezekiel
39:17-19 to describe great battles, while in Revelation 19:11-21 the
work of the faithful and true witness is to wage war with the sword.
Isaiah mentions Bozrah, an important Edomite settlement probably to
be identified with the modern Buseirah, about 60 kilometres [37 miles]
north of Petra.[5] Bozrah may have been a gathering place for Edomite
warriors as they set out on campaigns of pillage and carnage. The
warriors who fall by the sword are called 'wild oxen', 'young bulls',
and 'mighty bulls' in verse 7. Their death means that their blood and
fat are soaked up by the dry ground.[6]

8 Isaiah announces that the LORD has appointed 'a day of
vengeance' for Edom (cf. 63:4 where the same expression [*yôm*

---

[4]See ibid., pp. 40-42 for further discussion on the Edomites.

[5]With reference to Edom, see also the commentary on 63:1.

[6]The verb used (*râvâh* Pi.) is rare, and it is only in 34:5 and 7 that it occurs
with the meaning 'satiated'. Elsewhere Isaiah uses it three times in the sense
of 'to give to drink' (16:9; 43:24; 55:10).

nâqâm] occurs). In the Old Testament the concept of vengeance has a much more positive connotation than our English word would suggest. It has to do with lawfulness and justice. This is also suggested here since it is accompanied by the expression, 'a year of retribution for Zion's cause.' 'Retribution' (only occurring here and in Hosea 9:7 and Micah 7:3) has the idea of reward, and so vengeance has not only to do with Edom's punishment but also with Zion's blessing.

9-10a Fire is often used as a symbol of judgment. The geographic proximity of Edom to Sodom and Gomorrah may well have suggested the imagery of a judgment identical to that visited upon those cities (Gen. 19:24-25; the word 'sulphur' [*gofrît*] is used in both passages, and it has been used by Isaiah in 30:33). All of Edom—streams, dust, land—will come under fiery judgment that no one can quench.

10b-11 The permanent desolation of Edom will be the result of this judgment. The same message is conveyed in Jeremiah 49:17-18 and Malachi 1:2-3. What was once a prosperous land will become a desert. No one will wander over it. Only desert birds, such as the various owls and the raven, will find a home there. The second part of verse 11 contains a striking metaphor. Whereas normally a plumb line was used for building, it will now become an instrument associated with destruction. The result will mean that Edom is just like the state of creation mentioned in Genesis 1:2— 'without form and void' (here 'a plumb line of chaos and stones of void' [NASB]).

12 Difficulty in translating this verse goes back as far as the LXX and the Targums. If we start with the second part of the verse, the declaration is made that there will be no princes (*sârîm*) left in Edom. The opening word in the verse (*chorîm*) is used elsewhere of persons in positions of leadership and authority (cf. 1 Kings 21:8, 11; Jer. 39:6), and so these two words are synonymous. The following words say that there is no kingship (or possibly 'king') that they proclaim. This makes sense. If the nobles in Edom either participated in an election of the king, or else proclaimed it, their total disappearance from the land would mean that the Edomite monarchy was at an end.[7] The land will become a desert, and all the people, including all the nobility, will be gone.

---

[7] Two older commentators who come substantially to this position are F. Delitzsch, *Commentary on Isaiah* (Grand Rapids: Eerdmans, reprinted 1975), vol. 2, p. 72; and G. C. M. Douglas, *Isaiah One and His Book One*, op. cit., p. 279 n. 1.

13-15 The general picture is going to be one of complete devastation. Where there once was fortifications with watchmen on the walls, weeds are going to grow all over them, with birds and animals making their home in them. They will become resting places for wild animals, and birds will be able to have their nests there, knowing that they are safe from human disturbance. All that moves around the area are scavengers.[8]

c. Appeal to the Written Word (34:16-17)
16-17 Isaiah instructs his hearers/readers to search the LORD's scroll, and see what is written in it. In the context this cannot be anything else but a reference to what Isaiah himself has just written. Those who witness the destruction of Edom will be able to look at what Isaiah penned. He claims, 'for [by] my mouth he [the LORD] commanded [it].'[9] Isaiah is not the only Old Testament speaker to identify his own words with the words of God (some examples are found in 2 Samuel 7:14-16; 1 Kings 20:13, 42; 2 Chronicles 12:5). Indeed, all the birds will gather just as predicted, with none missing (note the repetition of 'each with her mate' from verse 15). This gathering is to be a work of God's spirit (or breath). Just as the allocation of territory to the tribes of Israel when they occupied the land of Canaan was a divine appointment, so also will be the territorial apportionment to the birds and animals. God is sovereign even over kingdoms like Edom and it will be a perpetual desolation. The verb, 'they will possess it,' is repeated from verse 11, while the time markers ('forever', 'from generation to generation') have been used already in verse 10.

---

[8]For a discussion on the problems of identifying animals and birds like those in this passage, and with a full listing of names, see Burton Goddard, 'Animals of the Bible,' *The Encyclopedia of Christianity* (Wilmington: National Foundation for Christian Education, 1964), vol. 1, pp. 219-49. One of the words in verse 14 is an *hapax legomenon*. This particular word (*lîlît*) may designate a bat or an owl that could have been an object of worship, though there is no mention of that in this context.

[9]This translation follows the MT, but early versions (LXX and Targum) suggest a reading 'his mouth', such as found in 1QIsa[a] (*pîhû* instead of *pî*). Some Hebrew manuscripts have 'the mouth of the LORD' (*pî yhwh*). While *pî* can be either 'my mouth' or 'the mouth of,' this alteration has all the hallmarks of an emendation to solve a difficulty.

d. Future Blessing for the Restored Exiles (35:1-10)

Whereas in chapter 34 a fruitful land is being turned into a wilderness, the reverse is pictured in chapter 35. In this way it parallels chapters 10 and 11. The desert is to become a fine, watered land, with prolific vegetation such as grass, reeds, and flowers. A road will lead to Zion, and on it all the redeemed will come with joyful singing. Many of the themes in this chapter have occurred earlier, and they will again feature in later chapters. This is part of Isaiah's technique as a theme receives progressive particularisation.

1-2 The contrast is very marked. What was once parched land will (metaphorically) rejoice as it is enabled to bring forth flowers like the crocus. The element of joy is emphasised by the use of several synonyms: 'be glad', 'rejoice', 'rejoice greatly', 'shout for joy'. The opening word 'they will be glad' has a suffix attached to it (third masc. pl.) that appears to be the indirect object of the verb: 'the desert and the parched land will be glad *for them.*'[10] It provides a link to bind chapters 34 and 35 together, thus bringing God's judgment and blessing into a close relationship. 'Them' has to refer to those who inhabit the wilderness. The renewed land will share in the glory of Lebanon, Carmel and Sharon. All three were noted for their fruitfulness, and have been linked together already in 33:9. They (the desert and the parched land of verse 1) will see this manifestation of the LORD's glory, a demonstration of his royal splendour.

3-4 Words are now addressed to those with weak hands and feeble knees, the symptoms of fading hope and unfulfilled longing. The command is to 'strengthen' the hands and 'make strong' the knees. Both of these verbs occur in Moses' charge to the people as a whole and to Joshua (Deut. 31:6-7; Jos. 1:6-7, 9, 18). The expression 'be strong and courageous' appears to have been a standardised one, for it is also used for Solomon (1 Chron. 22:13; 28:20) and for Hezekiah's military leaders (2 Chron. 32:7). Likewise the linking of the instruction 'do not fear' with these other verbs also appears in these other passages. What the people needed to know is that their God is indeed coming. He will come as a saviour, but this will also involve vengeance and retribution. The concept has already been brought to the fore in 34:8, but now the reassertion of redemptive judgment stresses both sides of

---

[10]Many commentators and translations (including NIV, REB) think the suffix should be deleted, but it occurs in the oldest manuscript available (1QIsa[a]).

God's coming—judgment on his enemies, but salvation for those whose hope is in him.

5-7 The result of the LORD's coming will be evidenced by physical healings and changes to the natural environment. That these verses continue on from the previous verses is marked by the word 'then' at the commencement of verses 5 and 6, and the phrase 'and the hot sand will be...' at the opening of verse 7. There is, of course, a marked contrast between what Isaiah says here and the message concerning his own ministry in his original commission (see 6:9-10). The world will become a new Eden, with all physical infirmities such as blindness, deafness, crippling disease and dumbness gone. In addition, the wilderness areas will suddenly have abundant water supplies, and the dry dens of the jackals will be changed into flourishing vegetation such as grass, reeds, and papyrus. Jesus takes up these words along with Isaiah 61:1 when he sends word back to John the Baptist (Matt. 11:2-4; Luke 7:18-23). His healing ministry pointed to his messiahship, and the breaking into time of his kingdom. But that ministry did not exhaust the prophetic word concerning eschatological days. It merely foreshadowed the even greater changes to take place at the end of time.

8-10 The theme of a highway for the redeemed has featured earlier in Isaiah's presentation of his message (see 2:3-5; 11:16). The MT says that there 'will be a highway and a way'. While 'and a way' may be an addition to the text, either to explain the rare word 'highway' or a scribe's writing the phrase twice instead of once, yet it is not totally out of place in this poetic description.[11] Four important facts about 'the way' are stated. First, it is 'the way of holiness', so-called because it leads to him who is the Holy One of Israel. Because it is so characterised it is not available to 'the unclean' and 'the foolish'. The first of these terms is borrowed from Mosaic law, and it describes the person who is ritually unclean. The second term is from the wisdom literature and it depicts the person who does not have spiritual understanding and hence goes astray morally. Secondly, it is specifically stated that this highway is 'for those who walk [the] way'. This points

---

[11]The word for 'highway', *maslûl*, only occurs here, but it is related to the more common word $m^e sillah$. The words 'and a way' are missing in 1QIsa^a, but this could be due to an attempt to correct a supposed doubling of the phrase.

to the fact that the way of holiness takes its character from those who use it, a fact emphasised by the terms 'ransomed' and 'redeemed'. It is for them and them alone. Thirdly, the normal dangers to pilgrims, such as attacks by wild animals, will be gone (cf. the contrast with what is said about Edom in 34:13-14). Fourthly, the pilgrimage to Zion will be intensely joyful. 'Sorrow and sighing' will disappear, and in their place will be 'singing' (*rinnâh*), 'everlasting joy' (*simchat 'ôlâm*), 'exultation' (*sâsôn*) and 'joy' (*simchâh*). The heaping up of descriptive terms for rejoicing highlights the festive joy that will accompany the return to Zion (cf. also 52:8-9). Redemption can be depicted in its various phases—return from exile in Babylon, the coming of Jesus as the Messiah, and his ultimate return when he comes a second time to bring salvation to those who wait for him (Heb. 9:28). Here, as elsewhere in Isaiah, these various 'comings' are coalesced into a descriptive passage.

Part 2

Historical Transition
(36:1–39:8)

After the descriptions of the future in the previous chapters, this new section of the prophecy brings the reader back to the reality of the days in which Isaiah lived.[1] They were crisis days, and this is portrayed vividly. Several factors should be mentioned concerning these chapters.

1. Chapters 36–39 of Isaiah have as their parallels 2 Kings 18–20 and to a lesser extent 2 Chronicles 32. While it is impossible to conclude definitively whether the accounts are original to Isaiah or to the writer of 2 Kings, yet preference should go to the view that takes Isaiah's account as the original one.[2] He was conversant with Hezekiah's reign, for the Chronicler records that 'the acts of Hezekiah and his deeds of devotion... are written in the vision of Isaiah the prophet' (2 Chron. 32:32; cf. how close the last phrase is to Isa. 1:1).

The parallels can be set out as follows:

Isaiah		2 Kings	2 Chron.
36:1	Sennacherib invades	18:13	32:1
36:2-10	Sennacherib's message	18:17-25	32:9-15
36:11-12	The request regarding language	18:26-27	————
36:13-20	Sennacherib's message continued	18:27-35	32:16-19
36:21-22	Report to Hezekiah	18:36-37	————
37:1-7	The LORD's message to Hezekiah	19:1-7	————
37:8-13	A renewed call from Sennacherib	19:8-13	————
37:14-20	Hezekiah's prayer	19:14-19	32:20
37:21-35	Senncherib's downfall predicted	19:20-34	————
37:36-37	The Assyrian withdrawal	19:35-36	32:21a
37:38	Sennacherib's death	19:37	32:21b
38:1-7	Hezekiah's illness	20:1-6	————
38:8-20	Hezekiah's prayer of thanksgiving	————	————
38:21-22	Hezekiah's desire for the temple	20:7-8	————
39:1-8	The Babylonian messengers	20:12-19	————

---

[1] I am indebted to the work of my successor at the Presbyterian Theological College, Melbourne, Dr. Gregory Goswell, for his fine study of these chapters in his doctoral dissertation, *'For Mine Eyes Have Seen the King': Kingship, Human and Divine in the Book of Isaiah with Special Reference to Isaiah Chapters 36-39*, pp. 111-336.

[2] See the extensive discussion by E. J. Young, *The Book of Isaiah*, vol. II, Appendix I, pp. 556-65, and also the summary assessment by J. A. Motyer, *The Prophecy of Isaiah*, pp. 285-86.

The Chronicler's account, though heavily dependent on 2 Kings, is much abbreviated. Both the account of the Assyrian invasion and the story of Hezekiah's illness are condensed, but much greater attention is paid to matters relating to Hezekiah's reforms.[3]

2. Many complicated factors impinge on the interpretation of these chapters, including the external evidence. Questions have been raised as to whether Sennacherib attacked Jerusalem once or twice. Reconciliation of the dating of events in Hezekiah's reign is also difficult. In this commentary attention is focused on Isaiah's record, with footnoted reference to other discussions that take up the wider questions.[4]

3. The account in 2 Kings 18:13-15 tells how, after the capture of 'all the fortified cities of Judah', Hezekiah sent a message to Sennacherib at Lachish. He confessed his wrong and offered to pay whatever was demanded of him. Sennacherib pressed his attack on Jerusalem, but before the tribute was paid God intervened, and after the death of 185,000 Assyrians, Sennacherib withdrew and returned to Nineveh (Isa. 37:36-37). Hezekiah had still to comply with Sennacherib's demands and the tribute (according to the Assyrian records) was sent after him to Nineveh.[5]

4. Though chapters 36 and 37 precede chapters 38 and 39, yet chronologically the events recorded in them took place later. This is clear from 38:6, where God promises fifteen more years to Hezekiah along with the assurance that he will deliver him and Jerusalem from the Assyrians. Other parts of the Old Testament show the same thematic presentation (cf. the account of David's victories in 2 Samuel 8 that chronologically fit between 2 Samuel 5 and 6).

---

[3]A summary of the differences are set out by Richard Pratt, *1 and 2 Chronicles* (Fearn: Christian Focus Publications, 1998), pp. 416-18.

[4]See the discussion of the difficulties by E. J. Young, *The Book of Isaiah*, op. cit., vol. II, Appendix I, pp. 540-55.

[5]What Sennacherib wrote was: 'I fixed upon him [Hezekiah] an increase in the amount to be given as *katre-* presents for my lordship, in addition to the former tribute, to be given annually. As for Hezekiah together with [various additional amounts are named] he sent me later to Nineveh, my lordly city. He sent a personal messenger to deliver the tribute and make a slavish obeisance.' See *DOTT*, p. 67. For the interpretation offered here and other aspects of Sennacherib's attack, see A. R. Millard, 'Sennacherib's Attack on Hezekiah,' *TB* 36 (1985), pp. 61-77.

5. Theological concerns lie behind the insertion of these chapters at this point in the prophecy. First, these chapters provide a fitting culmination to chapters 1–36, especially the role of Assyria in relation to Judah. All the might of Assyria cannot stand against the Angel of the LORD. Secondly, the vulnerability of Hezekiah to attack by the Assyrians and to illness is in the forefront. In both cases he is 'saved' by the LORD, and commits himself to praising him in the palace of the divine king (38:20). The final verse of chapter 39 points to a commitment by Hezekiah to the peace (*shâlôm*) and security (*'emet*) that come only from the LORD. Not surprisingly the remainder of the book shifts attention from human kingship to divine kingship.

6. These chapters are mainly in prose. The poetical sections in them (and in the parallels in 2 Kings) consist of the LORD's message for Sennacherib and Hezekiah (37:22-35) and of Hezekiah's thanksgiving hymn as he anticipates his recovery from illness (38:10-20).

A. The Assyrian Siege of Jerusalem (36:1–37:38)

1. Hezekiah: 'A Bird in a Cage' (36:1)

1 Two royal figures, Hezekiah and Sennacherib, confront one another. The time is the fourteenth year of Hezekiah's reign (701 BC). Assyrian records provide external evidence covering this period. What we have here is a summary statement. Sennacherib conquered many fortified settlements in Judah, and then proceeded to Jerusalem. He claimed to have captured 200,150 people and 46 towns, while Hezekiah was 'made a prisoner in Jerusalem, his royal residence, like a bird in a cage'.[6] Isaiah omits the account given in 2 Kings 18:13-16 of Hezekiah's acknowledgment to Sennacherib of his wrongdoing and the payment of a large tribute of gold and silver.

2. The Message for Hezekiah (36:2-22)

2 The Assyrians had come down the coastal route, and among the settlements taken was the important city of Lachish (about 30 miles [48 km] south-west of Jerusalem). From there Sennacherib sent a delegation of high-ranking officers to deliver a message to King Hezekiah (Isaiah only mentions one officer, but 2 Kings 18:17 notes

---

[6]J. B. Pritchard, ed., *The Ancient Near East, vol. 1: An Anthology of Texts and Pictures* (Princeton: Princeton University Press, 1973), p. 200.

that three came). To press home the message, a large army accompanied them. The leader of the delegation is Rabshakeh, a technical term from Akkadian meaning 'chief cupbearer', and designating a senior civil official such as a governor. Hence it should not be translated in English by military terms such as 'commander' (NIV).[7] He came as far as 'the aqueduct of the Upper Pool on the road to the Washerman's Field'. This was exactly the location where Ahaz earlier had been warned by Isaiah to put his trust in the LORD (see Isa. 7:1-17).

3 Three officials from the Judean royal court come out to meet Rabshakeh. Two of them, Eliakim and Shebna have already featured in 22:15-25 (see commentary). Shebna apparently was demoted from being 'over the house' (22:15) to the post of secretary, his original office now being in the hands of Eliakim. These men are given their official titles again in verse 22.

4 Rabshakeh commences his speech on behalf of Sennacherib, and several things are notable about it. The style, while in keeping with contemporary Near Eastern conventions in relation to messages to rebellious vassals, also has the format that the Old Testament prophets use: 'Thus says ....' The confrontation is between the LORD and Sennacherib. Here, and in several other places in the speech, there is overt use of prophetic language. It is a false prophet who speaks in the name of 'the great king, the king of Assyria'. The title 'great king' was frequently claimed by the Assyrian kings.[8] The message for Hezekiah concerns where his trust is placed, a theme that lies at the very heart of this speech.[9] It is also phrased in the second person singular throughout, and thus it is addressed personally to Hezekiah.

---

[7]H. Tadmor, *'Rab-saris* or *Rab-shakeh* in 2 Kings 18'*, in C. L. Meyers and M. O'Connor (eds.), *The Word of the Lord Shall Go Forth: Essays in Honor of D. N. Freedman* (Winona Lake: Eisenbrauns, 1983), pp. 279-85. I simply use the title 'Rabshakeh' throughout the commentary on chapters 36–39, as the MT treats it like a name, not using the preformative article with it.

[8]The title is also applied to God in the Old Testament. See Psalms 47:2; 48:2; 95:3; and Malachi 1:14.

[9]The Hebrew verb 'to trust' (*bâtach*) occurs six times in verses 4-10, along with the derived noun 'object of trust' (*bittâchôn*). It also occurs in verse 14 where Rabshakeh tells the people of Jerusalem not to let Hezekiah persuade them to put their trust in the LORD.

5-6 Rabshakeh's aim is to show how foolish it is for Hezekiah to trust in his own military might (verses 5-6), or to trust in the LORD (verse 7). Clearly Hezekiah had been under pressure to conclude an alliance with Egypt (see 20:5; 30:1-2). In rebelling against Sennacherib (the verb 'rebel' [*mârad*] is one of the technical terms for breach of treaty obligations) and depending on Egypt, Hezekiah is putting his confidence in a splintered staff. That reed will not hold his weight, but will splinter and cause him injury. The king should have known that the only dependable staff for himself and his country is the LORD (see Ps. 23:5 where the same word 'staff' is used). Ezekiel later uses the same illustration in reference to Egypt being a splintered staff to Judah (Ezek. 29:6-7).

7 The second object of false trust (according to Sennacherib) is reliance on the LORD. What Rabshakeh does is to give a purported quote from Hezekiah ('we trust in the LORD our God'), and set over against this the fact that Hezekiah had destroyed false altars and said to Judah and Jerusalem: 'You must worship before this altar.' The biblical record itself testifies to Hezekiah's actions in smashing the false objects of worship and even the altars (2 Kings 18:4; 2 Chron. 31:1). Archaeological finds have provided evidence of this altar destruction.[10] Rabshakeh is suggesting that Hezekiah is completely insincere as his actions show, and he may also be reflecting knowledge that many in Judah may well have disliked his spiritual reforms (2 Kings 18:3-6; 2 Chron. 29:1–31:21).

8 A new phase in Rabshakeh's approach is indicated by the opening words 'and now' (Heb. *v^e 'attâh*) that often mark another stage in an argument, though with continuity of subject matter.[11] The pattern of verses 5-7 is repeated in verses 8-10 in that reference to military power, Egypt, and God follow in the same order. The new stage in the argument is to accept a wager: 'Please negotiate.' The verb (*'ârav*) often in its basic form has the meaning of taking a pledge, but here and in the parallel in 2 Kings 18:23 it is used in another form (the Hitpael) in the sense of entering into a bargain. It is also followed by the small Hebrew word *nâ'*, which can show that what follows is the logical outcome of what has preceded.[12] Using psychological warfare Rabshakeh proposes

---

[10]See especially Y. Aharoni, 'The Horned Altar of Beer-sheba', *Biblical Archaeologist* 73 (1974), p. 6.

[11]Cf. the way that *v^e 'attâh* is used in Isaiah 5:3-5.

giving Hezekiah 2,000 horses if he can provide riders for them. It may not have only been the number of possible riders that is in question but the absence of experienced horsemen, for Israel and Judah rarely employed cavalry.

9 The challenge goes further, with Rabshakeh suggesting that even one of the minor Assyrian officials could succeed against Judah's forces. The assistance of Egyptian chariots and horsemen will not make any difference to the outcome of battle. In line with the personal address to Hezekiah throughout, the suggestion is that he *himself* is depending on Egyptian help.[13] The implication is that Hezekiah is relying on 'empty words' (verse 5), not on his own military strength or foreign assistance.

10 God again comes into the picture, as Rabshakeh claims to have divine authority for his attack on the land and his intention to destroy it. This may imply again that malcontents in the land favoured Assyrian intervention to bring cessation to Hezekiah's religious programme. It is also possible that Isaiah's earlier words (Isa. 10:5-11) could have been reported to the Assyrians. This is not the only time that a foreign king claimed divine authorisation for attacking Judah, for Neco of Egypt did the same in Josiah's day (2 Chron. 35:21).

11-12 An interlude occurs in which Hezekiah's representatives make no attempt to reply to the arguments that Rabshakeh has addressed to the king. What they challenge is the form in which the message comes. They want him to stop speaking in Hebrew and to use Aramaic, the *lingua franca* of the diplomatic world of the day. Hebrew is called here *yᵉhûdît*, doubtless this being the name given to the current Judean dialect of that time. The word 'Hebrew' (*'ivrî*) does not occur for the language of the Jews until used by Ben Sira in his prologue to *Sirach* (180 BC). The reason for the request is that the people on the wall can understand what is being said. Rabshakeh makes it quite plain in his response that the message is for all in Jerusalem. Using crude but pertinent language he describes those in the city. As though he is picturing the coming siege he describes them as those who 'will have to eat their own faeces and drink their own urine'.

---

[12]For the grammatical point, see T. O. Lambdin, *Introduction to Biblical Hebrew*, op. cit., p. 170.

[13]The Hebrew says not just 'rely on Egypt', but 'rely *for yourself* on Egypt' (*vativtach lᵉkâ 'al mitsrayim*); cf. NASB margin.

13-14 Rabshakeh is unmoved by the request made to him to speak in Aramaic, and so his second speech continues in the language of Jerusalem. What he says concerns Hezekiah, though nowhere does he refer to him as king. Four times he admonishes him (verses 14, 15, 16, 18; the first three all start with 'do not let ...', while the fourth is a continuation of a sentence and commences with 'lest'). The only king he acknowledges is Sennacherib (see verses 13, 15, 16, 18). Moreover, he clearly wants his message heard because he calls out with a loud voice.[14] He again adopts the prophetic pattern of speech: 'Listen to the words of the great king, the king of Assyria. Thus says the king ....' The first warning is a contradiction of what Hezekiah has said. Rabshakeh tells the people that their king is deceiving them when he claims to be able to deliver them. This theme of deliverance runs through the whole speech, occurring eight times (see verses 14, 15, 18, 19, 20).

15 The second warning is that the people must not think that their God will be able to deliver them. Hezekiah had clearly encouraged the people to trust in the LORD saying (according to Rabshakeh): 'He will certainly deliver you; this city will not be given into the hand of the king of Assyria.' The Assyrian mocks such assertions, pouring scorn on any thought that Judah's God or any other (see verse 19) can rescue Jerusalem and its people.

16-17 The 'false prophet' continues to speak against Hezekiah. Not only does he do this by counselling the people not to listen to him, but by encouraging them to come to terms with the present military situation. He wants them to yield to the Assyrian army, come out to him, and enjoy a good life. The expression used for coming to terms with the Assyrians only occurs here and in the parallel passage in 2 Kings 18:23. Literally it is 'make a blessing', where 'make peace' could have been expected. Presumably it indicates a token of compromise and acceptance of the Assyrian proposals. The promise is couched in terms of a new Eden – each person having his own grape vine and fig tree, and drinking water from his own well. This preliminary taste of the good life will be temporary until the people are taken to a land 'like your land' (presumably Assyria, though unnamed) where they will have grain, new wine, bread, and vineyards. Resettlement of people was a trademark of Assyrian policy (see 2

---

[14]The NIV omits the words 'with a loud voice' (*beqôl gâdôl*).

Kings 17:6, 18, 24-26 in reference to Israel after the fall of Samaria). Rabshakeh makes no attempt to hide the fact that removal to Assyria will take place, but tries to put it in the best light possible.

18-20 Verse 18 is a continuation of the sentence begun with the words of verse 16: 'Make peace with me ... lest Hezekiah deceive you.' What Sennacherib says via his spokesman is a reflection of the proud boasting of Assyria already noted in 10:8-11 at the time of previous invasion. The words are addressed to the people though they concern Hezekiah. He had assured the people that the LORD would deliver, but what Rabshakeh says is that the LORD is no more powerful than the gods of Hamath, Arpad, or Sepharvaim. These cities had all been captured by the Assyrians, sometimes more than once. While Hamath was under Israelite control during Solomon's reign (2 Chron. 8:4), it was clearly under Assyrian rule by the fall of Samaria in 722 BC (2 Kings 17:24). Arpad was devastated by the Assyrians on several occasions, and it is probably to be identified with Tell Rifa'ad (about 20 miles [33 km] NW of Aleppo in modern Syria). The location of Sepharvaim is unknown, but from the biblical references it appears to have been in Syria. These three cities are cited again by Sennacherib in his message to Hezekiah when he hears that the Egyptians are coming to the aid of Judah (37:13). 'Look', he says, 'what god has been able to save his land from my hand? How can the LORD deliver Jerusalem from my hand?' This blasphemy stands in marked contrast to the commitment to the LORD made by Hezekiah. Sennacherib sets himself up as a rival to the living God, the Holy One of Israel. The theme of deliverance is still central, as the verb 'deliver' (Heb. *nâtsal* Hif.) appears five times in verses 18-20.

21-22 No response comes from Hezekiah's representatives. The MT simply says that 'they remained silent and did not answer [even] a word'. Many English versions take the subject to be 'the people of Jerusalem', and they make a supposed distinction between the people and the three representatives by translating the opening of verse 22 as 'Then Eliakim ..., Shebna and Joah ... went to the king'. However, the people have not been the subject of a verb up to this point in the narrative, and the grammatical structure does not support the introduction of 'then'. The same subject is in view in both these verses. Moreover, the reason for the silence is 'because of (*kî*) the king's command', an instruction fitting for the representatives but doubtful if it is thought of as a command to the people as a whole. The three officials are noted as obedient servants of their king, and they proceed to report to him what Rabshakeh had said. The seriousness of the situation does not escape them, for they follow the normal mourning ritual and rend their clothes. The crisis facing Judah/Jerusalem is not over, for the sequel will show that the solution is quite different from what Sennacherib thought possible.

3. Jerusalem's Deliverance (37:1-38)

a. Sennacherib's Blasphemy Answered (37:1-7)

These verses record the interaction between prophet and king at a time of crisis. Their relationship is quite different from the earlier one between Isaiah and Ahaz (7:1-17). In the former case Isaiah, accompanied by his son, has to go and seek out the king. In this case the believing king, Hezekiah, sends his officials to Isaiah seeking prayer for the remnant.

1 Hezekiah, by his actions, proves that what the Assyrians said about him is true (cf. 36:7, 15, 18). He shares the grief of Eliakim, Shebna, and Joah, and shows that by adopting the customary signs of mourning (torn clothes, wearing of sackcloth). Moreover, he proceeds to the temple, doubtless because of the close connection between prayer and sacrifice, and because this was where his ancestor Solomon had declared that God would answer the people's prayers (1 Kings 8:30). The king's actions reveal more than just a token display of grief. Especially the fact that he dons sackcloth shows that he is expressing an attitude of humiliation and repentance. He sets the example for his people.

2 Hezekiah sends a deputation of civic and spiritual leaders to Isaiah. Eliakim and Shebna are joined by the 'elders of the priests'. This term could denote 'the leading priests' (see NIV), but it more probably designates the head of the priestly families.[15] All of them wear sackcloth as a sign of their united contrition.

3 The message is delivered to the prophet. The present crisis is said to be a day of distress, correction and disgrace. The first of these expressions is a common one, but the other two are rare. 'Correction' (*tôkêchâh*) occurs only here (and in the parallel in 2 Kings 19:3) and

---

[15]This interpretation follows that of J. A. Alexander, *Commentary on the Prophecies of Isaiah* (T. & T. Clark, 1873), vol. II, p. 52, and it was also adopted by E. J. Young.

in Hosea 5:9 and Psalm 149:7. The Hebrew verb from which it comes (*yâkach*) appears in judicial contexts, especially where God is accusing his people of breach of covenant obligations (cf. its use in Isa. 1:18). It also appears in passages in which judicial punishment is in view, as in the very next verse. The third word 'disgrace' (*ne'âtsâh*) occurs only here and in the parallel in 2 Kings 19:3. However, the verb from this root (*nâtsah*) has already appeared as early as Isaiah 1:4: ' ...they have *spurned* the Holy One of Israel' (NIV), and it also appears in 5:24. Combined in one clause these three nouns express the calamitous situation that Hezekiah sees has come on Jerusalem. The present situation is like a mother in childbirth, who after the entire pregnancy and pains, has no strength left to give birth.

4 While there is no mention of Hezekiah praying in the temple, yet he requests Isaiah to pray for the remnant that still exists. 'Remnant' in this context simply means those left after the deportation of many Israelites from the north after the fall of Samaria, and therefore signifies Judah/Jerusalem. The opening word in Hebrew (*'ûlay*) has a variety of meanings, including 'perhaps'. More probably here it means 'if', not in a doubtful sense but as an affirmation of hope.[16] Hezekiah's own prayer (verses 15-20) is an expression of confidence in the LORD, and nothing preceding it suggests a drastic change in his thought between his request to Isaiah and his own later prayer. What he wants is a divine rebuke for the Assyrian king, Sennacherib, because he had defied the living God (cf. the same expression used of Goliath defying the armies of the living God, 1 Sam. 17:26, 36).

5-7 When the officials come to Isaiah he responds with a message of hope. The similarity with Ahaz's experience continues (see comment on 36:2), for just as Isaiah passed on the LORD's message to Ahaz: 'Do not fear', so he does to Hezekiah. He is told not to concern himself about the things that Sennacherib's messengers have said. While the messengers are referred to as 'the Assyrian king's young men' (*na'arê melek ashshûr*) this may not be derogatory as the Hebrew word *na'ar* has a wide range of meaning including servants of a king, or soldiers.[17] The main part of his message is introduced by 'behold' which draws attention to the significant words to follow. No time frame is indicated

---

[16]See the range of meanings listed in *DCH*, vol. I, p. 152, and also the comments on affirmative adverbs by J. C. L. Gibson, *Davidson's Introductory Hebrew Grammar – Syntax*, op. cit., p. 141.

[17]Cf. our English use of 'boy' for soldier: 'Our boys are fighting over there.'

but four things are to happen. 1. God will put a powerful spirit on Sennacherib, i.e. bring a powerful influence to bear on him. 2. He will hear a report. 3. He will return to his own land. 4. There he will die by the sword.

b. Renewed Threat from Sennacherib (37:8-13)

A change takes place in the military situation. Another king comes into focus, Tirhakah, the Cushite king of Egypt. A report comes that the Egyptians, whom Sennacherib derided (36:5-6, 9), are coming to do battle with the Assyrians. That causes Sennacherib to make another attempt to threaten Judah into submission.

8-9a While on his mission to Jerusalem, Rabshakeh heard that his own king had broken camp at Lachish and was involved in a battle with Libnah. Both these centres were important fortresses on the south-west of Jerusalem. Lachish has been identified and excavated by an expedition in the 1930s and more recently by a team from the University of Tel Aviv.[18] Libnah's location is uncertain, though it appears to have been between Gath and Lachish (possibly Tel Burnat).[19] Sennacherib appears concerned that the Egyptians could get through into the Vale of Elah and proceed on to Jerusalem to lend support to Hezekiah. Tirhakah was over twenty years of age, and at this time he was the commander-in-chief of the Egyptian army for his brother Shebitku, king of Egypt.[20]

9b-10 Immediately Sennacherib gets word he sends unnamed messengers to Hezekiah, instructing them, 'Thus say to Hezekiah, king of Judah ....' This is typical Assyrian letter form. The message for Hezekiah is a simple one: 'How can you be deluded by your God on whom you rely when he promises that Jerusalem will not fall into the hands of the king of Assyria? (REB)' Sennacherib's aim is to discredit Hezekiah's God. Previously his message for the people was,

---

[18]For the most recent excavations see D. Ussishkin, *The Conquest of Lachish by Sennacherib*, Publications of the Institute of Archaeology, No. 6 (Tel Aviv: The Institute of Archaelogy, Tel Aviv University, 1982). Late in 1982 I was taken to visit Lachish by Professor Ussishkin, and shown over the sites dug by his team.

[19]Libnah means 'white' or 'whiteness', and it may be identified with the limestone cliffs at Tel es-Safi, known to the Crusaders as Blanchegarde.

[20]K. A. Kitchen, *The Third Intermediate Period in Egypt (1100-600 B.C.)* (London: Aris & Phillips, 1972), pp. 154-58.

'Don't let Hezekiah deceive you' (36:14). Now the deceiver, Sennacherib claims, is not the king but Judah's God.

11-13 The thrust of his message is supported by a reason, which is that none of the countries he mentions have been able to elude the military might of Assyria. Previous kings of Assyria had decimated many other countries, completely destroying them. The verb used (*châram* Hif.) is the one employed in the Old Testament for total destruction, such as Israel's destruction of the Canaanites (see, e.g. Deut. 2:34 and 7:2). Israel was not the only nation to employ this method of warfare. Sennacherib boasts that no god was able to deliver those who trusted in them – gods of Gozan, Haran, Rezeph, or Eden. All these places were located in Mesopotamia, and presumably the Assyrian conquests there were well-known by surrounding peoples, otherwise there is no point in citing these as examples for Hezekiah. Moreover, kings had been removed in Hamath, Arpad, Sepharvaim, Hena and Ivvah. The first three names in this list have already been mentioned in Sennacherib's earlier message to Hezekiah (see comment on 36:19). Hena's location is unknown, but it must have been in the same general locality as the other places mentioned. Ivvah is probably to be identified with Avvah, noted in 2 Kings 17:24 along with Babylon, Cuthah, Hamath and Sepharvaim from where settlers were brought to replace displaced Israelites.[21] The punch line as far as Hezekiah is concerned is the question at the end of verse 11: 'And will you be delivered?'[22] Sennacherib thinks that he can hem Hezekiah into one course of action when he considers all the previous conquests of Assyria. He must submit or see Judah and Jerusalem suffer the same fate.

c. Hezekiah's Prayer (37:14-20)

For a second time during the crisis the narrator mentions that Hezekiah goes to the temple, but there is a change. Rather than asking Isaiah to pray (lit. 'and lift up a prayer for the remnant that is left', verse 4), the

---

[21]This identification of the two places is all the more probable because the consonants in the MT for Ivvah (*'vh*) also occur in many manuscripts of 2 Kings 17:24 in place of the MT *'v'*. The pronunciation of the final syllable would be the same whichever spelling is used.

[22]There is no interrogative particle in the Hebrew text, but the context suggests that the question would have been indicated by tone of voice.

king himself prays. What he wants is that the LORD God will save his people from Sennacherib's power. There are many similarities with later sections in this prophetic book, with the Psalms, and with the conclusion of Daniel's prayer (Dan. 9:17-19). The prayer is also shaped in a chiastic pattern:

> *The Prayer Hearer:* 'O LORD God Almighty, God of Israel ... you alone are God'
>> *The Nature of God:* the God who sees and hears – 'Give ear ... open your eyes'
>>> *Assyria's Power*: 'They have laid waste all these peoples and their lands'
>> *The Nature of other 'gods'*: 'only wood and stone, made by human hands'
> *The Prayer Hearer:* 'O LORD our God, deliver us ... you alone, O LORD are God.'

14 Hezekiah's actions display confidence in his God as he receives a second communication from Sennacherib, this time in writing. He takes 'the documents' to the LORD's house. The Hebrew text has the plural, not the singular, as have the parallel passages in 2 Kings 19:14 and 2 Chronicles 32:17. Moreover, both the Kings' account and the one here in Isaiah say that Isaiah 'read *them*'. In addition to the direct message to Hezekiah, the documents could well have been accounts of Assyrian victories sent to validate the claims that were being made. At the temple Hezekiah spreads them out before the LORD.

15-16 Now the king himself prays, commencing with a long form of address: 'O LORD of hosts, God of Israel, enthroned [above] the cherubim'. The use of 'LORD of hosts' is significant coming as it does in a military context, for 'hosts' can mean 'the armies'. The warrior God is the 'God of Israel', a recognition that Hezekiah and others saw the southern kingdom of Judah as the true continuation of Israel as the people of God. The description of him as 'enthroned [above] the cherubim' is a standard expression, though only occurring here in Isaiah (cf. its use in 1 Sam. 4:4; 2 Sam. 6:2; Ps. 80:1; Ps. 99:1). This may well mean more than that he sits above the cherubim in the temple. It could also be a way of describing his heavenly enthronement, for he is said to be God over all the kingdoms of the earth and also the maker of heaven and earth. The uniqueness of Israel's God is asserted right at the start of the prayer, for a little later Hezekiah is going to depict Assyria's 'no-gods'. Appeal to the work of God as creator is an acknowledgment of his power to help, and Isaiah does this repeatedly in later chapters (see 40:12-17; 42:5; 45:11-12). The same appeal to the creator marks out the prayer of the early church recorded in Acts 4:24: 'Sovereign Lord, you made the earth and the sea....'

17 The appeal is couched in language typical of many psalms: 'Give ear, O LORD, and listen; open, O LORD, your eyes and see' (cf. Ps. 84:8), but it is also a form of prayer used by Daniel. Compare these words:

'Give ear, O LORD, and listen; O LORD, open your eyes and see' (Isa. 37:17)
'Give ear, my God, and listen;   open your eyes and see' (Dan. 9:18)

Hezekiah prays with deep intensity of feeling, asking God to have regard to the blasphemy of Sennacherib against the living God. What he asked Isaiah to pray about (verse 4) still forms the central point of his concern. The words 'to defy the living God' are identical in verses 4 and 17. He knows, however, that his God is able both to hear and answer prayer.

18-19 The central point of the prayer is that Hezekiah recognises the truth of the situation—indeed, the Assyrians have devastated all the lands previously mentioned, and their peoples.[23] Moreover, whenever they conquered they burned the 'gods' of that country in the fire. Their victories show that these 'gods' have no power, for they are simply the works of men's hands. Isaiah says they are 'no-gods', with the negative being linked with a noun to form a compound expression (*lô' 'elôhîm*). Other similar Hebrew expressions are 'a no god' (*lô' 'êl,* Deut. 32:21) and 'an unwise son' (*bên lô' châkâm,* Hos. 13:13).

20 Hezekiah returns to his opening theme. He again acknowledges that there is no other God but the LORD. The choice of LORD (*yhwh*)

---

[23]Gregory Goswell, '*For Mine Eyes Have seen the King': Kingship, Human and Divine, in the Book of Isaiah with Special Reference to Isaiah Chapters 36-39,* p. 180, argues convincingly that the word 'land' has occurred repeatedly in the context, and its repetition here in the central part of the chiastic structure of the prayer is by no means redundant. I also follow E. J. Young and John N. Oswalt in taking the second occurrence of 'land' in the sense of 'people' in accordance with Genesis 6:11-12.

used in connection with the verb 'to save' is significant. Its use as the favourite expression for God in the Old Testament dates from the time when the LORD's saving power was displayed towards Israel in Egypt (cf. Exod. 14:30; Deut. 33:29). The reason why Hezekiah wants deliverance for himself and his people ('save *us*', he prays) is that all the earthly kingdoms may know the uniqueness of Israel's God. Israel's role was to be a witness to the nations and to show that the LORD was near his people when they prayed (Deut. 4:7). Later Isaiah makes the same point when speaking of Cyrus' role and announcing that there is no other God besides the LORD. God's own declaration is: 'I am the LORD, and there is no other' (Isa. 45:6).

d. The LORD's Response (37:21-35)

The response falls into two parts, the first containing God's declarations concerning Sennacherib, with the second making specific promises to Jerusalem about her safety in the face of the Assyrian threat.

i. The Message for Sennacherib (37:21-29)

21-22 The LORD's response is to send a reassuring and comforting message to Hezekiah. In contrast to Rabshakeh's claim to speak for the great king (36:4), Isaiah speaks the message of the *real* king: 'thus says the LORD God of Israel.' True prophet succeeds false prophet. Since the prophet had directed his prayer about Sennacherib to his God, he now receives the direct answer, and one which, though addressed to Hezekiah, is really another speech against Sennacherib. It opens with a personification of Jerusalem, 'the Virgin Daughter of Zion'. Whereas the expression 'daughter of Zion' is common, this is the only time Isaiah uses it (cf. his use of 'Virgin Babylon' in 47:1, and the phrase 'Virgin Israel' in Jeremiah 18:13). The parallel phrase, 'Daughter of Jerusalem', is also an *hapax legomenon*, though 'daughter of Zion' is common. The attitude of Jerusalem towards Sennacherib is one of mockery, as he is told that she shakes her head 'after you'. This expression has to be interpreted by later references in this song such as the fact that Sennacherib and his forces will 'come and go' (verse 28) and that the LORD will make him return the way he came (verse 29).

23 Sennacherib is confronted with four things he has done, all descriptive of an attitude of pride on his part and an utter rejection of the LORD's claims as the mighty God. He has defied him, and committed blasphemy against him, for the Assyrian's message has maligned God's character. The following parallel phrases ('raised your voice', 'lifted your eyes') reinforce the pronouncement against Sennacherib. The first of these relates to the messages that he has sent to Hezekiah, while the second speaks of the proud boasting of Sennacherib. It merely emphasises what Isaiah has already said much earlier concerning Assyria (see 10:12). These four things are all directed against the Holy One of Israel, thus aggravating the blasphemy.

24-25 What transpired through the activities of his messengers (36:4-20; 37:9-13) was an act of defiance. Sennacherib made many claims for himself and his armies (as his inscriptions testify). Isaiah's words need not be regarded as a direct quotation of what Sennacherib actually said, but a representation of the tenor of his attitude and pronouncements. He indeed had many chariots, but they were not used in the mountains. In poetic language he is claiming that his army has been able to enter the most inaccessible places from the north (Lebanon) right down to the south (Egypt). No high peak was an obstacle to his troops, and they were able to find water when needed and cross the various branches of the Nile River in its delta.[24] These last claims are significant, for Sennacherib had not conquered Egypt. He sees himself as the mighty king subduing distant lands.

26 Whether or not Sennacherib's claims are true, the message to him is that all that has taken place has been part of God's plan. The expression 'you planned (or, 'formed') it from long ago' is very similar to what is said in 22:11 in reference to God's purposes for Israel. Not only had God planned, but he accomplished his purposes, 'he did it', and that even involved the destruction of cities so that they were reduced to being just a pile of stones. If the reference is to cities in Judah, God is the one who permitted judgment to come on his people by means of the Assyrian army. Just as God later used Cyrus to fulfil his purposes, so he also used Sennacherib as an instrument in his hand (45:4-7).

27 The people of the fortified cities have no power to resist any longer (lit. they are 'short of hand'), and hence suffer disgrace and shame before their conquerors. They are just like new green shoots, or grass that sprouts on the flat rooftops. As soon as the sun shines on

---

[24]The MT text has 'all the rivers of Egypt'. The Hebrew phrase *yeʾôrê mâtsôr* has already occurred in 19:6 (see commentary and footnote). The addition here is the word 'all'.

them they are scorched and wither. The comparison of people with grass is common in the Old Testament (see Pss. 37:1-2; 102:4; Isa. 40:6-8).

28-29 All details of Sennacherib's life are known by the LORD, both where he stays, and all his movements. 'Coming and going' is an Old Testament expression for the totality of someone's life (see Deut. 28:6; Ps. 121:8). Also, his rebellious attitude to God, stirring himself up in a rage, is known. The judgment that is passed on Sennacherib is a response to his rage and arrogance. The word 'arrogance' (*shâ'ᵃnân*) really means 'ease', so the idea is that he is resting on his own ability to carry out his threats against Judah and Jerusalem. The judgment is that the LORD will lead him and make him return from where he came. The reference to a hook in the nose and bit in the mouth is not just metaphorical language, for there is an extant stela depicting Esarhaddon leading captive Tirhakah of Egypt and Ba'alu of Tyre.[25]

ii. Promised Safety for Jerusalem (37:30-35)

The remainder of this message of Isaiah relates first to the fact that there will be restoration of the normal patterns of agriculture within a comparatively short time, and secondly to the announcement that Sennacherib and his army will not achieve the goal of subduing Jerusalem.

30 A sign is offered to Hezekiah that will confirm that God has indeed spoken (for the Heb. word 'sign', *'ôt*, see the commentary on 7:14). Probably the time frame is that within two full years the agriculture of Judah will return to its normal pattern. The implication is that Sennacherib attacked Judah and destroyed the crops in March/April, so that only crops from seeds dropped from the previous year's harvest will be available. If the Assyrian army departed in October/November, that will be too late for any planting, and hence it will be in the following year that the normal agricultural patterns will resume. One consequence of the Assyrian invasion was the inability of Judah and Jerusalem to draw upon two years' harvest from field and vineyards.

31-32 Hezekiah himself has already referred to 'the remnant' (see verse 4). While the normal word for 'remnant' (*shᵉ'êrît*) occurs in verse 32, another word (*pᵉlêtâh*) is employed in verse 31. It denotes

---

[25]*The Ancient Near East An Anthology of Texts and Pictures*, ed. J. B. Pritchard (Princeton University Press, 1973), vol. 1, illustration 121.

what has escaped or is spared, and may allude to those who migrated from the former territory of Israel to Judah in Hezekiah's time.[26] The message is that Judah and Jerusalem are not going to be destroyed, but a remnant will, like a young tree, take root downwards and bring forth fruit upwards. The picture is of continued life for Judah, as a remnant/escapees come forth from the siege of Jerusalem/Mount Zion. At the end of verse 32 there is the repetition of a phrase used in 9:7: 'the zeal of the LORD of hosts will do this.' The reminder is that the deliverance of Jerusalem is not going to be by human effort but by divine power.

33-34 The final words of the message concern Sennacherib. The assurance for Hezekiah and his people in Jerusalem is that the Assyrian army will be unsuccessful in their offensive. No breeches will be made in the city's walls, no arrows or shields will be used in battle, nor will Sennacherib erect a siege ramp (such as he built at Lachish) in front of Jerusalem. He will be forced to return by the way he came. There is a neat play on words in that in the clause 'by the way *he came by it* he will return', the words for 'he came' (*bâ'*) and 'by it' (*bâh*) occur next to each other, and while they are identical in pronunciation they differ in written form.

35 A divine promise is given that Jerusalem will be both defended and saved. The stated reason is important. It is not for Hezekiah's or his people's sake, but for the LORD's own sake and for the sake of the Davidic family that Jerusalem will be preserved. Daniel later is to give the same reason as he pleads in exile for divine mercy to be shown to Jerusalem. He prays: 'For your sake, O Lord, look with favour on your desolate sanctuary. Give ear, O God, and hear; open your eyes and see the desolation of the city that bears your name .... O Lord, hear and act! For your sake, O my God, do not delay, because your city and your people bear your name' (Dan. 9:17-19). God had chosen Zion as the place where his name would dwell (Deut. 12:11; Ps. 2:6) and there the Davidic rulers will have their enduring throne (2 Sam. 7:12-16; Isa. 9:7; 55:3).

---

[26]See the comment by D. J. Wiseman: 'Since many Israelites fled to Judah at this time, there is a sense in which Judah became the remnant of Israel' (*1 and 2 Kings* [Tyndale OT Commentaries, Inter-Varsity Press, 1993], p. 283).

e. God's Deliverance (37:36-38)

Isaiah's account of how God delivered his people from the Assyrian threat is given in an almost parallel account in 2 Kings 19:35-37. A much abbreviated account is given by the Chronicler (2 Chron. 32:21-22), which differs in two respects. First, God's intervention in the situation is described as annihilation of 'all the fighting men and leaders and officers in the camp of the Assyrian king' (verse 21). Secondly, instead of simply saying that Sennacherib, king of Assyria 'went and returned . . . and stayed in Nineveh' the Chronicler adds that he went home 'in disgrace' (lit. 'in shame of face'). This comment is significant as the Chronicler throughout his account mocks the Assyrian king who boasted of his ability to take Jerusalem.

36 The judgment on Sennacherib is in the form of a visitation of the Angel of the LORD. This angel was a divine messenger in human form, who was able to carry out functions that belong to God alone. He was able to claim that he was sent by God, while at the same time claiming divine attributes.[27] The Chronicler records how the Angel of the LORD was able to cause disease and death (1 Chron. 21:11-15, 17, 30). How the annihilation occurred is unstated, and though attempts have been made to link it with a statement of Herodotus, it is better to avoid speculation regarding the manner in which the Assyrians died.[28]

37-38 No mention is made of the location of the Assyrian camp. The writer simply notes that the army broke camp and that Sennacherib returned to his capital of Nineveh. Foreshortening takes place in that the gap of approximately twenty years between the end of the Jerusalem siege and Sennacherib's death is disregarded. Thus the summary account in these verses follows the prediction set out in verse 7. While Sennacherib was worshipping in the temple of his god Nisroch, two of his sons, Adrammelech and Sharezer, slew him with the sword. Jealousy may have been the motive, for clearly Sennacherib had designated Esarhaddon as his successor, not the sons who slew

---

[27]For an excellent discussion on the Angel of the LORD, see Geerhardus Vos, *Biblical Theology: Old and New Testaments*, pp. 72-76.

[28]Herodotus (II.141) records how the Assyrians retreated from Egypt after mice ate the thongs of their equipment in one night. The location is quite different, with the link only being the possibility that bubonic plague could had been carried by mice, and so destroying the Assyrian army within a very short space of time. Josephus (*Ant.* 10.17-23) also refers to a disaster that caused the Assyrians to depart.

him. Esarhaddon reigned from 681 BC till 669 BC (see the reference to him in Ezra 4:2). It is ironic that the foreign king who mocked Hezekiah's God was killed in the very house of *his* god, who was unable to protect him. The place where he thought himself completely safe turned out to be a convenient murder place where two of his sons killed him, and then fled to distant Ararat. This is most probably the Urartu (Armenia) mentioned in Assyrian inscriptions, a province to the north of present day Syria. The Chronicler adds an important note to the account here by drawing attention to the respect that was given to Hezekiah because of the LORD's deliverance of himself and his people (2 Chron. 32:23).

B. Hezekiah's Sickness and Recovery (38:1-22)

As already noted, chapters 38–39 chronologically precede chapters 36–37. Hezekiah's illness must have preceded Sennacherib's invasion, for 38:6 notes the promise of deliverance from that event. If Hezekiah died in 686 BC after a reign of twenty-nine years, and if he lived for fifteen years after his illness, then the illness itself must be dated as happening by 701 BC or earlier. Most probably it occurred in 702 or 701 BC. The account given here is a record of God's mercy and power, and also of Hezekiah's piety and trust in him, as his song of thanksgiving shows.[29]

The parallel account is contained in 2 Kings 20 with an abbreviated note in 2 Chronicles 32. These passages align as follows:

Isaiah	2 Kings	2 Chronicles
38:1-6	20:1-6	32:24
38:7-8	20:9-11	————
38:9-20	————	————
38:21-22	20:7-8	————

The Chronicler assumes that readers are familiar with the fuller parallel accounts since he simply refers to the 'sign' given to Hezekiah without any further explanation. The point he makes is that Hezekiah showed a repentant heart and that God heard the king's prayer, and answered speedily (see 2 Chron. 32:24-26).

The juxtaposition of Sennacherib's death in the temple of his god at

---

[29]See the excellent discussion of the dating of the events in Hezekiah's life by E. H. Merrill, *Kingdom of Priests: A History of Old Testament Israel* (Baker Book House, 1998), pp. 409-20.

the end of chapter 37 (verse 38) and Hezekiah's desire to go up to the house of his God at the end of chapter 38 (verse 22) is important. For the one king the visit to the temple meant death; for the other, the visit to the temple was part of his thanksgiving for restoration from illness and a prolonged life.

1. Urgent Praying and the Divine Response (38:1-8)

1 The opening words, 'in those days', do not relate back to the content of chapter 37 but are simply a summary of the earlier period of Hezekiah's reign. The king is seriously ill, with death imminent. At that moment Isaiah comes to him with a divine word: 'Thus says the LORD: Give your last instructions to your house, for you are going to die; you will not live.' The Hebrew verb 'to command' (*tsivvâh*) can be used in this sense of giving one's final instructions (see 1 Kings 2:1 of David's charge to Solomon). The same expression for attending to one's personal and family affairs is used concerning Ahitophel in 2 Kings 17:23. The use of the expression 'you are dying' (*kî mêt 'attâh*) has the idea of being on the point of dying, or about to die.[30]

2 The response of Hezekiah is to pray to his God. To do so he turns his face to the wall of his room. This probably indicates his desire to be alone with God, and his actions serve as a dismissal of the prophet. A major concern of Hezekiah may well be that he had at this time no heir, for Manasseh was only twelve years old when he began to reign (2 Kings 21:1). If this is so, Hezekiah is doubtless worried concerning the continuation of the Davidic line of kings.

3 The prayer does not focus immediately on the illness. Rather, Hezekiah wants God to remember how he has lived before him—'"walking before you in truth and with a complete heart, and what is good in your eyes I have done", and Hezekiah wept deeply' (lit. '[with] great weeping'). The language he uses is typical of laments in which the person praying cites past obedience as a motive for sparing him (cf. Pss. 7:8-11; 26:1-12). The appeal 'Remember' is virtually synonymous with a request for divine mercy. The description of his walk before the LORD places him in the tradition of his forefather David (see 1 Kings 11:4). Weeping is associated elsewhere in the Old Testament with pleading with God (see the experience of Hannah, 1

---

[30]The Hebrew participle is often used to denote imminent future action. For discussion on this point, consult *IBHS*, p. 627.

Sam. 1:7-10, or that of Esther, Est. 8:3). Hezekiah's prayer and its answer is of the same nature as Abraham's plea for Sodom (Gen. 18:23-33), or Elijah's prayer for rain (1 Kings 18:30-38), or the Syrophoenician woman's request for her daughter (Matt. 15:21-28).

4-5 God commands his servant Isaiah to go to Hezekiah with his response. He is to make formal announcement ('thus says the LORD') to him of two specific things. First, he is going to recover from his illness, and secondly, he is going to be delivered from the Assyrian menace. Hezekiah is also told that the message comes from 'the God of your father David'. The continued existence of the Davidic family is assured by God's gracious intervention. Fifteen years are added to Hezekiah's life, and this prolongation of his life was also symbolic of continuing existence and safety of Jerusalem.

7-8 The account concerning the sign given to Hezekiah is more abbreviated than that in 2 Kings 20:1-11, for it omits the choice that he had to make whether the shadow on the steps of Ahaz went forward or backward (2 Kings 20:9-10). The LORD's word to Hezekiah is confirmed by the addition of this sign, and the shadow retreats ten steps. It is possible that 'the steps of Ahaz' were not only functional steps but also served as a sundial. No further explanation is given of how this event occurred, but what happened is in line with reference to other miracles in the books of Kings, including the restoration of Hezekiah by divine action ('*I* have heard ... *I* have seen ... behold, *I* am adding ....').[31]

2. Hezekiah's Song of Thanksgiving (38:9-20)

Hezekiah responds to God's gracious intervention in his life, and the life of Jerusalem, by setting out in writing a song of praise. This song is very similar to psalms such as Psalms 85 and 89.[32]

9 It is unique to find a heading given for a song that occurs in a *narrative* setting of the Old Testament (Hab. 3:1 is in a poetic setting). The author is designated as 'Hezekiah, king of Judah', which immediately links him with his ancestor, King David, who was noted for his poetical and musical gifts. The term 'writing' (*miktâv*) in the

---

[31]For consideration of the wider question of miracles in the books of Kings, see Paul House, *1, 2 Kings*, op. cit., pp. 50-54.

[32]The Hebrew text of Hezekiah's song contains many difficulties. For discussion of them, see John N. Oswalt, *The Book of Isaiah: Chapters 1-39*, pp. 678-81, and footnotes 1-14.

ascription is also unusual as it is a rare word in biblical Hebrew, and never used in a title to a psalm. Though suggestions have been made that it should be altered to the musical or literary term *miktâm* that occurs in headings to Psalms 16 and 56–60, no manuscript evidence points in that direction. Many English translations render the last three Hebrew words of the verse with expressions like 'after his illness and recovery' (RSV, NASB, NIV, NJKV), but this makes the translation far too time specific. The Hebrew text simply says 'in his sickness, and when he recovered from his illness'. That is to say, the indication of time is not *after* recovery but during the period of his illness. Though Hezekiah is promised recovery (verse 5), even by the end of the chapter he is still not healed (verse 22).

The song is divided into three sections, correctly marked in the NIV by the way the text is set out. The first (verses 10-14) is a description of the king's distress, while the second (verses 15-19) anticipates restoration. The conclusion (verse 20) is a communal expression of thanksgiving in which king and people join in testimony to the LORD's saving power. The first two sections are marked off by 'I said' (verse 10) and 'What can I say?' (verse 15), with 'I said' probably implied before the conclusion.

10-11 The song begins with a declaration by Hezekiah concerning the danger he faces in the midtime of his life. She'ol awaits him, and he fears that he will be deprived of the years still ahead of him. The introductory 'I said' probably refers to the fact that the king had considered these matters and already given voice to some of the complaints. He fears that he will not see the LORD any longer in 'the land of the living' (see the use of this expression in Pss. 27:13; 52:5; 116:9; 142:5). The repetition of the divine name 'LORD, LORD' (*yâh yâh*) is a *hapax legomenon*, though *yhwh yhwh* occurs in Exodus 34:6. *Yâh* is essentially a poetic form, and the repetition may be to give greater solemnity to the expression. The final word in the MT of verse 11 (*chêled*) is also a *hapax legomenon*. This unusual word is altered, by interchanging two letters, to *chêdel* ('world') in some manuscripts. The best explanation is that it means something like 'land [or realm] of the dead', and so serves as a matching phrase to 'land of the living'.

12 Hezekiah compares his life to a piece of cloth that can be rolled up. While most English translations translate the first word in this verse (*dôrî*) as 'my dwelling', this is very dubious. Nowhere else in the Old Testament is it given this meaning. It is the word for 'generation', and here applied to an individual it means 'my span of life',[33] and thus forms an excellent parallel to 'my life'. Hezekiah says he is just like a tent that can be folded away, or a new stretch of cloth that can easily be taken off the loom. The last clause in the verse, 'from day to night you have finished me,' is probably a proverbial saying, and it reappears at the end of verse 13 as well. It is descriptive of the suddenness with which God can take life away, between morning and night.

13-14 In the presence of the LORD Hezekiah is quiet and submissive until dawn (cf. the use of the same Hebrew verb [*shivvîtî*] in Ps. 131:2). Distress, both physical and spiritual, can be compared to the breaking of bones (see Pss. 6:2; 32:3). The king sees the LORD as the one who comes like a lion and breaks his bones. Like birds such as swifts, thrushes and doves that make soft noises, so Hezekiah cries out in his distress. His vision is fixed upon the heavens, though his eyes grow weak from his intense looking to his God. The first part of the song ends with the words: 'O LORD, I am oppressed; go surety for me.' The verb 'to go surety' (*'ârav*) has the idea of taking responsibility for someone else, just as Judah assured his father that he would guarantee Benjamin's safety if he went down to Egypt (Gen. 43:9). Only here and in Psalm 119:122 is the verb used with God as the subject. The appeal is clearly for protection, just as a man would go surety for a friend in debt. Hezekiah wants divine assistance, a substitute to stand in his place.

15 The song moves over into thanksgiving at this point, not for healing already received, but in expectation of it (see comment on the next verse). It begins with a question: 'What shall I say?', and the answer is: 'He [the LORD] has spoken to me and he has done [this].' The final clause is very close to the concluding words of Psalm 22 ('for he has done [this]'), where they are a testimony to God's saving power and to the deliverance he can bring (22:31). Likewise Hezekiah is able to testify that God has heard his prayer and he has acted. As for himself he promises that he will live in future with a true spirit of humility (see Psalm 42:5 for the only other use of the same verb, *dâdâh*) since he has come to realise the real nature of his distress (lit. 'on account of the bitterness of my soul'; cf. Naomi's similar words in Ruth 1:13).

16 From early times this verse has proved difficult, as is shown by

---

[33] I am following the position taken by John N. Oswalt, ibid., p. 679, fn. 4.

the way in which the LXX and the Targum differ both from the MT and from each other. The RSV/ESV translation accepts the text without emendation and renders: 'O Lord, by these things men live, and in all these is the life of my spirit. Oh, restore me to health and make me live!' The reference to 'these things' seems to have as its antecedent God's speech and action just referred to in the previous verse. Hezekiah knows that he depends upon the sovereignty of God for life itself, and the threat of immediate death is past. The concluding clauses should be taken as speaking about the future, for the king is sure that God will restore him to health. The final verb is an imperative, 'Revive me!', and it is practically synonymous with the previous verb, 'you will restore me to health.'

17 Hezekiah looks back on his exceedingly bitter experience (lit. 'bitter to me, bitter') and acknowledges that is has been for his good (lit. 'peace'). The opening word 'behold' introduces the sense of wonder into his words, for he knows that the chastisement that he had been through has been for his good. This thought, that affliction leads to blessing, is reinforced in the New Testament (Heb. 12:11). In fact, he is conscious that God's love to him has preserved him from the grave. The verb used here for 'love' (*châshaq*) is the one employed in Deuteronomy 7:7 of God's love for Israel. Now the same verb is applied to God's commitment to Hezekiah. Many have suggested that the verb should be emended to mean 'hold back' (*châsak*), but the manuscript evidence supports the retention of 'love'. Possibly this verb had a nuance of loving so intensely that the direction of life was changed, and hence in this verse it could be translated 'you loved in a way that spared'.[34] Forgiveness of sins is also part of the divine mercy, and it is like God hiding sins behind his back.

18-19 In the grave there is no praise for God, as only the living can praise him. The opening words echo Psalm 6:5, while the expression 'those who go down to the pit', occurs in several psalms where it simply means 'the dead' (see Pss. 30:3; 88:4; 143:7). It is not the dead who demonstrate expectant waiting on God's faithful dealings. Rather, 'the living, the living, they praise' the LORD. The repetition of 'living' is another example of a stylistic feature that occurs in this song (see *yâh yâh* in verse 11, and *mar lî mâr* in verse 17), and it helps to accentuate the contrast between the dead and the living. Hezekiah himself is able

---

[34]This is the suggestion of David Talley in *NIDOTTE*, 2, p. 319.

to praise the LORD, just as fathers pass on to succeeding generations accounts that highlight God's faithfulness.

20 The song ends on a high note. There is a switch between first person singular ('the LORD will save *me*'; '*my* music') and first person plural ('*we* will sing', '*our* lives'). Those included in the 'we' cannot extend beyond those mentioned in verse 19, namely, the king (the royal father) and his sons. Hezekiah sets the pattern of true piety, and it is his songs that are sung. 2 Chronicles 29:30 tells of the king's concern for the temple music, and it would not be surprising if he composed songs for worship. The king and his sons give the lead for all of Judah. They will be found continually in the courts of the LORD's house. Experience of the LORD's saving mercy will find its response in heartfelt worship.

3. Hezekiah's Healing and Worship of the Heavenly King (38:21-22)

The conclusion of chapter 38 is more than just 'additional notes',[35] considered by many writers to be misplaced as compared with the account in 2 Kings 20. Many commentators suggest that the apparent chronological difficulty can be solved by translating the verbs in these verses as pluperfects in English, and this is followed in many translations: 'And Isaiah *had* said .... And Hezekiah *had* said....' However, Hezekiah's song *anticipates* recovery rather than praises God for what is already past, and the different wording as compared with 2 Kings 20:7-8 shows that these verses are here to form the climax of the account. Isaiah tells Hezekiah what to do so that *he will recover*, and Hezekiah's question points to the king's piety as he expresses a longing to go and worship the Great King in his temple. There is also a close connection between chapters 38 and 39, with the reference to Isaiah's and Hezekiah's speeches paralleled in matching pairs:

38:21-22	'and Isaiah said ...	and Hezekiah said ...'
39:3	'and Isaiah said ...	and [Hezekiah] said ...'
39:4	'and [Isaiah] said ...	and Hezekiah said ...'
39: 5, 8	'and Isaiah said ...	and Hezekiah said ...'

Prophet and king interact with one another, as first the king's recovery and worship at the temple are in view, before the narrative then moves

---

[35]The expression is that of John N. Oswalt, *The Book of Isaiah Chapters 1-39*, p. 690.

on to the episode with the Babylonian messengers.

21 The visible sign of Hezekiah's illness is said to be a 'boil' (*sh^{e}chîn*), a word used elsewhere in the Old Testament of a sign of God's wrath (Exod. 9:9-11, 4x; Deut. 28:27, 35; Job 2:7). A poultice of figs is to be applied to it, and there is some evidence from the Ancient Near East that such poultices were used both on humans and animals. But the main point is not the poultice, but that the narrative points to the sovereign God who is able to bring healing with or without visible tokens.

22 Hezekiah asks what is probably a rhetorical question: 'What sign [is there] that I will go up to the LORD's temple?' It is not the same request as reported in 2 Kings 20:8, but a further one. The Davidic king, Hezekiah, longs to be over the illness that prevents his personal presence at the temple. In making his request he shifts the focus away from the earthly kingship to the heavenly one.

C. The Prediction of the Babylonian Exile of Royal Treasures and Royal Sons (39:1-8)

The narrative dealing with the arrival of a Babylonian deputation occurs in the three historical accounts of the period: Isaiah 39:1-8; 2 Kings 20:12-19; 2 Chronicles 32:31. The Chronicler's account differs in a typical way in that he probes behind the outward actions to discover the hidden motives of the heart. Hence in his summary of the event he says that God left Hezekiah in order to test him and to know everything that was in his heart. In prayer David had spoken of how God was able to test the heart (1 Chron. 29:17), and now Hezekiah is to be tested. The Babylonian king was almost certainly concerned with far more than just Hezekiah's recovery from illness, for military considerations were always dominant in his thinking.

1 After Hezekiah receives healing from the LORD, messengers from the Babylonian king arrive at his court, along with the gifts appropriate to such an occasion. Merodach-Baladan was the local ruler of Babylon during Sargon's reign over Assyria (722–705 BC), but following Sargon's death he worked for independence from Assyria. The visit of his emissaries to Hezekiah was part of his diplomatic efforts to secure allies in the west. Hezekiah's illness and recovery may well have been the ostensible reason for the visit, but the Chronicler tells how the envoys came to ask about the miraculous sign that had occurred in the land (2 Chron. 32:31). This suggests that the sign given may have

excited expectation in Babylon that Hezekiah was a favourite with the
'gods' and therefore an alliance with Judah was highly desirable. That
these other factors are in mind is shown by the letters and 'gift'
(*minchâh*). This word for gift, while most frequently used for offerings,
is also employed in the sense of tribute money, such as that paid to
Eglon by the Israelites (Judg. 3:15-18), or that of the Philistines to
Jehoshaphat (2 Chron. 17:11).[36] Babylon is prepared to pay for a
western ally.

2 Hezekiah is extremely glad to receive the messengers (lit. 'he
rejoiced over them') and shows them everything – his treasury, his
expensive stores, and even his arsenal. Nothing in his palace or in the
whole of his kingdom is kept back from their inspection. The reference
to 'kingdom' suggests that the inspection was not cursory but rather a
leisurely investigation of Judah's resources. These same resources
became the desire of the Assyrians, Babylonians, and Persians in turn.

3-4 The prophet Isaiah comes, as he had done much earlier in his
career with king Ahaz (Isa. 7:3), to confront king Hezekiah. The text
specifically calls him 'the prophet' as a reminder that his visit to the
royal palace is as the LORD's messenger. He has two questions for
Hezekiah: 'What did these men say, and from where did they come *to
you*?' The NIV omits 'to you', but these words point to the significance
of the envoys' mission. They are not just incidental visitors, but they
come to deal directly with the king.[37] It is only the second question
that Hezekiah answers, and the answer is quite truthful: 'from a distant
land, from Babylon they came to me.' The follow-up question is: 'What
did they see in your palace?' Again, Hezekiah gives an honest answer:
'Everything in my house they saw. There is not a thing in my storehouses
that I did not show them.' The Chronicler's comment (2 Chron. 32:25)
points to the fact that Hezekiah was proud and he did not respond to
the kindness of God in giving him the extra years of life. He fails at a
crucial time, and though he is a great king yet he rests on human
achievement instead of on divine power.

5 The prophetic word to Hezekiah is announced in the name of

---

[36]See the discussion on the biblical usage by Richard E. Averbeck in
NIDOTTE, 2, p. 986, and also his reference to the Ugaritic parallels on pp. 978-
79.

[37]The verb in the first question may well be taken as suggesting a series of
'comings' that Isaiah foresees, whereas the verb Hezekiah uses only refers to
one coming (*yâvô'û . . . bâ'*).

'the LORD of hosts', the form of address that Hezekiah himself had used in 37:16 as he appealed to God to listen to the insults that Sennacherib had made against him.

6-7 The message itself contains no direct word of rebuke to Hezekiah over his showing the Babylonians all his kingdom. Instead, it is directed to the Davidic family (note the use of '*your* palace', '*your* fathers', '*your* sons'). The time in the future of the removal of the royal family and its accumulated wealth to Babylon is left unspecified. The opening of verse 6 can be translated as: 'Behold, days are coming when....' The introductory 'behold' draws attention to this significant event, while the indefiniteness of the prediction adds its own force to the content of the message. What Sennacherib was unable to achieve (the 'taking' of the people of Judah to Assyria, 36:17) will become a reality for the royal family when they are 'taken' (verse 7). The royal line is in danger, for some of the sons will be castrated, and hence unable to beget children. Becoming eunuchs will debar them from the LORD's temple (see Deut. 23:1 for the exclusion from the LORD's assembly of men who had undergone self-mutilation).[38] Instead of worshipping at the LORD's temple they will be servants in the palace of the Babylonian king.

8 The final verse of the chapter and section of the book contains Hezekiah's response to the LORD's message. A literal translation of the verse needs amplification to bring out its meaning. It reads: 'And Hezekiah said to Isaiah: "The word of the LORD you have spoken is good." And he said: "For there will be peace (*shâlôm*) and security ('*emet*) in my days."' The opening words are an expression of Hezekiah's piety, and of his submission to the LORD's will. He submits just as Saul had done long before to a proposal from his servant, saying, 'Your word is good' (1 Sam. 9:10). The second part of the verse must not be set in contrast to the first. Hezekiah is reported as saying something further. This could be spoken aloud, or else be what he thought (as interpreted in translations like NIV and ESV), though the thought/speech of the king had to become known for it to be inserted here in the narrative. The king's words are not a cynical expression of relief that at least there will be peace during his lifetime. Rather, they are a further expression of his piety as he realises that what has been

---

[38]I have commented on those excluded from the congregation in *Deuteronomy: The Commands of a Covenant God*, op. cit., pp. 209-12.

stated is for his benefit and is an expression of God's utter faithfulness (cf. the numerous uses of 'faithfulness' in the prayers in the Book of Psalms, and also the way that the Heb. word *'emet* is used in 42:3 and 43:9). From the Chronicler's account it is clear that Hezekiah both sinned and repented: 'Then Hezekiah humbled himself for the pride of his heart, as did the people of Jerusalem; therefore the LORD's wrath did not come upon them during the days of Hezekiah' (2 Chron. 32:26). Grace is operative, and Hezekiah is interested in the future well-being of his family. From all the revelation he has, he knows that in the highest sense this future is indeed secure since it rests on God's faithfulness.

This final comment is important for it helps to identify the link between chapters 36–39 and what eventuates in chapters 40 and following. Hezekiah knows that the only hope for the future rests on God's kingship, not on his. There is a shift in the book, in that there is no longer any interest in the Davidic kingship. What really matters are the blessings of peace and faithfulness that come from the heavenly king.

Part 3

The Book of Comfort
40:1–66:24

A. Israel's Restoration and Return (40:1–48:22)

The third and final part of Isaiah commences at this point. The previous section, and especially the reference to Babylon in chapter 39, has provided the bridge between the earlier part of the book and this one. The focus now changes to the coming situation when Israel will be exiled in Babylon. The writer's standpoint is still within Palestine, but he reinforces the lessons of divine judgment and mercy that had been set out long before in the Pentateuch (Lev. 26; Deut. 28). While Israel is to be punished for her sins, yet God will show great compassion to his people and restore them to their land.

Isaiah must have often felt that his work was unfruitful and his hopes disappointed. But amidst discouraging times and bitter experiences he must have been cheered by the thought of the remnant and even more by the prospect of the work of the servant of the LORD. He looked ahead to the release of the exiles from Babylon, and still further ahead to a greater day of redemption when the servant would die vicariously for his people's sins. While Isaiah's ministry was obviously directed to his contemporaries, yet he repeatedly points to the future work of the only God and redeemer.

This third part of the book can be divided in three, as there are significant markers present in the text—at the end of chapters 48 and 57 there is the statement that there is no peace for the wicked. The same thought occurs at the end of chapter 66, although the wording is different.

1. The Coming of the Lord (40:1–26)

a. The Forerunner (40:1-8)

1-2 The opening words of this section are known and loved because of their use in Handel's *Messiah*. In them there is no mention of Babylon at all (it first appears in 43:14). An anonymous voice calls out God's message: 'Comfort, comfort my people.... Speak to the heart of Jerusalem, and cry to her.' The three imperatives ('comfort', 'speak', 'cry') announce God's impending work, and there is a correspondence between the imperatives and the following paragraphs:

'Comfort'	—	verses 3-5
'Speak'	—	verses 6-8
'Cry'	—	verses 9-11

The opening imperative sets the tone for the whole section of the prophecy. It gives an assurance of comfort but presents it in the form of a command addressed to an unstated audience. The imperatives are plural, possibly addressed to the prophets in general. 'My people' is the object, not the person addressed (as the Latin Vulgate has it). What is important is that God still regards Israel as his people, a fact that will be brought out strongly later on (cf. 50:1; 54:8). Moreover, the command comes from the speaker who claims to be 'your God'.

Three reasons are given for this proclamation, all introduced by the Hebrew word *kî* (NIV 'that').

1. The first reason is that her hard labour is finished. The Hebrew word used here (*tsâv'â*) can refer to the military (Judg. 8:6), but it can also, as here, refer to hard service. That period in Israel's history is soon to end.

2. Payment has been made for her sins and God has accepted as sufficient what she has already suffered.

3. Israel has received 'double' for all her sins. 'Double' is not used in the sense of mathematical proportion, but to emphasise how fully she has been punished, though not more than she deserved.

b. Comfort Achieved (40:3-6)

3 This verse is applied to John the Baptist in Matthew 3:3, Mark 1:3, and Luke 3:4. The picture is of preparation for God visiting Jerusalem, which he did with the highest manifestation at the coming of the Messiah. The emphasis is on the LORD, not the returning exiles. Because the theme of the road as the one which Israel travels has already appeared in chapter 35, it is to be taken in the same way here, though the idea of it being the LORD's way as he comes to aid his people (Deut. 33:2; Ps. 68:3-7) may also be in mind. This road is used when the LORD marches with his people as he did in the exodus. The verb 'prepare' is used in Genesis 24:31 and Leviticus 14:36 of removing obstacles. 'Clear the way' brings out the meaning well. The second verb ('make straight') is used in the sense of making a rough surface smooth.

4 An explanation is given of the way in which the preparation is to be made. The normal contours of the country will be changed, so that hills and valleys all disappear as this new 'highway' appears. Right throughout Isaiah the theme of such a highway is present (see 11:16; 35:7-10; 40:3-4; 42:15-16; 43:19). Modern highway construction gives good illustrations of the picture presented here.

5 As soon as the highway is prepared the LORD will show himself. It will be a revelation of his glory, as he manifests his saving power. This salvation will be seen by all 'at that time' (or, alternately the Hebrew adverb can mean 'together'). The idea of universal acknowledgment of the LORD is going to be developed much further in successive chapters.

c. Human Frailty (40:6-8)

6-7 For a second time in this chapter a section commences with the Hebrew word for 'a voice' (*qol*), but this time the voice issues an instruction: 'Call', to which the response is: 'And he [or "one"] said, "What shall I call?" ' The NIV deviates from the MT to adopt a reading found in the LXX and in a major Hebrew manuscript from among the Dead Sea Scrolls: 'And I said.' There is no need to follow the NIV in making this alteration, for the anonymity of the speaker here matches the anonymity of the caller in verses 3 and 6. Human frailty is emphasised by likening 'all flesh' (i.e. all humanity) to the grass and flowers. They wither and fade when the wind blows on them, and Israel is just as vulnerable before the LORD.

8 The opening words repeat the commencement of the previous verse, but the conclusion is different. The thought climaxes in the assertion that God's word is enduring. Whereas the plot of heathen kings against Judah will not 'stand' (see Isa. 7:7), the LORD's word will.

d. Proclamation of Good Tidings (40:9-11)

9 The announcement is made by a female messenger. Some take this to be Zion/Jerusalem, so that these words stand in apposition to 'messenger of good news' (see this interpretation in the NIV footnote). Preference should be given though to the view that understands the proclamation being made to Zion and Jerusalem. The picture is probably based on the incident following the Exodus when Miriam sang about the LORD's victory (Exod. 15:20-21). Here the song is another one of good news. The Hebrew verb translated as 'bringer of good news' (*bâsar* Pi.) forms the background of the common New Testament verb (*euangelizomai*) for preaching good news. From prominent vantage points the voice is to announce loudly the imminent coming of the LORD. The command, 'Do not fear,' is one of a series in this part of

Isaiah (see 41:10, 14; 43:1, 5). The LORD's coming is announced by a series of statements all introduced by the Hebrew exclamation 'Behold' (*hinneh*); the NIV leaves out the first occurrence.

10-11 There are two figures used here to describe the LORD's coming. The first is that of the conquering hero, the mighty one, while the second is the shepherd of his people. The language describing the victor draws upon phrasing in Deuteronomy where the LORD's salvation is said to be with a strong hand and a stretched out arm (Deut. 4:34; 5:15; 7:19; 26:8). His victory is secure, and he brings the spoils of battle with him (cf. David in 1 Sam. 31:18-20). The second figure switches the idea from strength to tender compassion. Though his arm is still strong, it now serves to gather his flock and to hold it in protective care. This theme of the LORD as a shepherd is brought out in many ways in Old Testament passages (see Ps. 23:1; 78:52; Mic. 2:12; Jer. 23:2-3; Ezek. 34:1-31), while our Lord developed it further in his teaching ministry (John 10:1-18).

e. The Incomparable God (40:12-26)
Several features of this section stand out.

1. The whole passage is in Hebrew poetry and mounts to a climax in verses 30-31.

2. Stylistically there is a series of questions grouped into five paragraphs.

3. The whole section draws strongly on language from the Psalms. Compare:

verse 16	Ps. 50:8-13
verses 19-20	Ps. 115:4-8
verse 22	Pss. 104:2; 19:4, 6
verse 23	Ps. 33:10, 15-16
verse 25	Ps. 89:6-8
verse 26	Pss. 8:3-4; 147:4
verses 29, 31	Pss. 33:20; 103:5.

4. Of the five questions one is repeated with slight variations (verses 18 and 25) and in the main they are rhetorical (verse 27 is the only possible exception).

5. There is a mounting up of phrases that have to be seen in their totality. Thus verse 12 has terms related to the craftsman – 'measured', 'marked out', 'held', 'weighed', 'hollow', 'breadth', 'basket', 'scales',

'balance'. By contrast verses 13-14 are replete with terms related to wisdom – 'understood', 'instructed', 'counsellor', 'consult', 'enlighten', 'taught', 'knowledge', 'understanding'.

6. The language of the creation account in Genesis 1 is drawn upon for significant vocabulary.

12 To stress the incomparability of God questions are posed that highlight his power. Psalm 104:1-9 presents a similar picture of God with the world in his hand. This passage in Isaiah should also be compared with the questions put by Job to the LORD (Job 38:1-11). It is hard to be sure what answer is presupposed by the question 'Who?' While 'the LORD' has been suggested by many, perhaps 'no one' is better here and in the following verse. Attention is drawn to things that carry only trivial amounts in order to stress that God achieved his creative work with such ease. The Hebrew verb *kûn* occurs in this and the following verse, here with the meaning 'marked off,' and in verse 13 'who measured' or 'who has the measure of?'

13-14 Reviewing creation now from the aspect of planning, Isaiah points to the fact that no one had to teach the LORD. The opening question calls to mind his omnipotence, and in terms that imply his omniscience. It has been suggested that the phrase 'the Spirit of the LORD' should rather be 'the mind of the LORD' (so NIV footnote). The LXX took it this way and Paul quotes it twice in this sense in his epistles (Rom. 11:34; 1 Cor. 2:16). The emphasis is on God's creative power and therefore echoes of Genesis 1 are very appropriate. The repetition of words from Hebrew roots in these two verses ('to counsel', 'to make known', 'to teach') highlights the absence of any counsellor for the LORD. The series of questions is intended to show how vastly different God is from his creatures. In response to these questions Israel must acknowledge that God possesses absolute might and absolute wisdom.

15 Now thought concentrates on God's rule over the nations, which includes rule over the farthest islands (mentioned already in 11:11 and 24:15). The first comparison ('like a drop in a bucket', NIV) is uncertain, for the Hebrew words are difficult. A phrase dealing with 'dust' is to be expected and possibly it means 'dust of the balances'. 'Islands' may also include 'coastlands', 'shores', as Isaiah 20:6 suggests. To both 'nations' and 'islands' God calls attention with the repeated exclamation, 'Look!' (omitted in NIV).

16-17 Even if a nation wanted to present offerings to God, they could not do so in an adequate manner. Lebanon, renowned for its vast forests, for example, could not produce enough wood for the altar fires or animals for sacrifice. No nation has grounds for pride when compared with God. They are all reckoned as 'less than nothing' and 'formless', i.e. almost as if they did not exist. This last expression is another echo from Genesis 1:2, for it is the Hebrew word *tohû*, that is there normally translated as 'void'. It signifies what is without meaning or purpose.

18 The questions in verses 18-28 only make sense if some in Judah were thinking that the LORD was only one out of a number of gods. Again Genesis 1 provides some of the language in this section with use of the term 'likeness' (cf. Gen. 1:26, 28) and the verb 'overlay' (Heb. *râqa'*; cf. the use of the noun *râqî'a*, 'firmament', in Genesis 1:6-8). The question is put regarding any likeness of God. Can he be compared with any man-made image? The matter of idolatry will be developed much further later (see especially 44:6-23, and 46:1-13 where the gods of Babylon are just part of the baggage to be carried on carts).

19 For wealthy people the task of making an idol is a work for skilled craftsmen and it is costly. The idol when cast is often overlaid with gold beaten out thinly, or decorated with silver chains. These are probably not intended for dragging the idol but are part of the design (cf. chains on war memorials in the Western world).

20 For poorer people wooden idols have to suffice, though the effort is made to ensure that the idol is not just of a temporary nature. Wood is chosen which is durable, and the effort is made to set up the idol so that it is secure. But however great is the human effort in fashioning 'gods', they are nothing compared with the living God.

21 Like a father God chides the people and points them back to what they have known. Their knowledge of these things goes back to the origin of the universe (the Hebrew text has *'erets*, but this word is used in a manner closer to our English words 'world' or 'universe', as biblical Hebrew lacks any word for this concept). The description of God's work follows and contains three clauses all beginning with a participle, a style which is common in hymnic sections:

> 'he dwells ...'
> 'he stretches out ...'
> 'he brings (lit. gives)...'

In each case the participle is followed by further words that define the earlier expression.

22 The first of these expressions is that the LORD sits above 'the circle of the universe'. This expression for being enthroned (Hebrew *ha-yoshêv 'al*) is used of earthly kings as well as of the LORD (cf. of the LORD, 1 Kings 22:19; Psalm 29:10; of human rulers, 1 Kings 1:48; 3:6). The reference to the circle of the earth is unique but similar expressions do occur in Job 22:14 and Proverbs 8:27. Here the circle is either the heavens or the horizon. The word for grasshoppers may have been chosen deliberately because it sounds somewhat like the word 'circle', these words having two consonants in common (Heb. *chûg, chagâvîm*). For 'canopy', Hebrew uses a word that suggests fine material, a thin garment (cf. the use of a related word in verse 15, 'dust'). Psalm 104:2 also describes the heavens as being like a tent. This passage is typical of Old Testament descriptions of God; they are not negative, but are positive affirmations using anthropomorphic language. God needs the whole expanse of the heavens as his tent.

23 The LORD is the ruler of the universe. Great kings, including Sennacherib (Assyria) and Nebuchadnezzar (Babylon), are nothing before him (Heb. *'ayin* as in verse 17 of the nations). Rulers are made as nothing (Heb. *tohû*, cf. again verse 17).

24 Earthly rulers are compared to uprooted seedlings that are blown away by the wind. The rhythmical nature of the Hebrew of this verse and threefold repetition are well brought out in the idiomatic English of the NIV: 'no sooner ... no sooner ... no sooner ...' Those who think they are somebody will find that they are nobody. They do not endure for they are but chaff (cf. the use of this metaphor of the wicked in Psalm 1:4-6).

25-26 Earlier in verses 18-20 a contrast has been presented between the LORD and idols. In this section the implied contrast is between the LORD and heavenly bodies that are worshipped as gods. There was no reality behind these supposed gods as they are only heavenly bodies put in their place by the Creator (cf. Gen. 1:14). The living God speaks once more as 'the Holy One'. The indirect challenge is to the sun, moon and stars. The people are called to look at them and answer the question, 'Who created them?' The verb create (Heb. *bârâ'*) is used approximately fifty times in the Old Testament, and it is only ever used with God as the subject. Of this usage over half occur in Isaiah. The creator knows every star by name and the grandeur of the heavens is a reminder both of his infinite power and the weakness and frailty of man.

2. Strength for the Weary (40:27-31)

27 Several times in the Old Testament God's people are called lost sheep (cf. Isa. 53:6; Ps. 119:176). Already he has been declared to be the good shepherd who cares for the feeblest (verse 11). Now the LORD draws near to his people and even calls them by the familiar name 'Jacob', as well as 'Israel' (cf. Isa. 29:22-23). Jacob had been in exile in northern Mesopotamia too. Why should they claim that their rough way was hidden from the very God who was preparing their way (verse 3)? Why should they claim that their judgment had been passed over by God who was coming with his recompense (verse 10)? It would be easy for them to think that as God was so great he would not deign to care for them. However, the next verse shows that really God was too great to fail them.

28 The questions are now framed in the singular ('Have you not known?... Have you not heard?'), whereas they appeared in the plural in verse 21. The affirmation is that the covenant LORD is indeed 'the eternal God'. Once again the thought of the prophet goes back to the concept of God as the creator in order to convey the idea of him as the source of comfort and power for dejected Israel. As God he never grows tired and his understanding is infinite. No one is able to penetrate the depths of his knowledge.

29 God is able to bestow upon his frail creatures the strength that he alone possesses. The 'weary' he is able to endue with power, and the weak he is able to fortify abundantly.

30 The contrast between God and humans (his image-bearers) is drawn out further. Young men experience both faintness and weariness. The parallel expression in the second part of the verse draws attention to the way in which even the choicest of men (those noted for their physical strength) stumble with exhaustion.

31 Not all human beings experience the same desolation of weakness. There are some who are characterised by their confident trust in the LORD and the drawing of strength from him. The verb used here for 'waiting' (*qâvâh*) always denotes hopeful waiting, resting trustfully. It is a word that the psalmists use frequently to describe the character of God's faithful people (Pss. 25:5, 21; 27:14; 130:5). They find that they are able to exchange their weakness for God's strength (the verb is Heb. *châlaf,* 'to change' or 'exchange'; cf. the English 'caliph' that comes from Arabic). They are thus enabled to do things they earlier would have found either impossible (flying) or completely debilitating (running and walking). For those in exile the message is going to be that their frail condition can be overcome by divine power.

3. *Israel's* LORD *(41:1-29)*

a. *An Invitation to the Isles to acknowledge the* LORD *(41:1-4)*
1 Courtroom language is again used. A summons goes out to the foreign nations (the Gentiles) to acknowledge the reality of the living God. 'Coastlands' probably includes Greece and other eastern Mediterranean countries. The word occurs thirty-eight times in the Old Testament, and seventeen of these are in Isaiah. It is practically a technical term for the Gentile world. The nations are summoned to draw near to God and to speak their case in self-defence, and they are challenged to accept the offered strength from the God of Israel.

2 This is the first hint of Cyrus in the book of Isaiah, though at this stage not by name.[1] It is a frequent stylistic feature of Isaiah to introduce a person or concept without giving a name, and only later clarifying by an explicit reference. Isaiah will refer to Cyrus again in 41:25 but will only name him in 44:28. Here the thought is that a victorious king will come from the east. Verse 25 says from the 'north', as no king would try to cross vast desert areas to attack Palestine. The word 'north' also seems to be used several times by Isaiah as a term denoting danger or judgment. Cyrus did come from the east, then conquered in the north, and by 546 BC he had reached the west coast of Asia Minor. It is not surprising that nations trembled when they heard that he was on the move.

Some older commentators (e.g., Calvin and Matthew Henry) have assumed that the person indicated here is Abraham, but this does not really fit the context. Abraham did not strike the nations with terror as this person does, nor does it fit with the later reference to Abraham in this very chapter (see verses 8-9). Probably the rendering in the LXX

---

[1]See the discussion by John C. Whitcomb, Jr. on 'Cyrus in the Prophecies of Isaiah' in John H. Skilton, ed., *The Law and the Prophets: Old Testament Studies in Honor of Oswald T. Allis* (Presbyterian and Reformed Publishing Co., 1974), pp. 388-401.

introduced this idea. It has: 'Who has raised up righteousness from the east?', and this reference to 'righteousness' has led to the idea that the reference is to righteous Abraham. The word 'righteousness' (Heb. *tsedek*) can also mean 'victory', 'triumph', and it should not be taken here as a reference to Abraham's character. In his sovereignty God makes Cyrus victorious, so that he conquers nations with sword and bow.

3 This conqueror from the east will pursue after the nations and do so successfully (Heb. literally 'pass over in peace'). The second clause suggests the speed of approach. It will be such that seemingly his feet are not even touching the ground (cf. Dan. 8:5).

4 The coming of this conqueror (Cyrus) is not just by his own will. Rather, it is the LORD who will be seen to have brought him and to have accomplished his own purpose (Heb. uses two verbs, *pâ'al* and *'âsâh*, to describe this action). 'Call' is used in the sense of 'call into being', something that the LORD did from the first as he called generations into existence. Then follows the first of many such assertions by God regarding his own person and character: 'I the LORD [am] first, and with the last I [am] he.' He is the originator of all things, and the one who carries on his work throughout history. The New Testament expression of this is given by John the apostle: ' "I am the Alpha and the Omega," says the Lord God, "who is and who was and who is to come, the Almighty" ' (Rev. 1:8). These affirmations are solemn declarations by God of his own character and purpose.

b. The terror of the nations (41:5-7)

5 This verse expresses the reaction of the nations to the coming conqueror. Places far away will hear of what Cyrus has done, and be fearful. 'Coastlands' and 'ends of the earth' are used in parallel to describe far off places. They will draw near, but they have no case to state.

6-7 These versions clearly allude back to 40:18-20. The nations will try to support one another as they collectively come before the LORD. Mutual assistance will be provided, and with words of encouragement they will attempt to bolster each other's confidence as they make their approach. In practical terms the only response the nations can give is to try and refurbish their idols, hence the various craftsmen engaged in the making of idols will try and spur one another on. The idea is that the nations are vainly using idols to give them support, even though they themselves are the work of men's hands. No deliverance will be available for them from such human efforts, and their folly is highlighted by the final clause of the verse. The idols are so precariously positioned that they even need nails or pins to keep them from toppling over! No help could ever be expected from such false gods.

c. Abundant Consolation to Israel (41:8-20)

8 Israel is in a special relationship with God, and the prophet provides the reasons why she is not to fear. Several important names and terms occur in verse 8: 'Israel', 'my servant', 'Jacob', 'seed of Abraham', 'my friend'. These direct the thought back to the origin of the nation and the special relationship with the LORD that had already existed for centuries. The term 'Israel' comes from the new name that Jacob received at the brook Jabbok (Gen. 32:28). While the name 'Israel' is often interpreted to mean 'he struggles with God' (NIV), yet the form of the word suggests that God (Heb. *'êl*) has to be the subject. Hence the translation could be 'God strove', or 'God overcame'. Thus Jacob carried two reminders of his encounter with God, the brokenness symbolised by his disjointed hip and his new name. Isaiah applies the term 'Israel' either to the southern kingdom exclusively (see the parallel in 5:7, 'the house of Israel'//'the men of Judah'), or else he is taking a comprehensive view of people from both kingdoms. Israel (the northern kingdom) went into exile when Samaria fell in 722 BC, and its exile was never reversed, whereas Judah's exile was to finish when Cyrus issued his decree of restoration.

The term servant (Heb. *'eved*) is used in the Old Testament to describe the special relationship that individuals like the patriarchs (Exod. 32:13; Deut. 9:27) had with the LORD. Here it is used of the nation, as it will be later on as well (Isa. 44:1-2; 45:4). The servant Israel is also 'Jacob, whom I have chosen'. This is both a reminder of Israel's earlier name and of the fact of divine election. Repeatedly Isaiah joins together the verb 'chose' (Heb. *bâchar*) or the derived noun 'chosen' (Heb. *bâchîr*) with the word 'servant' (see, in addition to this passage, 42:1; 43:10; 44:1-2; 45:4). Election was both to privilege and an obligation to service, for the servant was to be a witness to divine power and grace.

Israel is also designated here 'the seed of Abraham, my friend'. God's people could never forget their origins. They were Abraham's children and as such were expected to show the characteristics of their forefather in his allegiance to God and obedience to his commands. Most probably here and in 2 Chronicles 20:7 the term 'friend' has the connotation of 'covenant partner'. James 2:23 links together a reference to Abraham believing God (Gen. 15:6) with the assertion that he was God's friend. The promise of blessing does not extend to all of Abraham's descendants, but only to those of the grandson called Jacob/Israel. The apostle Paul develops this idea when he shows that God's purposes would be fulfilled through Isaac, not Ishmael, and through Jacob, not Esau (Rom. 9:6-13).

9 The character of Israel is spelled out further. She was called by God from 'the ends of the earth'. The parallel expression, 'from its uttermost parts', only occurs here in the Old Testament, but the context demands a term denoting 'from afar'. Israel as a nation was laid hold of by God, called effectually, and given the designation 'servant'. All this is assurance of the fact that she is indeed chosen, and not rejected.

10 As a consequence Israel could be encouraged by the declarations that the LORD makes. Fear could be dismissed because of his presence with his people (for other passages with the same phrase 'do not fear', see 41:13, 14; 43:1, 5; 44:2; 54:4). Dismay could be banished because God is their God and will both strengthen and help them. His victorious right hand will continue to provide deliverance for them.

11-12 The future of Israel's enemies is depicted. Four descriptive terms are used in reference to these enemies. They are those 'who rage against you', 'those who contend with you', 'those who strive with you' and 'those who are at war with you'. These terms depict in increasing intensity the opposition to Israel. From rage, through legal arraignment and fierce quarrelling, the opposition progresses to outright war. The result for the enemies will at first be shame and disgrace, leading ultimately to complete destruction. The time will come when Israel will not even be able to find these enemies, and they will be as nothing on the world scene. Most of the nations who opposed Israel in Isaiah's day have disappeared from the map of world history. Even before Judah was taken into exile Assyria was gone. Her conqueror Babylon was taken by the Persians, and the territory she controlled was in turn taken by the Greeks, Romans and Arabs.

13 The reason why all this is going to happen is now explained. The speaker claims to be 'the LORD your God'. The promise to take Israel by the hand (verse 10) is repeated, with the assurance that the LORD will grasp her by the right hand. Hand-in-hand with God Israel will have nothing to fear. The command 'do not fear' is not just the prophet's word to the people, but is the express instruction of the LORD himself. The God who identifies himself as 'the LORD your God' is the one who speaks these words and who gives the assurance of his gracious assistance.

14 Once more the command is 'do not fear', but the description given of Israel is very unusual. Israel is called a 'worm'. The Hebrew word here (*tôlê'ah*) is used as a general description of insect larvae and worms. It is the word employed in Psalm 22:6 where the psalmist describes himself as 'a worm and not a man'. This verse may well be a conscious allusion to that passage, and now is used of the object of God's redemptive work. It emphasises the sense of weakness felt by Israel. The following phrase (Heb. 'men of Israel') has been felt by many commentators to be a poor parallel to 'worm'. They have suggested emending the text by changing to the word for 'maggot', or by obtaining the meaning 'louse' by comparison with Akkadian. There is no reason to question the integrity of the text. The unusual word for 'men' (Heb. *m^{e}tîm*) occurs in the expression 'men of number' (i.e., few men) in Genesis 34:30 and Deuteronomy 4:27. There is not complete parallelism in this first part of verse 14, for there is no parallel term to match the opening 'do not fear'. Here the expression is in apposition to 'worm Jacob' and is a further description of the poverty and weakness of Israel. In spite of her size and condition she was the one nation that did not need to be afraid.

The second part of this verse repeats the declaration of divine assistance already found in the preceding verse, but adds to it the assertion that the LORD is 'your redeemer, the holy one of Israel'. The Hebrew word for redeemer (*gô'êl*) comes from Israelite family law, with more than half the occurrences being in sections of the Old Testament setting out legal instructions (Lev. 25; 27; Num. 35; Deut. 19). This is its first occurrence in Isaiah. Just as God was the redeemer from bondage in Egypt, so will he be the redeemer from bondage in Babylon. Weak and puny Israel need not fear, for her deliverance will be secured by her redeemer.

15 The position of Israel as the redeemed people of God will ensure that she will overcome her enemies. The language of threshing is used to depict the victories that will be achieved. The threshing sledge was made of wood (cf. the fact that Araunah's sledge is offered as firewood, 2 Sam. 24:22), with teeth of iron or stone. The fact that the sledge here has new, sharp teeth is expressing the idea that it will be effective. God will sovereignly set Israel to this task, and hills will become as mere chaff. Isaiah uses the imagery of threshing elsewhere (21:10; 28:27-28), as does his contemporary Micah (Mic. 4:13).

16 The first part of the verse carries on the picture of threshing grain. The destruction of enemies will result in them being scattered, just like the wind carries the chaff away. By strength derived from the LORD the 'worm Israel' will be able to overcome the enemies. The second half of the verse describes the attitude of Israel to God. The people will rejoice in the LORD and praise the holy one of Israel. When deliverance comes they will attribute all praise and honour to God.

17-19 These verses give a picture of God's blessing of his people. The use of similar imagery regarding water has already occurred in Isaiah 35. The poor and needy, with tongues hanging out, search for water, but they search in vain. In their desperation they cry to God (implied by the verb 'answer' in 17b), for Israel's God will not forsake his inheritance (see Psalm 94:14). Just as he provided water in the wilderness for Israel, so will he again perform miraculous deeds. Places not customarily noted as sources of water ('barren heights', 'plains', 'desert', 'parched ground') will be abundantly watered. The second of these areas should not be translated by 'valleys' for it is a Hebrew term (*biq'âh*) which is used in parallelism with 'level ground' (Heb. *mîsôr*; see Isa. 40:4). The wonders of the earlier wilderness journeys will be repeated on a more marvellous scale. In verse 19 the picture is of a forest that will grow up in the desert. Trees that normally only grow in much better conditions will be able to survive in what was previously wasteland. As so often in this book trees form an important part of Isaiah's illustrative material.[2]

20 The reason is now given why the blessings are bestowed by God. It is in order that the nations may come to understand the great power of the Holy One of Israel. There is a cluster of four verbs here to emphasise the recognition that will come of God's power. The nations will 'see', 'know', 'consider' and 'understand'. In referring to the work of God Isaiah again uses the phrase 'the holy one of Israel', the distinctive title used throughout by him (for illustration, see 1:4; 5:19; 10:20; 29:19; 43:14; 60:9). Two of the verbs used of the original creation

---

[2]For a discussion on trees in Isaiah's prophecies, see Robert L. Alden, 'Isaiah and Wood', in J. H. Skilton, ed., *The Law and the Prophets: Old Testament Studies in Honor of Oswald T. Allis*, pp. 377-87.

are employed to describe this new creative activity of the Lord (*'âsâh*, 'make', and *bârâ'*, 'create').

d. Renewed Challenge to the Heathen Gods (41:21-24)

Legal language reappears in this section, as the Gentile nations are challenged to make a formal statement of their position. They are called on to let their 'gods' show their ability.

21 Opportunity is given to the Gentiles' idols to predict the future or explain about the past ('the former things'). The inability of heathen gods to predict is one of the reasons cited several times by Isaiah why these gods cannot be trusted (see 43:9; 44:7; 45:21). The regal call is made in the name of 'Jacob's king'. Isaiah could never forget his vision of the majestic king (6:5), and earlier he referred to the LORD as the king (see 33:17, 22). What they are to present is called 'strong [reasons]' (NIV 'arguments'), the only occurrence of this word in the Old Testament. The most powerful case the heathen gods can make will be required if they are to show their alleged superiority over the God of Israel. But Isaiah is clearly mocking them by using this word, as he soon shows (verse 25) that their reasons are really completely baseless.

22-23 NIV paraphrases the opening of verse 22 with the words, 'Bring in [your idols] to tell us what is going to happen.' The Hebrew is 'Let them bring near, and let them declare to us that which is going to happen'. Clearly those making the declaration are the heathen idols and therefore the NIV rendering is justified in order to make the meaning plain. The idols are challenged to reveal things that happened long ago ('the former things') or things that are still to occur ('the things to come') in order to prove that they are real gods. They have to do something, 'whether good or bad', to show that they exist and have power. Only such a demonstration will prove they are as good as or better than Israel's God.

24 But the word from Jacob's king is that the heathen gods have no power at all. In fact, they do not even exist. They are an 'abomination'. This word occurs 117 times in the Old Testament, normally of what is physically, ritually or morally offensive, especially of what is offensive to God (cf. its use in Deuteronomy 18:9, 12 of the Canaanite beliefs and practices). Alternatively, the term can be applied to the person who chooses the idol, but the reference to the idol itself is a perfectly acceptable interpretation of the Hebrew.

e. The Coming Deliverer (41:25-29)

25 The raising up of this deliverer ('Cyrus') has not been foretold by any of the heathen gods—only by the LORD. It is only Jacob's king who is able to predict his coming, for the arrival of Cyrus will be the direct outcome of God's will. The earlier description of Cyrus in the form of a rhetorical question had shown him as coming from the east (verse 2). Now the added description here says that he will come from the north and the east. The north is included because the Persians conquered territory in the north before they took Babylon, and the Persian empire stretched from Babylon in the east to the Aegean in the west. Also, invasion of Palestine was normally from 'the north' because of the desert, and again its use is a pointer to impending judgment. The main point being made by these compass bearings is that the deliverer will come from a far distance. Cyrus is said by the LORD to either 'call upon his name', or 'to proclaim his name'. The Hebrew expression can mean either, but here it is best to think that the intention is to indicate what Cyrus is to proclaim (see Ezra 1:2-4). He is depicted as a conqueror of rulers (using Heb. *sâgân*, a loan word from Akkadian employed elsewhere of Babylonian [Jer. 51:23, 57] and Assyrian [Ezek. 23:6, 12, 23] officials). Because of the Assyrian invasions a word like this would have become familiar in Palestine. With ruthless power Cyrus will come, using the nations just like a potter uses clay (see Isaiah 29:16 for use of the potter imagery).

26 The idols are unable to predict anything like this. The rhetorical questions point both to the inability of such revelation to come from the heathen gods and the fact that Israel's God is able to make such announcements. The denial that there is any such ability on the part of idols is made very emphatic, with the threefold repetition in Hebrew of the expression 'surely no one' (Heb. *'af 'ên*).

27 There are translational difficulties with this verse. Literally it reads: 'First, to Zion, behold, behold them! And to Jerusalem one proclaiming [good news] I will give.' Clearly ancient translations struggled with this verse. The LXX has a repeated 'I will give'. The Qumran scroll 1QIsa[a] has a different reading, *hnh hnwmh*, 'behold the speaker,' but this seems like an interpretation as the Hebrew word *nomeh* ('speaker') does not occur in the MT of the Old Testament. It is best to retain the Massoretic text and accept that the Hebrew, though lacking in smoothness, is dramatic in its force. The NIV paraphrases: 'I was the first to tell Zion, "Look, here they are!" I gave to Jerusalem a messenger of good tidings.' It still remains uncertain what is the 'they' to which reference is being made. It could be the words that are being spoken by the LORD or his messenger, in contrast to the absence of words from the idols (verse 26). Or, 'they are' could be a reference to coming events. 'Messenger of good tidings' has occurred already at 40:9, and in this verse it is a synonym for Isaiah himself as the spokesman of the LORD.

28 The response from the idolaters is absolute silence. Not one person is able to respond or give advice. When the prophet enquires there is no answer (cf. the use of 'counsellor' back in 40:13). Apart from God there is no true source of counsel.

29 All the idolaters are under a delusion and their actions are empty. The images that they construct are mere wind and confusion. A familiar word from Genesis 1:2 (*tohû*) is used to describe the images. Just as the original creation was characterised by confusion, so the heathen gods are simply waste.

4. The First Servant Song and a Song of Praise (42:1-17)
This chapter commences with the first of five 'servant songs'. For over a hundred years four of these passages (42:1-9; 49:1-7; 50:4-9; 52:13–53:12) have been designated by this descriptive title.[3] It continues as a conventional usage to refer to these sections. No evidence exists that they were ever sung, but certainly they are poetic passages that

---

[3] Bernhard Duhm, a German Old Testament scholar, in his commentary on Isaiah pubished in 1892, first grouped these passages. He was working from critical presuppositions, and regarded Isaiah 40–55 as the work of an author later than Isaiah of Jerusalem. These songs, he believed, were from the pen of an even later writer, and Duhm's argument that they are insertions into the text of Isaiah 40–55 was shown by their isolation from their contexts. Because he was working with chapters 40–55 explains why Isaiah 61 did not come within his reckoning as a 'servant song', whereas I believe it should be linked with them (see the later commentary on 61:1-3). Moreover, it can be shown exegetically that 'seams' bind these passages into their contexts, and each is followed by a doxology or call to praise God. Within the songs a transition takes place in relation to the identity of the servant between Israel and the coming redeemer. From the abundance of literature on the Servant Songs I suggest two books as the starting point: Henri Blocher, *Songs of the Servant: Isaiah's Good News* (London: Inter-Varsity Press, 1975), and F. Duane Lindsey, *The Servant Songs: A Study in Isaiah* (Chicago: Moody Press, 1985).

speak of 'the servant'. This term is used of individual servants (Abraham, Moses, Elijah, David), of both Israel as the nation and the faithful believers within it, and also to the coming deliverer, whom Philip the evangelist identified as Jesus (Acts 8:35). Within the songs there is considerable variety in the portrayal of the servant. 'He is spoken *of*; he is spoken *to*; and he even speaks *himself*.'[4] Likewise, many different descriptions are given of the servant's work, while the recipients of his ministry vary from the nation Israel to the many Gentile peoples. Within the commentary notice will be taken of the complexities in the presentation of the servant of the LORD.

a. The First Servant Song (42:1-9)

Cyrus has already been introduced but it is clear that he cannot be the subject of this song. His character and projected triumphs differ markedly from the character and work of the servant who is first announced here. This servant's ministry will not be restricted to the Near East, but is going to be world-wide in its scope. Though the servant is introduced, the theme reverts to idols in verse 8, so creating a link with the preceding section. There is no real reference here to the need of Israel, but rather everything is concentrated on the servant's work.

Five main thoughts occur in the opening section (verses 1-4).

1. There is an assurance that God will watch over and empower his servant (verse 1a-b).

2. There is a brief statement as to his work (verse 1c).

3. The gentleness of the servant is described (verses 2-3).

4. The confidence and ease with which the servant will carry out his task is stated (verse 4), and particularly noteworthy is the worldwide scope of his mission.

5. The servant's work will result in justice being brought to the nations (verse 4).

1 The opening verse commences with a word that draws attention to the proclamation. It can be translated 'behold' or, as the NIV does, 'here is'. Just as the idolaters have been identified in the preceding verse (see 41:29), so now attention is directed to a special person who is called God's servant (see comment on 41:8 for a discussion of this

---

[4]O. T. Allis, *The Unity of Isaiah: A Study in Prophecy* (Presbyterian & Reformed, 1950), p. 82.

term). It becomes clear that this servant, though closely related to the servant Israel, is yet to be distinguished from her. Everything that Israel was meant to be (but wasn't) will be realised in him. His relationship with God is spelled out by several specific statements.

First of all, the servant is held by him. The verb used here has already been used in 41:10 of the grip that the LORD has on Israel. The idea is that the creator of the heavens and earth (see verse 5) will exert his power to sustain his servant. It is also an assurance that no power will be able to overcome him.

Secondly, he is called 'my chosen one' by the LORD. This noun (*bâchîr*), derived from the verb 'to choose' (*bâchar*), is used exclusively in the Old Testament in describing a relationship with the LORD. Both verb and noun are used in parallel with 'servant' by Isaiah (see 41:8-9; 42:1; 43:10; 44:1-2; 45:4). To call the servant 'my chosen' is to stress the care that God has for him and for his mission.

Thirdly, he is the one in whom the LORD 'delights'. This verb can be used to describe God's people (Ps. 147:11) or the king (1 Chron. 28:4), or as here to designate the pleasure that the LORD has in his chosen servant.

Fourthly, God grants his Spirit in such measure that an abiding presence is indicated. The Spirit was given to kings (1 Sam. 11:6; 16:13), prophets (Num. 11:29; 24:2; 2 Chron. 24:20; Mic. 3:8), leaders (Num. 11:17; Judg. 3:10), and to artisans (Exod. 31:1-5). This description has to be compared with what is said about the endowment of the messianic figure 'the Branch' with the Spirit (Isa. 11:1-3). While the terms 'the Branch' and 'servant of the LORD' are never equated, yet the concept of endowment with the Spirit does link them. The chosen servant will receive such endowment that he will be upheld in his mission.

Fifthly, the servant will succeed in his mission of bringing 'justice' (Heb. *mishpât*) to the nations. This term is crucial in this servant song, occurring in verses 1, 3, and 4. The verb from which it comes (Heb. *shâfat*) is used of the exercise of governmental administration of various kinds, whether they be legislative, executive or judicial. The noun has a wide variety of meanings but here it designates 'a just order'. The accompanying verb (Heb. *yâtsâ'* Hif.) can mean either 'to speak forth', or 'to cause to establish'. The context favours the latter sense. The servant will ultimately bring about peace and just order among men.

2 The coming of the servant will be in marked contrast to that of Cyrus. In place of noise and glamour there will be no open display of royal pomp when the servant comes. He will come quietly and with modesty, and he will not need to lift up his voice in the public places. Instead he will carry out a teaching mission without seeking publicity. Matthew's Gospel quotes from this verse in order to show how Jesus fulfilled it when he withdrew from the crowds and instructed his hearers not to proclaim him publicly (Matt. 12:15-21).

3 His work will be directed towards the needy, and his gentleness will ensure that even a bruised reed will not be broken, nor a smoking flax snuffed out. He comes, therefore, not to destroy but to save, and in ministering to those whose lives are vulnerable he will act with concern and with gentleness. This has particular relevance to Israel in exile. She considered herself as almost broken off like a crushed reed, or extinguished like a spluttering wick. The servant will come as a healer of broken lives. The verse ends with a reaffirmation of what was said in verse 1c about the servant's work resulting in a just order. Here the same phrase is used with the added words 'in faithfulness' (Heb. *le'emet*). This addition draws attention to the fact that the reality will correspond with the prediction which is being made.

4 The character of the servant contrasts markedly with the character of Israel. This is indicated by the use of two verbs to describe him, verbs that have just been used in the previous verse. Setting out the translation helps to focus attention on the repetition:

3   A *bruised* reed he will not break,
         and a *smouldering* wick he will not snuff out,
         In faithfulness he will bring forth *justice*.
4   He will not *smoulder* or be *bruised*,
         till he establishes *justice* on the earth.

Judah was indeed a bruised reed and a smouldering wick in Isaiah's time. She could so easily be broken completely and her light snuffed out. How different it is to be with the servant! Weakness and fragility will not be characteristic of him, and his light will not be extinguished. The task of the servant is again stated in terms of the establishment of a just order and the fact that far distant places rejoice in his law. This is the third time that 'justice' has been mentioned in this song. Here the verb used is 'to set' or 'to establish' (Heb. *yâsîm*). The servant's work will lead to a successful conclusion with a just order prevailing.

In addition, the song says that the islands will hope in his law (Heb. *tôrâh*). 'Torah' is often used in the Old Testament as a description of the Mosaic teaching (see Deut. 1:5; 30:10; 31:9; Josh. 24:26), and a variety of English nouns can be used to translate it: 'statutes', 'ordinances', 'precepts', 'laws', 'commandments'. In the earlier description of the coming of Cyrus (41:3-7) it was said that the 'islands' will tremble before him. In contrast, when the servant comes, 'the islands' are going to hope in his teaching. 'Islands' once again designates far off places. The servant's mission will result in people trusting in his 'instruction', which is the best translation of 'torah' here.

5 While linking in with what has gone before, verses 5-9 turn away from the main subjects of verses 1-4 and concentrate on further assurances to the people. These assurances come in setting out the nature of the redemption that the servant will accomplish. It is God who speaks directly, and the message confirms the greatness of his power and his ability to carry out his purposes. He is 'God the LORD' (Heb. *hâ'êl yhwh*) who brought into being the heavens and who stretched out the earth and its produce (the Heb. word is restricted to Isaiah and Job and designates either 'off-spring', or as here, 'produce of the ground'). The description of the creative power of God resumes the ideas presented in 40:22-26 and they will be developed further in 44:24 and 45:18. The second part of the verse reflects upon God's plan to have the world inhabited (see 45:18). He gave animating breath to humans, and he maintains them in their various human activities ('walking').

6-7 The immediate application of the doctrine of creation is to the ability of the LORD to rescue and restore his people. A God with enough power to bring the world into being is well able to deal with the needs of his people. The connection between creation and redemption is always close in Isaiah's thought, as is shown clearly in the format of these verses:

> Thus says God the LORD
> > who created the heavens
> > who spread out the earth
> > who gives breath to the people on it
> > > and life to those walking on it
> I, the LORD have called you . . .

The servant is directly addressed by the LORD, with the first statement being a reminder that he is called in accordance with God's righteous purpose. This is a re-assertion of the first description of the servant in verse 1. The servant is not proceeding on a mission that is self-initiated, but one that originates within God himself, and it is 'in righteousness'. The use of this phrase creates a definite link with Cyrus, who is also said to be called in righteousness. In both cases the idea is that the person is called for a righteous purpose. This calling is given attestation in that the servant is declared to be held by God's hand, a re-affirmation of 'I uphold' (verse 1). In his work he will be upheld and strengthened by God so that the outcome will be assured. His relationship with God is such that he will be kept by him.

The most difficult phrase in this song is the statement that God will make the servant a covenant of the people (Heb. *b*^{e}*rit 'am*). Some suggested interpretations can be ruled out on grammatical grounds. Thus the idea that the reference is to the servant community is not a possible interpretation, as this would require a change in the word order (*'am b*^{e}*rit*). It has also been suggested that the word *b*^{e}*rit* does not mean covenant here but rather something that forms a parallel with 'light' in the following phrase. However, this is most unlikely not only because of the immediate context but also because covenant was such an underlying concept for Isaiah and his listeners/readers that to introduce a word here that looked and sounded like it would be most unusual. The best interpretation is that the servant is seen as constituting the essence of the covenant that is intended to be for the people. He sums up in his own person what the covenant really meant, and this will be spelt out by Isaiah and other prophets as they speak about the new covenant (see Isa. 54:10; Jer. 31:31-34; Ezek. 16:59-60). That the covenant was to bring blessings beyond Israel is made clear in the next phrase. The servant's work is also to bring light to the nations. The Gentile world will receive light, and as the second servant song describes it (Isa. 49:6), this will be salvation from the effects of sin, as referred to in 42:7, and not just the results of exile. Spiritual sight is to come to the Gentiles. They will come out of night into light. The word 'blind' is used in the Old Testament both literally and figuratively. It is a metaphor for the spiritual insensitivity of Israel (42:18-19; 59:10) as well as the spiritual deadness of the Gentiles. Moreover, the servant's role will extend to deliverance from prison and dungeon. Comparison should be made with Isaiah 61:1 and its application by

Jesus to his ministry as recorded in Luke 4:18-21. Release from the bondage of exile is going to be one application of the promise, but also, and more widely, it will result in deliverance from bondage to sin.

8 The LORD makes another declaration concerning himself that serves to separate him from the idols. He bears the name LORD (Heb. *yhwh*), which denotes the gracious redeeming God of the covenant. It was a name specifically associated with the exodus from Egypt (see Exodus 6:2-8 and the Song of Moses in Exodus 15:1-18). He will not permit his glory to be given to another (god) nor his praise to an idol. No idol could possibly match the redemptive work that the LORD is going to achieve through his servant.

9 'The former things' have already been referred to in 41:22. The reference is to events of long ago, probably those associated with the exodus from Egypt. They have already come to pass, while 'new things' are being declared by Isaiah. These are the things that the LORD is going to perform, first in the return of exiled Judah, but then later in the redemption of all those in darkness and the shadow of death. The idols are unable either to recite past events or tell of things to come. This is so different from Israel's God who brought into being the former things and who announces through his prophets the new things that are going to spring into existence. Interpretation of the past and prediction of the future belong to the LORD alone.

b. A Song of Praise to the LORD (42:10-13)

The first servant song is immediately followed by a doxology, a feature that occurs also with each of the other songs (see 49:8-13; 50:3; 54:1-8; 61:10-11). The thought of the coming of the servant calls forth a song of praise to the LORD. The theme and language are reminiscent of other Old Testament songs such as Psalms 95–99. The call to praise is repeated several times: 'sing' (verse 10); 'raise voices', 'rejoice', 'shout' (verse 11); 'give glory', 'proclaim his praise' (verse 12). The song is a variation of what has already been said in 24:14-15.

10 The opening is a call to sing 'a new song'. The use of the adjective 'new' can indicate the freshness of the song, or a song with an eschatological note, one linked in thought with the end times. This second option is preferable here, since the prophet has been speaking about the new things that are to occur. The coming of these days (the return from exile) is an event that will presage the fuller coming of God's salvation in new covenant days. After having described the

ministry of the servant to the Gentiles (verses 6-7) it is not surprising
to see that those taking part in this praise are those at the ends of the
earth. This thought is amplified in the second part of the verse by
reference to those who traverse oceans and to the far-off isles along
with their inhabitants. The work of the servant will reach far beyond
the borders of Israel, and Gentile peoples at the ends of the earth will
ultimately take part in the singing of a new song (see Rev. 5:9-10).

11 Turning to places nearer to Israel the call is for desert and
mountainous areas to join in the song of praise. Mention is made
specifically of Kedar and Sela. The first of these is the name of one of
Ishmael's sons and the father of the tribe that carried his name (Gen.
25:13). The area they occupied was south-east of Damascus. Sela is
a common noun in the Old Testament meaning 'rock', but it is also
used as a proper noun. While the name is linked with various sites, it is
most probably a reference to the Nabatean stronghold of Petra, some
90 miles (150 km) south-east of Jerusalem, as indicated in 2 Kings
14:7. 'Petra' is a Greek word meaning 'rock'. Even these Gentiles
living nearer to Israel are called upon to sing the LORD's praise. The
verb translated 'shout' in verse 11d occurs only here in the Old
Testament, but its meaning is clear from the use of 'sing for joy' in the
preceding phrase.

12 All those mentioned are summoned collectively to give glory to
the LORD, while the distant isles are called to declare his praise. The
parallelism here (as in verse 8) points to the idea of 'glory' being praise
or honour given to God. While the idea of giving 'glory' to a human
person occurs in the Old Testament (see the case of David in 1 Chron.
17:18), yet the expression relates most of all to ascribing honour and
dignity to God.

13 This verse gives the reason for the preceding summons. The
LORD is going forth to battle as a warrior, and he is going to be victorious
over his enemies. Twice in the verse the Hebrew root *gâvar* occurs.
First, it occurs in the description of the LORD as a warrior (Heb. *gibbôr*),
and secondly as the verb 'triumph' (Heb. *yitgabbâr*). While the noun
gibbôr is used of human warriors, it is also used in reference to God
as the commander-in-chief of his armies. His name is 'the LORD, strong
and mighty, the LORD, mighty in battle' (Ps. 24:8), and 'God of Gods
and Lord of lords, the great, the mighty, and the terrible God' (Deut.
10:17). He goes out like a warrior to battle, with 'zeal' or 'jealousy'
directed towards the salvation of his people. He will raise the battle

cry in order to startle the enemy. The verbal form used here and translated 'triumph' or 'show prowess' occurs only with the LORD as the subject (cf. Exod. 15:3; Ps. 24:8; 46:8-9; Isa. 61:1-6). He has the power to prevail against his enemies, and is able to bring his plans to fruition. When the LORD redeems his people this will be a demonstration of his power over all his and their enemies. As such it will feature as the subject of the new song which is sung in that day. Notice should also be taken of the contrast between this verse and the description of the servant in verses 1-3. There the servant acts quietly and with no outward show. Here the LORD is the violent warrior going forth to battle.

c. The LORD the Man of War (42:14-17)

These verses carry on the theme of the context. God depicts himself as having kept himself restrained for a long time, but now the appointed time has come to reveal his power. He is going to perform miraculous deeds as he leads his people (here called 'the blind') home again to Palestine. Deliverance from Babylon will be achieved by God who will not forsake his people (cf. Ps. 94:14), and that victory will bring shame on all the idol worshippers.

14 God pictures himself as holding back until the due time comes. The verb used is the same one as occurs in Genesis 43:31 of Joseph restraining his emotions while speaking with his brothers. This restraint has been 'for a long time'. This phrase can refer both to all of Israel's history up to the present time and also to the period of exile. Instead of continuing the thought of the warrior in the previous verses the LORD now compares himself to a pregnant woman waiting for the birth of her child. The use of the verbs 'cry out', 'gasp' and 'pant' are expressive of the intense desire of God for the achievement of his purpose for Israel.

15 The thought of changes in the geography again has prominence (for earlier occurrences of descriptions of a radically altered landscape see 35:7-10; 40:3-4), but here there is a difference. The idea is of violent judgment carried out by the LORD. He will so change the countryside that the vegetation on the mountain slopes will be destroyed, and the rivers will cease to flow. In the context of this section the judgment is presumably directed against Babylon, though she is not specifically named.

16 The promise is given of 'the blind' travelling on unfamiliar paths.

'The blind' is a reference to Israel, a concept that is going to be developed further in verses 18-19. Following judgment on Babylon God is going to lead his people out of their exilic bondage. The fact that he is the powerful one able to perform miracles for them is stressed by the repeated use of the first person pronoun: '*I* will lead'; '*I* will guide'; '*I* will turn' (lit. 'set'); '*I* will do'; '*I* will not forsake'. The rescue of Israel will take place only because of the LORD's power and grace. He will exercise his power on Israel's behalf and will perform all that he has promised.

17 When these things occur the heathen idols will be utterly discredited and those who trust in them will be put to shame. The claim they make about the idols, 'you are our gods,' will then be seen to be utterly false.

5. Israel's Only Saviour (42:18–43:13)

a. Israel Blind and Deaf (42:18-25)
18 This is probably a transitional verse between the description of divine judgment on Babylon and the resulting second exodus, and the accusations of disobedience against Israel. Spiritually Israel is both deaf and blind. She has little concern for God's laws, whether listening to them or reading them.

19 Israel the servant is now directly accused of being blind and deaf. She was chosen by God and promised strength and support (41:10), yet the messenger herself is in need of radical change. No one is as deaf and blind as Israel. A series of terms is used to define Israel: 'servant', 'messenger', 'the one committed to me', 'the servant of the LORD'. She is in a special relationship with God, denoted by the term 'servant', and in spite of her sin that relationship continues (cf. the later reference to the fact that no divorce had taken place, 50:1). This is the only time that the full phrase 'the servant of the LORD' (*'eved yhwh*) occurs in Isaiah. The term 'messenger' (or 'angel') is used for deputies sent by human leaders on business or diplomacy (Gen. 32:3-6), but it is also a term used of prophetic or priestly messengers sent by God (Hag. 1:13; Mal. 2:7). Often the formula drawn from diplomacy, 'thus says the LORD,' is used of these messengers (cf. the use of this phrase of Isaiah's ministry earlier in this chapter, 42:5). The third term (Heb. *meshullâm*) translated as 'the one committed to me' (NIV) or 'he that is at peace with me'

(NASB) is a passive form from the root from which 'shalom' ('peace') comes. Here it appears to denote one who is in a covenant of peace with the LORD, and so committed to him. This word then forms a very acceptable synonym for the following phrase, 'the servant of the LORD.' The seeming contradiction between verse 19 and verses 1-4 can be resolved by understanding that Israel has responsibility for the work, but can only accomplish it by divine endowment. As becomes clear later, only an individual servant, the Messiah, will be able to fulfil the role given to Israel.

20 Israel had been witness to many acts of God's power and grace, but did not take them to heart. She had ears ready and available for hearing the message of the LORD and yet did not really listen. Just what had been told to Isaiah at the outset of his ministry was indeed fulfilled in the way in which Israel failed to heed all the revelation that had come from God (cf. Isa. 6:9-10). Likewise the sin of Israel still consisted of the things of which Moses had accused them (Deut. 29:2-4).

21 God reiterates his purpose that the servant's work will be fulfilled and his law made great. For the sake of his own righteousness God was pleased to exalt his law and render it glorious. The use of the verb 'render glorious' creates a direct connection with the account of the exodus from Egypt, as its only other occurrence is in the Song of Moses (Exod. 15:4, 11). 'Law' has the same meaning here as in verse 4 and as it will have again in verse 24.

22 Israel (the nation) is unable to carry out its work for it is trapped and in bondage. It had been looted by the Assyrians (see Isa. 10:6) and was to be by the Babylonians, as Hezekiah had been told (Isa. 39:6). In this verse the verb 'to plunder' (Heb. *bâzaz*) and the related noun 'plunder' (Heb. *baz*) both occur. The symbolic name carried by one of Isaiah's sons, Maher-Shalal-Hash-Baz ('hasting to the spoil, hurrying to the prey', Isa. 8:1), was an early warning to Israel of what her enemies would do to her. While the description of Israel trapped in pits and hidden in prisons may relate to actual historical events, yet the description seems to point metaphorically to the greater bondage of being enslaved by disobedience and sin.

23 The theme is developed further in this and following verses with the idea that it is God who has given Israel over to the robbers because of the people's sin. The nation refused to walk in his ways and though punished still did not take it to heart (verse 25). In typical Isaianic style the message is addressed to the people by means of rhetorical questions. There is no need for anyone to answer these opening questions, as it is patently obvious that the people had not been listening to God's messages through the prophets. They might even speak of things to come and yet the people will not pay heed. The word for 'time to come' (*'achar*) is connected in Hebrew with what is behind, at one's back. It may well be used here as a shorter version of the phrase *'ach^{a}rît hâyyâmîm*, 'the latter days', 'days to come' (cf. Isa. 2:2 [=Mic. 4:1]; Hos. 3:5; Jer. 48:47; Ezek. 38:16).

24 The threat of being handed over to enemies was given in the covenantal warnings in Leviticus and Deuteronomy (Lev. 26:17; Deut. 28:25). The verb translated 'hand over' is the Hebrew word for 'give' (*nâtan*), but it is frequently used in this sense of delivering into someone else's power. When Israel and Judah fell under foreign domination it was not caused simply by the inability to repel foreign invaders. What took place was by the deliberate choice of God (see 2 Kings 17:7-23), and as a result of the people's sin. Here the cause of the sin is expressed as sinning against the LORD, not following his ways, and disobedience to his law. A literal translation of the second half of the verse is: 'They did not will to walk in his ways, and they did not listen to his law.' This expression is especially distinctive of Isaiah (see 28:12; 30:9, 15), occurring elsewhere only twice in Ezekiel. It literally means that they willed not to walk in his ways. The fault is pressed home to the people for their own punishment.

25 The outcome of the sin of Israel is the display of God's wrath. This is a repetition of the idea that occurs in the historical books (see 1 Kings 17:11, 18). God's anger is displayed against his own people, and they become part of the violence of war. An incorrigible people will be severely punished and yet not understand what is taking place, and also fail to lay the message to heart. The only escape from the fire of God's wrath will be by his mercy (see 43:2).

b. Israel's Saviour (43:1-7)

A new stage in the argument begins at this point. Continuity with the previous section is shown by the use of the Hebrew expression *v^e'attah*, 'and now' (cf. its use in 5:3-5). It is often used in the prophetic books to introduce some imminent activities of the LORD, either in blessing or cursing. Appeal is made to the character of the creator God, the holy one of Israel, who is able to reverse the exile and bring his people back to their land.

1 The verbs 'create' and 'form' can be used both of what God did in his activity in creation, as well as his forming of Israel as his own people (for previous use of 'create' in Isaiah, see 4:5; 40:26, 28; 41:20; 42:5; and for 'form', see 22:11; 27:11; 29:16; 37:26). Israel's God again speaks with authority, and this time it is a word of consolation for his people. His command to them is 'not to fear', and the reason for this is twofold. First of all, God is the one who has redeemed his people for himself. The verb used here (Heb. *gâ'al*) is used in the Pentateuch (Gen.–Deut.) of redemption of property or persons, and also of the role of the next of kin to effect payment of life for life. In the psalms and prophets it is a common word to describe how God will defend and vindicate his own people. The thought of near kinship may carry over from secular usage as well. The second reason is that God has called Jacob/Israel by his own name. He has placed his name on them to indicate ownership. Hence it follows that they belong to him. In spite of Israel's exilic experience nothing has changed the fact that Israel is the LORD's by creation and redemption.

2 A new exodus experience lies ahead for the exiles. Just as Israel was saved when passing through the waters of the Red Sea and of the Jordan River, so will the returnees be saved as they journey back home. The picture of the waters of judgment has already been used in 8:6-8, and one of the same verbs, 'sweep over' (Heb. *shâtaf*), is used here as well. 'Walking through the fire' may be a metaphor for acute affliction, though the experience of Shadrach, Meshech, and Abednego could well indicate the reality of such punishment (Dan. 3:25-27). God's wrath will not be poured out upon them, but rather he will save them when they pass through the fire. Emphasis is placed on the presence of God with his people in that the Hebrew word order stresses the fact that Israel is assured of God's presence.

3 The reason for this assurance rests in God's character. Four epithets are used by God to describe himself. He is 'the LORD' (*yhwh*), 'your God', 'the holy one of Israel', and 'your saviour'. The first of these is a reminder that the redeemer God of the exodus is still in covenant relationship with his people Israel. The second assures a people punished for their sins that there is still hope for them in that God remains their God. The third is the favourite expression for God used in Isaiah, drawing attention to God's purity and holiness. The final term gives further encouragement to them in that they are assured that there is hope for them in God's saving power. Whether Israel was in Egypt or Babylon, God is able to be the saviour. Some translations make the description of God the subject of the following verb 'give': 'I the LORD, your God,... give Egypt for a ransom.' While this is possible, the use of such an extended subject is unusual, and therefore it is better to understand the first half of the verse as an independent declaration by God in order to reassure his people concerning the certainty of their deliverance. The second part of the verse introduces the idea of a ransom price. The word used here for ransom (Heb. *kôfer*) occurs in the Mosaic law of a substitute price paid in exchange for a life. The idea is that nations such as Egypt, Cush, and Seba are exchanged for Israel. Cush seems to be the area south of Egypt (the upper Nile region), while Seba may well have been to its east. While the reference could be to the future conquering of these countries by Persia, the thought may be the more general one that Gentile nations are (or, were in the past) given up in exchange for Israel.

4 Israel occupies a special place in God's affection. She is 'precious', 'honoured' and 'loved', and due to this fact (NIV 'since') other nations (possibly the three just mentioned in the previous verse) are given up to judgment in her place. The verb, 'to be precious', is used theologically to convey the idea of the valuation of human life. While the ransom for the wicked is too costly (Ps. 49:8), this verse declares that Israel has great value in the sight of God (Heb. lit. 'precious in the eyes of'). The thought of God's love for Israel is one of the major themes of the book of Deuteronomy (cf. 4:37; 7:8; 10:15; 23:5). The second half of the verse continues the idea of ransom introduced in the previous verse. Men (the Heb. is *'âdâm* used generically) can be exchanged for Israel; Gentile nations can take her place. The thought of verse 3b is given greater emphasis by this repetition of the idea. It is another way of indicating the salvation of Israel, because she is the object of God's electing love. Israel stands in a totally different relationship with God than do any of the other nations.

5-7 Once more the declaration is made that Israel should not fear: 'Fear not, for I am with you.' The presence of God is not only reassurance to Israel but it is also the ground of future restoration. Just as the covenant curses were inflicted because of disobedience, so the promised blessing of restoration will apply because of God's faithfulness. In Deuteronomy 30:3-4 the promise was given: 'then the

LORD your God will restore your fortunes and have compassion on you and gather you again from all the nations where he scattered you. Even if you have been banished to the most distant land under the heavens, from there the LORD your God will gather you and bring you back' (NIV). The language echoes that promise, with the use of the verbs 'bring [back]' and 'gather'. From every point of the compass exiles will return. The actual people are described in various ways: 'your seed', 'my sons', 'my daughters'. 'Seed' (Heb. *zera'*) does not refer to future generations but to existing family members. They are not only sons and daughters of Israelite families, but more importantly they are regarded as God's sons and daughters.

The dispersion was extremely widespread. Prisoners taken in war were often sold on to other countries. From extra-biblical sources we know of Jewish communities existing in places not mentioned in the Bible. While Jeremiah was taken to Egypt along with others prior to the fall of Jerusalem (see Jer. 43:4-7), we do not know how there came to be a strong Jewish community in Elephantine on the Upper Nile. The important point here is that restoration will occur from all directions, and returnees will come 'from afar', 'from the ends of the earth'.

Two further things need to be noted about this restoration. First, it is to be the LORD's doing: '*I* will say to the north ... and to the south.' The longing for restoration may well have existed in the hearts of many exiled Jews, but the actual will to return is God's, not theirs. Secondly, the description of the returnees given in verse 7 reinforces what has already been said about them. They are a people God has called by his name, and therefore they are his. In addition he created, formed, and made them, stressing that the origin of Israel was God's creative work. It is just another way of reminding the people of their election, which was not designed to bring glory to them but to their Maker.

c. The Courtroom (43:8-13)

8 There is a clear link in thought with 42:18-19. Most modern translations take the first verb as an imperative ('lead out'), but the form is a Hebrew perfect ('he led out') and should be preserved. Isaiah is picturing a courtroom scene in which Israel and the nations take part. Though Israel is both blind and deaf, she is a witness for the LORD (see verse 10). The assembly has already been gathered together and at the forefront is the blind nation Israel (Heb. *'am*). The spiritual state of Israel is indicated in that the nation is described as blind, while having eyes, and deaf, while having ears. Ability to see and hear ordinary things does not mean spiritual perception.

9 All the Gentile nations (Heb. *gôyîm*) are assembled as well. They are also called 'peoples' (*l^{e}umîm*). This word is a rare poetic form, mainly found in the Psalms and Isaiah, and its meaning is dependent on the word used in parallel with it. Here it is clearly another word conveying the idea of 'Gentile nations'. The question is asked whether anyone has been able to foretell current events or has been able to tell of the distant past (Heb. lit. 'the first things'; cf. 41:22). If such were the case, then witnesses would be able to testify to this and so the account would be proved correct. The implication is, of course, that no such witnesses can be produced. The word for 'witness' (Heb. *'êd*) is a legal term referring to a person who is qualified to testify in court proceedings.

10 The LORD, however, is able to bring forth his witnesses, as his people were commissioned for that task. He makes a solemn declaration of this, with use of the formula 'declares the LORD' (Heb. *n^e'um yhwh*; see comment on this phrase at 1:24). In his sovereign love he had chosen Israel as his servant (cf. 42:1, with its similar language). The choice of Israel was made so that God would have a people for himself who would acknowledge him and put their trust in him. The verb 'know' (Heb. *yâda'*) is frequently used in the sense of recognising or acknowledging God (cf. with God's hand, Josh. 4:24; with God's name, Jer. 16:21). 'To believe' in a context such as this (and with the Heb. preposition *l^e*) has the idea of believing what is true. Belief and understanding are linked together. Israel had both to trust in the LORD and correctly perceive who he was.

The confession that Israel is to make concerns the self-existence of the LORD. It is the eternal God who makes the assertion regarding his person: 'I am he' (Heb. *'^{a}nî hû'*). This is an important phrase in Isaiah, and it also forms the background of the 'I am' sayings of Jesus recorded in John's Gospel. Several aspects of this phrase need comment.

1. The phrase itself does not make sense on its own but has to be understood in the light of the context. What is clear here is that 'I am he' is paralleled with 'I am the LORD' (cf. the similar parallelism in 52:5-6).

2. The phrase is only used by the LORD himself in Isaiah. No one

else can make that statement regarding oneself. Proud Babylon can only make a claim that approximates to it: 'I [am]' (Heb. *'ᵃnî*), but this presumptuous claim is clearly in contrast with the LORD's claim.

3. The phrase is an assertion of exclusive monotheism on the part of Israel's God. It expresses the conviction that there is no other God beside him (in addition to this passage, see also 44:6-8; 45:5, 6, 18, 21, 22; 46:9).

4. Jesus' use of the phrase 'I am' (Gk. *ego eimi*) is a conscious carry-over from Isaiah and is expressly an identification with the nature and actions of God.

The assertion of the LORD concerning himself is concluded with a sarcastic reference to the heathen gods: 'Before me no god was formed, and after me there will not be [any].' This is just another way of saying that there were no other gods at all. Any idol was just a pretend deity, without power and the ability to help its worshippers. In a culture rife with plurality of deities Israel is to know that there is only one living and true God.

11 What has already been declared is made even more emphatic by this verse; ' I, I [am] the LORD, and there is no saviour apart from me.' The form of the pronoun is the longer 'I' (Heb. *'ânôkî*, in place of *'ᵃnî*). While the longer form is often employed in earlier Old Testament books (e.g., in Deuteronomy), yet the shorter form definitely becomes far more common in later books. In Ezekiel the shorter form occurs 138 times as against a single occurrence of the longer form. It may be used here for emphasis or because it is fitting to do so when allusion is being made to earlier Old Testament passages. The assertion that follows is probably an echo of Deuteronomy 4:35; 'You were shown these things so that you might know that the LORD is God; besides him there is no other.' Common to both are the use of 'LORD' (Heb. *yhwh*), the idea of 'knowing', and the preposition 'besides him' (Heb. *lᵉvad*).

12 The LORD continues to speak (again with the emphatic 'I') and makes a declaration concerning his threefold activity: he has 'declared', 'saved' and 'caused to hear'. Such revelatory action and decisive redemptive work distinguishes him from any other so-called gods. The NIV translation, 'I have revealed and saved and proclaimed – I, and not some foreign god among you,' while it has a lengthy history of support among commentators, does not seem justified. The Hebrew grammar (including the use of the negative particle *'ên* and not *lô'*) suggests that the translation of the middle clause of the verse should be, 'and there is no foreign god among you.' This is simply stating the fact that there were no actual foreign or alien gods in existence, and so is equivalent to a declaration of monotheism. There does not seem to be any real difference between the phrase used here, 'foreign god' (Heb. *['êl] zâr*), and the comparable phrase, 'strange god' (Heb. *'êl nêkâr*). The declaration concludes with a repetition of the words, 'you are my witnesses, says the LORD,' from verse 10, coupled with a further statement of his own self-existence: 'and I am God.' In the context this last statement is the same as saying, 'I am [the only] God.'

13 Several translations, including the NIV, take the opening phrase as a reference to past time: 'also from ancient days' (Heb. *gam miyyôm*). However, it is best to take it as a reference to future time (cf. the same idiom in Ezekiel 48:35 and the NIV translation there, 'from that time on'). The translation will then be: 'Also, from now on, I am he.' This is stating the unchangeableness of the LORD. Both friend and foe can be assured that he is ever the same. The thought and much of the language comes from Deuteronomy 32:39. 'I am he' and 'and none delivers from his hand' are taken over exactly. When the LORD acts, no one else has the power to reverse those actions. The thought and language of the end of the verse is close to Isaiah 14:27: 'For the LORD Almighty has purposed, and who can thwart him? His hand is stretched out, and who can turn it back?' (NIV) There the prophet is asserting the LORD's purpose to crush Assyria and the inability of anyone to turn his hand back. Here the emphasis is more general. In respect to all of God's plans and actions, who is able to alter his sovereign will?

6. Israel's Unfaithfulness and God's Mercy (43:14–44:5)

a. The New Exodus (43:14-21)

The thought of a new exodus has already been introduced (see 41:17-20; 42:15-17), as well as the idea of 'new things' that are to take place (42:9). There is repetition of terms already used such as 'your Redeemer' and 'I am the LORD', but themes are developed much further. Babylon, already recognised to be the enemy of God's people (see chapters 13–14, 39) is shown to be the captor from whom the exiles are to be set free. Chaldeans are mentioned for the first time (verse 14; NIV 'Babylonians'). They were a Semitic people associated with the Euphrates valley, and established the Chaldean empire after the fall of Nineveh in 612 BC. Israel needed more than just redemption from bondage. Her spiritual state needed restoration and this could only be done by a God who could blot out transgressions for his own sake (verse 25).

14 The section commences with the LORD again making solemn declaration of his person and purposes for Israel. He identifies himself as 'your Redeemer, the holy one of Israel'. While their God is still the same, yet he is going to do things that far transcend the old or former things. The first of these concerns Babylon (see comment on 13:1). For the sake of Israel decisive action will be taken against Babylon, but the Hebrew is difficult to translate. The ancient versions struggled with it, but seem to be attempting to translate the Massoretic text as we still have it. The major Hebrew manuscript among the Dead Sea Scrolls, 1QIsa^a, has the same text except that it changes 'to Babylon' into the stronger 'against Babylon'. The most important question is: What is going to be brought down from Babylon? Translations provide an amazing variety of answers: 'nobles' (AV); 'bars' (RSV, NAB); 'prison bars' (JB); 'as they flee' (NEB); 'as fugitives' (NIV). If the parallelism of the verse is taken into consideration, the Hebrew word in question (*bârîchîm*) may well be another word for 'ships' or 'boats' corresponding to the following 'ships' in the next line (this is taking *ba* as the Heb. preposition). This may be supported by the fact that the verb 'bring down' is used in the Old Testament of embarking in a ship (see its usage in Psalm 107:23 and Jonah 1:3). Hence a translation such as this is quite feasible: 'For your sake I will send to Babylon, and cause all of them to embark in boats, and the Chaldeans in their proud ships.' The Babylonians lived by waters (see Jer. 51:13), and carried out extensive trading by means of the Tigris and Euphrates rivers and the Persian Gulf. The point of the message is that the ships in which they took such pride would one day become the means by which they would have to flee. The word translated 'proud' is actually 'their cry', i.e. their cry in joy or exultation.

15 The message against Babylon finds confirmation in the fact that the one making it is indeed the LORD, who describes himself to Israel as 'your holy one, the creator of Israel, your king'. While the expression 'your holy one' is unusual (this is the only occurrence of it in Isaiah), there does not seem to be any difference in meaning between it and the common 'the holy one of Israel'. At the opening of the chapter the LORD had announced that he himself had created Israel (verse 1). Now he expressly says to the people that he is 'the creator of Israel'. The God who created the heavens (40:26) and the ends of the earth (40:28) is the one who called Israel as a people and formed them into a nation. He had made them into a kingdom of priests (Exod. 19:5-6) and hence is indeed their king. This short oracle about the coming judgment of Babylon is prefaced and closed with an identification of the LORD that stresses his sovereign power over Israel and her enemies. He has the destiny of Israel and the nations in his hand, for he is the almighty creator of all things.

16-17 God has also a solemn word concerning Israel, and the new exodus will far transcend the former one. He was able to make a way for Israel through the waters and a pathway amidst the roaring waves. He led out the Egyptian chariots, the army (Heb. *chayil*) and the warriors (Heb. *'izzûz*). This last word occurs only twice in the Old Testament. It is used of the LORD strong and mighty (Heb. *'izzûz v^{e}gibbôr*, Ps. 24:8), and here in parallel with the word for 'army'. Though the NIV paraphrases it as 'reinforcements', a free translation like that is unnecessary. As it is linked with the word for 'army' it is best to translate it simply as 'warriors' or 'men of valour'. The fate of the Egyptian army is described in typically poetic language (for other examples, see Exodus 15:1-5 and Psalm 106:8-12). The Egyptian soldiers were drowned in the waters and their lives snuffed out like a wick. Another smouldering wick has already been mentioned (Isa. 42:3), but the contrast is evident. While the Egyptians were killed, weak Israel will be preserved by the LORD.

18 The command to Israel in this verse at first seems a little strange. God has just reminded them that he was the God of the exodus. Why then should he tell the people not to remember the former things or consider the things of long ago? There can be little doubt that the expressions 'former things' and 'things long ago' refer to the Exodus experience, as this is the subject being dealt with in the immediate context (and not the former prophecies concerning Cyrus). 'Do not remember' has the implication 'do not brood over' or 'do not only consider'. Thought should not be concentrated on the distant past, but rather directed to the immediate future when the events of the Exodus will be replicated in even more glorious fashion. The distant past events will pale into insignificance in the face of the 'new things'.

19 The introductory 'Behold I am ...' highlights the announcement that follows. God is doing a new thing, the use of the Hebrew participle *'oseh* giving the idea of imminent action. Judah is going to be led back out of Babylonian exile as a new creation. It is ready to happen just like a new plant springing out of the soil, but Israel is without spiritual perception to understand its true significance. A spiritually blind and deaf people could not grasp the wonder of the new thing. Just as in the past, so God will create a wilderness path for his returning people, and he will also provide streams in the desert. While desolate areas will have to be traversed by the returnees, yet God will make provision for them, including water to meet their thirst.

20-21 Creatures of the desert are also depicted as sharing in this sudden increase in water. Jackals and owls will give glory to God because of his wonderful provision. In 13:21 they are said to inhabit the ruins of Babylon, while in 34:14 they also appear in a message of judgment. The picture given of the return is not a literal description but a poetic account of the miraculous provision that God will make for his people. As the creatures will take part in his eternal kingdom (11:6-8), so they are here pictured as participating in the return from exile. The description of the provision is almost the same as in the previous verse (with a change from 'way' to 'water', and a change in the order of words, 'streams' and 'wastelands'). God's graciousness to the birds and animals is because he is going to provide drink for his people, his chosen one. What was said of Israel in 42:1 is repeated. The statement is an emphatic assertion of the place of Israel in God's affections. 'Chosen' is not here an adjective but the substantive, so that 'my people' and 'my chosen' stand in apposition to one another as two descriptions of the same group. Israel is both the people of God and the object of God's electing love. The explanation of the new thing God is going to do concludes with a comment about the nature of Israel. God had formed her (cf. 43:1), and part of her function was to declare his praise. Far off places had been spoken of as proclaiming his praise (42:12), but Israel's special relationship with God means that she was to have the special task of proclaiming his praise (see Deut. 10:21).

b. Israel's Failure (43:22-28)

Parallel to the transition in the previous chapter (42:18), at this point there is a change from presentation of the blessings to Israel to judgment upon her. Whereas Israel should have been fulfilling the LORD's mission as his servant, she has failed grievously and stands in need of God's forgiving mercy. He is the one who can blot out transgressions for his own sake.

22 The contrast with the preceding section is made clear in the way this verse commences. English translations need to start with 'yet' or 'but' in order to bring out the force of the Hebrew ($v^e l\hat{o}$' '$ot\hat{i}$ $q\hat{a}r\hat{a}$'$t\hat{a}$, 'but *me* you did not call [upon]'). The object of the verb ('me') is put in a position of emphasis. The verb 'call' (Heb. $q\hat{a}r\hat{a}$') is often used in the sense of calling upon God in prayer (cf. Pss. 14:4; 18:6), though it can also be used of calling out in proclamation. The first sense fits well in the context. In their self-satisfaction the people had failed to make their needs known to God. The situation was such that they even grew wearied with him. The verb 'to become weary' (Heb. $y\hat{a}ga$') has already been used in 40:29-31 in a completely different way. In reality the people have not waited on the LORD (40:31), but instead have grown tired of him.

23-24 It is hard to be sure whether the accusation of this verse relates just to the period of exile, or whether it applies to the whole of the prior history of the nation. On balance it is probably best to take it as referring both to the experience of the exile and to the preceding centuries. While the people could not present these offerings during the exile, their attitude had not changed. They did not bring lambs for the burnt-offerings, and failed to honour God with their sacrifices. What really happened was that God did not place unnecessary demands upon them. He did not force them into servitude in order to present gift offerings (the verb used is the causative form of the verb '$\hat{a}vad$). Though they were wearied with God, yet he did not weary them with demands for incense. From our knowledge of other cultures in the Near East, the ritual demands on Israel were not nearly as excessive as others experienced.

The list of sins relating to sacrifice are continued in verse 24. The people had not spent money on acquiring sweet cane. There is a play on sounds in that the first two consonants of 'acquired' and 'sweet cane' are the same (Heb. $q\hat{a}n\hat{i}t\hat{a}$, $q\hat{a}neh$). The whole clause is notable for its alliteration: $l\hat{o}$' $qanita$ $l\hat{i}$ $vakesef$ $q\hat{a}neh$, 'you did not acquire for me with money sweet cane,' 'you did not gain cane for me with cash.'[5] The sweet cane was an aromatic plant, possibly coming from

---

[5]C. R. North, *The Second Isaiah: Introduction, Translation and Commentary to Chapters XL-LV* (Oxford University Press, 1964), p. 129.

India, which was used as an ingredient in the sacred anointing oil (Exod. 30:25). Moreover, the fat of the sacrifices (the most desirable part) did not satisfy the LORD. The second usage of the verb 'to serve' occurs in this verse. The contrast is most acute: 'I have not *burdened/ belaboured* you with offerings' (v. 23c) ... 'but you have *burdened/ belaboured* me with your sins' (v. 24c). The sins of Israel pressed upon the LORD as a heavy burden. The contrast also occurs with the use of the verb 'to weary': 'I *did not weary* you [with requests]' ... (v. 23) 'but *you wearied* me with your iniquities' (v. 24). This is the repetition of a charge God had made at the very outset of this book (see 1:14, although a different word for 'burden' is used).

The essence of these verses is not a polemic against sacrifice in itself. It is a further reminder of the need for wholehearted worship and service. The people were going through the pretence of praying and offering sacrifices, yet there was no reality to their worship. A similar catalogue occurs in 1:1-15. There the people were invited to reason with the LORD and accept the full absolution of their sins. Here the passages move on to a similar declaration of God's forgiveness.

25 After describing their sin against him, the LORD indicates that he is the one who can blot out transgressions. The declaration is impressive in the way it opens with the repetition of the longer form of the personal pronoun, 'I' (Heb. *'ânôkî*), and the use of the third person pronoun, 'he' (Heb. *hû'*). There seems to be deliberate use of these features to echo the monotheistic formula (see comments on 43:11). What the LORD claims is that he (with the implication 'only he') can blot out transgressions. The verb for 'blot out' (Heb. *mocheh*, part.) is used at times in the Old Testament in connection with God's judgment (blotting out the memory of Amalek, Exod. 17:14; blotting out the name of the unrepentant, Deut. 29:20). But it also appears in passages like this which are speaking of salvation (cf. its use in the next chapter, 44:22). 'Transgressions' and 'sins' are used in parallel, while 'blot out' is paralleled with 'not remember'. To say that God 'will not remember' sin is equivalent to saying that he will forget it. While the verb is simply 'he will not remember', yet the addition of words such as 'no more' (NIV) in English translation are certainly warranted because of the synonym 'blot out' and also the general context. The motive for this divine action of forgiveness is the same as was given earlier for the salvation of Jerusalem from the hand of Sennacherib and his army, 'for my own sake.' Later Daniel will plead for the devastated city of

Jerusalem and the ruined sanctuary for exactly the same reason, 'for your sake' (Dan. 9:19). Salvation was not because of anything in the object, but solely because God was 'gracious and compassionate, slow to anger, abounding in love' (Ps. 103:8). When he saved, it was for his own sake.

26 Legal terminology occurs again, though it is not developed in such detail as in 41:1-7. Three things are demanded. First, the nation is instructed to put God in remembrance so that the case can be argued out in public. Secondly, they are called on to argue the matter out together in court. When the verb 'to judge' (Heb. *shâfat*) occurs in the *Nifal* form it is normally followed by one of the prepositions meaning 'with', but here the adverb 'together' points to the reciprocal nature of the legal case. Thirdly, they have to declare or relate the case, setting out the facts. The final clause, 'in order that you may be cleared', is probably the desired result of all three actions (and not just of the last one, as the NIV translation would suggest: 'state the case for your innocence').

27 Looking back to the patriarchal time, even their 'first father' sinned. The context does not make it clear whether Abraham or Jacob is meant. Clearly in Deuteronomy 26:5, in the ceremony of the first-fruits, a man had to confess that his father, Jacob, was a perishing Aramean.[6] But in Isaiah Abraham is expressly called 'your father' in 51:2, and so it is best to assume that he is intended here as well. No mention is made of any specific incident in which Abraham sinned, but the point is clear. Even the great forefather was not innocent before God (see, for example, the narratives in Genesis 12:10-20 and 16:1-6). Another group is specifically mentioned as rebelling against God. The Hebrew word used (*melîts*), from contexts such as Genesis 42:23 and 2 Chronicles 32:31, has the meaning of 'interpreter' or 'intermediary'. It is unclear whether priests or prophets are intended, and perhaps the use of 'spokesmen' is the best translation. Even prominent leaders of the nation are no more free from sin than Abraham.

28 As a consequence of Israel's sin, God pronounces judgment on the priests and the nation. The reference to the priests (Heb. lit. 'princes of the sanctuary') probably indicates that they may well be the ones

---

[6]In Deuteronomy 26:5 the adjective applied to Jacob can either mean 'perishing' (i.e. 'dying') or 'wandering'. While the latter is true, yet Jacob went down to Egypt as an old man ready to die, and hence the former rendering is preferable.

indicated as intermediaries in the previous verse. Whether the judgment is already past or still to come is uncertain from the form of the verbs used. It is quite feasible to translate both verbs in this verse as futures: 'And I will disgrace the princes of the sanctuary, and I will give Jacob over to the ban.' The reference is to a time in the future when the priests (see 1 Chron. 24:4-5) will be profaned. A group in the nation who were at the centre of the ritual concerned with holiness will find that they themselves will suffer the judgment of defilement. But something even more dreadful will take place. God will give Jacob/ Israel over to the 'ban' and to be abused with reviling words (Heb. *giddûfîm*). The word for 'ban' (Heb. *chêrem*) is the word that was used when things or people were given over irrevocably to the LORD, often for destruction (see Deut. 7:26; Jos. 6:17-18; 7:1, 11, 12, 15).[7] What was the judgment on Canaan and the Amalekites will become the lot of Israel. Here is the reversal of the situations regarding the holy place and the nation. The holy place will become a place of defilement (which happened when the Babylonians conquered Jerusalem in 586 BC), while Jacob/Israel will become like Canaan. Not surprisingly, the final aspect of coming judgment is making Israel the object of revilement. This is just what Sennacherib wanted to make them when he blasphemed their God (see Isaiah 37:6, 23, where the verb from which *giddufîm* comes is used).

c. *Future Blessing for the LORD's Chosen (44:1-5)*

Isaiah's style of writing continues at this point. He uses short statements with frequent abrupt changes of subject, except for 44:24-28 where there is a long statement with the use of many participles. However, there is a change in theme. In chapters 44 to 47 there is a concentration on the blessing in store for Israel. The only statements of rebuke are in 46:8 and 12. There is a marked contrast between the just given threat of utter destruction and handing over of Israel to derision (43:28), and the address to Israel in the opening words of a new section. Further words of comfort are addressed to Israel/Jacob, followed by a longer section showing in greater detail than before why idol worship is folly. This leads to a detailed description of the coming deliverance under Cyrus, who is now named explicitly as God's anointed servant (44:28; 45:1).

---

[7] See my note on *chêrem* on page 225, taken from my commentary on *Deuteronomy: The Commands of a Covenant God*, op. cit., pp. 97-98.

1 The transition at this point is made clear in the text by the introductory 'but now' (Heb. v^e '*attâh*). The call goes out to Jacob to listen. The description of Israel/Jacob is the same as has already been made (see 42:1; 43:10). The nation that has been called as the LORD's servant to fulfil his will is reminded that she is the one on whom God's sovereign choice had fallen. That choice was not determined by any intrinsic merit in her, but solely because of God's love (Deut. 7:7-8).

2 The opening words draw attention once again to the fact that it is a divine declaration that is being made: 'Thus says the LORD.' He defines himself as the one who has made, formed, and chosen Israel. This language of creation is most important in this section of Isaiah. The assurance is given that not only is God the creator of the world but he is also the creator of Israel. One addition here, as compared with the description in 43:1, is that Israel is said to be formed 'from the womb'. This adds tenderness to the description, as the words assure Israel that God cares for her just like a mother cares for her unborn baby. The consequence of this is that God will help or support her in the future. Though weak and frail, Israel can rest in the confidence that she will have divine support. Further comfort is provided in the latter part of the verse. Another 'do not fear' command is addressed to the chosen servant, using the same descriptive terms as in verse 1. However, there is a change in that instead of 'Israel' the term 'Jeshurun' is applied. This expression to denote Israel only occurs elsewhere in Deuteronomy 32:15; 33:5, 26. While it could be a diminutive, 'my little upright one,' there is no example in Hebrew of a diminutive ending in *-un*. The word is derived from the root *yâshar* which means to be upright. Hence, it may be that the word denotes the people to whom the law was given, one of the features that distinguished Israel from the surrounding nations (Deut. 4:8). She was to be the upright nation.

3 The theme of water again comes to the fore (see 35:6-7; 41:18; 43:20), though here there is change in that not only does the dry ground receive water, but God's Spirit is likewise to be poured out upon the people. What they had to realise was that they themselves were dry and thirsty ground, desperately in need of God's presence and blessing. This imagery occurs four times in eschatological passages in the Old Testament: Isaiah 32:15; 44:3-4; Ezekiel 39:29; Joel 2:28. Its use relates to the assurances of redemption being given to Israel, and the witness that God was with his people. The ultimate fulfilment of these prophecies came in New Testament times, as the use of the quotation from Joel in Acts 2:17-21 shows. Here the prophecy relates to the bestowal of the Spirit/blessing on the descendants in abundant measure. He is to be 'poured out' upon them. The fact that the source is from God himself is stressed by the verb ('*I* will pour out') but also by the use of the first person pronoun marker with each of the two nouns: '*my* Spirit', '*my* blessing'. Some of the consequences of this blessing are given in the following verses.

4 A comparison is made between rapid and luxuriant growth of grass and trees and the prospective increase in Israel's descendants. A part of the promise to Abraham was that his descendants would become like sand on the seashore. That vision seemed to be fulfilled when the nation was at its height under David and Solomon. However, the events in the period of the divided kingdom led to the ultimate dispersion of the people, leaving only the poor of the land in Palestine (2 Kings 25:12). Now the picture is of a future increase in number. The words following the verb in the Hebrew text have elicited a great variety of translations, and several possible emendations. The most plausible of these is that there is reference to a specific type of tree (a *bên* tree). While this emendation gives good sense with the parallel 'poplar trees' in the second clause, it involves other difficulties. The MT should stand: 'they will sprout up in the midst of the grass.' They will also become like the poplars growing by streams of water. The picture is one of luxuriant growth of vegetation that will serve as a model for the future increase in Israel.

5 Such increase will not take place *en masse* but individually. In the Hebrew text the demonstrative pronoun *zeh* occurs three times: 'This one ... this one ... this one'. The picture is of Gentiles making a profession of belonging to God's people. One will say, 'I belong to the LORD,' while another will be happy to be called by the name of Jacob. Still another will confess that he belongs to Israel. The NIV translation of verse 5c gives one possible rendering of the Hebrew: 'still another will write on his hand, "The LORD's".' The Hebrew is simply, 'This one will write his hand to the LORD.' There are two objections to the NIV rendering 'on his hand'. First, there is no preposition 'on' in the Hebrew text, and for it to be understood would be unusual. Secondly, there is the prohibition in Leviticus 19:28 of tattooing on the body. It is best to regard what is meant as a public written proclamation. Although 'Gentiles' are not mentioned, the idea is their incorporation into God's family. This is part of the missionary vision of prophets and psalmists.

7. The Folly of Idolatry (44:6-23)

At this point Isaiah reverts to the question of idolatry, and amplifies what has already been said regarding it. He includes detailed descriptions of how idols are made, and then points to the folly of trying to construct a god. In the midst of this there is the repeated assertion of the uniqueness of Israel's God (verses 6, 8) and the fact that he is the redeemer (verses 22-23).

6 A further declaration is made by the LORD, who proclaims himself as Israel's king, her redeemer, the LORD of hosts. The massing of titles together points to the glorious person to whom they all refer. Explicit reference to the LORD as king is rare in Isaiah, but adding to the previous references in 41:21 and 43:15, God again describes himself in this way. In addition he once more designates himself as her redeemer, and later in this section will expand on the idea (see verses 21-23). He is also 'the LORD of hosts', the God who has the armies of heaven and earth at his disposal. Though using slightly different phrasing than in 41:4 and 43:11, God reasserts himself as the originator of all things and the only God.

7 The language of this and the following verses has much similarity both to the rhetorical questions of 40:12-31 and the legal language of 41:21-29. If anyone wants to maintain that any so-called god is like the LORD, he should openly declare it. In addition, he should 'set out' before the LORD both things of the past and of the future (see 41:22, 26). The verb 'set out' basically means 'arrange in order', but it occurs in this and other forensic contexts in the sense of stating one's case in a legal way (cf. Job 13:18; 32:14; Ps. 5:3). The 'ancient people' could be taken as referring to humans of early times (as in Ezek. 26:20), but more probably is to be understood as Israel, the people God formed for himself.

8 Because of the character of God and his revelation Israel is not to tremble or be afraid. The verb 'be afraid' is a form that only occurs here in Hebrew (presumably from a Heb. root *râhâh*). The major Isaiah manuscript from Qumran (1QIsa[a]) actually has the common Hebrew verb for 'fear' (*yârê*'), but this looks like an attempt to solve the difficulty. The LXX and the Targum are clearly interpretative, and this suggests that the Hebrew manuscripts they were using had the reading of the MT. In the context a translation such as 'fear' or 'be terrified' is required. The reason for lack of fear is that God has already declared his purposes, including the future things that Babylon will suffer. He has done this already (the Heb. *mê'âz* does not require the interpretation 'long ago', but may mean the immediate past). Of his purposes Israel is witness, and testifies also to the uniqueness of her God and Rock. The term 'rock' for God is an old title (Deut. 32:4, 15, 18, 31, 37), and one used especially in the Psalms and Isaiah to denote the strength and safety he affords (see Isa. 17:10; 26:4; 30:29). The fact that other Near Eastern people used the same term for their god(s) probably underlies the final assertion: 'there is no rock; I do not know (any).'

9 From this point through to the end of verse 20, there is a sustained satire on the folly of idolatry. It commences with reference to the stupidity of the idol maker and the worthlessness of his work. The objects he makes, even though he treasures them as his 'darlings', are utterly without spiritual value. Those who would serve as witnesses for these idols are both blind and ignorant. The idols may have a fatal attraction but the end result is that the worshippers will reap their shame. They have chosen their gods in order that (Heb. *lᵉma'an*) they might be disgraced. Their blindness leads inevitably to shame.

10 These facts raise the inevitable question. Why would anyone go to the bother of shaping (Heb. *yâtsar*, the same verb used of God forming both the world and Israel) a (false) god or casting a metal image that is not going to bring profit? The thought of lack of advantage gained by idol worship has already occurred in verse 9. Worshippers should expect that various advantages would accrue because they worshipped a particular god, but the implication is that there is none.

11 Ultimately the folly of the craftsmen who make the idols will be made plain, when they are put to shame. Not only they but all who are associated with them will suffer this fate. They show that they are but mere men in their attempt to make gods. They are challenged to take their stand in formal court proceedings and together tremble and be ashamed as their folly is exposed. There is stress on 'all of them' being brought under judgment 'together'.

12 Two illustrations are used of the making of idols, the first one concerning the blacksmith (verse 12), and the second one in greater detail concerning the carpenter (verses 13-20). The Hebrew of this verse is awkward. Literally it is: 'he fashioned (Heb. *chârash*) iron [with a] tool, and he worked (Heb. *pâ'al*) with charcoal, and with hammers he fashioned (Heb. *yâtsar*) it, and he made (Heb. *pâ'al*) it with the might of his arm.' Both the words for implements ('tool', 'hammer') are rare. The context requires the maker of the idol to be a metal-worker, and therefore the NIV, though free in its translation, is close to the mark. The idol is made with intense human effort. But if the blacksmith has no food or water his strength diminishes and he becomes faint. Can any god whose making is so dependent on the maker be a real god?

13 The second illustration, given in much greater detail, is how an idol is made of wood. Several of the terms used for the instruments occur only here in the Old Testament, but the context must determine their meaning ('marker', 'chisels', 'compass') as well as the verb 'to make an outline' (Heb. *tâ'ar*). Two important statements are made about the idol. First of all, in contrast to man's creation in the image of God (Gen. 1:26-27) an idol is made in the image of a man (cf. Rom. 1:23). Secondly, it is made so that it can be placed in a 'house'. The Hebrew word 'house' is used both of heathen temples (*bêt ba'al*, 1 Kings 16:32) and the LORD's temple (*bêt yhwh*). Here it clearly refers to a heathen temple or shrine.

14 In order to get the wood needed for the basic form of the idol, a man would have to take special trees (cedar, cypress, oak and pine), and plant them in a forest. Their growth would be dependent upon that planting and on the needed nutrients from the soil and rain for them to grow to maturity. The idea is that the idol is a passive thing in the hand of its creator, totally dependent upon human minds for its origin and natural resources for the growth of the tree from which it is made.

15-17 The folly of the idol maker is worked out in detail. Half the wood is used for a fire, before which he warms himself and upon which he cooks his food (verses 15-16). The other half is used for the making of an idol (verses 15, 17). Before that idol he prostrates himself and worships. The word 'worship' (Heb. *sâgad*) is peculiar to Isaiah (44:15, 17, 19; 46:6), always being used in conjunction with the verb 'to prostrate oneself' and with reference to false worship. He gets satisfaction from the warmth of the fire and from the food he cooks on it, but to the other half of the wood, now fashioned as an idol, he prays. He addresses it as his god ('my god you are', verse 17) and expects it to deliver him from trouble. The illustration is a vivid reminder of the futility of idol worship.

18-20 This futility is spelt out further in these verses. The idol worshipper does not pause to consider the fact that he is worshipping the other half of his fuel for the fire. The idol he has made has no knowledge or understanding, and he has no more himself! Why should he worship what is just a block of wood (verse 19)! Not only is this folly, but the so-called 'god' is 'an abomination' to the LORD (verse 19). Here the word is used as a synonym for 'idol'. It is widely used in the Old Testament to denote what it is detestable to men and particularly what is 'an abomination' to God (e.g. human sacrifice, Deut. 12:31; sacrificing defective animals, Deut. 17:1; idolatry, Deut. 7:25). The ultimate result is that the idol worshipper 'feeds on ashes' (verse 20). Normally Isaiah uses the word 'feed' of the tranquil grazing of sheep or cattle, or to picture the good times in store for Israel and the land. Here the picture is of the attempt to find satisfaction from what remains of the burnt-out fires that have just been described. A 'deluded heart' deceives, so that the idol worshipper fails to recognise that the image he made is only a lie, and that he cannot save himself. Neither in himself nor in the things he makes can salvation be found.

21-22 Israel is called to remember 'these things', i.e. the arguments against idolatry that have just been given. She is reminded once more of her status before God, who had 'formed' her (see 43:1, 7, 21; 44:2, 9, 10, 12 for Isaiah's use already of this verb). Twice the assertion is made of the fact that Israel is the LORD's servant, and the second of these is given emphatic expression (lit. 'a servant to me you are'). Even when in exile Israel should never forget this truth. The final statement is awkward in Hebrew as it is a passive/reflexive form of a rare verb 'to forget'. Though the context may suggest an active verb is needed ('you must not forget me') to match the command 'remember' at the beginning of the verse, yet it is best to stay with the passive form of the MT. The LORD's comforting words, 'you will not be forgotten by me,' will be given additional weight by the assurance of forgiveness that follows in verse 22. God has blotted out Israel's sins so that they cannot be seen. The use of two nouns meaning 'cloud' is an appeal to the fact of their impenetrability. Hence it is best to translate them as 'cloud' and 'thick cloud', rather than using 'morning mist' (NIV) for one of them. This is just another way of emphasising that Israel's sin is covered. The final clause of verse 22 is a call to Israel to return in penitent faith to the LORD her redeemer.

23 The section ends with an appeal for nature to join in the thanksgiving. Heaven and earth, hills and trees, are commanded to rejoice with exuberant song because Jacob/Israel has been redeemed and God will be glorified in her. That is to say, God's glory will be manifested in Israel his servant, who will display to the world the wonders of his grace. Others will see in her what God has achieved.

8. *The Only Saviour (44:24–45:25)*

This section is composed of five stanzas all commencing with the statement 'Thus says the LORD' (verses 44:24; 45:1, 11, 14, 18). The earlier references to the coming deliverer (41:2, 25) had not specified exactly who he would be. Now God speaks again of this figure and tells that he is to be Cyrus, whom he calls his shepherd (44:28), his messiah (45:1). It becomes clear that not only is Israel to be saved, but that the LORD's salvation is to be announced to the ends of the earth (45:22).

a. *Judah's Restoration (44:24-28)*

The structure of verses 24-28 is carefully crafted in order to draw attention to the important announcement that is being made about Cyrus and about Jerusalem. It can be set out as follows:[8]

Thus says the LORD,
> your redeemer,
> and your fashioner from the womb
I am the LORD,

the one making all,

the one stretching out
the heavens by himself

the one spreading out the
earth: Who was with me?

| the one frustrating | and diviners he |
| the signs of liars. | makes fools of; |

| the one turning wise | and turns their |
| men backwards, | wisdom into folly |

---

[8]I am here following O. T. Allis as set out in his article 'The Transendence of the God of Israel; Isaiah 44:24-28' in *Biblical and Theological Studies by Members of the Faculty of Princeton Theological Seminary* (Princeton: 1912), 579-634, and reprinted in his book *The Unity of Isaiah*, op. cit., 62-63.

the one confirming the word of his servant	and the counsel of his messengers he fulfils	
he says of Jerusalem: she shall be inhabited	and of the cities of Judah: they shall be built;	and their waste places: I will build them up.
he says to the deep: dry up;	and your rivers I will dry [you] up;	
he says of Cyrus: he is	and all my pleasure he	even saying to Jerusalem:
my shepherd,	shall fulfil,	you shall be built.
		and of the temple: your foundations shall be laid.

24 The message begins with identification of the speaker. He is the redeemer, the one who formed Israel. He is indeed the LORD who made not just Israel, but everything! It was he who stretched out the heavens and the earth by himself alone. Was anyone with him? The question reminds us of the earlier ones in chapter 40:12-14. This verse is an emphatic declaration of the creative power of God, and serves to introduce the following statements.

25 False prophets did not take the creator into consideration when they made their prophecies. When they gave signs, he was able to thwart them, so showing that they were indeed false prophets. Diviners were no more successful in their divinations. They used methods such as throwing arrows from a quiver (cf. Ezek. 21:18-23), but the outcome showed that they were devoid of wisdom. The verb used to describe them (Heb. *hâlal* III) is used to depict someone who is mad, or acts like a madman (see its use in connection with David, 1 Sam. 21:13-15). God is able to overturn the wise (cf. what was said earlier in 29:14), and make a mockery of their knowledge.

26 On the contrary, God confirms the word he sends by his servant and fulfils the counsel of his messengers. 'Servant' is the rendering of the MT, but the Septuagint and Vulgate translations read it as the plural, 'his servants.' While the plural is possible (after revocalising the Hebrew word) it is better to stay with the MT. The 'servant' must be either Israel or more probably the prophet Isaiah himself. What was said of the word of the LORD in 40:8 is now applied to the message brought by Isaiah (the Heb. verb *qûm* occurs in both passages). By 'messengers' is meant the prophets in general, and the 'counsel' that they bring is the LORD's purpose (see Ps. 33:10-11). In a later passage also dealing with Cyrus, God will declare again that his purpose will be established (46:10).

Jerusalem's future is part of God's purpose. The message to her is that she is going to be restored. Likewise the cities of Judah are going to be (re-)built, while her ruins are going to be raised up. There is a play on words in the Hebrew text in that the opening word of the verse ('makes to stand', 'confirms', hif. part. of *qûm*) is matched at the end by another form (Poel) of the same verb, 'I will cause to stand.' The future of Israel and Jerusalem are inextricably tied together.

27 Allusions to the first exodus again predominate. The God who continues to speak is the one who dried up the water both of the abyss and of the river Jordan. The word for 'abyss' occurs only here in biblical Hebrew, but a cognate noun appears in Zechariah 10:11 for the depths of the Nile. The return from exile is going to involve similar interventions of God on behalf of his people.

28 As the message moves to its climax, revelation is given about the identity of the coming deliverer. He will be none other than Cyrus. The naming of someone long in advance is unusual but not without parallel. This is what happened when the unnamed prophet in 1 Kings 13:1-2 predicted the coming of a king by the name of Josiah. Cyrus is expressly called the LORD's 'shepherd', a term used in the Near East as a royal title from about 2300 BC and regularly employed in this way in the Old Testament (cf. 2 Sam. 5:2; Jer. 23:2). The reference to shepherd may be a play on the word Cyrus which in Elamite is 'shepherd'. He is going to bring the LORD's good pleasure to fulfilment. This phrase is virtually the same as that in verse 26, though 'pleasure' is used instead of 'counsel'. That good pleasure of God has Jerusalem as its focus, and Cyrus is going to proclaim its rebuilding and the laying of foundations for the temple. It was Cyrus' decree of 538 BC that authorised the return to Jerusalem of the exiles and the rebuilding of the temple.

b. Cyrus, God's Messiah (45:1-10)

1 The second of the messages in this section begins at this point. This continues revelation concerning the coming of Cyrus, who has already been named. Isaiah is still answering the question, 'Is the LORD truly God?' Unlike the idols of the heathen, he is God who moves the course of nations. On the other hand he who reduces 'rulers to nothing' (40:22-23) also raises up rulers and even foreign kings like Cyrus! God acts in the world and brings things to pass according to his will.

The surprising thing is that Cyrus is called God's *mâshîach*. From the Hebrew word used of Cyrus we get our English word 'messiah', of which *christos* is the Greek equivalent. The LXX translated this here as *tô christô mou*, 'to my anointed one [my Christ]'. Normally the Hebrew word *mâshîach* was applied to the kings of Israel (cf. 1 Sam. 24:6 of Saul; 2 Sam. 19:21 of David; Ps. 2:2 and Ps. 18:50 of the Davidic dynasty). Cyrus is given the two 'Davidic' roles of building the temple and ruling the nation that are noted in 2 Chronicles 36. Nothing is said about the house of Cyrus, for he stands as an individual.

Three main elements were involved in anointing. First, it was a declaration – an appointment was being stressed and declaration was made of this (cf. Ps. 2). Regular repetition of this act in the case of each Davidic king was a reminder that the real dignity and power of the office had always to be derived from the LORD. Secondly, it indicated close association with God of the person anointed. Injury done to the anointed one was therefore sacrilege. No one was to stretch out his hand against God's anointed (1 Sam. 24:6; 26:9; 2 Sam. 1:14). Thirdly, it also implied communication of something to the person concerned. He was fitted or endowed for a specific task.

What then does this reference to Cyrus imply? The naming of him is not as surprising as the giving of the title 'messiah' to him. He is a foreign king but he is given the title which had been reserved for the Davidic family. The nearest approach to this is the calling of Nebuchadnezzar 'my servant' (Jer. 25:9; 27:6; 43:10). The LORD also declares that he has taken hold of him by his right hand. The same phrase is used of Israel in 41:13 and 42:6. It indicates the close and intimate connection with the LORD. The phrase is also used in the Cyrus Cylinder, that tells how he captured Babylon without a battle, and then sent prisoners back to their homelands.[9]

His work is described in a fourfold way. 1. First of all he will bring

---

[9]For the text of the Cyrus Cylinder, see *DOTT*, p. 92-94.

nations into subjection to him. 2. He will also open the loins of kings, i.e. he will disarm them. This is exactly the opposite of being girded (see the same verb used of Cyrus in verse 5). 3. He will open doors before him, giving his armies access to other nations. 4. Gates will not be shut, as Cyrus' military exploits will be victorious.

2 Verses 2-7 are directly addressed to Cyrus, and the description of his work is given with stress on the LORD's role in his success. The Hebrew text draws attention to it, starting with the pronoun 'I', but continuing with the verbs '*I* will go before', '*I* will level', '*I* will break', and '*I* will cut down'. No hindrances will be allowed to impede Cyrus' progress. All impediments will be removed, both natural ('the mountains') and man-made ('gates', 'bars of bronze'). City gates were normally made of wood with metal bars. Herodotus mentions that there were 100 bronze gates around Babylon.

3 Treasures hidden away will fall to Cyrus. He will accumulate great hordes of wealth, including the temple treasures that had been taken to Babylon when Jerusalem fell (2 Kings 25:13-15). However, these he permitted the Jews to take back to Jerusalem (Ezra 1:7-11). It is as if Cyrus is to have the success of David and the wealth of Solomon. The LORD's ultimate aim is that Cyrus might acknowledge (Heb. 'know') that it was the God of Israel who was calling him by name—to the service of the LORD. The events would bring the recognition that they had been accomplished by the God of Israel. The Greeks viewed Cyrus as a wonderful example of what a king really was; the Jews saw him as a tool in God's hand.

4 God's purpose in using Cyrus is now related back to Israel, for the object or benefit is Jacob/Israel, the chosen servant of the LORD (for the description of the nation as 'servant' and 'chosen', see 42:1; 43:10). The choice of the names and the order in which they come (Jacob, then Israel) is significant. There is a reminder that Jacob had been changed into Israel (Gen. 32:28), and the new name given to the patriarch was a recognition of God's power. That power was still available to move even heathen kings in the service of God's kingdom. The titles given to Cyrus are honorific ones (the same verb *kânâh*, 'to give someone an honorary name') has already occurred in 44:5. From 2 Chronicles 36 and Ezra 1 we are tempted to think of Cyrus as really trusting in the God of Israel, but this and the following verse make it plain that he was used though he was not a true believer. The Cyrus cylinder confirms this as Cyrus says: 'Marduk the great god caused the big-hearted inhabitants of Babylon to ... me; ... At my deeds Marduk, the great Lord, rejoiced ... and graciously gave his blessing'.[10] Marduk was really the god whom Cyrus believed in and worshipped. No ground, therefore, exists for using Cyrus as an illustration of an inclusivist position in regard to recognition of divine beings. The whole context here in Isaiah, as well as the use the Lord Jesus made of the Isaianic background of his great 'I am' sayings (see, e.g. John 14:6), supports the exclusivist position.

5-6 To Cyrus the LORD repeats the assertion of his own being and uniqueness (see 43:11; 44:8). The claim made by Moses in Deuteronomy 4:35 is still as relevant for Isaiah's day. Whereas Cyrus will ungird others (see verse 1), the LORD will gird him. This verb 'gird' is often used of preparation for battle (Job 38:3; 40:7; Jer. 1:17). Here it has that metaphorical meaning but the context also requires the idea that Cyrus is being prepared for the assigned task by the LORD. Yet in spite of such demonstration of divine power Cyrus will not really know the LORD. However the acknowledgment will ultimately come from the Gentile nations. One important strand of the promise to Abraham was blessing to the nations through his seed (Gen. 12:3; 22:18). Cyrus' calling and consequent work was partial fulfilment of that purpose, as the 'second exodus' was to be integral to the ultimate vision of the salvation to the Gentiles. Blessing to the nations involves recognition of the LORD as the only God and redeemer. God's intentions embrace the whole world.

7 The LORD claims to be the one who forms light and creates darkness. He also establishes prosperity (using the Heb. *shâlom* in this common usage), and also brings about disaster (Heb. *ra'*, 'evil', but used as in Job 2:10 and Amos 3:6 in the wider sense of 'trouble', 'disaster'). This may well be said for polemical reasons to contradict Persian belief in two deities, one good and the other evil, though it is equally directed against polytheism. There may also be allusions here to what happened with the plagues in Egypt. The final declaration is that the LORD is the one doing 'all these things'. None of the things that are going to happen lie outside his control. There is poetic rhythm about verses 6d-7c:

---

[10]*DOTT*, p. 93.

> I am the LORD and there is no other.
> I form light and
> create darkness,
>   bringing prosperity
>   and creating disaster.
> I, the LORD, do all these things.

8 This hymn may be a conclusion to verses 1-7, or else an independent song of praise over God's salvation. It is very similar to the earlier song in 44:23, but because of the first person plural at the end of the verse ('I, the LORD,...') it is best to regard it as still part of the LORD's speech. There is a connection with the first message concerning Cyrus, in that the word 'righteousness' is common to both (41:2). The language is an exuberant description of righteousness coming down from heaven (cf. Ps. 85:11), and the earth opening up to produce an abundant crop.

9-10 These verses are best taken as a prelude to the next declaration by God in verses 11-13. The focus for the moment switches from Cyrus back to Israel (as is shown by the use of the plural verbs in verse 11). These 'woe' declarations remind of the 'woe' oracles earlier in Isaiah, especially in chapters 5–10. The background to these verses is probably the way in which many in Israel were questioning how God could use a foreign king to carry out his purposes for Israel. The nation could make a legal charge against God (the Heb. word *râv* has this implication; NIV 'quarrel', NKJV 'strive') but what right does a potsherd have to argue with its maker? Or what right does a child have to argue with its parents over its conception and birth? God is sovereign and he is able to carry out his purposes without his creature's will or understanding, and his purposes for Israel stem from his love and compassion for her. The same illustration comes in another 'woe' passage in Isaiah 29:16, and a broader application of the same principle is made in 10:15. It forms a very strong statement of the sovereignty of God in relation to man, and it is used by Paul in Romans 9:20-22.

c. God the Creator Controls History (45:11-13)

11 The third declaration by God in this section commences at this point. He identifies himself before proceeding to link together the repeated theme of these chapters: his role as creator and his actions in providing Cyrus as the deliverer of his people. The holy one of Israel and the one who formed Israel is not to face inquisition over his actions. The two predications, 'the Holy One of Israel' and 'his maker', have already occurred in a trial speech (43:15). While the words of God are statements ('Concerning things to come, they ask me about my sons, and about the work of my hands they give me orders'), yet the context requires them to be taken as indignant questions: 'Do they ask me about my sons? Do they give me orders about the work of my hands?'

12 God restates his creative role as a sign of his right to govern the affairs of men. He both made the earth and created mankind to live on it (see the later statement in verse 18 that he did not intend the earth to be void of inhabitants). The argument of 40:26-28 concerning the creation of the heavens is repeated with sharper focus. The Hebrew text emphasises that the work of creation was indeed the LORD's with the second half of the verse commencing, 'I, my hands have stretched out the heavens.' While an unusual grammatical expression it certainly stresses God's unique work in creation, before speaking of his providential rule over it ('and all their host I have commanded', NKJV).

13 The thought comes back to Cyrus who is not specifically mentioned in the MT but who is demanded by the context. The Hebrew text simply says 'I will raise *him* up in righteousness' (cf. NIV's insertion of 'Cyrus' into its translation). The same verb for 'raise up' is used as in 41:2 (Heb. *'îr* Hif.). The idea is: 'Will men who were made by God question his raising up this instrument to carry out his purpose?' The LORD is going to raise him in righteousness (the Heb. perfect expresses the certainty of the action) and will make his paths straight. These expressions have both been used in reference to Cyrus (41:2) and to the LORD himself (40:3). The thought of righteousness seems to be that God will uphold the demand of his covenant to redeem Israel (cf. 42:6 also 46:13). Cyrus' work will embrace both the rebuilding of Jerusalem (see 44:26) and the sending back of the exiles, called here by the LORD 'my exiles'. This is another note of comfort for them. No payment had been made for their 'sale' into captivity (see also 52:3), and hence no money is required for their release. The verse ends with the further comfort in the fact that 'the LORD of hosts', the God with everything at his disposal, makes the declaration.

d. Israel Saved by the LORD (45:14-17)

14 The fourth of the messages takes the thought another step forward. At some time in the future Israel will have domination over her enemies, and they will confess that Israel's God is the only one. The Egyptians, the Cushites (from upper Egypt) and the Sabeans are pictured as coming under the authority of Israel. What is not clear is whether this will be an enforced surrender or a voluntary action. The mention of 'chains' is probably figurative, conveying the idea of submission. Their actions will include bowing low in deference, pleading their case, and then making acknowledgment that God is with his people. In fact, they too will join with Israel in confessing that there is no other God. Later in this chapter the idea of conversion of the nations is carried further still (see on verses 22-24).

15 The idea of God hiding himself in wrath occurs elsewhere in Isaiah (8:17; 54:8), though here the meaning is rather that God does not reveal all his purposes. He veils from humans some of his designs, and his thoughts far transcend those of his creatures (55:8-9). The speaker identifies himself as 'the God of Israel, [the] Saviour'. Constantly God links his relationship with his people with his role as their saviour.

16 The teaching given in 42:17 and 44:9 is repeated in another form. A collective judgment is passed on all idol makers, for since there is only one God (verse 14) and Saviour (verse 15) there can be no other outcome. The word for 'idols' occurs only here and in Psalm 49:14, in both passages with the meaning of 'outward forms'. The use of the word is another way of mocking the idol worshippers, for their gods are only outward show without inward reality.

17 How different is the situation with believing Israel! The people are reassured that they will never have to suffer such shame as has just been mentioned, for they are saved by the LORD with an everlasting salvation. The return from exile ushers in an era of salvation that will never end. The mention of 'Israel' forms a bridge between earlier references to Israel and the concept of an ingathering of Gentiles along with Jews which is implicit here and becomes explicit in verses 22-25. The stress on the eternal nature of the salvation is clear from the expressions 'an everlasting salvation' and 'to ages everlasting'. The latter expression is made even more dramatic by the use of alliteration, as the three words in the phrase all start with the same Hebrew letter ('ayin).

e. A Just God and a Saviour (45:18-25)

18 The final declaration by God in this section of the book commences at this point. The Gentiles are depicted as coming over voluntarily and bowing before the LORD. The elaborate poetic introduction can be set out like this:

> For thus says the Lord —
>> he who created the earth, he is God;
>> he who fashioned and made the earth,
>>> he founded it;
>> he did not create it to be empty,
>>> but formed it to be inhabited.
>>>> 'I am the LORD, and there is no other.'

The division in the verse is marked by an accent (*atnach*) placed there by the Jewish Massoretes on the word translated 'he founded it'. The first part indicates the speaker and then the second part the words spoken. In the first part there are two parentheses. The first one affirms again that the LORD is God; the second that he made the earth for the intended purpose of man's habitation. In describing creation there is an accumulation of the language that Isaiah uses elsewhere of God's work: 'create', 'make', 'form', 'establish', 'waste'. The declaration of God's uniqueness is given in the identical form that has already occurred in verses 5 and 6.

19 The opening statement, 'I have not spoken in secret,' provides an immediate link with verse 15 ('you are a God who hides yourself'). God does not speak in secret or somewhere in the land of darkness (for 'darkness', cf. Gen. 1:2), probably a reference to dark caves in which soothsayers were consulted. On the contrary, Isaiah had invited the people to walk in the LORD's light (2:5) and later he will do so again (60:1). What is said here does not contradict verse 15, for God is unknown unless he reveals himself. Moreover, he does not deliberately obscure himself, so that men 'seek' (Heb. *biqqêsh*, often a cultic term) him by means of the occult. A clear contrast is being drawn between the LORD's prophecies and the messages from heathen occult practices. Instead of translating 'seek in vain' it quite possibly means 'seek me in the desert'. This may be an echo of Deuteronomy 32:10 that speaks of the LORD finding his people in the desert, yet he led them out of it to a good land. He speaks in truth and in righteousness

(Heb. *tsedek*). In other places this Hebrew word is used in contrast to what is a lie (see Ps. 52:3; Prov. 12:17). The last sentence of the verse asserts that the Lord declares what is 'right', using a word that combines the ideas of uprightness and moral integrity.

20 This verse introduces another court scene or trial speech (cf. 41:1-4; 41:21-29; 43:8-13; 44:6-8). The salvation of Israel now becomes the prospect of the heathen world as well. This provides another example of prophetic foreshortening, when the prophet gives a telescopic picture of the future, pulling distant events into closer focus. What he has just said of the Lord's revelation to Israel also applies to the Gentiles as well. The divine self-predication now becomes an appeal to 'the escapees of the nations' to come and assemble themselves together. They had to know that they could be the recipients of the same mercy as 'the escaped of Israel' (4:2). Instead of 'with one accord' or 'together' the Dead Sea Scrolls text 1QIsa[a] has 'and come'. While this provides good parallelism with the preceding clause, yet it is not otherwise supported. The use of 'with one accord' in the next verse suggests its retention here. The fugitives are idolaters, who carry about their idols in festal procession, and pray to a god which is 'a not-saviour' (cf. this expression with 'a no-god', Deut. 32:21; 'a son not-wise' Hos. 13:13). Again there is mocking of idol worship for the idols are so helpless that they cannot carry themselves.

21 There is an abrupt change from second person ('declare and present your case') to third person ('let them gather together'). If the matter is pressed then the subject of the latter verb would be the idols. However, we can follow the Targum and understand it as 'by all means take counsel together'. The antecedent of 'this' in the question, 'Who told this long ago?', is most probably a reference to the predictions regarding Cyrus, even though normally 'of old' refers to distant time in the past (Mic. 5:2; Hab. 1:12; Ps. 74:12; Ps. 77:11; Ps. 78:2; Ps. 143:5). The answer to the two questions is another self-predication, that asserts emphatically that there is no God besides the Lord, 'a righteous God and a saviour'.

22 The call goes out to the heathen to turn and find salvation with the Lord. 'Turn' here means 'repent and turn from your idols to me'. The New Testament uses the verb 'turn' in the same way (Acts 14:15; 1 Thess. 1:9). The form of the verb 'save' in Hebrew is passive – 'be saved', i.e. the Lord. They will find salvation in him alone. The appeal is to the Gentiles *en masse*, though individualisation follows in the next verse with reference to 'every knee' and 'every tongue'. The Abrahamic promise of blessing to the nations is still to come to its fullest realisation, but here is another anticipation of the full blessing to the Gentiles in the New Testament era. The verse ends with the reason why this call is given – there is no other God with whom they can find salvation.

23 The certainty of finding salvation with the LORD is assured by the fact that he has sworn by himself. The same phrase occurs in Genesis 22:16, and that passage may well be behind the usage here and the similar one in Isaiah 14:24. The same verb is used in Ezekiel 16:8 of the LORD pledging himself to Jerusalem. A word has gone forth from him that shall not be recalled (cf. Isa. 55:11 for the same Heb. phrase, *lô' tashûv*). The Hebrew text permits either the translation 'from my mouth has gone forth in righteousness a word' or 'from the mouth of righteousness (= 'truth') has gone forth a word'. It does not permit the translation 'righteousness has gone forth' because the verb is masculine, while 'righteousness' is feminine. Here, as compared with the previous verse, individualising takes place, for it is not mass but individual conversions that are depicted— 'every knee', 'every tongue'. Paul makes use of this passage when he is dealing with universal judgement (Rom. 14:11). The introductory words in that passage ('as I live, says the Lord') seem to be picked up from other Old Testament passages such as Isaiah 49:18; Jeremiah 22:24; and Ezekiel 5:11; and Paul also uses the words in the servant passage in Philippians 2:10-11.[11]

24 The first part of this verse is difficult because of the opening words that can be translated literally: 'Surely in the LORD to me he (or, one) said.' The opening words may be an oath, 'Yes, by the LORD,' as the medieval Jewish commentator Kimchi understood them. The LXX has 'saying' instead of 'said' and many follow it and wish to transfer it to the beginning of the verse – 'saying, in the LORD is righteousness and strength.' While this makes good sense, there is no textual justification for rearranging the order of the words. Both the NKJV and the NIV are similar in their understanding of the meaning:

---

[11]On this passage, see R. P. Martin, *Carmen Christi*, rev. ed. (Grand Rapids: Eerdmans, 1983), pp. 255-57, and his comments in *Philippians* (London: Tyndale Press, 1959), p. 105.

NKJV: Only in the LORD, it shall be said of me, are righteousness
         and strength.

NIV: They will say of me, 'In the LORD alone are righteousness
         and strength.'

These versions understand the words to mean that those turning to
the LORD will make a declaration that with him alone are victorious
deeds (i.e. salvation). Lest anyone should think such abundant grace
will cover even continued rebellion, the verse ends with a warning that
those who are unrepentant will be put to shame before him. This is an
echo of the even stronger words concerning those who are raging
against Israel (41:11).

25 The final verse of the chapter could be the continuation of the
LORD's words, or else the prophet's summing up. 'The seed of Israel'
are those of the Gentiles who have been converted (see verses 6 and
14) and thus become spiritual Israel. The Old Testament points to an
Israel within Israel, and the New Testament confirms that those who
believe are reckoned as children of Abraham (Gal. 3:7). Several English
versions render the first verb in this verse as a passive (NIV, 'will be
found righteous'; NKJV, 'shall be justified'). The verb is active in
form, and therefore RSV is better: 'in the LORD all the offspring of
Israel shall triumph and glory.' The singing of Hallelujah psalms such
as 104–106; 111–113; 115–117; and 146–150 would be an appropriate
way of doing this.

9. The Impotence of Babylon's Gods (46:1-13)

Chapters 46 and 47 are directed to Babylon, and combined they declare
victory over Israel's enemies. They enlarge on the earlier references
to Babylon in 13:1–14:23 and 39:1-8 (see commentary on these
passages). Isaiah knew that the gods of Babylon and the other Gentile
nations were impotent. This is the first time that heathen gods have
been specifically named in Isaiah, as the references till now have been
quite general. Bel was the Babylonian name for 'lord', and seemingly
was a synonym for 'Marduk', the chief god of Babylon. This is apparent
from the parallelism in Jeremiah 50:2:

> Babylon will be captured;
> > Bel will be put to shame,
> > > Marduk filled with terror.

In addition to this passage, Bel is used in Jeremiah 51:44. It is also found in the name 'Belshazzar' (*Bel has protected the kingship*). Cyrus was a polytheist and after he captured Babylon he vowed allegiance to his new god: 'Marduk, the great lord, was well pleased with my deeds and sent friendly blessings to myself, Cyrus, the king who worships him...'[12] 'Nebo' was the Babylonian god of learning and writing, with the centre of his worship being located at Borsippa, south-west of Babylon. The cult of Nebo continued to flourish down to 538 BC. The word appears in theophoric names such as Nebuchadnezzar and Nabonidus.

a. Downfall of the Idols of Babylon (46:1-2)

1-2 Not only is Babylon going to fall but her idols will as well. Her gods are going to be carried off into exile similar to how Judah was carried off (see verse 2: 'they themselves go into captivity'). The Hebrew word used elsewhere about Judah ($sh^evî$), is now used for the captivity of Babylonian gods (cf. Jer. 15:2; Ezek. 12:11). Isaiah notes that 'Bel has bowed down' and 'Nebo is [just now] stooping'. The change of verbal forms in the two phrases highlights the current position. The picture is of gods who are unable even to move themselves but have to be loaded as baggage on carts. Clearly they are unable to act as saviours as they themselves are carried off into captivity.

b. The safety of Israel in the Lord (46:3-7)

3 In the previous verse the gods of Babylon were being carried off into exile, but here by contrast, Israel's God carried her! Israel was 'loaded' on to him, who was both able and willing to accept the burden of carrying her right from her origin as a nation, just as a mother carries a child from the womb onwards. The call goes out from God to the 'remnant of the house of Israel'.

4 Such carrying of Israel is not going to cease, but rather go on until 'old age', 'unto grey hairs'. This assurance is given by the one who called Israel into being (see 43:7; 44:2). After a threefold mention of God carrying his people, at the end of the verse attention is called to the fact that he is going to do more than that. He will rescue them! Cyrus, 'the messiah', will be the means he uses to do that. God's role

---

[12]From the so-called Cyrus cylinder, see J. B. Pritchard, ed., *ANE*, vol. I, p. 207.

in protecting and saving is emphasised by the fact that five times in this verse the pronoun 'I' occurs in Hebrew in addition to the fact that the five verbal forms are all first person singular.

5 The character of idols and idol worship is dealt with in a manner reminiscent of the earlier presentation in 40:18-25 and 44:9-20. The incomparability of the LORD is emphasised again in language very close to that used in 40:25. The questions are rhetorical and no direct answer from the people is needed.

6 The third description of idol making is along similar lines to the previous ones. Their creation depends upon human skills! Gold and silver in the hands of a hired workman becomes a god before whom the people prostrate themselves.

7 The Babylonian gods were lifted up on the shoulders and carried by their worshippers. They were deaf and dumb idols (cf. the description of idols in Ps. 115:4-7). The actual making of the idol is not given as fully as earlier but the result is amplified. How foolish the heathen were to think that you could call out to a god for help when that god was something that could be picked up and transported elsewhere! The idol cannot move without help, and prayers to it go unheard and unanswered. It is unable to provide deliverance when a worshipper is in trouble.

c. God's Sovereign Pleasure (46:8-13)

8 At the beginning of a new section there comes a word of warning to the people. The message is addressed to the 'rebels', one of their hallmark characteristics, as Isaiah has already set out in 1:2 ('they have rebelled against me'). They are counselled to fix it in their mind and to take it to heart (lit. 'upon the heart'). The first of these verbs only occurs here, and its meaning has been interpreted in various ways, some requiring emendation of the text. It is reflexive in form and a meaning like 'show yourselves obedient' would be most appropriate.

9 In accordance with 41:22 and 43:18 'the former things' are the events of the exodus, which demonstrated the power and majesty of God. They had demonstrated his uniqueness, and appending another declaration to that effect is entirely appropriate. It takes a form unlike any of the previous self-asseverations, but the central thrust of it remains unchanged. There is no one who can compare with him!

10 Already mention has been made of the fact that God does not speak to mankind from a land of darkness (45:19). From the earliest times he had revealed himself and had spoken of the end times (Heb. *ach^{a}rit*), the events relating to the end of the epoch. He declares that his purpose will stand. The verb 'stand' is used of a plan being fulfilled (cf. Isa. 7:7), while 'pleasure' has the idea of intention and will. Doubtless what is in view is God's plans for Babylon and Israel, as the next verse makes plain.

11 Cyrus' coming is described a second time as being from the east (for the first time, see 41:2), and the suddenness and the vigour of his attack are linked in thought to the attacks of a bird of prey. From a distant land he will come with the swiftness of an eagle or vulture. He is said to be 'a man of his counsel', though the Massoretic note says to read this as 'a man of my counsel'. The MT is slightly awkward, as this phrase is part of divine speech. However, the meaning is clear enough, as God's counsel has just been mentioned in the preceding verse. The latter part of the verse expresses the absolute certainty in the fulfilment of God's purpose. When he speaks, it happens. When he forms an idea in his heart, he does it. The verb 'form' is used frequently by Isaiah (21 times), often in connection with the idea of creation. It is utilised here in its other sense of God forming something in his mind (cf. 2 Kings 19:25; Ps. 139:16; Isa. 37:26).

12 The third admonition in this chapter is a repetition of the first: *Listen* to me (verse 3); *Remember* this (verse 8); *Listen* to me (verse 12). It is addressed to 'the strong of heart'. The only other occurrence of this phrase means 'the stout of heart' (Ps. 76:5), but here the context demands a meaning such as NIV's 'stubborn-hearted', for it is used as a synonym for 'rebels' (Heb. *pôsh'îm*). These are the people who are 'far away from righteousness'. That is to say, they decline to receive the words of promise from the LORD and so will not participate in the saving deeds of the return from exile.

13 To those who doubt the promises reaffirmation is made of the impending revelation of God's victorious deeds. The victory will be his when his salvation is made known to Zion. The final phrase can be taken as a description of Israel ('Israel my glory'), but it is better to understand it as governed by the verb 'I will give' and therefore 'my glory' is parallel to 'salvation'. When deliverance comes it will be a display of the LORD's glory.

10. The Fall of Babylon (47:1-15)

The fall of Babylon has already been spoken of in chapter 14 (see commentary) and now there is a fuller development of that theme. It is not only the gods of Babylon that are to fall but Babylon herself. She is personified as a royal virgin who will be humiliated. Instead of being a queen she will become a servant or a prostitute. The form of the song in Hebrew is that of a taunt, and follows a metrical pattern in which there is a long phrase followed by a shorter one (see the 3:2 pattern of stressed syllables coming out in English translations of verse 2a and verse 2b). The contrast between the gods of Babylon and the saviour God of Israel continues, for it is made plain that the Babylonian gods cannot even save themselves (verse 14). The poem falls into four strophes: verses 1-4; verses 5-7; verses 8-11; verses 12-15.

a. Babylon Dethroned (47:1-4)

1 The opening strophe commences with direct address to Babylon that is continued throughout, except for the reference to the redeemer of Israel in verse 4 (see commentary on that verse). Babylon is addressed as 'the virgin daughter of Babylon', a personification of the city. The parallel phrase is 'daughter of the Chaldeans', using the alternative word for the Babylonians. The proud city is called upon to go and sit in the dust, on the ground (cf. 3:26), as a sign of abject humiliation. No longer will she be on a throne, for the delicate daughter will be compelled to carry out menial work. From pampered existence she will be reduced to servitude.

2 The picture of the completely changed condition of Babylon continues with reference to a task normally performed by women, especially slaves (see Exod. 11:5). Grinding flour with millstones was a daily occurrence. The remainder of the verse depicts the queen becoming a captive. She sets aside her veil, and in order to cross streams as she goes into exile she has to lift up her skirts and bare her legs.

3 The downfall of Babylon had been described earlier by Isaiah (see especially 13:18-20), and here the language finds a parallel in Ezekiel 16. Babylon the prostitute who had uncovered herself in her adulteries will be uncovered in judgment. God will take vengeance upon her without sparing anyone. This accords with Jeremiah's teaching on the same subject (Jer. 50:15, 28).

4 This verse is a response by Isaiah to the teaching just given from the LORD. God is spoken of as 'our redeemer', and the statement forms an antiphony to the preceding verses (for a similar antiphony, see 45:15). The coming fall of Babylon is intimately connected with the fact that the LORD of hosts, the holy one of Israel, is the redeemer of his people. Israel's redemption and Babylon's fall are two aspects of the same truth.

b. Babylon's Greatness to End (47:5-7)

5 The second strophe begins at this point. Babylon is again commanded to sit in the dust (see verse 1) and to do so in silence. This will be in contrast to the way in which Babylon previously had dictated the rules to others. Now she will be deprived of that status, as she goes into imprisonment herself (taking 'into darkness' to be an allusion to captivity/imprisonment). In the same language as already used in verse 1b, Babylon will no longer be called 'Queen of the Kingdoms'. She was noted in the ancient world for her beauty, 'Babylon, the jewel of kingdoms, the glory of the Babylonians' pride' (Isa. 13:19, NIV). That appellation will not be appropriate any more for just as she will no longer be 'tender and delicate' (verse 1), so her status will be reduced.

6 The accusation here is a repetition of what the history of Israel declares. Because of the people's covenant rebellion, God was very angry with them (2 Kings 17:18-20), and they were taken away from Palestine into captivity. The manner of description is that the inheritance of the LORD was profaned (the same language is used as in 43:28). There is an ambiguity as 'inheritance' is used both of Israel as the chosen heritage of the LORD (Exod. 34:9; Deut. 4:20), and less frequently of Canaan the land. The former meaning is intended here, for God was no longer regarding his people as holy before him. Submission to Babylon was part of God's purpose, and even the treatment meted out to the aged was part of foretold judgment (Deut. 28:49-50).

7 Though Nebuchadnezzar could boast about Babylon (see his words in Dan. 4:30), yet her glory was not going to last for ever. Even though she considered herself an everlasting queen, yet her time was short. She did not give a thought to that possibility, nor consider her 'latter end' (the same Heb. word as in 46:10). Babylon's greatness will come to a sudden conclusion.

c. Impending Judgment (47:8-11)

8 The third strophe that begins at this point stresses the self-satisfaction of Babylon. She is an irresponsible creature (the Heb. adj. used occurs only here in the Old Testament), thinking she was secure and there was no possibility that she would ever be deprived of her husband or her children. Her boastful claim was that there was none like her, which amounted practically to a claim that she was divine. The language used is very similar to that used earlier by God when he asserts his uniqueness (see 43:11; 45:5-6, 18, 22).

9 Sudden calamity will overtake Babylon in spite of all the magical precautions she takes. Archaeological discoveries have shown how elaborate were the magical ceremonies of ancient Babylon. Decipherment of clay tablets has revealed some of the various methods used to determine the future. The king of Babylon is pictured in Ezekiel 21:21 casting lots with arrows, consulting idols, and examining the liver of a slain animal to determine which road he should take. Two of the terms used here for the sorcerer and the charmer (Heb. *keshâfîm* and *chavârîm*) are from the list of banned Canaanite practices in Deuteronomy 18:10-11. No magical practice will be able to ward off the inevitable judgement.

10 Babylon had been confident in making and carrying out her plans. Her trust was in herself, not realising that in God's sight those plans were evil. She thought that there was no god who saw her wickedness. Isaiah had earlier condemned those in Jerusalem who tried to hide their plans from the LORD (29:15). Even though Babylon prided herself in her wisdom, yet that very same wisdom led her astray. She claimed to be divine, saying, 'I am, and there is none besides me' (the exact words that have already been used in verse 8).

11 What proud Babylon did not realise was that her boasts would not save her from God's judgment. When disaster came no magical spells would be able to deliver. When calamity (the Heb. word *hovâh* occurs only here and in Ezek. 7:26) fell there would be no possibility of paying a ransom price to avoid it (see the same message in the oracle against Babylon, 13:17). The Medes would not accept any bargaining; they demanded absolute surrender. Moreover, the devastation that would encompass her was both unpredictable and sudden.

d. No Saviour for Babylon (47:12-15)

12-13 The fourth and final strophe commences with verse 12. Babylon is encouraged to continue with her spells and sorceries (cf. the earlier reference to the same practices in verse 9) that have been a lifetime pursuit. The choice of verb here (Heb. *yâga'*) may well be intentional, suggesting that there is both hard labour and futility in what she practises. Babylon falsely thought that these things might be successful or cause terror. However, as verse 13 makes plain, all this activity with magicians and sorcerers was utterly futile. Babylon was notorious for the prevalence of astrologers and stargazers, as Daniel 2 confirms, but none of this frenetic activity will result in deliverance. The challenge to the Babylonian magicians to come forward is going to fail, for though they prophesy month by month, yet no salvation results.

14 In reality, Babylon is doomed to destruction, just like chaff waiting for the flames to devour it. The sorcerers and magicians are no more powerful than the gods they claim to represent. In this they differ so markedly from the God of Israel who has repeatedly been declared to be the saviour (see 43:3, 11; 45:15, 17, 21; 46:13). So far from saving others, they cannot even save themselves! So sudden and complete is the coming destruction that it is likened to a fire that leaves no coals before which people can sit and warm themselves. This is an allusion to the fact already mentioned that wood was often the material out of which idols were made (see 44:15).

15 The final pronouncement about the folly of Babylon is that none of the magicians can offer any hope for the inhabitants of that city. A lifetime of involvement with them cannot hide the reality that every one of them is just proceeding in his own erroneous way. No salvation can be found in any of them. The difference between them and the Lord is absolute. He is the saviour; they are not.

11. The Lord's Rebuke to Israel (48:1-22)

As the prophecy moves towards the close of this section (chapters 40–48), attention turns to the stubbornness of Israel in the face of the announcement of the coming deliverance from Babylon. Whereas previous chapters have dealt with the idolatry of the Babylonians, now the accusation of idolatry is directed towards Israel. Cyrus is not mentioned in this chapter by name, but the reference clearly links him with the previous proclamation. He is the one who has been called, and whose mission will be successful (verse 15). The Jewish exiles are encouraged to flee from Babylon (verse 20), this being the last time Babylon is mentioned by name in Isaiah.

a. Stubborn Israel to be Refined (48:1-11)

1 The message is directed to the Jewish people, identified as 'Jacob', 'Israel', and 'Judah'. These varied expressions indicate that Isaiah's message is to the entire nation as such. It mattered not if they were from the 'house of Jacob', or were 'called by the name of Israel', or 'came out of the waters of Judah' (AV). The last expression is awkward and has provoked various suggestions, with many wanting to emend the text to read 'from the bowels of Judah' (cf. Gen. 15:4; 2 Sam. 7:12; and 2 Chron. 32:21). However, since Israel is called a 'fountain' in Deuteronomy 33:28 and Psalm 68:26, it is better to take the reference here to be similar to that usage. Hence NKJV is close to the mark when it translates 'and have come forth from the wellsprings of Judah'. While God's concern is with the entire nation, yet the primary focus of Isaiah's message is to Judah. Descended from Jacob and Judah, the people are 'beloved for the sake of the fathers' (Rom. 11:28). Outwardly they show signs of covenant allegiance, swearing by the name of the LORD and solemnly ascribing praise to the God of Israel. However, in reality they are acting hypocritically because they are not doing so in truth and righteousness.

2 The people indicated their outward attachment to the LORD by being called 'the holy city'. This is the first occurrence of this title for Jerusalem, and it appears elsewhere only in Isaiah 52:1; Nehemiah 11:1, 18; and Daniel 9:24. Their attitude was like those whom Jeremiah mentions who thought they were safe because they constantly repeated 'the temple of the LORD', 'the temple of the LORD', 'the temple of the LORD' (Jer. 7:4). They claimed to be relying on the LORD of hosts, but this claim must be viewed as a pretence in light of the previous verse.

3-4 Here the message moves again to the ideas of the old and new things. God had not acted without making his will known to his people. 'The former things' probably stands here for all of the previous history of Israel up to the announcement concerning Cyrus, which were 'the new things'. God spoke ('from my mouth it went forth') and his people received the message ('I caused them to hear'). Then fulfilment came, with the word 'suddenly' (Heb. *pit'om*) indicating its commencement. The stress is on how surprising God's actions were, even when his people had prior warning of them. The character of the people had not changed over the years. They were obstinate, with an attitude to their God that was as if their neck was composed of iron, and their brow bronze.

5 The message of verse 3 is repeated in a slightly altered form. The LORD had announced his plans beforehand lest anyone was tempted to attribute them to their hand-made deities. The three words used for idols are practically synonymous. The thrust of the argument is the same as in 44:17-20.

6 There are sudden transitions in this verse from singular to plural. A literal translation of it is: 'You (2 s.) have heard. Look at (2 s.) it all. And you (2 pl.), will you not make it known (2 pl.)? I make known to you (2 s.) new things from now on, and hidden things and you (2 s.) do not know them.' Such transitions are not unknown in other parts of the Old Testament, especially in Deuteronomy. The change could be to stress the responsibility of all in Israel to acknowledge the truth of God's accusations. In contrast to the former things (verse 3), 'new things' are being made known. These new things relate first to the restoration from exile, but they may well also include the events of the messianic era (cf. 65:17, 'new heavens and a new earth'). Paul's words in Romans 16:25-27 speak in similar terms of a gospel 'hidden for long ages past but now revealed and made known' (NIV).

7 These 'new things' were not revealed long ago. Though they were part of God's purpose they had been kept secret until this time. Had they been revealed earlier the people could have boasted that they already knew about them, or that they were the work of their idols (cf. verse 3).

8 This verse expresses the reason why God had not revealed all these things to Israel. She was unfaithful to her husband, the LORD, the verb used here being used elsewhere of unfaithfulness in marriage (Exod. 21:8; Jer. 3:20) and also of unfaithfulness of Israel to the LORD (Jer. 9:2). She was both treacherous and a rebel from birth. The opening of the verse, through the threefold repetition of the Hebrew adverb *gam* ('also') emphasises this fact. They had not heard or known, nor had they had their ears opened. The repetition of the expression 'from of old' for the fourth time in this passage helps to tie together the general theme. None of the English translations is able to show this by rendering it identically in all four verses (3, 5, 7, 8), though NASB comes close ('long ago' 3x, 'from long ago' 1x).

9 The thought of this verse is also expressed in Psalms 78:38-39 and 103:14-16. For his own name's sake God does not cut Israel off, that is, destroy her. The Hebrew expression for making a covenant is 'to cut a covenant' (Heb. *kârat* b^e*rît*), and the punishment for disobedience to the covenant was 'to be cut off from Israel' (Gen. 17:14).[13] For his own glory God does not punish Israel to the ultimate.

10 In the events of the destruction of Jerusalem and the captivity in Babylon God had been trying Israel. However, he had placed limits on this, or otherwise Israel would have been destroyed utterly (i.e. refined as silver). If they were given what they deserved they would have perished. Previously they had been through 'the furnace of affliction' in Egypt (see for the use of the similar phrase 'the iron furnace': Deut. 4:20; 1 Kings 8:51; Jer. 11:4). The exile was a repetition of this testing, but reassurance is brought to the people by a reminder that God had chosen Israel. Instead of 'I have chosen you' the Qumran manuscript 1QIsa[a] has 'I have tested you'. The change is only of a single letter in Hebrew. The uniformity of the MT tradition and the fact that God's election of Israel has been so prominent up to this point (cf. 41:8-9; 43:10; 44:1-2) suggest that the reading 'I have chosen' should be retained.

11 Repetition of the words 'for my own sake' emphasises that it is not Israel's merit that prompts the heralded restoration. When Daniel prays for the restoration it is for this same reason, 'For your sake, O God' (Dan. 9:19). Dishonour had been brought to God's name because of the scattering of the Jewish people (see Ezekiel 36:20-23). While God's name had been profaned, in the final analysis he would not yield his honour to any other (the Heb. phrase is identical with Isaiah 42:8). Failure to fulfil his promises and restore Israel would only result in his enemies gloating over his inability to deliver.

---

[13]As a covenant sign God commanded the rite of circumcision to be performed on all the males in Abraham's family, and thereafter on all male children. If obedience was not shown to this requirement, then death would follow. The language used plays on the fact that the expression in Hebrew for 'make a covenant' is really 'cut a covenant'. Thus the penalty was being cut off from Israel, so that it was no longer just a token sign, but the real thing. It was a constant reminder of the need to keep God's covenant, and thus enjoy his blessing, or else suffer the consequences of disobedience.

b. Israel Redeemed (48:12-22)

12 As this whole section of the prophecy (chapters 40–48) moves to its close, God addresses Israel again, reaffirming his own unique character and urging the exiles to leave Babylon. Jacob/Israel is addressed by the LORD as 'my called one'—a reference back to his choice of Israel as his people (see commentary on 42:6). Once more the LORD declares that he is the first and the last (see the previous occurrences in 41:4 and 44:6). The origin of everything is with him, and he will see his purpose through to completion.

13 The theme of God as creator is given again as the basis for God's ability to predict the future and to act with almighty power. The heavens and earth were brought into existence by him. He had only to speak the word, and the creation resulted (cf. Ps. 33:9; both in this psalm and here in Isaiah the verb 'to stand' is used in the Heb. text of the response to God's creative voice).

14-15 The call to 'assemble together' could be addressed to the nations, or alternatively to the idols. Most probably it is to the nations as in 43:9, as the following question is very similar in both passages. Isaiah 43:9 has 'Who among them will declare this?' while here it is 'Who among them has declared these things?' Quite a few Hebrew manuscripts and early versions like the Targum and the Syriac have 'Who among you?' However, this seems to be a deliberate alteration to the text to have it addressing the idols. It becomes clear that 'these things' is a reference to what has already been said about Cyrus (see 41:2, 25; 44:28–45:5; 45:13; 46:11). Not only is Cyrus the Lord's anointed (45:1), but he is also 'his beloved'. The LORD loves the one who will succeed in carrying out his desire (i.e. Cyrus' desire) on Babylon. God's desire and that of Cyrus merge. What Cyrus is to do in reference to Babylon will be accomplishing God's desire. Moreover, the assurance is repeated that the LORD has indeed spoken (see 46:11 for almost the exact words) and Cyrus' work will come to fruition. The Hebrew idiom at the end of verse 15, 'his way will prosper', is used of the even greater servant of the LORD in Isaiah 53:10: 'the pleasure of the LORD will prosper in his hand.'

16 The great surprise in this verse is that the speaker refers to himself as the one on whom God has sent his Spirit. Several factors suggest that it should be taken as an interjection by the servant of the LORD. The previous chapters have only designated one person as Spirit-endowed and that is the servant (see 42:1). Moreover, the designation of God used here, 'Sovereign LORD' (NIV; Heb. '^{a}donai yhwh$) occurs again in Isaiah, in the third servant song (50:4, 5, 7, 9) and in 61:1 in what is probably another servant song (see footnote on, page 283). The servant calls for attention, declaring that from the first pronouncement about Cyrus (see 41:2) he has not attempted to hide the message (cf. 45:19, 'I have not spoken in secret'). When the predicted events come to pass, then the servant will be involved in them. The final part of the verse speaks of the mission of the servant. He is sent by the eternal God as his messenger, yet later it becomes clear that he himself is divine. There is ambiguity in the Hebrew text regarding the final phrase, 'and his Spirit'. Grammatically this could be part of the subject ('the LORD God and his Spirit') or part of the object ('the LORD God has sent me and his Spirit'). The context in Isaiah suggests that the first of these is preferable. The sending of the servant is an activity of the eternal God and his Spirit.

17-19 The LORD, before calling for the exiles to leave Babylon (verses 20-21) reassures them as to his purposes. He identifies himself using a cluster of titles: 'the LORD', 'your redeemer', 'the holy one of Israel', the LORD your God'. He affirms yet once more by this usage that he is the faithful covenant God of Israel, who still stands in relationship with his people. In spite of all their sin he acknowledges that he is their God. In addition, he directs attention to the fact that he is the one who instructs them in the paths of righteousness, and obedience to him will always be for their profit. Immediately after a command to 'listen' (verse 16) there is a reminder of how Israel failed to follow the LORD's commands (cf. the same pattern in Ps. 81:11-16). Three things are said about what Israel forfeited by her disobedience. First, she surrendered her right to peace and righteousness, which could have come in abundant waves, just like the mighty waters of a river in flood or the rolling waves of the sea. Secondly, she could have still been a large nation in fulfilment of the promise to Abraham that his descendants would be like sand on the sea shore (Gen. 22:17). That promise was realised in the Davidic/Solomonic empire (1 Kings 4:20), but the exile dramatically reduced the numbers belonging to Israel and Judah. Thirdly, though the experience of the exile was to be judgment on God's people, yet their name was never going to be obliterated completely. This is the second time in this passage the concept of 'cutting off' has been mentioned (see verse 9).

20-21 Finally, the call goes out to the exiles to leave Babylon and to flee from the Chaldeans. Babylon is not mentioned by name any more in Isaiah. This call is to be announced with 'shouts of joy', the Hebrew word (*rinnâh*) being used both of expressions of joy and sorrow. Here it is clearly a joyful shout, as they proclaim it far and near. This is an expression of the universalism that occurs in this part of Isaiah, as the message of God's redemption is proclaimed to the world. That message is of God's action in freeing 'his servant Jacob' from bondage and exile. Redemption is God's work. The thought that it is to be a second exodus is presented in verse 21 by reference back to the first exodus. In the desert Israel did not suffer thirst for God provided for her, even making water to flow from the rock (see Exod. 17:6; Num. 20:11). The implication is that the returning exiles will also find that God will provide similarly for them.

22 This section of Isaiah (chapters 40–48) closes with a statement that is going to be repeated almost exactly at the end of the next section as well (57:21). For those who are rebellious ('the wicked') there will be no prosperity ('peace'). No one among the exiles should think that they will be safe simply because they bear the name 'Israel'. That does not make them immune from God's judgment. The promised blessings only apply to those within Israel who seek the LORD in truth and righteousness (cf. 48:1).

B. The Messianic Salvation (49:1–57:21)

The new section beginning at this point continues to the end of chapter 57, when the refrain, 'There is no peace for the wicked' (57:21), will be heard again. Just as the previous section was dominated by messages concerning Cyrus, so this one is dominated by the promised servant. With increasing clarity Isaiah sets out the servant's role, his preparation for ministry, and his ultimate vicarious death. As in the short interjectory speech in 48:16, the servant himself speaks in this passage (49:1-7) and in the following one (50:4-11). However, in chapters 52:13–53:12 the message is given in the third person.

1. The Second Servant Song (49:1-13)

Clearly this servant song has many similarities with 42:1-7, especially with renewed description of the servant being a light to the Gentiles (cf. verse 6 with 42:6). There is also reference to the distant islands or coastlands (cf. verse 1 with 42:4) and to the ends of the earth (cf. verse 6 with 42:10). What is said about the servant in verse 3 still equates the servant with Israel in some respects as in 42:1-3. However, a subtle change of meaning appears in that although the servant is called Israel, he is also differentiated from Israel (see verse 5).

a. The Call of the Servant (49:1-3)

1 The song opens with an address to the distant nations as in 41:1. This type of appeal to 'listen' is characteristic of Isaiah (see also 46:3, 12; 51:1, 7; 55:2). The servant is the speaker and addresses distant peoples, ones to whom he has already been commissioned. 'Islands' probably includes both islands and coastlands of the Mediterranean (cf. its use in 11:11; 41:1, 5; 42:4), as the use of 'distant nations' in the parallel expression makes clear.[1] The servant now reflects on his calling. From the womb he was called, and from the body (lit. 'inward parts') of his mother his name was mentioned. The call of Jeremiah is given in similar terms (Jer. 1:5), while the apostle Paul was also called from birth (Gal. 1:15). The point in these three cases is the sovereign action of God who calls before there is any indication of ability to fulfil their respective missions.

2 The preparations for his work consisted especially of things connected with speech, for here it is his prophetic (rather than kingly) role that is in view. His speech is likened to a sharpened sword and polished arrow, designating the ability to reach the target in view. An arduous task is ahead of the servant and he is not sent to it until he has been properly equipped. In Revelation John depicts the exalted Lord with a sharp sword coming out of his mouth (Rev. 1:16; 19:15, 21). The second and fourth clauses in this verse describe the protection afforded him by the LORD ('hidden in the shadow of his hand', 'concealed in his quiver').

3 While the context of the first servant song makes it plain that the servant is Israel, the identification is not explicit. Yet here the LORD addresses the servant directly, calling him both 'my servant' and

---

[1] The word 'nations' is preceded by the Hebrew preposition *l* that normally means 'to' or 'for'. Here it is used in a vocative sense. For illustrations of this usage drawn from the Psalter, see M. Dahood, *Psalms III* (The Anchor Bible: New York: Doubleday & Co., 1979), pp. 407-08.

[2] Many commentators have suggested that the word 'Israel' should be deleted, but this judgment stems from theological reasons. The only Hebrew manuscript that omits it is Kennicot 96.

'Israel'.[2] This address is part of the oscillation in these songs between the collective and individual identifications of the servant. It becomes clear in verse 5 that there are two Israels in view, one (the individual) who has the special task of bringing the other (the nation) back to the LORD. Through him God will be glorified, and ultimately through those to whom he ministers, this glory will also be revealed (see 61:3, for the use of the same Heb. verb *pâ'ar*).

b. The Mission of the Servant (49:4-7)

4 The servant is discouraged and depressed and feels all his labour has been in vain. The emphasis on himself is made emphatic by the inclusion of the pronoun 'I' together with the verb 'I said'. He declares that all his hard toil has achieved no real results. There is only emptiness (Heb. *tôhû*; this word from Genesis 1:2 occurring eleven times in Isaiah) and a void. The third colon in the verse starts with the word 'yet' or 'nevertheless' which marks a contrast to 'I said' at the commencement of the verse. He knows that though visible results may be lacking, yet the LORD is going to use him to perform his appointed mission. What the servant says is: 'my judgment is with the LORD.' 'Judgment' (Heb. *mishpât*) can mean either one's activity in establishing justice, or the receiving of justice. The former gives the better meaning here, as the parallel expression is 'my work'. Though the servant on the one hand has a low perception of his own work, yet he knows that the ultimate outcome will be success and that he will be vindicated. There were to be occasions in Jesus' ministry when he faced unbelief and rejection that could well be the fulfilment of this verse.[3]

5 The LORD's description of the servant repeats part of verse 1. Even from before his birth the servant was destined for this particular mission. His task is to restore Jacob/Israel to a living relationship with God. In other words Israel (the servant) has the role of turning Israel (the nation) back to the LORD. There is a textual question regarding the Hebrew word *lô'* preceding the verb 'be gathered'. The written text has it as the negative 'not', but the Qumran scroll 1QIsa[a], the LXX, and the Massoretic marginal note have it as the preposition *l*

---

[3]See the excellent comments on this point in J. A. Motyer, *The Prophecy of Isaiah*, p. 387, fn. 1.

[4]Exactly the same translational problem occurs in the Hebrew text of Isaiah 9:2 (Eng. text Isa. 9:3).

('to') plus the masculine singular pronoun. This makes excellent sense of the passage, as 'bring Jacob back to him' then has as its parallel, 'and Israel shall be gathered to him'.[4] The final stanza describes the servant's exaltation in God's eyes and his declaration that support for his mission comes from God's strength. The mission to be accomplished will be testimony to God's grace and power.

6 After the parenthesis in the previous verse the opening 'he says' directs attention to God's words, which commence with the expression, 'it is too small a thing to be my servant.' While these words are certainly unusual they do have a parallel in Ezekiel 8:17. The servant's task is not limited to the role of restoring the dispersed Jews (those God has 'kept' during the exile) but includes the much greater task of bringing salvation to the Gentiles. Also, the reference to 'light to the Gentiles' is a repetition of 42:6, with the indication that in reality this is a bringing of God's salvation to the ends of the world. The latter part of this verse is quoted by Paul and Barnabas in Pisidian Antioch as justification for their Gentile ministry (see Acts 13:47).

7 With solemn formality the LORD here describes the effect that the servant's mission will have on rulers. The one who speaks is 'the redeemer of Israel, his holy one'. Though the servant is despised (cf. the double occurrence of this same description in Isaiah 53:3) and abhorred by the nation,[5] yet he is going to have a dramatic impact on rulers and princes. Those who normally sit on thrones (kings) will see the servant's saving work and will rise in his presence. Courtiers (princes) who normally stand in the royal presence will prostrate themselves before him. This description of royal response to the servant is further developed in 52:15. Just as the nation of Israel was chosen by God, so the servant, who fulfils all that the nation was meant to be, is also chosen by him.

c. Confirmation of the Servant's Mission (49:8-12)

The delimitation of the servant passages is difficult, and while some want to conclude this song at verse 7, it seems that verses 8-12 are closely allied to what has preceded, so it is best to include them as

---

[5]Though the Heb. word *gôy* is usually used of the Gentiles, it can on occasion, as here, be applied to Israel. See Genesis 18:18. It appears in conjunction with the common description of Israel as *'am* in Exodus 33:13 and Deuteronomy 4:6-7.

[6]For discussion of the name 'Sinim', see commentary on verse 12.

confirmation of the servant's mission. As elsewhere there is oscillation between the work of the servant in the ultimate future and his role in the return from exile. Several factors suggest that something more than the return from exile is envisaged. First, reference to the time of favour echoes the language about the year of jubilee (Lev. 25:8-55) and in Isaiah 61:1-3 (cf. Luke 4:16-21) it is applied to the messianic deliverance. Second, the exiles will come not just from Babylonia but 'from afar; Look! Those from the north and the west, and these from the land of Sinim'[6] (NKJV). Third, the message that precedes, along with the first servant song, speaks of the work of the servant affecting the Gentiles. While return from exile was not first and foremost a ministry to non-Jewish people, it certainly had relevance for them, and of Israel they would say, 'The LORD has done great things for them' (Ps. 126:2).

8-9a A further significant declaration is made by the LORD. This time of God's favour or goodwill lies in the future. Paul quotes these opening clauses in 2 Corinthians 6:2 when he speaks of the manifestation of God's grace that has been shown in the coming of the Lord Jesus. The servant's prayers will be answered in that he will be 'kept' to be a covenant for the people. The same verb 'keep' (*nâtsar*) is used of the servant as has already been used of 'the preserved of Israel' in verse 6, for the LORD keeps him ready for his mission. This is the second time that this phrase 'a covenant for the people' has occurred (see commentary on 42:6). In his person the servant embodies all that is intended in the covenant. Part of the promise that had been given to Israel concerned restoration to the land. Here it is expressed not simply as return to the land, but also a reassignment of its regions. Joshua originally carried out the assignment of land (see Josh. 14:1-5), but when the returnees from exile come back there will be an assignment of the desolate inheritances. This means that the messianic servant is going to be both a new Moses and a new Joshua. He is going to call for 'the prisoners' (a synonym for 'the exiles') to come out, and for those in 'darkness' (a synonym for 'imprisonment') to be released.

9b-10 On the journey back to Palestine the people will be fed by the LORD, just as when the first exodus took place. Not only will they feed like cattle grazing by the roadside, but even in unexpected places (barren hills) they will find food. They will neither hunger nor thirst (see the earlier reference to God's provision of water in the wilderness in 48:21). Scorching heat will leave them untouched, while the strong rays of the sun will not strike them. The reason for these blessings lies in the fact that their compassionate God, like a good shepherd, will lead them beside springs of water. The picture transcends anything that actually happened during the return from exile, and seems to point to an eschatological ingathering of Jews and Gentiles (see verse 12).

11 As in chapter 40 the physical environment is going to be transformed to provide a pathway that is easy and level. God regards the mountains and highways as his, and he is depicted as ensuring that the returnees will be able to traverse the countryside easily.

12 The servant's work is going to extend far beyond the exiles in Babylon. From far off lands there is going to be a pilgrimage back to Zion. From north and west they will come, even from *sînîm*. This obscure Hebrew word has been interpreted in various ways. The early versions do not give much assistance, with the LXX translating it as Persia, while the Vulgate renders it as *terra australis*. The traditional English rendering has been China, but there is nothing to confirm this. In more recent times it has been conjectured that it is really Aswan in southern Egypt. Another very plausible suggestion is that it denotes some far off country whose exact location is deliberately not given with precision. This would mean that God was claiming that pilgrims will come even from unmapped areas.[7]

d. Doxology (49:13)

13 The description of the servant's work is followed by a song of joy. Heaven and earth are personified, and are called upon to sing in joyful exaltation of the LORD. There is much similarity with passages earlier in Isaiah (see 12:6; 42:10; 44:23), and it is to be noted especially that the phrase 'burst into song, O mountains' is identical with 44:23. The reason for this joy is appended. The LORD both comforts his people and has compassion on his afflicted. In the context 'people' can hardly be restricted to Israel, but must include all those depicted as coming from afar (see the previous verse). The idea of God's compassion is picked up from verse 10 and given wider application.

---

[7]For this suggestion, see J. A. Motyer, *The Prophecy of Isaiah*, p. 392, or his Tyndale commentary on *Isaiah* (Inter-Varsity Press, 1999), p. 312.

2. The Restoration of Israel (49:14–50:3)

a. Zion's Complaint (verses 14-21)

As in 40:27 the complaint from Israel is that she has been forgotten by God, though here the answer is fuller and more triumphant. Family analogies predominate in God's response – mother, baby, sons, children. Israel is neither forsaken nor forgotten.

14 Judah in exile claims that she has been forsaken and forgotten by the LORD. The message that Isaiah received at the time of his call (6:12) specifically mentioned the forsaking of the land. It is true that Judah was forsaken (see also 54:7), but it was not true that she was forgotten. As long as the covenant bond stood, there was no danger of God casting off his people (cf. Paul's words in Romans 11:1).

15 Here is the reassurance that the Judaean exiles need. It is far easier for a mother to forget her baby than it is for the LORD to forget his people. Maternal compassion may fail, but God's compassion is enduring. His character is that of the compassionate God. He revealed himself to Moses as 'the LORD, the LORD, compassionate and merciful' (Exod. 34:6), and in this context he is already called 'He who has compassion' (verse 10). Whatever maternal forgetfulness could occur, God in no way could forget his people. In the Hebrew text 'I' is emphatic, stressing the contrast.

16 Before any further declaration of God's never-ending concern for his people is made, attention is called to what follows, by the opening word 'See'. God's care of his people is so certain that it is like having them engraved on his hands. Zion's walls ever live before the LORD. This may be a reference to the fate of Jerusalem in her desolation, or, alternately, a reference to the future rebuilding of the walls.

17-18 The theme of children is taken up at this point and is developed in the following verses.[8] The children will return, while those who brought God's punishment on Israel will hasten away. Her seemingly lost children will gather to her, henceforth to be hers for ever (the promise of the gathering was made back in 11:12). Her downcast eyes can now be lifted up and fixed on the returning children. Their return will be a time of glory for Israel, as the returnees will be

---

[8]The LXX, the Targum, and the manuscript 1QIsa[a] have *bônayik* ('your builders'), the MT has *bânayik* ('your sons'). While 'your builders' would make good sense, yet the whole context favours retaining the MT reading.

to Zion as ornaments are to a bride. The solemnity of this assurance is enhanced by the use of an oath formula: 'As I live, says the LORD.'

19-20 The picture is of exiles and their children born in captivity returning to Palestine. They will come back to places that have been devastated by aggressors called here 'those who devoured you'. The Hebrew verb 'to swallow' is used (*bâla'* Pi.), and it is often employed as in this verse with the figurative sense of consuming or devouring (cf. Ps. 35:25; Eccles. 10:12; Lam. 2:16). These oppressors will be gone, and as Israel settles in the land she will find that she needs a larger stretch of territory to accommodate the numbers returning. The children in particular will find the territory very restricted and consequently will ask for greater room in which to live.

21 Judah will muse to herself (lit. 'in her heart') over the change that is coming. She expresses surprise by her first question that as a captive widow she now has all these children. Though desolate and rejected, she finds herself surrounded by a new family, and this causes astonishment. There is a strong contrast drawn between her and her new children by setting the emphatic 'I' over against the thrice repeated 'these' ('Who has born *these*'; 'Who brought *these* up'; 'But *these*, where are they from?'). Her questions simply enhance the idea that she herself was incapable of bearing these children. Just as in the case of Abraham and Sarah the gift of life was due to the grace and power of God.

b. All Flesh to Know the Redeemer (49:22-26)

22 Again a solemn declaration is made by the LORD.[9] He intends to beckon the Gentile nations and attract their attention by an ensign or banner. Such signalling has been mentioned earlier in this book (5:26; 11:10-12; 13:2). The same idea, that the Gentiles will be used by God to restore the dispersed Jews, is mentioned in 14:2, 43:6, and 60:9. The manner of the return, with the sons in the arms and daughters on the shoulders, indicates that it will be done with the care and compassion that mothers or nurses bestow. The same imagery will reappear in 60:4 and 66:10-11.

23 The concept of the previous verse is repeated but this time by using the illustration of the actions of kings and queens. They too will

---

[9]The Heb. text has ' *a*dônay yhwh. Where this combination occurs the Jewish Massoretes indicated that what was said was *'a*dônay *'e*lôhîm (NKJV 'the Lord God'; NIV 'the Sovereign LORD').

act with paternal and maternal care, and whereas it was the children in view in verse 23 it is now appears to be Zion herself who is the subject. There will also be a reversal of roles in that Zion will no longer be in subjection to others but will herself be honoured by the leaders of Gentile nations bowing in subjection to her. 'To bow before' and 'to lick the dust' are synonymous expressions of subjection (cf. Ps. 72:9; Mic. 7:17). This will be further proof to Israel that her deliverance is to be achieved by the LORD's mighty power. The ultimate outcome will be that those who wait for him, i.e. whose trust is in him, will not be disgraced or let down.

24 The need for divine power to achieve release for the captives is indicated by the two questions in this verse, which find their reply in verse 25. The first one points to the need for Israel to be taken from the grasp of her captors. The second one asks the question whether those who rightly have captives in their possession can be deprived of their lawful gain? The Hebrew manuscript 1QIsa^a, the LXX, the Syriac and the Vulgate all had difficulty with the word 'righteous/ness' (*tsâddeq*) in this context. But no change is necessary to 'fierce' (Heb. *'ârîts*) as in the NIV or NRSV, for the questions are raising the issues of force and right as grounds for holding captives. In both cases, when God's grace intervenes, they will be on Israel's side.

25-26 The answer to these questions comes in another formal response by the LORD. Indeed, the captives will be released from the grip of warriors and what is taken in plunder will be retrieved. The promise is also given that God will take up the cause of his people. He will defend them (see also the assurance given in Jer. 50:34). The threat is made that those who have oppressed the exiles will themselves engage in cannibalism, just as some in Jerusalem did when it was razed (Lam. 4:10). The ultimate aim of this is that the LORD will be acknowledged by all mankind. Previously it had been said that the purpose of divine actions was not only that Israel might know that their God was the LORD (see 45:3) but that those from east to west might know him as well (see 45:6). That latter promise is now repeated in verse 26 with the claim that all mankind (Heb. *kol-bâsâr*, 'all flesh') will know God's character. The combination of names for him ('LORD', 'saviour', 'redeemer', 'mighty one of Jacob') reinforces the point that Israel's God is able to overcome all earthly rulers and ensure that the captives are freed.

c. Israel to be Delivered in Spite of Her Sin (50:1-3)

1 The LORD now takes up the matter of the relationship between himself and his exiled people using a similar metaphor of a bride and her children as appeared in the previous chapter (49:14-21). The first question concerns whether a certificate of divorce is in existence. The normal practice was for a husband to provide his wife with such a certificate when he sent her away (see Deut. 24:1-4). The implication is that no such document was ever given to those taken to Babylon. That was just as well because there could not be a restored marriage after a divorce document was issued. Jeremiah certainly says that the northern kingdom of Israel was given a divorce certificate (Jer. 3:8). Even though the southern kingdom was unfaithful, there was no divorce. What occurred was a temporary separation between God and his people (see 54:7), which was initiated by the people themselves when they forsook him. The second question concerns whether there was a debt that had to be paid by selling the people. Certainly not! God is debtor to no one. In fact what transpired was that Judah was sold because of her sins, and Zion (the mother) banished because of her transgressions.

2 The radical sin of the people was disobedience to the word of God. He had spoken, but there was no response on their part. The prophets had spoken God's message but the people were deaf to them. Then other questions are posed that relate to the LORD's attitude and ability. Did the LORD lack the power to redeem (Lev. 25:26, 28, 47-48)? The LORD's hand was never shortened (Num. 11:23). He who rebuked the Red Sea is still the God able to deliver and redeem his people. The mention of fish dying is a reference back to the plague that caused all the fish to die in the Nile. The verb used here for 'rot' is the same one that appears in Exodus 7:18.

3 The LORD's power is such that he is able to cause darkness, whether by an eclipse or by some other means. The root of the word 'darkness' (Heb. *qadrût*) is used in 1 Kings 18:45 of the sky being darkened by clouds. Some have thought that this is a reference to what happened at Mount Sinai, but in the context in which the Exodus experiences are prominent it is more probably an allusion to the plague of darkness (Exod. 10:21).

3. The Third Servant Song and a Message of Comfort (50:4-11)

a. The Servant's Humiliation (50:4-9)

This passage has been called 'the Gethsemane of the Servant'. Much of the song is unclear without the light of the New Testament. The noun 'servant' (Heb. *'eved*) does not occur within it, though it does come immediately afterwards (verse 10). Some distinctive features of this song stand out: (1) it is the most personal of all the servant songs; (2) the servant himself speaks in a soliloquy; (3) in the first two servant songs, the servant is a teacher, but here he is a disciple, who is fitted and prepared for his work; (4) suffering is an integral part of the servant's experience; (5) it is abruptly introduced, and where it ends is unclear.

4 Throughout the song the servant refers to the fact that it is the LORD God (NIV 'Sovereign Lord') who has spoken to him (see the fourfold use of the Heb. *'adonai yhwh* in verses 4, 5, 7, 9). This gives added solemnity to the message. There was preparation of both the servant's tongue and ear. He is given the tongue of disciples (Heb. *limmudîm*; cf. Isa. 8:16; 54:13). The purpose of this gift is expressed by a very rare Hebrew verb, which occurs only here in the Old Testament (Heb. *'ût*). A meaning such as 'sustain' or 'comfort' is needed in the context. This consolation is given to 'the weary', who are probably both Israel and the Gentiles. The ears are also prepared continuously ('morning by morning') for this saving ministry. The servant is made ready to receive the LORD's commission.

5 The thought of preparation of the ear is continued, but with the added concept that the servant, unlike Israel, is not rebellious when the message is received. This stands in marked contrast to the behaviour of the collective servant: 'You have neither heard nor understood; from of old your ear has not been open' (48:8). The servant neither refused to obey the message he received nor did he pull back from the suffering that was set before him.

6 As distinct from the other prophets, the servant is equipped for his task through special suffering. The best commentary on this verse is Hebrews 5:8-9 with reference to the obedience that Christ learned through his earthly sufferings. The mention of 'strikers' points to some public chastisement, not just a private quarrel. Plucking the beard was an insult (see Neh. 13:25), while the phrase 'mocking and spitting' is a compound expression to denote all sorts of insults, whether by speech or by actions. The description of the mistreatment of the servant finds its fulfilment in the mockery and shame that Jesus endured prior to and during his death on the cross.

7 The ground of the servant's confidence lies in the LORD's help and twice he repeats this (verses 7 and 9). The predicted suffering will not mean that God withdraws his support, nor that he suffers disgrace in God's sight. The verbs 'be disgraced' and 'be ashamed' occur together thirty times in the Old Testament, and there is no real difference in meaning between them. In spite of suffering the servant perseveres with his mission, setting his face like a flint. This is a forceful simile to denote the firm determination of the servant. The New Testament records how Jesus set his face steadfastly to go up to Jerusalem, even though he knew the suffering that awaited him there (Luke 9:51).

8 The language of the lawcourt appears in this and the following verse. The confidence from the LORD encourages him to ask his adversaries to come and bring their charges. He knows that his vindicator is close at hand, and therefore is quite ready to stand at the judgment seat with any accuser. He gives the challenge to his accuser (lit. 'lord of my judgment') to draw near with his charges. In its fulfilment this prophetic word came to pass when even Pilate acknowledged that he was handing over to death an innocent man (Matt. 27:24).

9 This verse opens with repetition of the assurance of the LORD's help. The phrase is identical to that in verse 7, except for an introductory 'behold' in the Hebrew text. Some versions like NKJV bring this out by the use of a word such as 'surely'. The challenge is again given for anyone to condemn him. 'Justify' and 'condemn' are exact opposites, the one to declare just, and the other to declare guilty. The question is posed in a striking way: It is not simply 'Who will condemn?' but 'Who (Heb. *mî hû'*) is he that will condemn me' (NIV)? All those who oppose him will fall apart like an old garment. This same imagery appears in Job 13:28; Psalm 39:11; Psalm 102:26; and Isaiah 51:6, 8. God's righteous purposes will outlast any human malice.

b. Comfort to those Obedient to the Servant (50:10-11)

10 This and the following verse seem to be the words of the LORD, just as the opening verses in the chapter are. The servant is referred to in the third person, and the LORD speaks about 'my hand' (verse 11) even as he has already spoken of 'my creditors' in verse 1. The responsibility is set out for anyone who truly fears the LORD (taking the Heb. *mî* as the indefinite 'whoever') to act with full reliance upon him, even though the pathway ahead is dark. The two verbs used for faith ('trust', 'rely upon') are both used repeatedly in the Old Testament of putting one's confidence in God, and there is no apparent difference in meaning between them. What is required is obedience to the servant and trust in the LORD. Those walking in darkness need the light that comes by trusting in him.

11 The destruction that the wicked prepare for the servant of the LORD falls upon themselves. The section closes on this ominous note. The wicked are like a man starting a fire with a flint and then the fire he has kindled surrounds him. They are called on to go on with that course of action if that is their mind-set, but the fire of wrath they kindle now becomes to them a fire of judgment from the LORD's hand. The final word is that those who walk in the light of their own fires will lie down in torment. This is the only time in the Old Testament that this word 'torment' occurs. It comes from a root meaning to hurt or to grieve, and here designates a place of pain that is the result of God's judgment.

4. The Joy of Restoration and Preparation for the Return (51:1–52:12)

From the beginning of chapter 51 to 52:12 there is a series of calls, which may well be understood as the result of the awakening of the servant (50:4-5). These calls (with their opening words) are as follows:

51:1-3	'Listen'
51:4-6	'Hearken'
51:7-8	'Listen'
51:9-16	'Awake, awake'
51:17-23	'Rouse yourself, rouse yourself, arise'
52:1-6	'Awake, awake'
52:7-10	'How beautiful . . . break forth into joy'
Supplement	The New Exodus 52:11-12 'Depart, depart'

These calls are framed by the third and fourth servant songs. Zion is to take comfort and encouragement from the assurances God gives and to prepare for the imminent departure of the exiles from Babylon.

Days of sorrow are going to be replaced by a time of great joy when the LORD makes the oppressors drink the cup of his fury and when he redeems Jerusalem.

a. The New Eden (51:1-3)

1-2 This opening call is directed to those who 'pursue righteousness', the same group as those who 'know righteousness' (verse 7). They are clearly the believing community 'who seek the LORD', not the whole number of exiles. They are asked to consider where they sprang from, as God's faithfulness in fulfilling his promises to Abraham and Sarah should encourage fresh confidence in his purposes for them. Elsewhere God is called 'the rock' (see Deut. 32:4; 1 Sam. 2:2; Ps. 89:26), but here it is Abraham who is 'the rock' and the 'quarry'. The calling of Abraham and God's dealings with him and his descendants are summarised in the second part of verse 2: 'When he was one I called him; then I blessed him and made him many.' Genesis 11–21 is dominated by the theme of God's promise of a large family coming from the childless marriage of Abraham and Sarah (Gen. 11:30; 15:2; 16:1; for the same language of Abraham only being 'one', see Ezekiel 33:24; also possibly Malachi 2:15). The commencement of fulfilment of the promise came with the birth of Isaac, and from him ultimately there was a large family, 'as numerous as the sand on the seashore' (1 Kings 4:20). The use of the verbs 'bless' and 'make many' re-echoes the repeated promises to Abraham.

3 If God had been faithful to his word of promise to Abraham, would he not also fulfil his promises to the exiles? Isaiah has already spoken of God's comfort and compassion for his afflicted ones (see especially 49:13). The theme of the desert being changed into a new Eden has been developed in chapter 35, though without specifically naming it 'Eden'. The present barrenness will be replaced with lush vegetation, so much so that the new Eden will also be 'the garden of the LORD' (cf. the way in which Ezekiel calls Eden 'the garden of God' and 'the holy mountain of God', Ezek. 28:13, 14). This restoration of Eden will be accompanied with joyful singing as an indicator of the changed circumstances of Jerusalem and Judah (see similar references in Isaiah 35:6, 10; 51:11; 52:9). The description of transformed nature points to an eschatological realisation for the prophecy.

b. Justice to the Nations (51:4-6)

4 The exiles have to understand that God's purposes include the Gentile nations. Hence God calls to his people (here designated by the two Hebrew words *'am* and *lᵉ'ûm*) to pay attention to the message that his law/justice is going to reach the nations. Whereas the servant was earlier the light (42:6; 49:6), now it is God's law/justice that is to be the light. There is no conflict between the two ideas, for part of the servant's role is to bring justice (see 42:4, and cf. 2:2-4).

5 The opening clause of this verse has produced various translations (cf. NASB 'For I will set my justice for a light of the peoples', and in contrast the NIV: 'My righteousness draws near speedily'). There are two Hebrew verbs that are identical in form (Heb. *râga'*), the one meaning 'to have rest', and the other 'to do something quickly'. On balance it is better to take it as the NIV does, for the context here in the following chapters is on the near approach of the restoration from exile. Also, it seems best to make it the first word of verse 5 rather than attaching it to the conclusion of verse 4 (see NKJV). The remainder of the verse asserts that God's salvation will reach to the Gentiles, and his power (twice in the verse 'arm' is used in this sense) will come to those who wait for him (the same verb as in 40:31). The experience of salvation will not be for the Jews only.

6 The contrast is between the transient things that belong to the heaven and the earth and the abiding salvation of God. Similar references to the dissolution of heaven and earth have already occurred in this book (see 24:4; 34:4). The same comparison of a garment rotting away comes in Psalm 102:25-28 where the idea is that God remains the same throughout time while the creation itself will perish. This point is made emphatically in Hebrews 1:10-13, with use of a quotation from Psalm 102. Just as God's word abides for ever (cf. 40:8), so does his saving power.

c. A Message for the Faithful (51:7-8)

7 This call is addressed to those who know what is right and who have God's law in their hearts. These expressions are synonymous with those in verse 1. To have God's law in the heart is an expression found in the Book of Psalms (see 37:31; 40:8; 119:11). It means much more than just being able to recite that law. Rather, it clearly indicates living in accordance with God's directives. This couplet is to strengthen such people. They should not fear the reproaches of men nor let their insults disturb them. Isaiah has already told his Jewish compatriots that others would pour scorn on them (43:28), but now he presents God as the comforter of those who are abused.

8 One of the similes in this verse has appeared earlier (see 50:9: 'the moth will eat them'). Now is added the similar one of a worm eating up wool. Both reassert the point made in verse 6. Those who set themselves against God's people will themselves utterly perish just like a worn-out piece of cloth. The contrast, though, is that God's salvation is abiding. Even from generation to generation his saving mercy will be in evidence. As over against his enemies, God is unchanging.

d. The Mighty Redeemer (51:9-16)

9 This call is different from the preceding ones in that it is addressed to God. A double call to the arm of the LORD to awake commences it, and then this call is repeated later in the verse. 'The arm' is frequently a symbol of God's power, especially as it was seen in the Exodus (cf. Exod. 6:6; Deut. 4:34; Ps. 77:15; Isa. 63:12). The appeal is for a fresh demonstration of this power in the new exodus. Both 'Rahab' and 'monster' are used in the Old Testament as symbols for those who oppose God. 'Rahab' comes from a Hebrew root meaning 'to behave proudly', and it is used of Egypt (as here and in Ps. 87:4) while 'monster' (Heb. *tannîn*) is applied to both Egypt (as here) and to Babylon (Jer. 51:34). The appeal is to remember the mighty deeds of God in overcoming all human efforts at the time of the Exodus from Egypt.

10 The crossing of the Red Sea is recalled as a specific demonstration of divine power. The 'great deep' had been conquered with God making a way for the redeemed to cross over. Back in 50:2 the same event is referred to as a rebuke that dried up the waters. The word used here for 'redeemed' is the verb that God himself used to describe what he was going to do for his people in Egypt (Exod. 6:6), and which in the Song of the Sea is used to designate the people whom God had led out (Exod. 15:13). Though the depth of the Red Sea was apparently not very great, yet poetic hyperbole magnifies it to be the 'great deep' (see also 63:13).

11 This verse (apart from some insignificant variations) is identical to Isaiah 35:10. It speaks of the future time when sorrow will disappear, as the LORD's redeemed return from exile with joyful songs on their lips. Praise is a spontaneous response to divine mercy. The connection with the context is probably that it is an answer to a further unexpressed question such as: 'And has it not been already said that ...?'

12-13 After the questions of verses 9-11 God himself speaks in response. Again the emphasis falls on the great power of the creator God. He is able to bring the prisoners out of their dungeon, and also to reassure them that they are still his people (verse 16). The response commences with another affirmation of both God's self-existence and the fact that he is the one who comforts his people. The form of the self-affirmation is identical with that in 43:25. The assurance is directed to 'you' (pl.), presumably here the people as a whole. Their present trouble is that they fear their oppressors who are but men, as temporary as the grass of the field. Coupled with fear is their forgetfulness of God. The forgetfulness was not on his part (see 49:14-16); it was on theirs. In spite of the fact that their comforter was the creator God, they lived under abiding terror (the Heb. text emphasises this by saying that their fear was 'continually all the day'). The challenge in the final question of verse 13, 'Where is the wrath of the oppressor?' is intended to show how insignificant that wrath is when compared with God's ability to deliver his people from Babylon's control.

14-15 The prisoners need to know that their present captivity (depicted here as a cowering before their oppressors) is soon going to end. Death in a foreign dungeon is not going to be their lot, nor will they perish because of lack of food. The reason is that their God is indeed the LORD, the LORD of hosts. This combination of titles highlights the capacity of God to keep his people and to ensure their return to Palestine. Their covenant God (*yhwh*) is also the omnipotent God (*yhwh ts^{e}va'ôt*), who has the ability to cause the sea to be churned up (cf. Job 26:12; Ps. 107:25).

16 This verse explains further the two ideas of verse 15. On the one hand he is their LORD, and therefore he can say: 'You are my people.' On the other hand he is the almighty God of creation who established the heavens and the earth. His 'words', presumably the law given through Moses (see the earlier reference to the law in the heart in verse 7), has been put within them, while they can rest secure in the shade of his hand. This imagery of shade is frequently used in the Old Testament to denote the protection that the LORD gives to his people (cf. Pss. 17:8; 36:7; 121:5; Isa. 25:4).

e. The Cup of God's Wrath (51:17-23)

17 The dominant note in this section is the fact that Judah had been made to drink the cup of God's wrath, but that cup has been taken away. God's judgment is often depicted as though it was a drink of strong wine, especially so when the judgment is on the Gentile nations (for typical examples see Isa. 29:9; 63:6; Ps. 60:3; Jer. 25:15-16; Ezek. 23:32-34). But even the chosen nation was not exempt from this punishment. The people in exile had to realise that the cup has been removed (see verse 22). Hence the call to 'rouse themselves' (the reflexive form of the same verb as in verse 9), for God's deliverance draws ever nearer.

18-20 Family imagery is used to depict the suffering that has been endured as a consequence of God's judgment. Children, who could have been expected to aid and support the mother, are gone. Double calamities of desolation and destruction, famine and sword, have come upon them, with no one able to give consolation. The first pair relate to the ruined city of Jerusalem, the second to its inhabitants. There are two questions relating to comfort. The first one is: 'Who will have compassion on you?' The second question, which parallels the first, is awkward. The Hebrew text has: 'Who I can comfort you?' While this could mean 'Who but I can comfort you?', the context favours taking it as synonymous with the first question: 'Who can comfort you?' This is how the early translations of the Old Testament interpreted it. Verse 20 reverts to the question of the state of the sons. They are no use as they are faint, lying down in the streets like an antelope caught in a net. They are the objects of God's wrath, and have experienced his rebuke. There can be no expectation of help from this source.

21-22 Now a direct word is addressed by God to his afflicted people. The idea of drunkenness already used (see verse 17) is taken up again. The exiled nation had not become inebriated with wine but rather with the cup of wrath that God had given her. The promise is given that this cup of wrath has been taken away so that the people no longer will be forced to drink from it. By direct intervention of the Lord God (using the double appellation of *'ªdonay yhwh* as in 50:4, 7, 9) that period is finished, and now he is ready to take up their case (cf. 49:25) and contend for them.

23 This new period in the history of God's people is marked by the fact that it is now Israel's oppressors who are to drink from the cup of wrath. These enemies of Israel and Judah have not escaped God's justice. They had humiliated and subjected them to abject cruelty. The language here of walking on the backs of captives is more than just figurative language (see Ps. 129:3). Stepping on the necks of captives occurred (Jos. 10:24), while Damascus was accused of threshing Gilead with sledges having iron teeth (Amos 1:3). The principle in this summary message against Babylon is expanded elsewhere in the Old Testament, especially in the oracles against the nations (Isa. 13–23; Jer. 46–51; Ezek. 25–32; Amos 1–2; Obadiah; Nahum). While judgment begins first with the house of God, sinful heathen nations will not escape their just reward.

f. 'Awake, awake' (52:1-6)

1 The call is to Zion and it is expressed in similar terms to the call already issued in 51:17, though the form of the verb 'to awake' reverts to that used in 51:9. The form in 51:17 may well suggest that the drunken Jerusalem has to make a strenuous effort to stir herself. Here Zion awakes just as easily as the arm of the LORD awakes. She had called herself 'the holy city' (48:2), and now the LORD calls her this. Back in 1:26 the promise had been given that she would be called 'the city of righteousness, the faithful city'. Zion is urged to put on festive garments as she anticipates her approaching deliverance, possibly an allusion to priestly garments (see the same term used in reference to the garments of Aaron and his sons in Exod. 28:2, 40). No longer will any uncircumcised or unclean foreigner come within her gates, as they were prohibited from participating in the worship of the LORD. This description is part of the picture of what Jerusalem will be at the time of restoration, not necessarily what she will always be, for clearly the Romans, 'the uncircumcised and the unclean', later occupied Jerusalem.

2 Zion has to rouse herself from the dust in which she lies, and cast off her bands of captivity. It is strange to find a command to sit (Heb. *shᵉvi*) coming straight after the imperative 'Rise'. If it is retained then the idea will be that Jerusalem, after picking herself up out of the dust and putting on her festal robes, then sits again in stately splendour. Alternatively it may be taken as synonymous with 'captive' (Heb. *shᵉviyyâh*), which occurs in the next line, and the translation will then be, 'Rise up, O captive Jerusalem' (NASB).

3 This and the next three verses are in prose, not poetry, though some traces of parallelism appear. Zion's children had been sold for nothing, and they will be redeemed without money. The Hebrew word *chinnâm* can be used to indicate 'for no reason', but here the parallelism makes it certain that the meaning is 'without money'. This confirms what has been said already, that there was no payment when Israel went into exile, and similarly there will be none when the return takes place (cf. 45:13; 50:1).

4 Two important points in Israel's history are recalled. The people had experienced the bondage in Egypt. God had taken Israel down there to live as a foreigner, a sojourner (Heb. *lâgûr*). Once more a reference back to the Exodus sets the pattern for God's impending activity of restoring his people to Palestine. The second important event was the captivity by Assyria. The cruelties of Sennacherib and his troops is still vividly before Isaiah's eyes, and this had taken place 'lately' as opposed to the 'at first' in reference to the Egyptian bondage. While the translation 'lately' is unusual for the Hebrew expression in question (b^e'*efes*), there is no reason why it cannot apply to a limit of time as well as its normal usage in regard to limits of space (it appears most commonly in the phrase 'to the ends of the earth').

5 The question with which the verse opens (Heb. v^e'*attâh mah-lî-fôh*) is used in a variety of settings, but here the idiom seems to mean something like our 'Now, what have we here?' In this context 'here' cannot refer to Egypt or Assyria, but must be a reference to Babylon. The LORD responds to both the misery of his people and to the dishonour done to his name. Even those who rule over Israel (i.e. their own rulers, not the foreign ones as the NIV takes it to mean) mourn, while God's name is continuously a thing of derision. In Ezekiel 36:20-23 mention is similarly made of the mockery by Gentiles of God's name because *his* people had to leave *his* land.

6 When the LORD's people are redeemed from their bondage in Babylon they will acknowledge both that it is their God who foretold that event and who accomplished it. The declaration with which the verse ends is reminiscent of earlier ones (especially the use of 'I am he', Heb. *^{a}ni hû*'). It is made even more emphatic by the final 'behold [it is] I'. The expression 'in that day' can certainly have eschatological overtones, but here it refers to the impending return from exile, which in itself is a picture of the messianic deliverance to occur through the work of Christ.

g. 'How beautiful . . . break forth into joy' (52:7-10)

7 The address is to Jerusalem, the ruined city, and hence the mountains are those surrounding it. The idea of gladness is implied by the verb 'to bring good news' (Heb. *m^{e}vassêr*) but then made more definite by the words 'peace', 'good [things]', and 'salvation'. This passage contains echoes of 40:1-11. A number of important themes are brought together—peace, salvation, the kingdom of God—and all just preceding the description of the servant's vicarious work. The climax of the proclamation concerns the LORD's kingship, just as in the royal psalms (see Pss. 93:1; 97:1; 99:1), and in the triumphant declaration of the multitude of redeemed saints in heaven (Rev. 19:6).

8 The prophets seems to be addressed, for 'watchmen' here and in 66:10 is applied to them. The difficulty with this is that desolate Jerusalem did not have prophets. However, the whole scene is treated dramatically and they see the LORD coming back to Zion as near as one man looking into the eye of another (Heb. 'for eye to eye they see'). The watchmen burst into song at the sight of the LORD's return.

9 A word is now addressed to desolate Jerusalem, which will be able to rejoice because the LORD has redeemed and comforted her. This is a repetition of the message already given in 44:23 and 49:13, sharing with the latter passage the parallel expression 'he has redeemed Jacob/Jerusalem'. Both the verbs for singing used here ('burst forth' and 'sing') have also occurred in these earlier passages. Faith is able to lay hold of God's promises and to rejoice.

10 The LORD's salvation is not just directed to Zion and Jerusalem but it also concerns the whole world. As a warrior he 'bares his arm'. This phrase occurs here and in Ezekiel 4:7 as an expression of his saving power. Like a warrior who pulls back his upper garment so that he may fight more easily, so the LORD is ready to demonstrate his might in redeeming his people. This supplements the call given earlier to the LORD's arm to awake (51:9). The impending salvation will be seen by all the Gentile nations, even to the ends of the earth. While all may not be touched personally by this salvation, yet it will provoke universal acclaim.

h. Supplement: The New Exodus 'Depart, depart' (52:11-12)

11-12 The most obvious display of the LORD's salvation will be in the liberation of the exiles. They are called to come out of Babylon (Heb. *misshâm*, 'from there', another indication that the writer was not himself in Babylon). The double imperatives ('Depart, depart, go out ... go out'; NIV fails to preserve consistency by translating 'go out ... come out') stress the urgency, yet it is not to be pressured flight. Their coming out is to be different in some respects from those who came out of Egypt long before. The exiles will be able to get themselves ready for the new exodus, unlike the Israelites of old who had to go out 'in flight'. This word (Heb. *chippazôn*) only occurs in Exodus 12:11, Deuteronomy 16:3 (in connection with Passover) and here in Isaiah 52:12. It is probably a technical term referring to hasty or fearful flight. Whereas the Israelites spoiled the Egyptians, the exiles are not to touch any unclean thing. This is probably because Jerusalem is cleansed anew. The reference to those who carry the vessels of the house of the LORD is an indirect prophecy fulfilled when Cyrus allowed the exiles to take the temple vessels back to Jerusalem (Ezra 1:7-11). Those who were to carry the temple vessels had themselves to be cleansed and purified. There is also the reassurance that the LORD will both protect them in the front and in the rear, just as he did in the first exodus (cf. Exod. 13:21-22; 14:19-20).

5. The Fourth Servant Song: The Suffering of the Servant (52:13–53:12)

a. Introduction and General Summary of the Whole Subject: To Glory Through Suffering (52:13-15)

This is the longest of the servant songs, and also the most explicit in regard to the servant's ministry. It is also the passage of the Old Testament that is most frequently quoted in the New Testament. There are five stanzas in it, each containing three verses. Up to the end of verse 6 the first person plural is used ('*our* message', '*our* infirmities', '*we* esteemed him stricken', '*we* all, like sheep, have gone astray'), then the third person singular ('*he* took', '*he* was oppressed', '*he* was cut off'). This song is also distinguished by the numerous words that are repeated throughout, giving not only the sense of unity but the integration of ideas.[10]

13 Attention is called immediately to the servant, designated as

---

[10]Two very good studies on this question are Paul L. Raabe, 'The Effect of Repetition in the Servant Song', *JBL* 103, 1 (1984), pp. 77-84, and Ronald Bergey, 'The Rhetoric Role of Reiteration in the Servant Song Poem (ISA 52:13–53:12), *JETS* 40, 2 (1997), pp. 177-78.

'my servant'. This is the same expression as used in 42:1, but it becomes clear now that the servant is the one who is able to perform tasks that Israel is unable to do. He is the servant *par excellence*. Since 50:10 the term 'servant' has not been used. The Aramaic Targum goes further and says 'my servant *the messiah*', indicating that early Jewish interpretation certainly took this passage as messianic. The servant's ministry is going to be successful, because the verb 'act wisely' indicates prudent and intelligent action. He shall see the fruit from his work and his struggle shall be crowned with blessing. Three verbs of similar meaning are used to describe the messiah's status; 'he will be high and lifted up, and greatly exalted' (NASB). The first two are used in 6:1 to describe the LORD's throne that Isaiah saw 'high and lifted up', and from John 12:41 it becomes clear that Isaiah saw Jesus.[11] While the trilogy of verbs should not be pushed to mean Jesus' resurrection, ascension and sitting on God's right hand, yet it is clearly indicative of the ultimate glory of the suffering servant. The New Testament points in this direction. Echoes of this passage can be found in the use of the phrase 'your holy servant' (Acts 3:13, 26; 4:27, 30), and in the use of the expression 'exalted to the right hand of the Father' (Acts 2:33; cf. also Phil. 2:9). This verse looks to the end of the servant's work. The course of his life and ministry passes through night to light, *per ardua ad astra* ('through hardship to the stars').

14 Immediately the message switches to the servant's humiliation. Translations of verses 14-15 differ considerably, partly because of the way that the repeated use of the preposition 'from' (Heb. *min*) and the particle 'so' (Heb. *kên*) are understood. It is best to take the structure of the verses as:

'Just as . . . . . . , so (similarly) . . . . . . ,
So (as a result) . . . .'[12]

This way of understanding the text means that the humiliation of Israel is first mentioned, followed by a reference to the similar humiliation of the servant. Then verse 15 notes the ultimate result of that humiliation in the servant's accomplishments. In exile Israel was regarded with revulsion, the verb 'appalled' (Heb. *shâmêm*) being frequently used of astonishment in the face of divine judgment. While

---

[11] In John 12:41 the Greek text says 'Isaiah said this because he saw *his* glory', but the context requires the object to be 'Jesus' glory'.

[12] I have adopted this viewpoint from A. A. McRae, *The Gospel of Isaiah*, op. cit., p. 131.

many follow two Hebrew manuscripts, the Syriac and the Targum alter the Hebrew 'at you' to 'at him', it is better to retain the harder reading. Israel is being reminded of the reaction to her exile, especially since sudden switches of person are not uncommon in biblical Hebrew. The idea of the humiliation of the servant has already been introduced earlier in 49:4, 7 and especially in 50:6. Now the message is that the servant's humiliation, while similar in some ways to Israel's, goes much further. Those who see him will even wonder if he is human, so great will be his disfigurement. The reason for this disfigurement is given later in the song.

15 The result flowing from the servant's humiliation is that he carries out a priestly sprinkling of the nations, and their kings will stand amazed when they understand something of his mission. The traditional rendering 'sprinkle' is often objected to for three reasons: first, the causative form of this verb is always followed by a preposition, not a direct object as here ('many nations'); secondly, this rendering does not present a satisfactory contrast to 'were appalled' (verse 14), nor a parallel to the 'kings shall shut their mouths at him' (verse 15); thirdly, the reference to a priestly servant is out of place at this point. None of these objections are insuperable.[13] The verb in question is normally used of priestly sprinkling of water (Num. 8:7), blood (Lev. 4:6) or oil (Lev. 14:16). Here it fits the context admirably in summarising the result of the servant's humiliation. Blessing to the nations has already been part of Isaiah's message, and now he intimates that there will be a priestly ministry to them as a result of the Messiah's suffering and death. This verse forms an integral part of the whole song (52:12–53:12) and should not be interpreted without reference to the totality of Isaiah's presentation. This word of prophecy was fulfilled when believers in many nations were called 'God's elect ... chosen according to the foreknowledge of God the Father, through the sanctifying work of the Spirit, for obedience to Jesus Christ and sprinkling by his blood' (1 Pet. 1:1-2). Gentile rulers will be amazed and made speechless when they hear for the first time that it is through the servant's humiliation that he will be victorious (cf. Paul's use of this verse in Rom. 15:21).

---

[13]For an excellent detailed note, see G. C. Douglas, *Isaiah One and His Book One*, pp. 366-69. See also E. J. Young, 'The Interpretation of *hzy* in Isaiah 52:15', *WTJ* 3 (1941), pp. 125-32.

b. Prevailing Unbelief: The Servant's Unpromising Appearance (53:1-3)

1 The speaker appears to be the prophet himself, speaking as a member and representative of Israel. The expression 'our report' could mean either 'what we heard' or 'what we announced for others to hear'. However, the word 'report' (Heb. *sh^{e}mû'âh*) when used of prophets seems to combine both meanings: 'the message received from God for transmission to the people.'[14] The preposition in the phrase 'to whom' is unusual (Heb. *'al* instead of *'el*), but as these two prepositions are often interchanged in the Hebrew Bible it is unwise to try and extract some special meaning from it. The point of the questions is to highlight the unbelief of the Jews and of mankind in general. Even though God revealed his mighty arm (see 52:10), yet Israel did not believe. Jesus applied this verse to the Jewish unbelief of his day (John 12:38), while Paul's application of it is to the refusal of the Jews to accept the good news of the gospel (Rom. 10:16).

2 The description of the servant's humiliation follows. He is compared to a 'tender shoot' and to 'a root'. The same idea has already been presented in Isaiah 11, where the Messiah has been called 'the root of Jesse' (verse 10). Here the emphasis is on the insignificant appearance of the servant and the unglamorous environment from which he will come. The phrase 'before him' could refer to his growing up 'before God' but may be a Hebrew idiom for growing straight up (see the same usage of Dagon 'fallen straight forward', 1 Sam. 5:3). Moreover, his 'form' (Heb. *to'ar*) has already been mentioned (52:14), and now it is said that he lacks the outward appearance of 'form' and 'beauty' that would attract people to him. It is as if the prophet says: 'We look at him, but there is nothing to look at.'

3 The general description of the servant's humble appearance in verse 2 is followed by a more detailed one. The first part is very similar to what is said in 49:7. He is not only despised but is forsaken by friends (cf. John's description of Jesus' rejection even by his own kindred, John 1:11-13; Peter's denials, John 18:15-18, 25-27; and the action of the entire band of disciples in fleeing, Mark 14:50). He becomes an object of abhorrence and a man of sorrows. The plural 'sorrows' probably points to a man whose chief characteristic is sorrow. He is a sufferer in the fullest sense of the word. Not only that, but he is

---

[14] See *CHAL*, p. 375; *TWOT* 2, p. 939.

acquainted with sickness. Clearly sickness here has a wider meaning than our English expression, as we see from the way in which this verse is applied by Matthew to Jesus' healing ministry (Matt. 8:17). Jesus was not vicariously sick for us, but his miracles were 'signs of the time' pointing to the great redemptive deliverance he had come to effect.[15] His appearance is such that others can only look on him with abhorrence. Once more the idea of being despised is given, followed by a confession of Israel's sin ('we did not reckon him'). Though the prophet uses the plural form ('we') yet he himself is not necessarily involved in person, but he speaks as a member of Israel. The verb 'reckon' in this context has the idea of valuing or esteeming. Those who saw the servant's sufferings failed to judge them aright, wrongly thinking that he was smitten by God (see verse 4).

c. A Substitute for Sinners (53:4-6)

In this stanza there is an explanation of the servant's marred appearance. It becomes clear that his sufferings are not for himself but on behalf of others. Furthermore, God's design in this is made plain, in that he is the one who places iniquity on the sin-bearing servant. The contrast between 'him' and 'us' is maintained throughout.

4 In the previous verse Isaiah has told how the servant knew sorrow and grief. Now he tells how he carries and bears ours. The particle with which the verse opens can be translated 'assuredly'. Two synonymous verbs (Heb. *nâsâ'* and *sâval*) are used to describe the action of carrying sin, or carrying it away (= forgiveness). They appear in parallel here, and then also in verses 11-12. Both verbs are used in the literal sense of carrying a burden, but then signify to bear punishment or guilt. In his own person the servant takes upon himself the spiritual diseases of others, and carries them up to his death on the cross (1 Pet. 2:24). The servant's vicarious work is unrecognised by many, who think of him as 'stricken, smitten of God and afflicted'. The Vulgate and some early rabbinic scholars took the word 'stricken' (Heb. *nâgûa'*) to mean 'leprous'. It is true that the verb from which this word comes is used in passages speaking of being stricken with leprosy (see Lev. 13:8; 2 Kings 15:5), yet there is no indication that 'stricken' can be equated with the normal word for 'leprous' (Heb. *m^etsôrâ'*). Here the word refers back to the already-mentioned bodily suffering.

---

[15]For an excellent discussion of this point, see Geerhardus Vos, *The Self-Disclosure of Jesus* (Grand Rapids: Eerdmans, 1954), pp. 259-60.

The servant's experience is a divinely inflicted punishment, as verse 5 makes clear.

5 This verse expresses over and over again the truth that the servant not merely shares our griefs but actually suffers in our place as sinners. Four times the contrast between 'he/him' and 'we/us' appears.

> *He* is pierced . . . *our* transgressions.
> *He* is crushed . . . *our* iniquities.
> The chastisement of *our* peace . . . upon *him*.
> *His* wounds . . . *we* are healed.

On account of our transgressions he is 'pierced through' (i.e. mortally wounded), while for our iniquities he suffers under incalculable emotional and spiritual pressures (cf. the use of the verb *dâkâ'* in Ps. 51:17, 'a broken and a *crushed* heart'). Moreover, 'the chastisement that makes us whole' (RSV) is part of the redemptive judgment that he vicariously bears, while our healing is at the cost of his wounds. In this context 'wounds' implies death. The healing effected is spiritual, for the Messiah's death brings believers into a new relationship with God. The verb 'to heal' (Heb. *râfâ'*) is used here as in 6:10; 19:22; and 30:26, since diseases and sorrows ultimately flow from sin. All these references probably go back to the promise, 'I the LORD am your healer' (Heb. *'anî yhwh rof'ekâ*, Exod. 15:26). The servant is to suffer not simply as a consequence of sin but as an efficacious remedy for guilt.

6 The verse begins and ends with confession of sin, and places emphasis on 'all of us' (the Hebrew text starts and finishes with the same word, *kullânû*). Comparison is made with sheep who go astray, but the wonder is that there is a shepherd who will care for such wandering sheep (Isa. 40:11; cf. also the prayer in Ps. 119:176). Not only do sinners leave God, but they also break relationships with one another. The remedy that God provides is to place human iniquity on the servant. The verb used (Heb. *pâga'* Hif.) is a strong one, denoting laying a burden on someone (for another use of this verb in the sense of 'intercede', see verse 12). Many echoes of this whole passage are found in 1 Peter 2:21-25, that speaks of the suffering of the sinless Christ, bearing our sins in his own body up to the cross. His wounds provide healing for us, straying sheep, who are now safely in the fold of the good shepherd. This verse ends the portion of the song using 'we/us', and hereafter the third person is used.

d. The Servant's Submissiveness and Purity (53:7-9)

The picture presented in this fourth stanza is of a meek servant who is silent in the face of accusations, and then who dies for the transgressions of others. Though he himself committed no violence, he is condemned unjustly and does not react to the physical violence done to him.

7 The opening of the stanza focuses attention on the manner of harsh and unjust treatment given to the servant. His oppression is described by use of the verb that is employed in Exodus 3:7 to denote the harsh treatment measured out to Israel in Egypt (*nâgas*). It implies the use of physical violence. The next phrase is made emphatic by the use of the personal pronoun 'he', while the form of the Hebrew verb ('*ânâh*, Nif.) certainly allows for a reflexive meaning: 'and he allowed himself to be afflicted' (cf. Jesus' insistence that he gave his life freely for his sheep, John 10:14-18). The death of the servant is depicted in sacrificial terms, emphasising his silence in comparison to a lamb or adult sheep being slaughtered. The figure of a dumb sheep appears elsewhere in Jeremiah 11:19. The servant unresistingly stands before his persecutors, uttering not a word in his own defence. Peter seems to have this passage in mind when he speaks of the meek endurance of Christ (1 Pet. 2:23). While the servant is depicted as a lamb, it is only in the New Testament that the phrase 'lamb of God' appears (John 1:29; see also Acts 8:32-33, 35; 1 Pet. 1:18-19).

8 It is by coercion and (false) justice that the servant is taken away, either to execution or from life itself. The rest of the verse has been translated in various ways. The best interpretation seems to be the NASB or NIV margin: 'Yet who of his generation considered that he was cut off from the land of the living for the transgression of my people, to whom the blow was due?' (NIV mg.). This translation makes several factors very clear. He is cut off from the land of the living, i.e. he suffers death. This was because he was vicariously bearing the guilt of his people, to whom the penalty rightly belonged. 'My people' here must refer in the first instance to the prophet's people, Israel, though the New Testament makes plain that Jesus' death was for Jew and Gentile alike. The people of his own day misunderstood his death, a theme already mentioned in the first verse of this chapter. Even when Jesus taught his disciples that the Son of Man was going to be betrayed, they did not understand his teaching (Mark 9:30-32).

9 There is here the strange intermingling of the actions of wicked men and the purposes of God. It is the LORD who places the burden of sin on the servant (verse 6), yet men take the innocent sufferer and put him to death, and his body is placed in a rich man's grave (see the New Testament expression of this in Peter's words, Acts 2:23). Here 'wicked' and 'rich' are used in parallel, for in Old Testament times many became rich through wicked means, just as many still do. The prophecy was actually transcended when a devoted rich man, Joseph of Arimathea, placed Jesus' body in his own tomb (John 19:38-42). The servant's innocence is asserted again, for his death and burial takes place in spite of the fact that he had done no violence. The Hebrew expression is unusual in that the negative stands in an odd position: 'he did not violence' (cf. the testimony of one of the criminals crucified with him, Luke 23:41: 'this man has done nothing out of place'). Peter, in encouraging his readers to endure unjust suffering and so follow the example of Christ, quotes the second part of this verse (1 Pet. 2:22).

e. The Glorious Success of His Completed Propitiation, and also His Intercession (53:10-12)

The final stanza of this servant song explains what lay behind the miscarriage of justice towards the servant. The events concerning him were part of the divine purpose as he suffered on behalf of others. The picture of him is as a later poet put it:

'Tis finish'd – The Messiah dies
　　for sins, but not his own;
The great redemption is complete,
　　and Satan's power o'erthrown.　　(Scottish Paraphrase 44)

Though humiliated in his vicarious suffering, the servant by his death provides the means for bringing justification to many. This final stanza returns to the opening theme of ultimate triumph in 52:13.

10 The stanza opens by pointing to the fact that the messiah's sufferings are grounded in the sovereign good-pleasure of God. It is the LORD who has been pleased to bruise him (verses 5-6) and to put him to grief (verses 3-4), and now it is declared to be the LORD's pleasure expressed in his exaltation. The LORD has no delight in the blood of bulls and goats (Isa. 1:11), but he is satisfied through the servant's offering of himself. The servant is crushed and broken by suffering (the verb can mean 'wounded', as it is used in the cases of

Ahab [1 Kings 22:34] and Joram [2 Kings 8:29]). The offering of himself is not an ordinary sin offering, but a trespass offering. The servant makes his soul an *'âshâm,* the trespass offering that had the idea of a payment for withheld value (Lev. 5:7, 15). He makes up for the blemished lives of those he represents, who are reckoned as his spiritual children (Heb. 'seed'). The statement that 'he prolongs his days' could refer to the eternal existence of the Messiah, or to the prolonging of his work through his body, the church. With all its faults the church still continues the ministry of her risen head. The final statement in the verse indicates that the LORD's affairs will prosper under his control, a phrase taking up the theme of exaltation already stated in 52:13.

11 There is a translational problem in this verse. The AV translation 'he shall see the travail of his soul' does not fit the Hebrew text well, for it simply says 'from (or possibly 'after') the travail of his soul he shall see ..., he will be satisfied'. Normally this verb 'see' has a direct object following it, which actually occurs in two Hebrew scrolls from Qumran (1QIsa[a] and 1QIsa[b]) that add the word 'light'. The LXX also supports this textual reading, and English versions such as RSV, NASB, and NIV insert it. 'To see light' is a reference to resurrection after death (cf. Job 3:16b; 33:28; Ps. 36:9; Ps. 49:19).[16] 'To be satisfied' is probably a shortened form of the idiom 'to live long' (for the full form 'to be satisfied with days' see 1 Chron. 23:1; 2 Chron. 24:15). By his knowledge and understanding of God's mind, the righteous servant is able to bring acquittal to many. The theme of 'the many' that occurs here and in verse 12 is echoed in Jesus' declaration regarding the mission of the Son of Man (Mark 10:45). The final verb in the verse picks up the word 'bear' that has already occurred in verse 4. The servant's ministry is characterised by a bearing of the sin and guilt of others, the iniquity of 'the many'.

12 The ministry of the servant is not completed with his death and resurrection. He administers gifts, the spoils of his victory, to 'the many', sharing with them what his death achieved (cf. Paul's statement regarding the gifts of the ascended Christ, Eph. 4:11-13). Having poured out his soul in becoming a trespass offering (see verse 10), he has achieved the acquittal of those who believe and the consequences of

---

[16]For an alternative interpretation without adding the word 'light', see J. A. Motyer, *The Prophecy of Isaiah,* op. cit., p. 441.

his death flow to them. Though he was sinless, yet he was numbered with sinners from the time of his baptism right up to his death (see the use of this reference in Luke's account of the crucifixion of Jesus between two criminals, Luke 22:37). This has not been mentioned explicitly before, though implied in verses 5-6. At the conclusion of the verse and this song, the servant's ministry is characterised once more as a bearing of sin (the verb *nâsâ'* has already been used in verse 4), but to this is added the concept that he also engages in an on-going intercessory ministry for sinners. A Hebrew verb already appearing in verse 6 (*pâga'*) is used with one of its other meanings of 'intercede' (for other examples of this use see Isa. 59:12; Jer. 15:11; 36:25). The prophetic servant, who offers himself for sinners, is also the one who carries out continual intercession for them. He stands in their place.

6. Salvation for the World (54:1–55:17)

a. The rejected Israel received back into blessedness by her husband (54:1-10)

This chapter is first of all a poetic response to the message regarding the servant (for such a response after earlier servant songs, see 42:10-12; 49:13). It also returns to the theme of Israel the bride who after a brief separation is brought back into the marriage relationship.

1 Exiled Israel (or possibly the desolate Jerusalem as representative of Israel), the childless wife, is called upon to sing with exuberant joy. The association of these three verbs denoting singing is quite typical of Isaiah (cf. 12:6; 24:14; 44:23; 49:13; 52:9; 55:12). Israel had been barren (cf. 49:21) like Sarah (51:2). However, like Sarah she will be transformed for joy because of her many children. Childlessness was regarded as a disgrace in the Near East. Here the assurance is given of a drastic change that will result in a large family. This verse is quoted in Galatians 4:27 of the heavenly Jerusalem, which will have many children called in by the gospel message.

2 The increase in children will be so great that dwellings have to be enlarged. In 33:20 Zion has already been compared to a tent. Those who are seemingly in a hopeless position are called to show no restraint in making housing provision for the unexpected enlargement of the family. The verb 'to stretch out' is third person plural and active in form. It can be translated like the NKJV: 'let them stretch out the curtains,' or regarded as an imperative as the NIV does: 'stretch your tent curtains wide.'

3 Israel is viewed as spreading to the right and to the left. These terms are used elsewhere in the Old Testament of the directions 'south' and 'north' (for Heb. *yâmîn* as 'south', see Psalm 89:12; for Heb. *s^em'ôl* as 'north', see Ezekiel 16:46). The verb 'to spread out' is used repeatedly in reference to Jacob and his seed (Gen. 28:14; 30:30, 43) and his family in Egypt (Exod. 1:12). The restricted boundaries of the exilic period are to give way, and Israel will spread out into the towns now occupied by Gentiles. The language here (especially 'spread out', 'your seed' ['descendants'] and 'dispossess') recalls the promises relating to the first occupation of Canaan. For a second time the Jews will dispossess the existing occupants of Palestine and live in the towns they presently inhabit. The fulfilment came as the Jews returned in several stages (as related in the books of Ezra and Nehemiah) and carried out the work of rebuilding—altar, temple, the city walls.

4 The verse commences with 'Fear not', one of Isaiah's repeated refrains (see 41:10; 41:13; 41:14; 43:1; 43:5; 44:2; 44:8). The exile had indeed been a humiliation, but the return to Palestine will be a reversal of that. Joyful Israel will be able to put that experience behind her and no longer dwell on the reproach she suffered. There is a seeming contradiction here with the statement in Jeremiah 51:5 that says that Israel and Judah were never widowed. To many the exile did suggest that the bond between God and Israel had been permanently severed as if by divorce or death. However, both Jeremiah and Isaiah (see comments on 50:1 and verses 5-8 of this chapter) show that there was only temporary separation, no divorce or widowhood.

5 The confidence that the people can have is founded on the fact that the one making the promises and fulfilling them is none other than the 'husband'. The Hebrew text actually uses plural forms for both 'maker' and 'husband'. This may be compared to the use of the plural 'our' in Genesis 1:26 or of 'us' in Isaiah 6:8. It is possible that they are assimilations to the word *^elôhîm* for God, which looks like a Hebrew masculine plural form. Another possibility is that there is deliberate avoidance of the singular form *ba'al* (meaning 'lord' or 'husband') so that there is no association with the Canaanite god of that name. The 'husband' is none other than 'the LORD of Hosts', 'your redeemer', 'the holy of Israel'. The accumulation of titles points to the majesty of Israel's God who is also the God of the whole earth. Isaiah's understanding of Israel's God is that he is the one with universal authority.

6-7 The first half of verse 6 has suggested to many commentators that the ancient marriage bond is in view (the verb is '*he has* called you'). The terms used to describe the bride, however, do not fit a reference to the distant past. Israel in exile is described as 'deserted' and 'distressed in spirit', a youthful wife who has been rejected. The LORD's call will then be understood as the recent call to return both to him and to the land of Canaan. The exile is regarded as only 'a brief moment', 'a moment of time' (Heb. *rega*') in Israel's experience, and because of the abundant compassion of God, he will 'gather' (Heb. *qâvats*) her. This is practically a technical expression for gathering the scattered exiles and restoring them to the land. It occurs in God's pledge in Deuteronomy 30:3-4 to assemble his scattered people, and is used in descriptions of the event after it had taken place (Ps. 107:3).

8 Looking at the period of the exile God declares that it is a time in which his anger is expressed and his face is hidden from his people. The opening phrase, one notable for its assonance (Heb. *beshetsef qetsef*), is variously translated because the word *shetsef* occurs only here in the Old Testament. Early translations take it to mean a short period: 'in brief wrath' (LXX); 'in an atom of time' (Aquila); 'in a brief hour, for a time' (Targum). A reference to time, however, seems unnecessary as the word already used in verse 7 for 'a brief moment' comes shortly afterwards. Probably it is a variant of another Hebrew word (*shetef*) meaning 'flood', which does occur along with 'anger' in Proverbs 27:4 ('a torrent of anger'). Hence the NIV translation is good: 'in a surge of anger', and this fits in well with the reference to Noah's flood in the next verse. The contrast then is between the short period of overwhelming anger and the everlasting mercy and compassion of the LORD the redeemer. From the next chapter (55:3) it is clear that this compassion is linked to the everlasting covenant.

9 This is an echo of Genesis 9:11, 15. God declares that there is a similarity between the present circumstances ('to me *this* is like ...') and the time of Noah. The NIV and several other versions accept a slight change in the Hebrew text to obtain the reading 'like *the days* of Noah', but this is unnecessary, as the emphasis is on divine judgment and the repeated mention of waters is telling. God gave the pledge that the earth would never again be destroyed by a flood. Similarly he has pledged himself by oath that he will not be angry or rebuke the people. Whereas in an earlier message Isaiah declared that God's anger was not turned away (see 9:12, 17, 21), now he can proclaim the reality of averted anger.

10 The compassionate God reaffirms his commitment to his people. Even if the mountains were to move, yet his covenantal love (Heb. *chesed*) and his covenanted peace (Heb. *b^erît sh^elômî*) will still remain. Both Isaiah and Ezekiel 34:25 and 37:26 use the expression 'covenant of peace' (cf. also its use in Num. 25:11-13), and it is probably no different in meaning from Jeremiah's 'new covenant' (Jer. 31:31). Here it follows on the description of the servant's suffering in chapter 53 and the declaration that his ministry was one of 'peace' (Isa. 53:5). In the next chapter the promised blessings are linked with the 'everlasting covenant, the sure mercies of David' (Isa. 55:3). All that the earlier Old Testament covenants intended will find fulfilment in the new covenant.

b. Zion Resplendent (54:11-17)

The section starts abruptly without any introductory formula but ends by concluding 'thus says the LORD'. The picture here is not really the Jerusalem to be found or experienced by the returning exiles but forms the background to the eschatological scene in Revelation 21:10-21. It is concerned with the glory of the new Jerusalem (verses 11-14a) and its protection by the LORD (verses 14b-17).

11-12 These verses depict the glory of God's people in the future. The imagery is of some great building constructed out of precious stones. Clearly, afflicted Jerusalem is in view (see the appellation 'afflicted' already used of Jerusalem in 51:21), and she is regarded as a tempest-driven city (the translation 'storm tossed' is too nautical) that lacks comfort. Verses 11b and 12 are descriptions of the city adorned with precious stones. Some have understood that a bride with her cosmetics is being described, but although one particular Hebrew word (*pûk*) can be used of eye-shadow or something similar (see 2 Kings 9:30; Jer. 4:30), it is also used of mortar (1 Chron. 29:2), which fits the building imagery here. The rebuilt Jerusalem is going to be notable for its costly and attractive embellishments, though even it will be transcended by the new Jerusalem (see John's description of it and the use made of this passage in Revelation 21:10, 18-21).

13-14a The verse division should come in this way as verse 14b is linked with what follows, not what precedes. Two characteristics are mentioned of Jerusalem's children. First, the picture is of spiritual teaching to be given to the children by the LORD, a matter highlighted in Jeremiah's description of conditions under the new covenant (Jer. 31:33-34). Secondly, their peace is to be great, the peace that was mentioned in verse 10, and that is procured by the atoning work of the servant. Verse 14a is probably a strong echo of Isaiah 28:16. Jerusalem may well have been known as the 'city of righteousness' (cf. 1:26). The renewed city will be safe and secure, without conditions engendering fear. The verb 'to be far off' is actually an imperative ('be far off'), but this only serves to give greater emphasis to the promise.

14b-15 The remainder of this chapter deals with the difficulties yet to face God's people. The assurance is given of God's presence with them and their ultimate vindication by him. In contrast with all the military attacks that Jerusalem had suffered in the past, there is to be enduring safety, for even when an attack takes place, the attacker will be forced to surrender to Jerusalem. Attacks on it will fail, because it is the city under God's protection. The picture is an extension of the idea of 'peace' that has been presented already as the work of the LORD's servant (53:5; 54:10). It is an idealised description of the messianic conditions that will prevail at the second coming of Christ. While opposition rises repeatedly against the believing community during the progress of church history, yet at Christ's appearance all such opposition will fall.

16-17 Repeated verbs and pronouns give emphasis to the LORD's work in raising up nations such as Assyria and Babylon; '*It is I* who created the blacksmith ... *it is I* who created the destroyer' (NIV). The fashioning of weapons of war is ultimately God's doing, but now the weapons will be unsuccessful and accusing words will fail to achieve their end. Blacksmiths, warriors, and accusers are all in God's control, and he will ensure that Jerusalem's safety is preserved. No hostile weapon can 'prosper' against them (verse 17), because the pleasure of the LORD 'prospers' in the servant's hands (53:10; the same Heb. verb *tsâlach* is used in both passages). The concluding statements reaffirm that this is the heritage of God's servants and he will be their vindicator. After chapter 53 all the occurrences of 'servant' are plural as here (see also 63:17; 65:8-9, 13-15; 66:14). These servants, the 'offspring' of the Messiah (53:10), i.e. the beneficiaries of his vicarious work, probably includes both Jews and Gentiles. They are all those who are faithful in their commitment to the LORD. His oath in verse 9 is balanced by the final 'says the LORD'.

c. The Divine Invitation to Spiritual Life (55:1-5)

This chapter picks up many of the themes already treated in the preceding chapters, especially those in 40:1-11. Some of the themes are:

Forgiveness	40:2 // 55:6-7
Return from exile	40:3-5 // 55:12-13
Participation in future return	40:4 // 55:12
The word and its enduring effect	40:8 // 55:10-11

The new exodus theme also comes into focus again, picking up the ideas of the miracles of water and manna in the wilderness (cf. 41:17; 48:21). But now the thought is of 'wine and milk', festive foods that would be suitable for a marriage feast. This expression may also have some connection with the common reference to Canaan as a land flowing with milk and honey. Sennacherib's invasion (701 BC) had brought famine to the people. There is mention in 30:20 of 'the bread of adversity and the water of affliction', while Isaiah's message to King Hezekiah mentions the plain food used in the sabbatical year and the year of jubilee (37:30). Here, however, the picture is of abundant provision without cost.

1 God appeals to the people to return and find spiritual nourishment with himself. The promise has already been given of water for the thirsty land (44:3). No cost is involved in the provision, for not only are those invited who have no money but it is also said that wine and milk are available 'without money and without price'. The intensity of the invitation is seen in the thrice repeated 'Come', while it is extended without discrimination to all who are thirsty. For fulfilment in the messianic era we must look to what Jesus said to the Samaritan woman (John 4:10-14) and also his words in John 7:37-39.

2 The main idea is that many people have grown comfortable in their exilic situation, and some at least did not realise that ultimate satisfaction was not to be found there. Their present condition may seem to satisfy their immediate needs, but it is only temporary satisfaction. The tone is chiding, as the prophet presents God's call with urgency: 'go on listening' (Heb. *shim'û shâmô'a*; the use of the Heb. inf. absolute after the imperative stresses the continuing aspect).

3 The Davidic covenant (2 Sam. 7) was an expression of God's steadfast love. In verse 15 he promised of David and his family: 'My grace (*chasdî*) shall not depart from him, as I took it away from Saul,... but your house and kingdom will be made sure (*ne'emân*), forever (*'ad 'ôlâm*).' When it was given David responded in amazement that God had dealt so graciously with him and his family (2 Sam. 7:18-19). Psalm 89 is a poetic expansion of the 2 Samuel 7 passage, and it affirms repeatedly the gracious and lasting nature of this covenant. This passage in Isaiah re-echoes the words of 2 Samuel 7, affirming again the abiding nature of the Davidic covenant and using three of the key words from 2 Samuel 7 ('eternal', 'mercy(ies)', 'sure'). The call is to pay heed to the invitation and so find spiritual life within the scope of this covenant.[17] Paul clearly saw in Jesus' resurrection from the dead the eternal nature of the Davidic covenant (Acts 13:34).

4 The verse commences with a word calling attention to what follows: 'Look.' David had been appointed not only as a leader and commander over Israel (1 Sam. 13:14) but as a witness to the nations. In his initial response to God's covenant David recognised that there was going to be blessing for humanity in general from this new and special relationship between God and David's family (2 Sam. 7:18-19).[18] In fulfilling the role to the nations David praised and exalted the LORD among them (2 Sam. 22:47, 50-51). It has already been shown that David's greater son, the Messiah, would also be such a witness, both personally (49:6) and through his messengers (Acts 13:47).

5 A second consecutive verse commences with the word 'Look', linking together the complementary missions of David and Israel. The picture is of something more than just an expansion of the Davidic empire to embrace other nations as well. Here the spiritual mission of the nation is in view, for the holy one of Israel had adorned her with beauty (cf. what was said in 54:11-12). There are to be Gentile nations who will be attracted to her from the farthermost parts of the earth (cf. 2:1-5; 60:1-14), coming so eagerly that it can be depicted as 'running' to her. The opening section of the chapter comes to a climax at this point.

d. An Invitation to Seek the Lord (55:6-7)
6 The call of verse 1 is repeated in even stronger terms. It contains both a promise and a caution. The promise is that God will be found of

---

[17]See the article by W. C. Kaiser Jr., 'The Unfailing Kindnesses Promised to David: Isaiah 55:3,' *JSOT* 45 (1989), pp. 91-98.
[18]See W. C. Kaiser, Jr., 'The Blessing of David: The Charter for Humanity,' in *The Law and the Prophets*, ed. John Skilton (Presbyterian and Reformed, 1974), pp. 298-318.

those who seek him, while the caution is that the invitation is not going to be held out for ever. 'To seek the LORD' often designates in the Old Testament the desire to cleave in faithfulness to him. It occurs especially in the books of Chronicles, and the words to Solomon in 1 Chronicles 28:9 are particularly relevant: 'If you seek him (Heb. *dârash*), he will be found (Heb. *mâts'â*) by you; but if you forsake him, he will reject you for ever.' Jeremiah reports God's invitation to the exiles using the same two Hebrew verbs: 'You will seek me and find me when you seek me with all your heart. I will be found by you ...' (Jer. 29:13). The alternative way of expressing the same idea ('call on him while he is near') simply reinforces both the promise and the caution.

7 The promise of mercy is put in the context of repentance. The turning to God can only be effective on his terms. Two things are needed: the sinner needs to change his thoughts, and then his actions. When he returns to the LORD he will find abundant pardon. Mercy will be displayed and sins blotted out. This is just another way of expressing the assurance of pardon given in 43:25 and 44:22. When sin is forsaken then overflowing mercy will be shown. The exiles need reassurance that God will deal with them in grace when they return to him.

e. The Spiritual Nature of the Return from Exile (55:8-13)

8-9 The thought of verse 7 is now put differently, for the words 'thoughts' and 'ways' are picked up and utilised again. Isaiah conveys God's solemn declaration that his thoughts and ways are so different from man's. The reference to heaven and earth is very typical of Isaiah. There is an immeasurable gap between God's thoughts and actions and those of humans. Man's thoughts are futile (Ps. 94:11), while the greatness of God is beyond man's ability to fathom (Ps. 145:3). Furthermore, it is not just that God's ways are inscrutable; they are so different morally (cf. verse 7). To be walking in obedience to the LORD requires abandonment of our ways and adherence to his.

10-11 Just as the rain and snow accomplish the purpose of watering the earth, so the word of God does not fail to accomplish the purpose for which it is sent. This example from the natural world teaches a spiritual lesson. Just as the moistened earth becomes productive, so God's word goes out but does not return empty, i.e. it will achieve the purposes for which it is intended. His word and promises can be relied upon, as they are eternally true. 'Word' here may well primarily refer to the promises already stated in the immediate context (cf. verses 3,

5, 7). Hebrews 6:7-8 probably contains echoes of this passage.

12-13 The restoration from exile is pictured in dramatic language. The people are to be led out [of Babylon] with joy, a thought that ties in with earlier references such as 52:8. The LORD is the one who will lead his people out of slavery and bring them by streams of water (Jer. 31:9). The curse of exile (see 5:6; 6:11-13; 7:21-25; 32:12-13) will be reversed, and plantations of pines and myrtle will replace the thornbush and briars. The reference to literal peace and joy is replaced by metaphorical references in verse 12b, as nature joins in the joyful acclamation. In verse 13 the literal appears again, as reference is made to the productive use of the land when the exiles re-settle in Palestine. The restoration will in itself bring glory to the LORD and it will be confirmation of the promises made to the dispersed of Israel. The LORD's deliverance of his people will never be forgotten.

7. Incorporation of Gentiles in God's Redemption (56:1-8)

The main part of chapter 56 (verses 1-8) deals with the question of the involvement of others in the redemption of Israel, particularly foreigners and eunuchs. The 'foreigner' (Heb. *nêkâr*, not *gêr*, 'sojourner') was someone who was excluded from worship at the sanctuary (Ezek. 44:9), while the 'eunuch' (Heb. *sârîs*) was a term originally applying to court officials. Because many of these were castrated, the word later came to mean 'eunuch'. Though the law did not use this expression, it did exclude from worship those who were castrated (Lev. 21:20; Deut. 23:1). Just as Gentiles were to be ingathered into God's kingdom, so were strangers and eunuchs, for none would be excluded because of nationality ('strangers') or because of mutilation, either accidental or deliberate. The New Testament shows how Gentiles generally and eunuchs in particular could be incorporated into the Christian church (see Acts 8:27, 38-40).

1 To the community of Israel the direction is given that as the LORD's salvation draws near, they must exhibit close adherence to what is just (Heb. *mishpât*) and right (Heb. *ts^edâqâh*). Too often Israel deviated from these norms. Previously this has been mentioned in poetic terms (45:8), but now is directly commanded. The near future, says the LORD, is going to see his saving power and his victory revealed when he uses his servant Cyrus to fulfil his will (see commentary on 44:24–45:13).

2 Blessing is pronounced on the faithful observance of these things, especially on sabbath keeping and refraining from doing evil. The sabbath was intended to be kept unto the LORD ('holy to the LORD', Exod. 31:15) as part of the covenant commitment of Israel after the redemption from Egypt. In the new order to follow redemption from Babylon (55:12), the sabbath will again be prominent (see 56:4-6; 58:13-14; 66:23). There must be no desecration of that holy ordinance, and holiness of life in general is depicted as keeping one's hand away from 'all evil'. Everything that stands opposed to God and his ways is to be shunned.

3 Changed religious circumstances are going to create altered conditions affecting hitherto excluded persons such as the eunuchs and the foreigners. If they attach themselves to the LORD, becoming devoted worshippers, then they will no longer have to declare that they are not part of God's people. No longer will the foreigner have to declare his separation from the covenant people, while the eunuch will no longer have to declare himself an unproductive tree. This is a reference to his impotence, which meant that even if he was accepted into the community of Israel his name would be blotted out.

4-5 Special provision is made for the incorporation of eunuchs into God's kingdom. Sabbath observance was a central requirement of the covenant, and it provided a visible mark of God's people (cf. Jeremiah's message relating to the Sabbath, Jer. 17:19-27). Likewise a true worshipper is to be characterised by commitment to the things that please the LORD, and adherence to *his* covenant. The promise is that the eunuch will indeed have a place in God's house and a reputation even better than those who already belonged to the covenant community ('sons and daughters'). That position will be secured for them, and there is no possibility that they will be ever be excised from God's people. The threat of being 'cut off from his people' (for this expression, see Gen. 17:14; Lev. 20:3, 5, 6) is never going to apply to them.

6-7 A somewhat fuller description is given both of the 'foreigner' and of his expanded privileges. He will also be brought into a new relationship with God. Again, Sabbath keeping features as a sign of covenant commitment and service, though in comparison with what is said in verse 4, the foreigner is said to refrain from defiling the Sabbath and treating it as something common. He will also love the name of the LORD and be devoted to him, with the aspect of service being mentioned twice ('to serve him', 'to be his servants', NIV 'to worship him'). The picture of the foreigners coming to the house of prayer on

Mount Zion ('my holy mountain') recalls the pilgrimage of Gentiles to God's house mentioned in 2:2-3 (cf. also 4:3-6). They will do what was previously forbidden (offer burnt offerings and sacrifices) and these will be accepted by God. The widening of privileges is made clear by the assertion that God's house will be a house of prayer to all nations. Solomon, in his prayer at the dedication of the temple, made specific mention of the foreigner coming to pray there and his prayer being heard (1 Kings 8:41-43). Now the LORD's message is that this will no longer be an exception but the rule, for all nations will be welcome there. When Jesus cleansed the temple he quoted this verse, indicating that what had become a den of robbers should rightly be 'a house of prayer' (Matt. 21:13).

8 This section on the eunuch and the foreigner concludes with the assurance that the Lord Jehovah is going to gather others in addition to the dispersed Jews. The gathering is going to be of Jew and Gentile together into God's kingdom. This ultimately could only be fulfilled when Jesus made atoning provision for both so that they could be saved in the same manner (Acts 15:11). The prayer of Christians continues for the fulfilment of this vision:

> Let Zion's time of favour come;
> O bring the tribes of Israel home;
> And let our wondering eyes behold
> Gentiles and Jews in Jesus' fold.

William Shrubsole 1759–1829,
'Arm of the Lord, awake, awake!'

8. Adulterous Israel (56:9–57:13)

The date of this section seems definitely to be pre-exilic, as the description of conditions does not seem applicable to Palestine or the exiles in the period of captivity, nor is it in tune with the preceding promises of restoration (see the Introduction, pages 23-24). The focus is on unfaithful watchmen who fail to warn of the impending dangers, and a people who have forsaken the LORD. The passage records the folly of the people in forsaking the LORD and proving false to him (56:8, 11). Lack of godly leadership has its impact for evil upon the believing community.

9 God calls for the nations surrounding Israel to come and attack. The imagery is of beasts of forest and field attacking the garden (Israel).

The same imagery occurs in Psalm 80 where wild boars of the forest ravage the vineyard and beasts of the field feed on it (verse 13). Psalm 89:40 is similar in that the attackers have broken through the walls of the garden. God in his rule over the nations invites Gentile nations to invade Israel.

10-11 The messengers sent to Israel were God's 'watchmen'. The term is used of those stationed on walls to raise the cry when danger was at hand (see 1 Sam. 14:16; 2 Kings 9:17-20). While it may well include the political leaders, it is taken over especially as a descriptive term for the prophets, who were given the responsibility of alerting the nation of impending danger. The term is particularly important in Ezekiel, as God appoints him as a watchman for the house of Israel (Ezek. 3:17; 33:7). Here the watchmen are depicted as blind and lazy. They are dumb dogs who sleep while danger is at hand, and ravenous dogs whose appetites are never satisfied. Another term for the prophets is also used here. They are 'shepherds'. The verb (*râ'âh*) is used of God's appointment of David as the one who feeds or cares for Israel (2 Sam. 5:2), though the title 'shepherd' is never applied to Israelite rulers.[19] While God was the principal shepherd of Israel (cf. Pss. 74:1; 78:52; 80:1; Ezek. 34:31), the prophets were his under-shepherds (in addition to this verse, see Jeremiah 3:15 and Ezekiel 34:1-10). Emphasis is placed on their lack of knowledge, with mention of this in both verses 10 and 11. Just as those within the covenant community were said to turn to their own ways (Isa. 53:6), so also the prophets, who regarded financial gain as a greater motivation than obedience to the LORD.

12 The message to the prophets returns to a theme already dealt with in 28:7-8. They desire the intoxication of wine and beer, and even expect tomorrow to be better than today. The spirit of their words is also displayed in the longing of the rich fool in the New Testament (Luke 12:19).

57:1-2 Various terms are used to describe the godly. They are 'the righteous', 'men of covenant faithfulness', and 'those who walk uprightly'. Another group of synonyms is used for death: 'perish', 'gathered', 'come into peace', and 'rest upon their beds' (Heb. 'biers'; cf. the use of this idiom regarding the dead king Asa, 2 Chron. 16:14). They are taken away from life by the LORD and so are spared evil.

---

[19]It is applied to Cyrus, whom God calls 'my shepherd' in Isaiah 44:28.

Their death means that they are at rest and in peace. The contrast with the wicked is that there never will be any peace for them (see verse 21). Also, the reaction of the ungodly is that they fail to learn from this as they lack spiritual discernment.

3-4 These verses give the divine verdict on the ungodly, while verses 5-10 describe the actual behaviour being condemned. When this has been done, God addresses them in verses 11-13, spelling out the consequences of their actions. The sin of idolatry is presented using the idea of spiritual adultery. The command is to the offspring of sorceresses, adulterers and prostitutes to come and hear the charges against them. The questions in the opening part of verse 4 are intended to direct the people to the real object of their mockery. What they do not realise is that when they make faces to show their contempt, it really is against themselves. This is taking the last part of the verse as the response to the questions: 'Against whom do you delight? Against whom do you make a wide mouth and stick out the tongue? It is you ...'[20] Their attitude to others is only a reflection of their own character. Their lives are characterised by transgression and deceit.

5-6 The message now focuses on the type of religious practices the people indulged in, with all the associated immorality. The locations in view are clearly Palestinian, not Babylonian, with the reference to trees, hills, and cliffs. The people burn with lust as they come to the places where the gods are worshipped ('among the terebinth trees', 'under every green tree', 'in the valleys', 'under the crags', 'behind doors', 'high hills'). Reference is made to a variety of idolatrous practices including sacred prostitution, child sacrifice, and worship of stones worn into suggestive shapes by the waters of the river. Whereas the LORD is the believer's portion and lot (see Psalms 16:5; 73:26; Lamentations 3:24), these idols are the trust and confidence of those who worship them. This assertion is made very emphatic by the statement: 'They, they are your lot.' The LORD has been renounced and in his place they have put their idols. The question at the end of verse 6 is simply: 'Concerning these, shall I comfort myself?' The Hebrew construction here (*nicham 'al*) is used elsewhere of a change of heart regarding something, and so relenting (cf. Exod. 32:12). This

---

[20]Most versions take the last part of the verse as a question, but Oswalt's explanation is to be preferred. See John N. Oswalt, *The Book of Isaiah: Chapters 40-66*, p. 472.

meaning fits well as God indicates so emphatically that he has set aside compassion and consequently his judgment will come.

7-8 Cultic practices on high hills were a regular feature of Canaanite worship, and at times were permitted even for God's people (see the case in 1 Samuel 9:11-26). However, sacred prostitution was often a feature of this worship, and here the picture is of people who go up on the hills not only to offer sacrifice but also in order to have their sinful beds there. Behind the doors and doorposts of what was really a brothel they hang their 'remembrance'. This could be something like the mezuzah that orthodox Jews still put on their door frames, but this would mean that once the door was shut the symbol containing portions of Scripture would not be visible to them while they were sinning. More likely the 'remembrance' was some form of pagan symbol (so NIV) that they placed there. The following part of verse 8 is cryptic in the Hebrew text. Literally it says: 'For from me you uncovered, and you went up, you enlarged your bed.' As Hebrew often uses the preposition 'from' (Heb. *min*) to signify a comparison, it is quite possible that the meaning is 'for you have uncovered yourself *to those other* than Me' (NKJV). The worshipper gets the bed ready and makes a pact with the lover. In breaking the covenant with the LORD they in effect make a covenant with the false gods (Heb. 'You cut for yourself [a covenant] with them'). They delight in committing adultery and looking on the nakedness of their lover.

9-10 The imagery changes to relationships with foreign kings. Judah has failed to trust in the LORD and now turns to find help from the great kings of countries such as Egypt, Assyria and Babylon. Ambassadors go bearing gifts such as oil and perfume. The reference to descent to the grave is a way of expressing total humiliation before these kings. All these journeys caused great weariness, but Judah will not acknowledge the folly of it all. She will not even bring herself to say, 'It's hopeless, it's no use.' Later when in exile the people would make this confession (see Ezekiel 37:11). For the present Judah manages to gather up strength to persist in this way. The Hebrew text is difficult to interpret as it says, 'you have found the renewal of your hand,' or, 'the life of your hand.' This appears to mean that enough strength has been found so that she does not become weak or tired, but as the expression is unique we cannot be sure of its meaning.

11 By means of questions the accusation is made that the nation has been false to the LORD, neither remembering him nor pondering over him and his ways. The suggestion is that the people have been so much in fear of someone else that they have failed to give due honour and obedience to their covenant God.

12-13a However, the day is approaching when God will expose (Heb. 'declare') their false righteousness and their works, which will fail to provide any help to them. Their righteousness is like filthy rags in God's sight (Isa. 64:6). In time of trouble they should call upon their collection [of idols] and see if they will deliver them, The word for 'collection' (Heb. *qibbuts*; cf. modern Heb. *kibbutz*, a collective farm) occurs only here in the Old Testament. The language is ironic, as the truth is that those idols cannot possibly deliver them. They are so ephemeral that even a puff of wind can carry them away.

13b The section ends with a declaration concerning another group in the community. There are those who instead of trusting idols have put their confidence in the LORD, and made him their refuge. The promise to them is that they will inherit the land and possess God's holy mountain. These promises speak of security and access to God's presence. The 'holy mountain' is Zion (see 11:9; 65:25) which stands as a symbol for the heavenly city of God (see Hebrews 12:22).

9. Comfort for the Contrite (57:14-21)

14 This verse serves as a bridge between the declarations concerning the idolaters in verses 3-13 and the word of comfort to the contrite in verses 14-21. The language and thought are reminiscent of Isaiah 40:1-5 as God calls for preparation of the road on which the returning exiles will travel. Everything that could cause stumbling is to be removed out of the way. The words here also anticipate those in Isaiah 62:10.

15 The speaker identifies himself as the high and lofty one, using two words that have been used earlier of the exaltation of the servant (52:13). There is added that he 'dwells for ever' (Heb. *shokên 'ad*) and 'his name is holy'. The first of these expressions should be compared with the statement about the messianic child in 9:6 that he will be 'the father of eternity' (Heb. *'ᵃvi 'ad*). God dwells in a high and holy place, yet condescends to live with those who are contrite and lowly in spirit. This combination of 'broken' and 'contrite' occurs in Psalms 34:18 and 51:17, describing the result of conviction of sin. The result of God's abiding with such people is that their spirits and hearts are restored. The manifestation of divine grace brings cheer to those who are cast down.

16 The first part of this verse is very similar to Psalm 103:9 (the words 'accuse', 'forever', and 'always' occur in both, but a different verb is used for 'be angry'). God declares that he will not forever contend with Israel for that would mean that man, his creature, would be reduced to weakness. 'To contend' is to bring formal charges against someone (cf. its use in 3:13; 49:25; 50:8; 51:22). God was compassionate towards his erring people, restraining his anger. He understood their frailty and remembered that they were but flesh (Ps. 78:39). 'Spirit' and 'breath' are synonyms for 'soul'.

17 The past history of Israel was a record of wilful sin that had invoked God's anger. The people had gone after their own gain (Heb. *betsaʻ*, NKJV 'the iniquity of his covetousness'; NIV 'his sinful greed'). When such acquisition for personal gain dominates, then it sets aside honesty and obedience to God's laws. The stress on his anger is made plain by the repetition of the verb 'to be angry', the reference to smiting them in judgment, and the hiding of his face (cf Isa. 1:15). In spite of this the people went on wilfully sinning, continuing to backslide, with their hearts set on their own ways.

18-19 Israel's waywardness is in clear view, but yet God announces healing, and this promise forms the first and last of the promises in these verses (cf. the Messiah's healing ministry already discussed on 53:5). Moreover, he will guide Israel and restore comfort to her and her mourners. This message of comfort had been spoken of at the very outset of this section of Isaiah's prophecy (40:1), but now it can be seen as a result of the messianic work of the servant of the LORD. Those who previously had been rebels will show genuine repentance and grief for their sins. The internal change of heart will be reflected on the outside by praise that is the fruit of the lips (cf. Heb. 13:15). The theme of 'peace' runs right through Isaiah's prophecy (see 9:6, 7; 26:3, 12; 27:5; 32:17, 18; 48:18; 52:7; 53:5, 54:10, 13; 55:12; 57:2). Both inward change and outward expression are part of God's creative work. It is possible that the words 'peace, peace to those afar and those near' indicate the content of the praise being offered. Those near will be the covenant people, while those afar will be Gentiles. The New Testament records how the message of peace indeed came to Jew and Gentile alike, to those near and those afar (see Acts 10:34-36; Eph. 2:13, 17). The verse ends with the indication that this message is God's solemn declaration, and the assurance of healing is repeated: 'I will heal him' (the singular *him* is required, contrary to NIV's *them*).

20 The contrast between those who have been spoken about in the preceding verses and this one is most marked. Whereas the believers are at peace with God, the wicked are characterised as entirely lacking such peace. They reject God's salvation and resemble the roaring sea that cannot be stilled and that tosses up slime and filth. Not only do they fail to obtain peace, but the metaphor suggests they progressively bring to light more sin and uncleanness.

21 This section of Isaiah (chapters 49–57) closes with a repetition of the words already used at 48:22. The only difference is that 'my God' is used instead of 'the LORD'.

C. The Ultimate Salvation (58:1–66:24)

This section of Isaiah's prophecy ends at 66:24 with a description that parallels in meaning (though not the precise wording) the refrain used in 48:22 and 57:21. The glory of Zion features even more prominently throughout, but there is a vision of something even grander. God is going to create a new heaven and a new earth (65:17; 66:22). The prophecy also returns to a theme set out in chapter 2 in depicting a pilgrimage of the Gentile nations to Jerusalem (cf. 2:2-3 and 66:19-20). While judgment will feature in the end times, yet the glory of the LORD will be seen and declared. The title 'the servant of the LORD' as an individual figure does not occur in this section, 53:11 being its final occurrence. Instead, there are only the plural forms – 'my/your/his servants'.

1. The Marks of God's People (58:1-14)

1 The prophet is to shout loudly to the people and not 'hold back' (the same verb as used in 54:2 of Israel not holding back from enlarging her tent). Like the trumpet at Sinai (Exod. 19:19), he is to declare to God's people their transgression and sin. Everyone needs to hear the message concerning their rebellion, for despite their seeming religious ways they are far from pleasing God.

2 On the surface the people seem so holy, even making a pretence of seeking God day by day. Likewise they appear to desire his ways, i.e. they seemingly are eager to know his direction for their lives, whereas in reality they are a nation that has forsaken him. They pretend they are righteous, acting the part of an upright nation that obediently follows the LORD's commands. They even expect God to manifest his righteous acts of judgment to save them, and pray for his coming in saving power. They seem eager for a meeting with God (for the only other use of same Heb. word *qir^evâh*, see Psalm 73:28).

3 The people have gone through the motions of fasting, and yet God has not looked favourably on them. Fasting was prescribed for the Day of Atonement (see Leviticus 16:29, 31), and it became so much a mark of that day that 'the fast' came to be a way of describing the day itself (Acts 27:9). Other fasts came to be observed but they did not have divine sanction or authority. These fasts were something around which the religious life of the exiles later revolved (Zech. 7:5). The people assert that they have afflicted their souls (NKJV; NIV 'humbled') and yet God had taken no notice. But the truth of the matter is that instead of humbling their souls they make these days times of pleasure, and rather than safeguarding the rights of their workers they exploit them.

4 Peaceful religious observance on a fast day is replaced by strife and conflict. Fighting takes the place of a penitential approach to God. A rare word for 'strife' is used (Heb. *mattsâh*) which is identical in writing and pronunciation to the much more common word for the unleavened bread used at Passover. Perhaps there is a play on words to enforce the message that solemn religious festival days have been turned into occasions for fisticuffs. If the people wanted their voice to be heard in heaven (lit. 'on high') then the fast days would have to become what they were really meant to be.

5 Rhetorical questions are used to press home the folly of pretending that their outward observances are really spiritual worship. Would God choose a fast like the one just described? Would he be satisfied with a mere bowing of the head, or even the appearance in the traditional sackcloth and ashes? They however went so far as to declare that this was indeed a fast pleasing to God, but in reality it was only an ephemeral exhibition of humility.

6-7 These verses put in question form the type of worship with which God is pleased, and positive answers are expected. The fast he chooses is characterised by the true administration of justice and letting slaves go free as required by the law (see Lev. 25:39-54). Moreover, God requires of his true worshippers that they feed the hungry, give shelter to the homeless, and clothe the naked. In particular, they must care for their own kith and kin (Heb. 'from your flesh'), fulfilling all due diligence to meet their material needs. The principles of care for the needy set out here are amplified further in Jesus' words in Matthew 25:35-36.

8 This and the following verse both commence with the adverb 'then' (Heb. *'āz*; see also its use at the start of verse 14) that points to the consequence and also to the connection between obedient response to God's demands and enjoyment of promised blessings. The prosperous future days are described using terms such as 'light' and 'healing'. The analogy with the first exodus appears again in the reference to the LORD going before his people as well as being their rearguard (cf. the use of this same term already in 52:12 and the references quoted in the comments there). 'Righteousness' in this context is equivalent to God's presence or his saving power. Just as in the first exodus, so in the return from exile God will both lead his people and protect them against attacks from the rear.

9a Another certainty is that the LORD will be ready to answer the cries of his people. Cries for help will produce a response. A call for salvation (the Heb. verb is the one from which the common word *t'shû'âh*, 'salvation' comes) will have as its sequel the LORD's declaration that he is at hand to deliver (cf. the use of the repeated 'Here am I' in 65:1).

9b-10 Future blessing is not going to be automatic. There has to be a change of attitude and behaviour. The yoke of oppression has to be removed, and both accusatory signs and words stopped. The Hebrew text just speaks of pointing the finger, but in the context it looks as if a gesture of contempt is intended. On the positive side there has to be provision for the hungry and satisfaction of the needs of the oppressed. These actions will herald the dawning of a new day when the darkness of the past will be succeeded by midday light.

11 God will show compassion to his people in continually leading them. The verb for 'lead' only occurs twice in Isaiah (here and in 57:18), but elsewhere in the Old Testament it is used of God's gracious and compassionate actions towards his people (see Exod. 13:17, 21; 15:13; Deut. 32:12; Ps. 23:3). Abundant provision will be made for their experience in the desert and their bodies (Heb. 'bones') will be rejuvenated. More than that, there will be abundant renewal so that Israel, a garden without water (Isa. 1:30), will have abundant water and because of its constant flow it will never be a spring that deceives.

12 The promise of a restored Jerusalem, already made known in the prophecy concerning Cyrus (see 44:26), is again described. Ruins will be rebuilt and old foundations utilised afresh for the new habitations. Breaches in the city walls will be restored, and streets will again be lined with houses. This prophetic word found fulfilment in the work of Nehemiah who on his return to Jerusalem encouraged the people to rebuild its walls so that they would no longer be a disgrace (Neh. 2:11-18).

13-14 The last two verses in the chapter revert to the theme of the sabbath (see comment on 56:1-7). It pointed back to both creation and redemption (cf. Exod. 20:11 and Deut. 5:15),[1] while its keeping was a mark of covenant obedience (Exod. 31:13, 16-17). The point is made explicit that the sabbath was the LORD's 'holy day', 'the LORD's holiness' (Eng. versions in general render this second expression 'the LORD's holy day', but the word 'day' does not appear in the Heb. text). It was intended as a day for the LORD's pleasure, not the people's. That involved keeping the rest day and so refraining from turning one's feet to other pursuits. It had to be a day of 'delight' (Heb. *'oneg*), a rare word derived from the verb (Heb. *'ânag*) used at the commencement of verse 14. Some English versions (NASB, NKJV) manage to show the connection by rendering 'delight' and 'take delight in' or 'delight yourself'. Verse 13 ends with the statement that the people must not 'speak a word'. 'Word' here is probably a collective noun, 'words', and refers to idle words or words related to their normal business pursuits that misdirected their hearts away from the LORD and his day. The promised blessings for sabbath keeping are stated in terms drawn from the song of Moses (Deut. 32:13) and his dying blessing (Deut. 33:29). If they honoured his day, then God would honour them and they would find that the heritage of their father Jacob was still theirs. The final statement of verse 14, 'the mouth of the LORD has spoken', was used earlier in 1:20 and 40:4.

2. Redemption for Penitent Israel (59:1-21)

a. Israel's Sinfulness (59:1-2)

1-2 These two verses re-assert the LORD's power to save even a people who have been alienated from him. What was presented as a question in 50:2 is now given as an emphatic statement: 'Behold the LORD's hand is not shortened that it cannot save' (NKJV). The fact

---

[1]Notice the wording of the Westminster *Larger Catechism* on this point: Question 121: 'The word *Remember* is set in the beginning of the fourth commandment ... to continue a thankful remembrance of the two great benefits of creation and redemption'.

that the LORD would answer prayer has already been given in other words (30:19). Now the reassurance is presented that his ears will be ready to listen to a cry for salvation. The people's sins have become like a dividing wall between them and their God, and their iniquities have hidden his face. Just as the word 'hand' in 28:2 is the ultimate hand, God's hand, so here 'face' is God's face, which is obscured because of their sins. Most English versions depart from the MT here and follow the reading in the early versions of 'his face', but this is unnecessary. While this separation continues, there will be no answer to their prayers, a fact that had been presented at the very commencement of Isaiah's prophecy (1:15).

b. Specification of Israel's Sin (59:3-8)

The general statement of verses 1-2 is now given greater specification, as the description focuses on the depth and extent of their depravity.

3 Hands, fingers, lips and tongue are all instruments of sin. The four descriptions of sin are 'blood[guilt]' (see verse 7), 'injustice', 'deceit' and 'perversity'. The verb used for the staining of hands (Heb. *gâ'al*) is not the verb 'to redeem' but another one that means 'to defile', 'to become impure', and it reappears in 63:3. Actions and words are both represented as being completely defiled by sin.

4 Both the vocabulary and the syntax of this verse make translation and comment difficult. The verbal forms may be intended to convey the idea of habitual action, while the range of vocabulary powerfully describes the extent and intensity of sin. Different words are used for 'lies' in verses 3 and 4 while the people are said to rely on what is empty or confused (the Heb. word *tohû*, borrowed again from Genesis 1:2). Two similar sounding words are used in verse 3 and at the end of verse 4 (*'âvon* and *'âven*), the former meaning what is crooked, while the latter has more the meaning of what is unjust or false. The picture is of a people perverting justice, swearing falsely, trusting in what is empty, speaking vainly, conceiving distress, and giving birth to injustice. The final statement in the verse appears in an almost identical form in Job 15:35.

5-6 The plans that sinners make are worthless to themselves and harmful to others. What they devise is likened to vipers' eggs and spiders' webs. Danger is present whether the eggs are eaten or crushed. The webs are worthless as a type of covering for they cannot form any useful part of clothing. The latter part of verse 6 emphasises that the people's works are evil in themselves and their intention is to cause hurt to their neighbours. The reference to acts of violence ties in with what has already been said in verse 3 regarding hands stained with blood.

7-8 The description continues with phrases that depict readiness to sin coming from a corrupt heart. The opening sentence of verse 7 is practically identical to Proverbs 1:16. Stemming from innate evil their actions are directed to violence and corruption. The combination of 'ruin and destruction' (NIV) is clearly a fixed pair[2] in biblical Hebrew, for it also occurs in Isaiah 51:19, Isaiah 60:18, and Jeremiah 48:3. The fact that their lives are marked by the absence of peace is stressed by both the beginning and end of verse 8. This is a reaffirmation in different words of the refrain in 48:22 and 57:21. The theme of the perversion of justice in both these verses picks up the earlier expressions in verses 3-6. Paul draws upon parts of these verses as he quotes from the Old Testament in Romans 3:10-18 to prove that Jew and Gentile alike stand under condemnation because of their sins.

c. The Consequences of Sin (59:9-15b)

As the prophet now includes himself in the description he writes in the first person plural ('we', 'us', 'our'). The repetition of words such as 'justice', 'far off', 'righteousness', 'wait for', 'grope', 'transgression', and 'growl' adds to the intensity of his words as he confesses the sins of the people and notes how universal sin is.

9-10 Whereas justice should have been at the heart of Israelite life, it is remote. Whereas there should have been light, there is darkness. Amos, another eighth century BC prophet, uses similar language to dispel the idea that the coming day of the LORD is going to be light and joy for the people (see Amos 5:18-20). Like blind people they grope (Heb. $n^e gash^e sh\hat{a}h$) along a wall; like people without eyes they grope (Heb. $n^e gashsh\hat{e}sh\hat{a}h$) for their way. This Hebrew verb occurs only here, but it closely resembles another rare verb in the covenant curses of Deuteronomy 28. Moses gave the warning to the individual Israelites that they would grope ($m^e mash\hat{e}sh$) at midday, and like a blind man they would grope ($y^e mash\hat{e}sh$) in the dark (Deut. 28:29). The parallels

---

[2]The term 'fixed pair' refers to words that regularly occur in parallel expressions in Hebrew, e.g. head//skull, earth//dust, mouth//lip. The same phenomenon occurs in Ugaritic, another early North-West Semitic language.

in thought and language suggest a conscious dependence on the passage in Deuteronomy. The picture is of the pathetic spiritual blindness of Israel and the fact that the people cannot enjoy peace while they remain under covenant discipline. They are like the dead (cf. Ezekiel's description of the exiles in 37:1-14).

11 The mournful state of the people resembles the murmuring of a bear as it awaits its prey, or the cooing of a dove. Deliverance is what the people seek, but there is no sign of it, for it remains afar off. This is virtually a repetition of verse 9a, except that 'salvation' has replaced 'righteousness'. The fact that on three occasions the people are said to be 'afar off' (verses 9, 11, 14) emphasises not merely their geographical isolation from Palestine but their separation from their God.

12-13 Isaiah's confession on behalf of his people resembles Ezra's (Ezra 9:6-7) and Daniel's (Dan. 9:1-14). He acknowledges that their sins testify against them, and they are 'with them' in the sense that they are conscious of them. As in other passages, such as Psalm 32:1-2, three common words are used to describe their rebellion in God's sight: 'transgression', 'sin', and 'iniquity'. In verse 13 there is a catalogue of their sins, with the first three being against God ('rebellion', 'treachery', 'turning our backs on God'), while the second three are against their fellow-men ('oppression', 'revolt' and 'lies'). Their state of heart towards their covenant LORD inevitably results in expressions of sin against others. When the vertical relationship is broken, the horizontal one inevitably suffers as well.

14-15a The description of the moral state of the people continues. 'Justice', 'righteousness', 'truth' and 'honesty' are all absent. All these qualities should stand at the very heart of life, but they are either removed or prevented from making their impact. Justice is turned away, while righteousness is remote. Truth fails in the city square and is also said to be lacking (the verb used occurs only six times in the Old Testament and on every other occasion it is preceded by the negative particle *lo '*). Only after the return from exile will Jerusalem be called 'the city of truth' (Zech. 8:3). The final sentence in the section is hard to translate and to explain. The LXX renders it very freely: 'They have turned their mind from understanding.' While this makes good sense in the context, it is not a translation of the Hebrew text that says: 'and the one who turns aside from evil allows himself to be taken as spoil'.[3] The meaning of the Hebrew is that in a society so

lacking in moral rectitude a person may soon give way to self-interest
and permit himself to act wrongly towards others even before he himself
is wronged.

d. Salvation from the LORD (59:15b-21)

The scribe who copied the text of Isaiah in 1QIsa[a] left a blank in the
middle of the verse, indicating that he thought that a new section
commences at this point. He was correct, as what follows does not
continue the catalogue of sins but after beginning with threats focuses
on the LORD as the redeemer. He is going to come to Zion as the
covenant God (verses 20-21).

15b-16 Israel's condition did not please the LORD for he noted the
absence of justice and was dismayed that there was no intercessor
(the same verb for 'intercede' is used as in Isa. 53:12). Earlier it has
been noted that the LORD's arm is able to effect salvation (see 51:9;
52:10). Later the same message is going to be given in almost identical
terms (63:5). God does not need anything external to himself when he
acts in salvation, nor does he require support from anyone else.

17 God is the divine warrior who girds himself for battle. His
righteousness, salvation, vengeance and zeal are regarded as part of
his armour (cf. Paul's description of the Christian in armour prepared
for spiritual warfare, Eph. 6:10-18). Attention has already been called
to God's vengeance (see 34:8; 35:4; 47:3), but it should be noted that
the Hebrew term has a much more positive connotation than the English
one. While vengeance does refer to God's actions in vindicating his
name, yet it also relates to maintenance of justice and the provision of
salvation for his people. It is linked here with 'zeal' as in Nahum 1:2
(Heb. *'êl qannô' v^e noqêm yhwh*, 'the LORD is a jealous and avenging
God', NIV). As Israel's covenant God he will both visit iniquity and
show mercy.

18 Part of God's future actions relate to his judgment upon the
unbelieving world. It will receive its just reward (Heb. k^e ... k^e, 'as ...
so') and even the far off places ('the islands'; see 11:11; 20:6; 40:15;
41:1, 5) will not escape what is their due. Twice in the verse the verb
'repay' (Heb. *ye shallêm*) is used of God's enemies and foes. However
in 65:6 the same verb is going to be used of God's judgment on the sins
of Israel. Jew and Gentile alike will experience his judgment since

---

[3]The Hebrew verb is *shâlal* in reflexive form (Hitpoel), and hence can be
given the meaning of 'allowing oneself to be taken as spoil'.

both are under sin. This is the conclusion that Paul comes to in Romans as he quotes Old Testament Scriptures to prove that the whole world is accountable to God (see Paul's quotations in Romans 3:9-20).

19 Mention has already been made to the fact that far off nations in east and west will come to fear the LORD (45:6; 52:10; 56:8). The last prophet of the Old Testament, Malachi, repeats this promise of the exaltation of God's name among the nations from the rising to the setting of the sun (Mal. 1:11; both the NKJV and the NIV make Malachi's words a declaration concerning the future, not a contemporaneous reality). The latter part of the verse contains several difficulties, and this is reflected in the variety of translations:

NASB   'For He will come like a rushing stream,
        which the wind of the LORD drives.'
NKJV   'When the enemy comes in like a flood,
        the Spirit of the LORD will lift up a standard against him.'
RSV   'For he will come like a rushing stream,
        which the wind of the LORD drives.'
NIV   'For he will come like a pent-up flood
        that the breath of the LORD drives along.'
NIV (mg) 'When the enemy comes in like a flood,
        the Spirit of the LORD will put him to flight.'
NEB   'His glory will come like a swift river
        on which the wind of the LORD moves.'

The difficulties revolve around several words.

1. The expression 'rushing stream' or 'swift river' is indefensible from a grammatical point of view unless a change is made in the MT, for the word translated 'rushing' (Heb. *tsâr*) does not have the article with it if it defines 'river'. Moreover, while it may mean 'pent-up' it is hard to see how this can be stretched to mean 'rushing'.

2. The fact that this word has just been used in the previous verse makes it much more likely that it again means 'enemy'.

3. The choice between 'wind of the LORD' and 'Spirit of the LORD' becomes easier when it is realised that in verse 21 the LORD speaks of his 'Spirit', and this is in keeping with the preceding context that has emphasised the power of God to effect salvation.

4. The final verb (Heb. *nos^e sâh*) could either be from a Hebrew root meaning 'flee' (*nûs*) or one meaning 'lift up a banner' (*nâsas*).

Since this form of the verb occurs only here in the Old Testament either is possible. Probably the traditional rendering is as near the mark as any; 'When the enemy shall come in like a flood, the Spirit of the LORD shall lift up a standard against him' (AV). The imagery is that when the ingathering of the nations takes place the enemy will come to disrupt, but the Spirit of the LORD will lift up the battle standard against him (for battle standard, see also 49:22 and 62:10).

20 Again the assertion is made that the redeemer is returning to Zion (for redeemer, see 41:14; for returning to Zion, see 52:8), and this coming is especially directed to the repentant within Jacob/Israel. The same expression for repentance has already been used very early in the prophecy (1:27). The return from exile was to be one expression of this, but the ultimate one was to be the coming of the Christ. Paul uses this passage when speaking of the ingathering of Jewish people after the full measure of the Gentiles has come in (Rom. 11:25-27).

21 Linked with the thought of the redeemer's work is mention of God's covenant with repentant Israel. God enters into a new expression of his relationship with his people upon whom he places his Spirit. While it is not expressly called 'the everlasting covenant' here, yet it is said that the words being put in the mouths of the people will not depart from that time on and forever (Heb. *mê'attâh v^e'ad 'ôlâm*). This covenant is the new one (Heb. *b^{e}rît ch^{a}dâshâh*) of Jeremiah 31:31-34 or the everlasting covenant of Ezekiel 16:60 (Heb. *b^{e}rît 'ôlâm*). Joshua was instructed not to let God's word depart from his mouth (Josh. 1:8), and now the people collectively are given the same instruction. From generation to generation they must adhere to the stipulations set out in this covenant if blessing is to flow to them.

3. The City of the LORD (60:1-22)

Though couched in Old Testament language the descriptions in this chapter point far beyond the return from exile. The walls are not going to be built by Jews but by foreigners, and the gates of the city will ever be open. It is an idealised Jerusalem that is depicted—one that speaks of the eschatological days of redemption and bliss.

1 The double command is addressed to Jerusalem/Zion, as the feminine suffixes show. As she is suffused with light from the LORD, so must she reflect that light. The reference to the glory of the LORD picks up the theme from 58:8. Just as the pillar of cloud and fire demonstrated God's glory to Israel at the time of the exodus, so will there be a further manifestation of that glory when God's saving power again is shown.

2 The picture is of a world living in darkness, but Jerusalem lit by the LORD's glory. The idea of darkness has been used several times by Isaiah to depict times of oppression and sin that will only be changed when the messianic salvation appears (cf. Isaiah 9:1, and the quotation of it in Matthew 4:15-16 in reference to Jesus' ministry in Capernaum). The parallelism in this verse serves to emphasise both the condition of the world (darkness/thick darkness) and the contrasting situation with Jerusalem (the LORD shines on you/his glory will be seen on you). The verb 'to shine' used in these two opening verses of the chapter (and the derived noun 'shining' in the next verse) is often used of the sunrise. Just as it describes the sudden disappearance of darkness when the sun rises, so it depicts the way darkness and gloom are banished before the blazing light of God's glory.

3 The illuminated city of Jerusalem will be an attraction to the non-Jews who will make their pilgrimage to it. Even rulers will be drawn irresistibly to the blazing light that envelops the city. While using different language from 2:2-4, this verse introduces more references to the pilgrimage of the Gentiles (see verses 5, 9, 10-12, 14). Jerusalem will become a beacon that attracts the nations to its glow.

4 Earlier in 49:18 and 22 the main ideas of this verse were presented as a partial depiction of the return from exile. In this context the description goes far beyond that event, as the return of sons and daughters is linked with extraordinary events such as foreigners coming with their wealth to Jerusalem (verse 5) and joining in praise of the LORD (verse 6). The sons are coming 'from afar', which may imply they are Gentiles who now qualify as the LORD's children. The daughters are carried at the side, which may have the meaning that the NIV gives to it, 'carried on the arm', as young children often are.

5 The first half of this verse contains several idiomatic expressions which, as comparison of different English versions shows, can be variously translated. What Jerusalem sees is unstated. It could be the event just described in verse 4, or it could be the LORD. If the latter is meant, then the idea may well be that as the LORD shines on them, so their faces become radiant. The following words literally are, 'your heart shall fear and be enlarged.' The verb 'to fear' can be used both of quaking with terror or delight (cf. for the latter, Psalm 119:161). As the people see the LORD, then with enlarged affection they will rejoice.

Not only will Gentiles come to Jerusalem, but riches both from the sea and the nations will also be brought to her. Revelation 21:26 may well be an echo of this idea.

6-7 Various countries are selected for mention: Midian and Ephah (Abraham's son and grandson through Keturah, Gen. 25:2), Sheba (in southern Arabia), Kedar (the Bedouin Arabs living south-east of Damascus), and Nebaioth (an Arabian tribe named after Ishmael's firstborn son, Gen. 25:13, and possibly the ancestor of the later Nabatean kingdom). These countries are representative of the nations who will come bearing their goods for trade and their gifts for the LORD's house. They will participate in worship (proclaiming the praise of the LORD), and provide the necessary sacrifices for the altar ('Kedar's flocks', 'the rams of Nebaioth'). Through all this the LORD will be praised and he will beautify his temple. The whole picture is of Gentile nations participating in true worship in the end-time kingdom of the LORD.

8-9 The picture continues in poetic terms of Gentiles flying like birds to Jerusalem, while those who belong to her as children (cf. the same phrase 'your sons' in verse 4) will come on 'ships of Tarshish'. Tarshish was probably Tartessus in south-west Spain, though various other possible sites have been identified (e.g. Tarsus in Asia Minor and Tharros in Sardinia). The Hebrew word *tarshîsh* may have originally meant 'refinery', and so 'ships of Tarshish' could designate any ore-bearing vessel. Vessels of this name plied the Mediterranean and the Red Sea and the Arabian Sea (cf. 2 Chron. 20:36). People and precious metals will both be transported from the distant isles, who are 'waiting' for the LORD, a Hebrew verb (*qâvâh*) often used in the Psalms and prophets to denote expectant waiting on him. This will be for the LORD's name, he who is the holy One of Israel. Not only the temple in Jerusalem is to be made glorious (verse 7), but Jerusalem herself will be glorious. City and temple will both be endowed with splendour.

10 The reference to foreigners rebuilding the walls of Jerusalem has often been taken as relating to the decree of Artaxerxes allowing Nehemiah to rebuild them, but it comes here in a context demanding a fulfilment in the distant future. While the return from exile was a second exodus, it also served as a pattern for an even fuller redemption to come in messianic days. Even foreign kings are going to bow in submission and become servants. The second part of the verse is similar in thought to 54:7. Again, the pattern for the future is to be governed by the experience of the exile and return. The time of God's judgment is going to be followed by a fresh demonstration of mercy.

11-12 Jerusalem's gates will be for ever open, for no longer will there be any need of defensive measures. Moreover, foreign kings will have to yield submission, and as they are led in triumphal procession the wealth of their nations will be surrendered to Jerusalem. John's description of the heavenly Jerusalem draws upon this passage, especially with reference to the doors never being shut and kings of the nations bringing their splendour into it (Rev. 21:22-26). Comparison should also be made with James' use of Amos 9:11-12, with its imagery of rebuilding, in his speech at the Jerusalem assembly (Acts 15:15-18). The thought of submission of foreign kings comes in again in verse 12, coupled now with the threat of extinction if they do not become servants of the new Jerusalem and its inhabitants.

13 The renewed city is going to be even more glorious than it was at the height of Solomon's kingdom, as Lebanon will be called upon again to provide the pine, fir and cypress (see 1 Kings 5:10). God refers to the sanctuary as 'the place of my sanctuary' and 'the place of my feet'. The first of these terms is regularly used in the Old Testament to describe the tabernacle, while the second one (often with the addition of Heb. word $h^a dom$, 'footstool') designates the ark as the place where figuratively God's feet rest.

14-15 The reversal of fortunes will also be seen when the children of those presently oppressing Jerusalem/Israel come and bow in humble submission. Also, those showing disdain to God's people will have to come and make due acknowledgment of the position of Jerusalem. She is to be called 'the city of the LORD' and 'Zion of the Holy One of Israel'. These titles add to the picture of Jerusalem given in the opening chapter of this book, 'the city of righteousness, the faithful city' (1:26; see also the further description of the new Jerusalem in 62:4). Zion stands in a special relationship to the LORD, for she is his. The deserted city attracts no trade, and hence travellers are absent from her. However, in place of being hated and deserted, Jerusalem will become a city of pride and joy, and this new-found character will last ('everlasting pride', 'joy of generation after generation').

16 The imagery here is very similar to the depiction in Near Eastern art of princes being suckled by goddesses. Converted Gentiles will give of their wealth and energies to Jerusalem, just like a mother giving milk to a young child. From foreign kings will come vital strength and power. The Old Testament use of this analogy goes back to the description in Deuteronomy 33:19 of Issachar and Zebulon suckling the abundance of the seas and the treasures hidden in the sands. This will be a further demonstration of the saving power of the LORD, who is also called here 'your redeemer, the mighty one (Heb. *'âvîr*) of Jacob'. This word as a descriptive title of God only occurs in poetical passages in the Old Testament. It first occurs in Genesis 49:24, and appears three times in Isaiah, always as a parallel to LORD (1:24; 49:26; 60:16).

17 Jerusalem was noted for its gold and silver during the reign of Solomon (1 Kings 10:21, 27). Here the assurance is given that there will be replacement of what is inferior in wealth or strength: gold will take the place of bronze, silver instead of iron, bronze instead of wood, and iron in place of stones. In addition to changes in the materials from which the city is to be built, there will also be changes in the administration. Peace and righteousness will be characteristics of the new city as the guards and overseers replace the former sinful officials of the past.

18 The city of the LORD will consequently be marked by the absence of violence, while ruin and disaster, mentioned previously as characteristics of the city (see 51:19), will be conspicuously absent. Since the new city is of the LORD's making its walls will be called 'Salvation' and its gates 'Praise'. On the one hand there is recognition that the creation of this new city is God's work, while on the other the people respond by their praise.

19-20 The extraordinary features of the city include the fact that the LORD himself will be its light, and this will be its lasting nature ('an eternal light'). Moreover, the LORD will be the glory (*tif'eret*) of Jerusalem, picking up on the expression 'house of my glory' (*bêt tif'arti*) in verse 7. This Hebrew word occurs seven times in Isaiah 60–64 in reference either to God's inherent or ascribed renown. Because of this fact Jerusalem will not need the sun or moon any more. Revelation 21:23 and 21:25 take up this concept and re-iterate that the heavenly Jerusalem will be filled with God's light so that there will be no need of natural light-bearers (sun and moon) or artificial ones (lamps). The perpetual absence of a setting sun or waning moon means that God is the everlasting light of the city, and sorrow will be banished for ever. This idea has already been expressed in 35:10 (though using different vocabulary) in connection with the return from exile. If that was true of that demonstration of God's power and grace, how much more it will be true of the perfected salvation!

21 In character the heavenly Jerusalem is going to be far different from the earthly one. All the people will be righteous and their status as the redeemed of the LORD will be forever secure. This thought is expressed by the idea of possession of the land of Canaan. This was one of the promises made to Abraham, fulfilled in the conquest of Canaan (Neh. 9:8), and realised again in the return to the land after exile. The heavenly Jerusalem will be eternally all that the possession of the land signified. As in 57:13 possession of the land is equivalent to the fullness of blessing. The second half of the verse contains some difficulties. It reads literally: 'the shoot of *his* planting, the work of *my* hands, to display oneself glorious.' Because pronouns need to be consistent with one another, the choice has to be either 'his planting' and 'his hands', or 'my planting' and 'my hands'. The latter choice is preferable as the first person singular pronoun has occurred several times already in the chapter and will do so again in the next verse ('I, the LORD'). The RSV, NIV, and NKJV all translate it in this way. Through the LORD's power a righteous people will be gathered who will be a testimony to his glory.

22 The idea of a vast increase in the number of the people has already been mentioned in 51:2 and 54:3, both passages having the promise to Abraham of numerous descendants as their background (Gen. 12:2; 15:4-5; 17:16). A vast increase in numbers will be a sign that the covenant curse (Lev. 26:22) is no longer in force. The final declaration in the verse and section reaffirms that the speaker is the LORD who will speedily bring his plans to fruition. At the appointed time he will see to it that his purpose is quickly fulfilled.

4. The Fifth Servant Song (61:1-9)

Though not normally classified as a servant song, this passage should be reckoned along with the earlier songs. Like Isaiah 49:1-7 and 50:4-9, it is in the first person, and testifies to an anointing by the LORD for a ministry that is to include proclamation of good news, liberty to captives, and gladness in place of mourning. Many of its phrases are similar to ones already used and it sets out the manner in which the LORD is going to fulfil the vision of the new Jerusalem that has just been described in chapter 60. Like the earlier servant songs it is followed by a hymn of praise in verses 10-11 (cf. 42:10-13; 49:13; 50:3; 54:1-3).

The prophetic office of the servant is in view. He is to preach the good news that a healing and comforting ministry is to be inaugurated. Moreover, there is going to be release for prisoners and comfort for those who mourn.

It is notable that at the beginning of his ministry Jesus read part of this passage in the synagogue at Nazareth where he had been brought up. Luke 4:16-19 records how Jesus unfolded the synagogue scroll of Isaiah and read verses 1-2a. His sermon started with the words: 'Today this scripture is fulfilled in your hearing.' He clearly saw his own ministry as a fulfilment of what was spoken long before by Isaiah.

It helps to set out the passage in a manner that shows some of the connections in thought.

> The LORD has anointed me
> > to preach good news
> He has sent me
> > to proclaim freedom
> > [to proclaim] release of prisoners
> > to proclaim the year of the LORD's favour
> > [to proclaim] the day of vengeance
> > to comfort all who mourn
> > to give to those who mourn in Zion
> > > a crown instead of ashes
> > > oil of gladness instead of mourning
> > > a garment of praise instead of despair.

These will be called oaks of righteousness, a planting of the LORD to display his splendour.

1 The servant declares that he has been anointed by the Sovereign LORD in order to carry out a ministry that is designated in the following clauses. Nine times the infinitive form of verbs is used ('to proclaim [good tidings]', 'to bind up the broken-hearted', etc.) as the speaker specifies the tasks for which he has received the Spirit of the LORD. Anointing in the Old Testament was used not only to set someone apart for specific service but also to equip for that service. The servant is to be a messenger of good news (the same verb is used as in 40:9) and a healer to the broken-hearted. The captives are going to receive a message of 'freedom', a technical term used in Leviticus 25:10 of the Year of Jubilee, and in addition to this passage only used elsewhere in Jeremiah 34:8, 15, 17 and Ezekiel 46:17. Those in dark prisons will also be affected by this ministry in that they will be able to see. Release from captivity in Babylon was only a forerunner of the greater release to be effected by Jesus' ministry. Paul declares concerning himself and his fellow Christian believers that the Father planned that ministry 'in order to rescue us from the dominion of darkness' and to bring us 'into the kingdom of the Son he loves, in whom we have redemption, the forgiveness of sins' (Col. 1:13, NIV).

2 The expressions 'time of favour' (49:8) and 'day of favour' (58:5) have already occurred. Now the term 'year of favour' is used, and the context requires it to refer to the same period of deliverance spoken of in verse 1. The eschatological days will see a deliverance far greater than that depicted by the Year of Jubilee, and Jesus in his sermon in the synagogue at Nazareth declared that that year had come. Later Isaiah is going to use the expression 'year of redemption' (63:4) for the same period, also calling it 'the day of vengeance of our God'. 'Vengeance' in its Old Testament usage has a much more positive connotation than our English word suggests. It has to do with lawfulness and justice, and is often associated (as here) with salvation. God's vengeance forms part of the eschatological picture of the removal of all obstacles before the coming of the great day of the LORD. Moreover, that day will see mourning replaced by joy. The mourning is not so much individual sorrow over a loss in one's family, but rather mourning over the present state of affairs (see Jesus' use of the idea of mourning in the Sermon on the Mount, Matt. 5:4).

3 The focus on mourning continues. What is to happen will be a complete transformation. This is implied by the choice of the Hebrew verb and following preposition in the opening clause (*sîm l^e*; cf. its use in 42:16 for the transformation of darkness into light). The phrase 'those who mourn in Zion' describes steadfast waiting upon God in the expectation that he will intervene in saving mercy. This will include those who like Simeon and Anna waited for the consolation of Israel (Luke 2:25-32, 36-38). The following three phrases describe states that will be exchanged for something else (the Heb. preposition *tachat*, 'instead of', is used in each of these clauses). In the first one, mourning (symbolised by the use of ashes) will be replaced with joy (symbolised by the ornate headdress). There may also be a play on words 'headdress' and 'ashes' in that in Hebrew they each have the same consonants but in a different order (*p^e 'êr* and *'êfer*). The following phrases carry on this idea with reference to mourning/spirit of despair being replaced by oil of gladness/the garment of praise. They will become like oaks planted by the LORD (for the simile, see Psalm 1:6 and Jeremiah 17:8), and in so doing they will display his glory (cf. the repeated use of this verb in 60:7, 9, 13, 21; the word for 'headdress' also comes from this same root).

4 The ultimate salvation of God is depicted using the language of return to Jerusalem after the exile. Just as the returnees had to set about rebuilding, in like manner those in God's final kingdom will live in renewed habitations. Later Isaiah will point to God's declaration concerning the heavenly Jerusalem that will be created as a delight (Isa. 65:18-19). The language is a typical example of Hebrew poetic parallelism. The use of 'renew' paves the way for the declaration concerning the new heavens and earth in 65:17.

5-6 Just as foreigners are to be builders in the new Jerusalem (see comment on 60:10), so are they to serve as shepherds and farm workers. They will give themselves to menial tasks so that the true Israel will be able to realise her calling of being priests to God (cf. Exod. 19:6). There does not seem to be any real distinction between 'priests' and 'ministers', as 1 Kings 8:11 uses both terms concerning 'the priests' not being able 'to minister' because of the cloud of glory that filled the temple. The reference to 'the wealth of nations' picks up what has already been said about Gentile wealth coming to Jerusalem in 60:5-6.

7 The transformation of circumstances will mean that shame and disgrace are banished and in their place will come lasting joy. Israel had experienced double punishment for her sins (40:2; note that the word for 'double' is a different one there) but now like a firstborn son (see Deut. 21:17) she will be favoured with a double portion. The word 'portion' is often used in the Old Testament to describe a piece of land received as an inheritance, such as was allotted at the time of the conquest of Canaan (Jos. 19:9). Not only will the new Israel possess territory but it will be far more extensive than that allocated originally at the conquest. Not surprisingly, the allocation of this double inheritance will bring forth expressions of joy as the people realise that their shame and disgrace have been put away for ever. Once more the heavenly realities are described in terms borrowed from the original inheritance of Canaan by Israel at the time of the conquest.

8 The opening of this verse is important as it marks out the reason why this reversal of fortunes will take place. The LORD loves justice and will see to it that rewards and punishments are administered appropriately. He hates 'robbery in the burnt offering' (NASB). The NIV translation 'I hate robbery and iniquity' involves accepting a revocalisation of the MT so that instead of 'in burnt offering' (Heb. b^e '$ôlâh$) the Hebrew is read as 'and iniquity' (b^e '$avlâh$). While this translation or something near to it is found in the LXX, the Syriac and the Latin Vulgate, yet the alteration is not convincing. In fact it is inappropriate to render the Hebrew preposition b^e as 'in' and to remove the idea of burnt offering from a context that is replete with allusions to priestly anointing and dress (see 61:1 for anointing; 61:10 for priestly dress; 62:3 for the priestly mitre; 62:9 for sanctuary). What God requires is total commitment and this involves offering the prescribed sacrifices. Anything else is robbery. Current practice in Judah concerning blemished sacrifices that are unacceptable is drawn upon in the midst of an eschatological message. The LORD will fittingly and faithfully recompense like an employer handing out wages, and enter into 'an everlasting covenant'. This phrase is used in Isaiah 55:3, Jeremiah 32:40 and 50:5, and Ezekiel 16:60 and 37:26, and it appears to be identical with 'new covenant' (Jer. 31:31).

9 Another scattering will take place, but this time it will result in blessing to the nations, in accordance with the promise made to Abraham (Gen. 12:2-3). These covenant keepers will be observed by others who will realise that they are indeed blessed by God. The connection in thought with the Abrahamic covenant is closer than most English versions suggest, as the final clause in Hebrew is 'that they are a *seed* the LORD has blessed'. This word 'seed' occurs frequently in reference to descendants of Abraham (Gen. 12:7; 13:15; 15:5, 13-16, 18; 17:7-9, 12, 19; 22:15-18), and used here it carries overtones of the gracious promises of God to him. The Jewish Diaspora in Hellenistic times resulted in some proselytes or God-fearers, as the New Testament confirms (Acts 2:11; 6:5; 13:43), and from whom many of the early Christian believers came.

5. The Saviour Comes! (61:10–62:12)

10 As with the earlier servant songs, the fifth one is also followed by a song of praise. There is no express indication of who the speaker is, but most probably it is Zion personified. She rejoices greatly on account of the revelation of salvation and righteousness made to by her God, the covenant LORD. The traditional marriage ceremony, with its joyful celebration and festive garments, is made the symbol of the rejoicing that will accompany the final salvation. Clothing, headdress and jewels depict the special nature of the occasion, as already indicated by the bestowal of gifts set out in verse 3. The idea of clothing and jewels used in both Old and New Testaments makes it plain that salvation is not inherent in people themselves but is indeed a gift of God.

11 Just as in 44:3-5 and 45:8 the idea of a garden is utilised to depict the way in which God will bring forth his righteousness and praise. The garden sprouts forth plants from seed, while God makes righteousness to sprout forth so that it becomes an object of praise before all the Gentile nations. Once more indication is given that the eschatological salvation is going to reach out to the Gentiles as well as to the Jews. That salvation will have reference to the needs of all.

62:1 Sudden switches in speakers are not unusual in Isaiah. Here it is the LORD who now speaks. Whereas at times he had been silent (see 42:14; 57:11; 64:12), for the sake of Zion/Jerusalem he will proclaim her coming glory. She will be visited with righteousness that will shine like the dawn of a new day, and her salvation will be as apparent as a blazing torch. The coming deliverance will not happen in secret nor without due proclamation. Moreover, the salvation is not just outward deliverance but something that involves inward change as well.

2 Salvation for Jerusalem will be something that the Gentile nations will see for themselves. Just as they were amazed at God's deliverance of his people from Egypt (Deut. 4:6-8), so they will see the radical change that is coming. The term 'righteousness' is repeated and the term 'glory' is added. These expressions highlight the transformation to be effected in desolate Jerusalem. She is also to be given a new name by the LORD. This idea of a new name complements all the other expressions concerning 'newness' that Isaiah has, or is yet to use: a new song, new things, and new heavens and earth. These are eschatological terms that find their ultimate fulfilment through the work of Christ. Not surprisingly, the expression 'a new name' reappears in the book of Revelation (2:17; 3:12).

3 The prophet takes up an idea already mentioned in 28:5. Israel's new position will be an exalted one, as though she is entitled to be marked out as both king and priest. She is to be a crown of glory in the LORD's hand, using a term employed for a regal crown or appropriate symbol of authority (cf. 2 Sam. 12:30; Zech. 6:9-14). The second part of this verse is clearly parallel to the first, with 'royal diadem' replacing 'crown of glory', a different word being used for hand (Heb. *kaf* instead of *yâd*), and a change from 'LORD' to 'your God'. Israel will be returned to a position of honour and responsibility before God.

4-5 The important concept of name is taken up again with greater detail. Two Hebrew names could be used of Jerusalem during the exilic period. She could be called both Azubah ('Deserted') and Shemamah ('Desolate'). The coming of God's salvation will bring about a change in status, so that Jerusalem will become Hephzibah ('my delight is in her') and Beulah ('married'). These two names were already in use as Jehoshaphat's mother was called Azubah (1 Kings 22:42), while Manasseh's mother was Hephzibah (2 Kings 21:1). The reason for this change is because God delights in Jerusalem and the land will be reckoned as married. This is the theme already dealt with in chapters 50 and 54. While the northern kingdom of Israel was divorced (see Jer. 3:6-10), the southern kingdom of Judah was only separated for a short time. The reasons given for this naming in verse 5 are that just as a young man marries a maiden, so Jerusalem's sons will marry, i.e. be committed to the covenant relationship with the LORD. Also, just as a young man rejoices over his bride, so will the LORD rejoice over the restored Jerusalem.

6-7 The speaker is the LORD, who declares that he has appointed watchmen on Jerusalem's walls. This most probably refers to the prophets (see 52:8 and 66:10) sent by him to declare the good news. Their role was a continuous one in making declaration on God's behalf so they were never silent. As in 52:8, this section contains a graphic picture of the ministry of the prophets, with hyperbolic language to emphasise the intensity of their mission. They are referred to as those who make mention of the LORD. The verb used here (*zâkar* Hif.) is frequently used of mentioning God's name in worship, or invoking his name in prayer (for previous use in Isaiah in this sense, see 26:13 and 48:1). They are to give themselves no rest as they pursue this task, nor give any rest to the LORD until Jerusalem is restored. The intensity of this work of prayer is similar to the intensity that was evident in David's prayer as he sought a place of rest for the ark of the covenant (see Psalm 132:1-5). The restoration of Jerusalem was intended to be something that was an object of wonder and praise among all nations.

8-9 Isaiah has previously mentioned how God swears by himself (see 14:24; 45:23: 54:9), while his arm of power works salvation (33:2;

59:16). He could not swear by anyone else (Heb. 6:13), nor was there any other saving arm. Among the curses of the covenant set out in Deuteronomy 28 were ones involving the use of the produce of the land by invading armies (see Deuteronomy 28:33-51). Now Isaiah proclaims God's solemn oath that never again will this take place. They will drink their own new wine, and feast upon their own grain harvest. Those who harvest the grapes will drink the wine produced from them before the LORD at his sanctuary. No longer will God's courts be profaned by a sinful people (1:12), for on festival occasions a believing company will drink of the tithe that they bring to the LORD. The vision transcends the immediate restoration of Jerusalem as recorded in the books of Ezra and Nehemiah. The rebuilt temple was defiled by the installation of the 'abomination of desolation' (a pagan altar or statue) by Antiochus Epiphanes in 167 BC, while Pompey in 63 BC captured the temple. In AD 70 the Romans destroyed it. Perhaps the picture Isaiah gives is to be linked with the fuller reference to the 'new' Jerusalem in chapters 65 and 66.

10 In each of the last three sections of Isaiah there is a call to prepare the way (for the earlier ones, see 40:3 and 57:14). The one here is the fullest of them and there also seems to be progression in thought. The first calls for the preparation of 'the way of the LORD', while the second only mentions 'the way', though the context makes it plain that it is the way of Israel. This third passage enlarges the idea to embrace the Gentile nations, who will be attracted by the banner which is raised. No fuller explanation is given of the gates through which the procession is to go, but the wider context makes it virtually certain that they are the gates of Babylon. All impediments are to be removed so that there is a highway for those returning to Jerusalem, and a signal is to be given to the nations that God's saving mercy is being displayed.

11-12 The two final verses in this section speak of the LORD's proclamation of the coming redemption of the exiled Israelites. It has affinities with 40:9-11, including the identical phrase, 'Behold, his reward is with him, and his work before him' (40:10//62:11). The recipients of the message are not just Jews but Gentiles as well, for it has gone forth to the ends of the earth. When the LORD saved Judah in the time of Hezekiah, this salvation was made known to the ends of the earth (see 2 Chron. 32:23). Now a further act of saving mercy will be made known as Jerusalem experiences the LORD's salvation. The attitude to both the people and the city will change too, as the people will no longer be called 'Deserted' (see verse 4) but rather 'the holy people, the redeemed of the LORD'. This is an allusion to Exodus 19:6. At last Israel will be what the LORD intended her to be as his chosen and special people. The city will also be recognised as having changed in character. She will be called 'Sought After', a passive form from the Hebrew verb *dârash* that can have the idea of being cared for. Another prophet, Jeremiah, using the same verb, later speaks of Jerusalem as not being cared for (Jer. 30:17). However, the prophecy here looks beyond the fate of Jerusalem after the devastation of 586 BC and pictures her as the object of the LORD's care. The period of desolation will pass away, and no longer will anyone call her 'forsaken'.

6. The Day of Vengeance (63:1-6)

In the history of interpretation many have understood the figure in this passage to be the servant, and thus taken the reference to blood-stained garments as relating to Jesus' death on the cross. However, this cannot be the correct interpretation as the blood on the garment is not that of the figure coming from Edom but the blood of his enemies. Clearly the blood relates to the judgment meted out on these enemies. This section has many affinities with 59:16-18, more apparent in Hebrew than in translation. The first question concerns the identity of the warrior figure coming up from Edom. This is the fourth prophecy in Isaiah relating to Edom (for the earlier ones, see 11:14; 21:11-12; 34:1-17), and there is progression in that the judgment on Edom becomes greater and greater. This is consistent with the evidence for the whole of the Old Testament. Whereas Edomites (descendants of Esau) are regarded earlier on as brothers (see especially Deut. 2:4 and 23:7-8), curses are later invoked against them (see Amos 1:11-12; Obad. 1-21; Jer. 49:7-22; Mal. 1:2-5). Edom is presented as a symbol of a world opposed to the people of God, but here also of the judgment of God upon his enemies.

1 A question is asked by the prophet as to the identity of the figure coming from Edom and from her capital of Bosrah (probably the modern Buseirah, about 60 kilometres [37 miles] north of Petra). The names 'Edom' and 'Bosrah' are significant. 'Edom' comes from the same root as the word 'red' in verse 2, while 'Bosrah' is from a Hebrew verb that means 'to gather grapes'. The warrior's garments are vivid in colour (the NKJV's 'dyed garments' is closer than the NIV's 'garments stained crimson'), splendid in appearance as he strides in great strength. The answer comes from the figure himself, as the LORD is the one speaking in righteousness, the one mighty to save. He is able to speak with authority and to save by his own power.

2 Further questions are posed. Why is the LORD wearing garments that are stained red? Why is he clothed in a manner like a man treading the winepress? The prophet compares him to a man involved with crushing the harvest of grapes, whose juice stains his clothes red. The imagery of the winepress as symbolic of divine judgment also appears in Joel 3:13 and Lamentations 1:15.

3 The LORD speaks of his work of judgment as a treading out of the winepress (the word used is technically the 'trough' but here it indicates the whole press). He did this alone, i.e. he did not employ others to carry out this mission. In respect of Edom, the LORD sovereignly administered the due judgment, a demonstration of his righteous anger. The use of both 'anger' (Heb. *'af*) and 'wrath' (Heb. *châmâh*) stresses the fact that God's actions are an expression of his righteous indignation against sinful nations. The imagery of the winepress is carried further, with reference to the spattering of the clothes with blood, and the staining of all his garments.[4]

4 The declaration is made that this will be a day in which God's inner desire for vengeance will be displayed, while at the same time his saving actions will be seen in the redemption of the exiles. This linking of vengeance and salvation is typical of Isaiah and other prophets (see commentary on 61:2, and cf. Isa. 34:8; 35:4; 59:18; Jer. 51:36; Nah. 1:2). Vengeance on Israel's enemies and her redemption are intimately linked, because one is the reverse of the other. An act of God can be a demonstration of both judgment and salvation at the same time, a fact coming to its highest expression in Jesus' messianic death on the cross.

5 The essential thrust of Isaiah 59:16 is repeated here, though it is now stated in the first person singular instead of the third person singular. The parallel phrases are:

---

[4]The Heb. word for 'staining' is unusual in form in that it has the prefix of an imperfect and the suffix of a perfect. There are some other examples of this in the OT and in extra-biblical texts, and hence no emendation is needed. See the note by Cyrus H. Gordon and E. J. Young in *WTJ* 14, 1 (November, 1951), p. 54.

Chapter 59	Chapter 63
He saw	I looked
there was not a man	there was no one to help
and wondered that there was no intercessor;	and I wondered that there was no one to uphold;
Therefore his own arm brought salvation for him;	therefore my own arm brought salvation for me;
and his own righteousness, it sustained him	and my own wrath, it sustained me.

The message of both verses is identical. The situation demanded a divine response and there was no other able to intervene and effect deliverance. Once more wrath precedes salvation, just as it does in Jesus' teaching (Matt. 13:30, 41-43).

6 The imagery from grape harvesting continues. Just as the harvesters crush the grapes, so will the LORD tread upon the nations in his anger, and the resultant wine, in his wrath, he will make them drink. God's own people at times had to drink 'wine of confusion' (Ps. 60:3), but his enemies had to drink wine of judgment.

7. God the Father and Redeemer (63:7–64:12)

The prophet now moves from the thought of judgment on unbelieving Gentiles to the great compassion that God has shown to Israel. He, as the father, has bestowed great blessings on them his children. After the declaration of this truth, the prophet prays on behalf of the people, appealing particularly to the fact that the LORD is their father (63:16; 64:8 [Heb. 7]). Past mercies and present circumstances intermingle in the intensity of the petitions. Much of the language is similar to, or may even be based upon, the Book of Psalms. In particular, the appeal 'Do not remember iniquity [or, sin]' 64:9) occurs in Psalms 25:7 and 79:8, and is in effect an appeal for forgiveness. There is also a general affinity between this section and communal appeals such as Psalms 44 and 74.

7 The prophet announces the covenant mercies of God (NKJV 'lovingkindnesses'; NIV 'kindnesses') that call forth praise. Mention of them begins and ends this verse. The covenant overtones come through this double use of an important covenant term, the mention of the 'goodness' (Heb. *tûv*) shown to the house of Israel, and the occurrence of a special word for showing mercy (Heb. *gâmal* instead of the more common '*âsâh*). 'Goodness' is a term used elsewhere of the special blessings that a covenant afforded (see especially its use by David in his prayer of response to Nathan's oracle concerning the Davidic dynasty, 2 Sam. 7:28). The verb *gâmal* is used elsewhere along with 'good' (Heb. *tov*) to indicate the bestowal of blessing on someone (see 1 Sam. 24:17 regarding David's actions toward Saul). It is also a term connected with the family, as derivatives of the word denote a weaned child, and hence most appropriate in this context in which the father/child relationship is in view.

8 God had declared the relationship he had to the people of Israel as one that depended upon his adoption of them as his people. They in turn were expected to be obedient to his laws and not prove false to him. However, Isaiah at the very commencement of his prophecy has shown that they were in fact unworthy children (Isa. 1:4), a statement that probably relies upon Deuteronomy 32:5-6. God's concern for them as his people resulted in him becoming their saviour, not only from the bondage in Egypt but on many later occasions as well. 'Saviour' means more than just a national deliverer, for it includes the spiritual dimension as well, as the vocabulary in the context shows.

9 There is a translational problem in this verse, as in 9:2, 11:3 and 49:5.[5] The Hebrew word for 'not' (*lô'*) and 'to him' (*lô*) are pronounced identically, though written differently. Here it is best to follow several of the early versions of the Old Testament and most modern English versions in accepting that this word is the Hebrew preposition 'to' together with a third masculine singular suffix. The meaning of the opening of the verse is then that when Israel was afflicted God identified with them in that affliction ('In all their affliction he was afflicted'). This principle later found expression in the way in which Jesus identified with his sinful people in submitting to John's baptism (Matt. 3:13-17). That identification with Israel's afflictions brought about their salvation by the Angel of the Lord as promised (Exod. 23:20-23). In his love (the only occurrence of the Heb. noun '*ah^avâh* in Isaiah) and pity he redeemed, then carried them as a father does his children.

10 Israel's general attitude to their God, unlike that of the servant (50:5), was one of rebellion (the same verb has already been used in 1:20; 3:8; 30:9). The statement here of their rebellion and God's consequent grief is based on words in Psalm 78:40 (see that psalm for a full description of Israel's repeated rebellion). The attitude of Israel

---

[5]See the comment on 9:2.

grieved the Holy Spirit,[6] who is mentioned three times in this passage (63:10, 11, 14). Twice he is declared to be the Holy Spirit, and once the Spirit of the LORD. In Psalm 106:33 the rebellion is said to have been against the Spirit of God. Since they had turned from him, he turned from them and set himself as their enemy. The end result was that he fought against them.

11 As focus shifts to the events of the Exodus, verses 11-14 form a unit recalling these past events. There are problems in translating verse 11 in particular. There is abruptness in the syntax, and the variety of translations shown in ancient versions indicates that the difficulties were apparent even in pre-Christian times.[7] In the context the subject at the beginning of the verse must be God. There is a sequence in the verbs leading up to this verse: 'they rebelled ... they grieved ... he turned ... he remembered'. There is no need to make the verb 'remember' plural (as does the NIV). 'Remember' is used fairly frequently in the Old Testament of God's actions in acting according to his promises (see Gen. 8:1; 9:15; Exod. 2:24). The time he remembered was 'the days of old', which, along with the prior usage of the phrase in verse 9, refers to the bondage in Egypt. Whom did he remember? The Hebrew text is abrupt in answering, 'Moses, his people.' There is no need to emend to the common expression, 'Moses his servant,' as a plural subject is required by the later words 'he brought *them* up' and 'the *shepherds* of his flock'. It is best to supply 'and': 'Moses [and] his people.' The LORD brought them up from the [Red] Sea, and he also put his Holy Spirit among them, which is probably a reference to the bestowal of spiritual gifts for the leadership in Israel.

12 The Exodus was accomplished by God's power (his 'glorious arm') and through the instrumentality of Moses ('by the right hand of Moses'). God divided 'the water', which may well include the Jordan as well as the Red Sea. The purpose of these actions was to bring glory to himself, which is expressed by saying that he was making for himself an enduring name (Heb. *shêm 'ôlâm*; cf. the use of the 'name' in a similar way in 55:13, where it is called 'an enduring sign', Heb. *'ôt 'ôlâm*).

---

[6]Cf. the exhortation of Paul in Ephesians 4:30: 'Grieve not the Holy Spirit of God.'

[7]For a discussion of all the difficulties, see John N. Oswalt, *The Book of Isaiah: Chapters 40–66*, pp. 601-03.

13 He also led them through 'the deeps', an expression that can also be applied to the Red Sea (see Psalm 106:9). Even though the chronological sequence may suggest 'the Jordan' here, yet it is safer to understand it of the Red Sea, or else of the Red Sea *and* the Jordan. Their progress through the waters was as unimpeded as a horse running in open country. They did not stumble as they crossed over.

14 This verse forms a conclusion. Israel's progress into Canaan is likened to a beast going down into a valley and finding rest there. All the major early versions (LXX, Syriac, and Latin), instead of reading 'the Spirit of the LORD gives him rest', translate it as 'the Spirit of the LORD leads him'. While the two verbs have two consonants in common (cf. *nâchâh* and *nûach*), the MT is the harder reading and should be maintained. This verb is also used of the occupation of Canaan (Deut. 3:20; 12:9-10; 25:19; Josh. 1:13; Ps. 95:11). Each stage of the journey to Canaan was an expression of the rest the LORD was giving, but ultimately the rest prefigured the heavenly rest of God's people (Heb. 3:16-4:11).

15 Following the historical recollections in verses 7-14, the prophet goes on in verses 15-19 to lament on behalf of his people and make confession of the sins of Israel. Though the people of Israel are still God's children, they have strayed from his ways. The urgent appeal is made to God to 'look down from heaven and see from your glorious throne'. There is not enough specific information given in the text to try and suggest a possible historical background.[8] Though most English versions translate 'from your *habitation*', yet the rare Hebrew word in question (*zᵉvûl*) comes from a root (*zâval*) that appears to mean 'exalt, honour'. The noun then probably means 'throne', 'palace', or 'dais'.[9] The prophet questions whether God's zeal, strength, and compassion are held in check. The Hebrew word for 'held in check, restrained' is the one used of Joseph as he tried to contain his emotions when he saw his brothers (Gen. 42:31). The same verb will recur in the final verse of this section (64:12, Heb. 11). If God loved more than an earthly father, could he restrain showing his love and mercy to an erring people?

16 Indeed, the LORD was their father, a fact stated at the beginning

---

[8]See John N. Oswalt, *The Book of Isaiah: Chapters 40–66*, 'Excursus: The Historical Setting of 63:15-19,' pp. 616-17.

[9]This last translation is the one chosen in *DCH*, III, p. 81.

and the end of this verse. Even if the patriarchs disowned them, as it were, still the LORD would claim them as his own children. Speaking on behalf of the people the prophet calls the LORD 'our redeemer'. The more common form used when addressing Israel is 'your redeemer', but here and in 47:4 the acknowledgment is made of this special family relationship as the people base their claims on having God as their redeemer. And not only that, but he was their redeemer from eternity, and that meant that that relationship antedated any with the patriarchs.

17 Israel's experience in the past had not been of unconditional obedience to the LORD. A sinful people had strayed from his ways, and he let this happen. The words are not necessarily saying that God caused them to go astray (as NIV and NKJV suggest), but rather that he allowed this to happen. In the fourth servant song confession has been made of the fact that 'all we like sheep have gone astray, and each of us has turned to his own way' (53:6; cf. also the psalmist's use of this verb when he says: 'I like a lost sheep went astray', Ps. 119:176). Hard hearts were made still harder as sinful stubbornness showed itself (cf. Exod. 4:21; Isa. 6:10; Ps. 95:8). Appeal is made to God to return and show favour since the people are his servants, the tribes of his inheritance. The term 'servant' is a reminder of the covenant relationship between God and his people, while 'tribes of your inheritance' draws attention to the fact that Israel was God's chosen heritage (Exod. 34:9; Deut. 4:20).

18 Israel's occupation of Canaan and the presence of the ark in Jerusalem was only for a relatively short period. When the Babylonians ('our enemies') came, they trampled upon the holy place, showing their utter contempt for even the most sacred Jewish site. The historical records in 2 Kings 25:9 and 2 Chronicles 36:19 state that they burned the temple with fire, a fact confirmed in poetical passages in Psalm 74:7 and Isaiah 64:11.

19 The commencement of this verse is very cryptic in the Hebrew. It simply says: 'We are [or, 'have become'] from of old.' Something has to be added. Several English versions such as RSV, NASB, and NKJV translate it as a comparison: 'We have become *like* those over whom you have not ruled, *like* those not called by your name.' The NIV makes a contrast: 'We are yours from of old; but you have not ruled over them, they have not been called by your name.' Certainly the idea of contrast is there already in the previous verse, though it is hard to press the first word (Heb. *hâyînû*) to have the meaning 'we are yours'. Israel's state was just like the Gentile nations over whom the LORD had not ruled, and who had never been called by his name. The question the Jews were facing is: 'Are we still God's chosen heritage, or has he let us become like the other nations?'

64:1-7[10] These verses describe an appearance of God in times past, when he intervened in the affairs of his people. The language and thought echo what is said about God's appearance at Mount Sinai. The recollection of past actions is meant to encourage the people to call upon their God and experience his saving mercy. But first, they have to repent of their sins.

1 The language here is similar to that in other Old Testament passages, such as Psalms 18:7-15; 68:7-8; 77:14-20 and Habakkuk 3:3-7, that describe a visible appearance of God (a theophany). Contrary to most English translations of this verse the tenses should be past: 'Oh that you *had rent* the heavens, that you *had come down*, for the mountains quake at your presence!'[11] The heavens are described as being like a curtain that can be split in order for God to descend. Even the mountains are said to tremble before such a majestic divine appearance. The second clause of this verse is repeated in identical wording in verse 3.

2 God had come in fiery display, a demonstration of his power when he manifested himself (see Deut. 5:22; 1 Kings 18:38; 19:12). The fire sets twigs ablaze and causes water to boil (Heb. *bâʿâh*; only here and in 30:13 in the Old Testament does this verb 'to boil' occur). The purpose of the appearance was to make the LORD's name known to his enemies, and so that Gentile nations would tremble before him. A theophany was intended to produce a response, not just to be a dramatic display of God's presence and power.

3 When God appeared to Israel it was not something that the people were expecting. However, the appearance involved awesome events. The Hebrew uses a participle from the verb 'to fear' (*nôrâ'* from the root *yârê'*) to speak of the great redemptive acts of God (see its use

---

[10]There is a difference in chapter division in the MT and the English versions. What is verse 1 of chapter 64 in the English, is part of verse 19 of the previous chapter in the Hebrew. Hence in Hebrew there are eleven verses in chapter 64.

[11]Both John N. Oswalt, *The Book of Isaiah: Chapters 40–66*, pp. 618-21, and J. A. Motyer, *The Prophecy of Isaiah*, p. 518, rightly take this as a reference to a past appearance, not an appeal for a future one.

in Deut. 10:21, 2 Sam. 7:23; 1 Chron. 17:21 and Ps. 65:5). These events were so beyond human power to perform that they induced awe in those who saw them. The second clause in this verse is a repetition in exact words of verse 1b.

4-5 The exclusive claims of the LORD have already been asserted frequently in previous passages (see especially 43:11; 45:5, 21). Now Isaiah points to the fact that even since 'ancient times' (probably meaning the patriarchal period) no one has heard, perceived, or seen any other God than the LORD. This is what Moses had already declared at the time of the renewal of the Sinai covenant in the plains of Moab (see Deut. 4:7, 32-36). However, for those who truly trust in him and 'wait for him' he acts. Isaiah has used this verb 'to wait for' (Heb. *châkâh*) twice earlier in his prophecy (8:17; 30:18) where it refers to believing confidence and devout waiting for him. God had indeed met with those who joyfully do what is right. They also show their devotion to him by remembering him in his ways, not just conforming in a legalistic manner to his commands. Their focus is on the person of their God. The latter part of verse 5 is difficult, as a literal translation shows: 'Behold, you were angry, and we sinned. In them for a long time— and we are saved.' The essential point is that in spite of the fact that God was angry when sin was committed, his people, even though they knew this, continued to sin, and that over a long period of time. The final clause is best taken as a question: 'And how can we be saved?' In the face of such provocation, will God intervene to show his saving mercy?

6 Isaiah had earlier made confession that he and his fellows had all wandered from God like sheep going astray (53:6). Now he declares that all of them have become ritually unclean before him. The word he uses (Heb. *tâmê'*) describes various kinds of ritual uncleanness and it occurs most often in Leviticus 10–16. Instead of being clad in robes of purity, their righteousness is reckoned by God as being like defiled garments. While the word for 'defiled' is used of menstrual impurity, yet it often has a wider connotation of physical ritual impurity. This description certainly applied to pre-exilic Judah with whom Isaiah identified ('we', 'our righteousnesses', 'our sins', 'us'), but is not a universal truth applying to every human action. The people's standing before God is also like a leaf that withers, or one that is carried away by the wind.

7 The sinfulness of the people is so great no one calls upon God in prayer nor grasps him in an attitude of prayerful dependence. The people lack the characteristic that so marked their ancestor Israel, who struggled with the angel at the brook Jabbok (Gen. 32:22-32). At times like this God appears to have hidden his face from his people, a concept already mentioned earlier in the prophecy (see 8:17 and 54:8). The iniquities are so great that they have caused the hearts of the people to melt within them and they have become completely dispirited (see verses 9 and 12).

8-9 The concluding verses of chapter 64 (verses 8-12) revert to the theme of God as father. The communal nature of the concept and the united prayer of the people continue—first person plural pronouns occur ten times in the space of five verses. On behalf of the people Isaiah pleads with God for his forgiveness and an end to his wrath. Verse 8 contains another declaration of God's fatherhood (cf. 63:16) and also the thought that Israel was merely clay in the potter's hand (cf. 45:9-10). In spite of present circumstances the people appeal to the past and the fact that the relationship between them and God was established as a father/son relationship. Therefore they can pray (verse 9a) for God's anger against them to cease (cf. the assurance of 54:8 that this anger was not going to continue for ever—only for a moment!). They also plead for God not to remember their sins perpetually. The prayer in verse 9b is a powerful request to God to be gracious to them. The phrasing of the request is pointed, impassioned, and based on the fact that they are indeed his people. The NKJV brings out the force of the Hebrew text admirably with its rendering: 'Indeed, please look—we all *are* Your people!' The use of the Hebrew particle *nâ'* after the verb both softens it and also may indicate that the request is the outcome of the existing situation.[12]

10-11 The description of the land is that everything is a wilderness, including Zion. Not only are the people God's people but the towns in which they live are his towns. They and everything they possess really belong to him. That did not spare them from being objects of God's judgment. These 'holy' cities may well have included many of the places at which the ark of the covenant resided, such as Shiloh, Nob, and Gibeon. Even the temple with all its glory ('our beautiful and holy temple') and with its long historical associations ('where our fathers

---

[12]For this use of the particle, see T. O. Lambdin, *Introduction to Biblical Hebrew* (New York: Charles Scribner's Sons, 1971), p. 170.

praised you') will not be spared. There is no need to think that verse 10 is describing the state of the temple after the final fall of Jerusalem and the devastation of all the cities. The Hebrew text simply says that the holy house is ready for burning, and the desirable things are ready for devastation. Since the Hebrew word for 'desirable thing' is used in Ezekiel 24:21 of the temple, it may be used here simply as a parallel expression for 'temple'. This statement is perfectly consonant with a pre-exilic setting, such as the attack by Sennacherib. It is a declaration of future destruction, not necessarily a description of past devastation.

12 The final prayer is made on the basis of the things that have already been stated (Heb. *'al 'êlleh*, 'on account of these things'). The appeal is that God will not continue 'to hold himself in check', the second time within a short space that this Hebrew verb has been used (see comment on 63:15). The people clearly think of God as declining to answer them ('Will you hold your peace?') and continuing his afflictive judgments upon them. The plea is clearly for an end to the present circumstances by God showing his saving mercy.

8. A Patient and Compassionate God (65:1-16)

As the prophecy moves to its close it returns to themes that have been present from the opening chapters. The distinction continues to be made between the true servants of the LORD, and those who provoke him by their false sacrifices and blatant disregard for his laws. These concluding sections of the prophecy provide the answer to the people's prayer given in chapters 63 and 64.

1 God's revelation to Israel was sovereignly given. The people did not approach him with their requests ('ask', 'seek'), yet he was 'sought' and 'found' by them. While the NIV's translation 'I revealed myself' is free, it does capture the sense here. Divine revelation was also made to a people who had not approached him, nor called on his name. This clearly refers to Gentile nations. God announced himself to both in repeated terms of his immediate presence, 'Here I am' (Heb. *hinnênî*, 'Behold me', words that Isaiah himself used in response to God's call, 6:8).

2 God's mercy was such that he held out his hands continually to an obstinate people. This is a wonderful picture of God's forbearance. Paul quotes the first part of the verse along with verse 1 in Romans 10:20-21 where he is dealing with Israel's rejection of God. Israel could not plead ignorance of God's demands, for she had received revelation. So far from influencing her to do what was right, she continued to walk in evil ways, following her self-made ideas. The parallel use of 'ways' (or synonyms) and 'thoughts, imaginations', is relatively common in the Old Testament, and the usage depicts just how feeble man's evil plans are in God's sight.

3-5 These three verses provide a detailed description of 'the people', with a succession of participles defining its nature. They can be set out as follows:

> the people [who are] continuously provoking me to my face,
>   sacrificing in the gardens,
>   offering incense on altars of brick;
>   sitting among the graves,
>   and spending their nights in vigils;
>   eating the flesh of pigs,
>   and their vessels hold broth of unclean meat;
>   saying 'Keep away; don't come near me, for I am holier than
>   you'!
> These are smoke in my nostrils, as fire that burns all day.

Instead of living in obedience to the LORD, Israel sinned openly and in a provocative manner. Constantly she did what caused vexation to him. Several illustrations are given, with the first two concerned with offering sacrifices in gardens and burning incense on altars of bricks. In two other passages Isaiah refers to gardens that seem to have been dedicated to idol worship (1:29; 66:17), and also associated with other flagrant sins. While the Hebrew text says simply that the incense is burned 'on bricks', yet most English versions correctly interpret this as 'an altar of bricks'. In place of true worship of the living God, Israel so often substituted idolatrous worship and sacrifice.[13] They were also engaging in some cultic practices associated with the dead, and also sinfully transgressing the food laws by eating pig's meat and other ritually unclean food.[14] Moreover, those who were engaging in these

---

[13]The phrase 'offering incense on bricks' was difficult as far back as the second century BC, for the Qumran manuscript 1QIsa[a] has 'they emptied hands on the stones'. Possibly the text means that they built altars with brick, not the stone that the law prescribed, for the bricks are in keeping with Babylonian building customs in which brick was widely employed.

[14]The word used for this food occurs in Leviticus 7:18 of a sacrificial offering that has become unclean because it was not eaten in the specified time.

practices considered themselves holier than others and tried to prevent them from coming near. God's attitude to these people is that they are smoke in his nostrils, a fire that burns all the day. The meaning appears to be that God's anger is provoked just like a continuously burning fire, though it should be noted that nowhere else in the Old Testament is the phrase 'smoke in my nostrils' associated with anger.

6-7 The direct response to the prayer of 64:12 is now given by the LORD. The forthcoming judgment on the people has already been decreed, and it stands sure. The LORD intimates that he will not keep silent any longer but will repay in full their sins. This idea is stressed by the repetition of the Hebrew word 'I will repay', with the added words, 'into their bosoms'. This is a Hebrew idiom used here and twice elsewhere (Ps. 79:12; Jer. 32:18). The use of this language appropriate to the payment of a debt points to the exact nature of God's judgment. In these three passages it is best to keep the word 'bosom' in the translation (as with NASB and NKJV), rather than render it by a similar English idiom 'into the lap' (NIV). The switch from third person ('*their* laps') to the second person plural ('*your* sins') brings home the coming judgment in a very personal way. It is not just the sins of that generation that invite God's judgment, but the cumulative sins of the past generations as well. Their fathers had committed such sins, and they had continued with them, and now recompense will come. The idea is not that one generation has to be punished for the sins of past generations, but rather that the former sins have been consistently committed by the present generation who face God's wrath for their idolatrous actions. They continue to sacrifice on the mountains to Baal, and so defile the LORD by their syncretistic worship. God promises to give them full measure. In the Hebrew text the word 'first' (Heb. *rîshônâh*) follows 'their work'. A number of translations (e.g. AV, RSV, NIV) take it as modifying 'their work' and so render 'your former work'. For grammatical reasons it is best to take it as an adverb modifying 'measure out'. The meaning is then that *first of all* God will measure out their work, before proceeding to do anything else as he responds to their appeal.

8 Verses 8-12 present again the distinction within the nation. On the one hand there is a believing remnant, for God will not destroy all the people (verse 8). He makes promises to his chosen people (verse 9), and will bless those who seek him (verse 10). On the other hand those who forsake the LORD and disobey him (verse 11) will be subjected to judgment (verse 12). A formal declaration of blessing and cursing is now made in verse 8. An illustration is given from the vineyard, a particularly fitting one, for early in this book Israel was compared to a vineyard that had produced bad grapes (5:2, 4, 7). The point is made that there may be juice remaining in a bunch of grapes. Likewise there is the prospect of a remnant being found whom the LORD calls 'my servants'. This will be the holy seed that will be the stump in the land (Isa. 6:13).

9 The promise is made that God's true servants, the chosen people, will come from both Jacob (Israel) and from Judah. The old division will no longer be in force in the restored community, for as the LORD later said through Ezekiel, his purpose will be to 'make them one nation in the land, on the mountains of Israel' (Ezek. 37:22). 'Mountains' here and in Ezekiel 37 is just a synonym for the land of Canaan. The restoration after the exile will be another stage in the history of redemption, and will prefigure even greater changes to come when there will be a new heavens and a new earth (see verses 17-25 of this chapter).

10 Two areas in Canaan are chosen as reference points. Sharon was the rich coastal plain extending from about the present day Jaffa for about 50 miles (83 km) to the north, while Achor was the valley near Jericho where Achan was executed (Josh. 7:24-26). They probably represent the extent of the land, and their lush vegetation ('a pasture for flocks' and 'a resting place for herds' respectively) denotes the abundant provision that will be made for the remnant, 'my people who seek me' as the LORD describes them. In Hosea 2:15 the prospect is given that the valley of Achor (which means 'trouble') will be so transformed that it will become 'a door of hope'.

11-12 Now a word is addressed to the unbelieving community. Those who belong to it are characterised as being 'those who forsake the LORD', a term used over a hundred times in the Old Testament of covenant breaking (for examples, see Deuteronomy 29:25[24]; Jeremiah 2:13, 17, 19; Daniel 11:30). They also do not keep the land of promise in their thoughts and affections (contrast the unnamed author of Psalm 137 who calls down curses upon himself if he forgot Jerusalem). Moreover, they are also charged with being involved in worship relating to Fortune and Destiny. These two Hebrew words (transliterated in the Jerusalem Bible as Gad and Meni) are rare, the first occurring only here and in Genesis 30:11, though it probably occurs in names such as Gaddiel (Num. 13:10, 'El is my fortune') and Gaddi (Num. 13:11, 'my fortune'). The second one occurs only here. They seem to refer to two deities, but no certain identification can be made. To these deities they made offerings of food and drink. The same judgment that God's enemies will face ('the sword') will be destined for unbelieving Israel.[15] It was not that they were unaware of God's claims on them, but they did not heed his messages and persisted in wrong-doing. The words 'for I called ... what displeases me' are repeated in almost the same terms in 66:4.

13-14 The final words in this section announce the doom of unbelieving Israel, with the terms of the coming judgment echoing the passages in the Pentateuch containing the covenant curses (Lev. 26, Deut. 28). In Hebrew there is a striking rhythm about the message. Four times the expression 'behold my servants' occurs in succession (preserved in some English translations such as NASB and NKJV). God's servants, already spoken of in verses 11 and 12, will have full satisfaction, whereas the unbelievers will lack the very necessities of life. While 'the chosen people' will rejoice, the unfaithful ones will be put to shame and cry out in anguish of heart.

15 The curse of death is to come upon the rebels, and all that will remain will be their name and it will serve as a curse. This particular expression is apparently based on Numbers 5:21 that speaks of 'the oath of the curse'. Often in the Old Testament 'oath' and 'curse' are closely related (see Genesis 26:28; 1 Samuel 14:24; Nehemiah 10:30; Daniel 9:11). The idea is that in future when a curse is pronounced it will contain the names of unbelieving Israel as an illustration (cf. the similar case of the names of Zedekiah and Ahab in Jeremiah 29:22). However, to the faithful he will give 'another name', most probably the 'new name' of 62:2 (see comment on that verse).

16 In contrast to cursing there are those who are going to bless themselves. This means to invoke a blessing on themselves (cf. the use of the Heb. reflexive form in Genesis 22:18 and 26:4). When they bless or take an oath it is to be by 'the God of the Amen', a phrase that is unique to this verse. The Hebrew word *'âmên* comes from a root that means 'confirm', 'support', or 'be established'. The Hebrew verb for 'believe' is the causative form of it, i.e. you pronounce your 'amen'

---

[15]There is a play on words in that the noun 'destiny' (*$m^e n\hat{\imath}$*, verse 11) and the verb 'destined' (*mân\hat{\imath}t\hat{\imath}*, verse 12) are from the same Hebrew root.

over what God has said. 'Amen' is also often used in the Old Testament following the pronouncement of solemn curses (see Numbers 5:22; Deuteronomy 27:14-26; Nehemiah 5:13 and Jeremiah 11:5). Invoking a blessing or taking an oath had to be done with fitting solemnity for they were done using the name of the God of the Amen. The New Testament in two passages sheds further light on this practice (see 2 Corinthians 1:20 and Revelation 3:14). The final sentence of this verse asserts that God is able to set aside former sins so that they no longer come into his reckoning.

9. The New Heaven and the New Earth (65:17-25)

A new Jerusalem has already been announced (54:11-12) but now there is a further vision that transcends that picture. In fact, there are to be a new heaven and a new earth, and mortality will no longer apply. The reference to death in verse 20 may suggest that there is a blending of heavenly/future and earthly/present realities in this passage. There is considerable overlap between this passage and Isaiah 11:6-9, though in place of the final statement that 'the earth will be full of the knowledge of the LORD as the waters cover the sea' (Isa. 11:9), this one ends with the words, 'says the LORD'. This ending is fitting, for it calls to mind the creative word of God in Genesis 1 when 'God spoke and it came to be' (Ps. 33:9). So will it be with the new creation. John in Revelation 21:1-5 fills out the concept from the New Testament point of view.

17 The announcement is prefaced with the words 'behold, I ...', a form that often occurs when the speaker is the subject of the following verb. The previous use of 'behold' in verses 13 and 14 calls for attention, but then focuses on God's servants. Here the focus is on the creator God who is forming a new heaven and a new earth, the climax in a succession of newness of which Isaiah speaks (see 'new things', 42:9; 'a new song', 42:10; 'a new thing', 43:19; 'new things', 48:6; 'a new name', 62:2). When the new heaven and earth are realised, then 'the former', i.e. the previous order in the first creation, will not be remembered, nor will it trouble human hearts.

18-19 The stress on God's creative work continues with a double mention of what he is going to do.[16] The new creation will call forth

---

[16]The Hebrew participle of the verb 'create' (*bôrê'*) is used once in verse 17 and twice in verse 18. In Hebrew the participle can be used to convey the idea of what is going to happen.

intense joy, and the new Jerusalem and its inhabitants will elicit praise. Not only will humans note the entirely changed Jerusalem, but the LORD himself will take delight in his own new creative work and the inhabitants of the new Jerusalem. No longer will weeping and crying be part of the experience of the people of God. Revelation 21:4 picks up this feature of the new order and describes a day when

> His gracious hand shall wipe the tears
> > from ev'ry weeping eye:
> And pains and groans, and griefs and fears
> > and death itself, shall die.   (Scottish Paraphrase 67)

20 The altered conditions in the new Jerusalem are illustrated by two examples. No longer will infants die young, while adults dying at a hundred years of age will be considered mere youths. Anyone who fails to reach a hundred years must be under some form of curse. The longevity calls to mind the situation in the days prior to the flood (cf. the reference to Noah in 54:9-10).

21-22 The removal of covenant curses will mean that the people will be able to build houses and plant vineyards, knowing that they will have permanent dwellings and secure food supplies. In accordance with the curses given through Moses (Lev. 26:14-17; Deut. 28:30), the experience of the people was that they were uprooted from their own homes and consequently were unable to profit from the vineyards they had planted. The expectation here is that with the inauguration of the new kingdom dramatic changes will take place when the LORD appears, for

> He comes to make His blessings flow
> > far as the curse is found.
>
> > > > Isaac Watts 1674–1748,
> > > > 'Joy to the World'

Just as a tree is used elsewhere to denote endurance and permanence (cf. Ps. 1:3; Jer. 17:8), so is it here employed to characterise the enduring kingdom prepared for God's people. These, called here by God 'my people' and 'my chosen ones', will fully enjoy the fruits of their labour.

23 Constant toil will not bring weariness (the same Heb. verb *yâga'* is used as in 40:30, 31), nor will their children have to endure 'sudden terror'. This Hebrew word (*behâlâh*) is rare, occurring only four times in the Old Testament. Its first occurrence is in one of the covenant curses (Lev. 26:16), where untimely terror is a judgment to be visited upon disobedient Israel. Apart from its use here in Isaiah 65, the two other occurrences are in Psalm 78:33 and Jeremiah 15:8. In all the occurrences God is the agent who brings 'sudden terror'. Once more the picture is of the reversal of a covenant curse in the world, for instead blessing extends to the people and their descendants.

24 In the previous chapter the people had complained that God did not hear them when they called on him. How different will the situation be in the eternal kingdom! Even before the people call, God will hear, and his answer will come so quickly that it finds them still speaking. The use of the first person singular pronoun twice (in addition to the first person singular verbal form) emphasises the fact that God is pledging himself to be so attentive to the needs of his people.

25 The language of Isaiah 11 is called on to provide the final words of this section, with the words 'They shall not hurt or destroy in all my holy mountain' being quoted exactly. The imagery is that of an idyllic situation in which there is no disharmony at all in nature, and animals such as the wolf and the lamb and the lion and the ox, will be able to coexist without strife. The reference to the serpent is based on the curse of Genesis 3:14, where eating the dust is a way of expressing the abject humiliation awaiting Satan. No destructive forces will prevail in the LORD's eternal kingdom.

10. Distinguishing True and False Worshippers (66:1-9)
The position of this chapter after chapter 65 and the earlier messianic passages may seem chronologically out of place. However, this chapter balances chapter 1, and while it contains eschatological features, yet it does point to abuses in Isaiah's day. The distinction continues to be made between true and false worshippers of the LORD. The true ones tremble at his word, whereas the false ones do not respond to his calls, continuing in their evil ways. Certain judgment is coming on those who delight in their abominations. Temple worship had been part of Isaiah's inaugural vision in chapter 6, and now at the conclusion of his prophetic book the temple theme reappears.

1-2 The LORD makes a declaration concerning where he is to be worshipped. He cannot be contained within buildings made by human hands. This was recognised by Solomon in his dedicatory prayer for the Jerusalem temple when he said: 'Behold, heaven and the heaven of heavens cannot contain you. How much less this temple which I have built?' (1 Kings 8:27). Stephen also thought it important in the New Testament era, for he declared that 'the Most High does not dwell in temples made with hands' (Acts 7:48). The king of the universe, the creator whose 'hand made all these things' (verse 2), regards the heavens as his throne and the earth his footstool. Moreover, those who worship with acceptance before him are characterised by being humble, contrite in spirit, and trembling at his word. Twice in this section 'trembling' is mentioned (verses 2 and 5) as a mark of devout worshippers. It is the same sort of trembling as Eli had for the ark of God (1 Sam. 4:13), or the trembling of the faithful after the return from exile (Ezra 9:4; 10:3).

3-4 Part of the early messages of Isaiah from the LORD concerned unacceptable sacrifices (Isa. 1:11-15). Now the condemnation of false worship occurs again at the conclusion of the book. So abhorrent was it in God's eyes that the worshippers might as well have been committing the heinous sins of murder, of using pigs or dogs as sacrificial offerings, or of burning incense before an idol. Since they had chosen their own ways, delighting in abominations (verse 3) and the things displeasing to God (verse 4), he in turn will choose to bring judgment upon them. What the judgment will comprise is said to be 'harsh treatment' and 'what they dread'. The first of these is the translation of a Hebrew word (*ta'alûlîm*) that occurs only in Isaiah 3:4 and this verse. In the context 'harsh treatment' is a better translation than the older 'delusions' (AV, NKJV). The sentence 'For when I called, no one answered, when I spoke, no one listened' is a repetition of 65:12, except that the third person is used instead of the second person.

5-6 The distinction between the two religious classes in Israel is expressed in another declaration by God. Those who tremble at his word are asked to give heed to this message. It concerns those of their fellows who hate them (see earlier indication of hatred in 60:15) and who thrust them out. The Hebrew verb for 'thrust out' is rare (occurring only here and in Amos 6:3), and in post-biblical Hebrew it is used to describe 'excommunication'. The reason for their exclusion is adherence to the LORD's name. These enemies taunt them by sarcastically asking them to rejoice in the LORD's glorification (cf. Isa. 5:18-19 and Ps. 22:8 [partially quoted in Matt. 27:43]), but yet the enemies' fate is certain for they will be put to shame. Verse 6 describes uproar in Jerusalem, even from the temple, as the LORD executes full judgment on his enemies. No historical circumstance is indicated, and it is best to take this as a prophetic announcement of the final judgment that will take place just prior to the new Jerusalem coming into being.

7-9 The supernatural nature of the latter-day events is enforced by introducing the concept that a new nation can be born in a day. Before the mother even goes into labour, the child is born. This is something beyond normal experience, and yet it is going to happen to personified Zion. She who had no children (54:1) will suddenly give birth to children. Pregnancy will certainly result in birth, and far more than one child is to come, for the LORD will not close up Zion's womb. It becomes clear too at the end of verse 9 that the one being addressed is Zion, for the suffix on the Hebrew word 'your God' is second person feminine singular.

11. Zion Triumphant (66:10-24)

The final scene in this prophecy is an eschatological picture of the new Jerusalem as the mother who will succour and comfort her children. Jerusalem, called by the LORD 'my holy mountain', is going to be the gathering place for people from all nations, and those who belong to him are going to endure for ever. Just as the two major preceding sections of Isaiah 40–66 have ended on a note concerning the absence of peace for the wicked (48:22; 57:21), so this one ends on the note of judgment for those who rebel against the LORD.

10 The LORD's call is to join with Jerusalem in her joy. In Hebrew there are three different verbs for 'rejoice' in this verse, though the English versions tend to have only two. The variety of expression serves to highlight the intensity of joy that is expected. The NASB translation captures this with three English verbs: 'Be joyful ... rejoice ... be exceedingly glad.' Those to whom the call comes are described as loving Jerusalem and mourning over her. These descriptions are not contradictory, for those whose affection is set on Jerusalem will also be those who are deeply distressed over her misfortunes. The faithful in exile are like those in Psalm 137:5-6 and Lamentations 1:16 and 2:11 who weep for the desolate Jerusalem.

11 There is a close connection with what precedes, for both clauses are introduced by 'that' or 'so that' (Heb. *l^ema 'an*). 'Rejoice greatly ... that you may nurse ... that you may drink deeply' (NKJV). Whereas Jerusalem previously was pictured as drinking the milk of the nations

(60:16), she is now the mother who, from her full breasts, will give satisfaction to her children.

12a The idea of peace being likened to a river has already occurred (see 48:18 and comment). Here the LORD announces his plan to stretch out peace like a river and the wealth of the Gentile nations will come to her as swept along by a flooding stream. The new Jerusalem is going to be renowned for her peace and prosperity. Nothing that causes pain and grief will be present (Rev. 21:4), while the glory and honour of the Gentile nations will come to her (Rev. 21:26).

12b-13 The imagery of Jerusalem the mother continues. Satisfaction and safety are promised to those who love her. Her children will be carried at her side and play on her knees. Just as a mother comforts a child, so will all who love Jerusalem be comforted in her (NIV renders the Heb. preposition b^e as 'over', but the meaning 'in' should be retained as in NASB and NKJV). The picture is of the abounding blessings *in* the new Jerusalem, rather than comfort *for* her.

14 Verses 14-17 indicate that the distinction between godly and ungodly manifested in life will continue through to the eschatological finality. Joy for the godly is contrasted with terror for the ungodly. Whereas the godly will find joy and comfort in the new Jerusalem, the ungodly will meet their end as they come under God's judgment. In verse 14 the verb 'to see' has no object, but clearly something like 'this' or 'these things' has to be supplied. Participation in the eschatological events will be a matter of joy for the believing community, and their 'bones' will flourish like the grass. While 'bones' can be used as simply the equivalent of 'persons' (cf. Ps. 6:2), it is better not to follow the NIV here ('*you* will flourish'). Possibly it refers to national strength or identity that will flourish 'like grass'. Elsewhere in Isaiah and other parts of the Old Testament 'grass' is a symbol of frailty (cf. Isa. 40:6; Ps. 103:15-16), but here it represents luxuriant growth. In the final events of history God's hand, i.e. his power, will be displayed to his servants, while his 'indignation' will be shown to his enemies. There does not seem to be any clear distinction between the Hebrew words for 'indignation' (*za'am*) and 'anger' (*qetsef*), especially seeing they occur in parallel (Jer. 10:10). The next three verses spell out more fully how this indignation is going to be displayed.

15-16 Universal judgment is to follow the coming of the LORD, what the writer to the Hebrews calls the appearance of Christ 'a second time' (Heb. 9:28). In the Old Testament one use of the word 'fire' is to symbolise divine judgment. It separated Adam and Eve from the tree of life (Gen. 3:24), while it consumed disobedient Nadab and Abihu (Lev. 10:1-2) and the sons of Korah (Num. 16:1-35). Here the LORD proclaims that his coming will be a display of his power ('his chariots', 'his sword') and of his great anger (lit. 'to give back in wrath his anger'). This coming is expressly declared to be judgmental on all flesh (a Heb. idiom which here and in verse 23 has one of its common meanings, 'all human beings'). The finality of the judgment is shown by the last phrase in verse 16. Many will be 'slain of the LORD', a phrase that can mean 'murdered' (cf. Deut. 21:1-3) but is often descriptive of those slain in battle. Here the phrase means that the judgment will be unto death.

17 All who commit flagrant sins and follow idolatrous practices will be consumed. The first part of this verse is clearly referring to known practices, but there are insufficient references either within or outside the Bible to be sure of the details. The ungodly in Israel dedicated themselves in gardens set apart for false and idolatrous worship (for such 'gardens', see 1:29 and 65:3). They go there 'after one in the midst', which can refer either to following an idol or else some cult leader. Their evil practices extend to eating wild pigs, rat meat, and other abominations. They blatantly flout the restrictions of the Levitical law (see Lev. 11:7, 29), and though professing to be holy their practices bring destruction upon them.

18 Verses 18-23 depict the final assembly that is to take place before the LORD. People will be gathered from many countries (some of which are specified in verse 19), and in fact all mankind will come and bow in subjection to him. The commencement of this verse is a very broken sentence, as if someone is speaking under intense emotion. A literal translation is: 'I—their actions and their thoughts— ... [it, fem. sing.] has come to gather all the nations and the languages and they will come and see my glory.' A glance at the various English translations shows how various attempts have been made to understand the text, often with the addition of words or help from early versions (e.g. adding with the LXX the verb 'know': 'I know their actions ...'). Certainly 'actions' and 'thoughts' seem to refer to the previous verses, and now the LORD proclaims a universal gathering of nations when his glory will be revealed to its fullest extent, a fact anticipated in 40:5.

19 The promise is given that a sign will be set 'among them', i.e. among the Jews who have been just mentioned in verse 17. The word 'sign' (Heb. *'ôt*) can be something that is meant to propel people to action, or else to serve as confirmation after certain predicted events have come to pass. Here the first meaning is intended, though it is hard to be certain of the fulfilment. In the context the sign could well be the judgment that has just been described, though various commentators have linked it with the inauguration of the Christian era[17] or with the cross of Christ.[18] The survivors, i.e. those who have survived the judgment, are to be sent as missionaries to the nations who have not heard about the LORD's fame or witnessed his glory. The nations chosen are a representative sample and the following list gives an indication of their identification:

Tarshish—Probably Tartessus in south-west Spain. It has already occurred in 2:16; 23:1; 60:9.

Pul and Lud—unknown locations, but they are mentioned together in Jeremiah 46:9 and Ezekiel 30:5. Possibly they were both on the Mediterranean coast west of Egypt, and hence may be the Libyans and Lydians. The designation of Pul and Lud as archers may be meant to signify that the missionaries were going to those who already had a reputation for their hostility and military prowess.

Tuval— the Caucasian area in the north-east. See Genesis 10:2.

Yavan—the Ionian coast (modern Turkey) has been suggested, but the LXX translated it as *hellas*, and in Arabic *yûnân* is Greece. See Genesis 10:2.

Far off islands—strictly speaking, 'island' designated an area of land bounded by sea. In passages such as this it is paired with 'nations' and seems just to be a general term for far off places.

20 The 'missionaries' will bring to Jerusalem their 'converts' in pilgrimage (see Isaiah 2:1-4), in a similar manner to the way in which Israelites brought their offerings to the LORD's house in ceremonially pure containers. They will come using all different sorts of transport as they make their way to Jerusalem, the LORD's holy mountain. Gentiles now become 'brethren'. Paul's description of the Gentiles as an offering to God (Rom. 15:26) may rest on this verse. It could also be the background of the thought that the early converted Gentiles were the first-fruits of the harvest.

21 As part of the new order even Gentiles will be able to participate

---

[17]See, for an example, E. J. Young, *The Book of Isaiah*, vol. III, p. 532.
[18]See J. A. Motyer, *The Prophecy of Isaiah*, p. 541.

in priestly functions, for from those gathered to God's holy mountain a choice will be made for service as priests and Levites. In Hebrew there is no 'and' between these words, and hence the same problem of interpretation has to be faced here as elsewhere in the Old Testament. Are priests and Levites identical? The answer seems to be that all priests had to be from the family of Levi, but not all Levites were automatically installed as priests. The main point here is that even Gentiles will have a legitimate place of service in the new kingdom of God, something to which 1 Peter 2:5, 9 draws attention for the New Testament church.

22 God who is the maker of the new heavens and new earth declares that they will last. The Hebrew verb used is 'to stand', but especially in poetic passages it has the meaning 'endure'. Just as God himself 'stands' (Ps. 102:26), so do his plans (Ps. 33:11), and that includes the total new order that has been proclaimed through Isaiah. The participants in the new kingdom will also endure, and they will have a name that cannot be cut off.

23 The time of judgment by sword and fire will have passed, and those who have survived it will come and bow in worship before the LORD. Clearly 'all flesh' in this verse means those of the human race who are reconciled to God. They will join in perpetual praise before him. 'Sabbaths' and 'new moons' will come and go, but the praise continues.

24 The final verse in this section (chapters 58–66) and the conclusion of the whole book ends on the same note as the two preceding sections (see 48:22 and 57:21). Instead of specific reference to the lack of peace, this verse describes it using alternative language. All those who bow before the LORD will also be witnesses of the final judgment of unbelievers. They will go out and look, not for the purpose of rejoicing in the fate of the condemned, but to be solemnised by the sight. 'The worm' and 'fire' are symbols of the enduring punishment of rebels, and Jesus himself used part of this verse when teaching his disciples the fate awaiting those who cause others to sin (Mark 9:48).[19] The final word of the LORD through Isaiah is that these condemned rebels will be 'loathsome', using a Hebrew word (*dêrâ'ôn*) only used elsewhere in Daniel 12:2 in a similar context. The contrast here is the

---

[19]The Textus Receptus adds the quotation twice more in this passage (verses 43 and 45), but they are lacking in important early Greek manuscripts.

same as is set out more fully in New Testament teaching. The Lord is coming 'to be glorified in his saints and to be admired among all those that believed', while 'those who do not obey the gospel of our Lord Jesus Christ ... will be punished with everlasting destruction from the presence of the Lord' (2 Thess. 1:8-10).

Subject Index

Persons Index

Scripture Index

Other books of interest in the *Focus on the Bible* series

Focus on the Bible

Deuteronomy

The Commands
of a covenant God

"who will look at the third commandment in quite the same way after reading Dr Harman's comments?"
Dale Ralph Davis

Allan Harman

Deuteronomy
The Commands of a Covenant God
Allan Harman

'Deuteronomy' is a misnomer, it means 'the second law'. The name is taken from Deuteronomy 17:18 where the expression really means having a *copy* of the law. Deuteronomy is therefore not a second, different, law but a renewal of the covenant made on Mount Sinai. For a people on the brink of entering their promised land Deuteronomy confirmed God's gracious promises as they prepared for new horizons and adventures.

Allan Harman shows the covenant structure of Deuteronomy throughout its 5 key sections

> Historical introduction (1:1 to 4:49)
> The Foundation of the Covenant Relationship (5:1 to 31)
> The Exposition of Ten Commandments (6:1 to 26:15)
> The Re-affirmation of the Covenant (27:1 to 30:20)
> The Continuation of the Covenant (31:1 to 34:12)

"Allan Harman's exposition is as clear as crystal... This is a work of fine scholarship lightly worn."
Geoffrey Grogan, International Christian College

"He keeps the connectedness of the text before us and yet can dash off to capture a Hebrew participle or suffix, pilfer a bit of Near Eastern background, or serve up the succinct result of a word study – all to light up a passage." **Dale Ralph Davis**

Allan Harman has recently retired from the posts of Principal and Professor of Old Testament at the Presbyterian Theological College in Melbourne Australia. He has taught graduate courses on Deuteronomy at Ontario Theological Seminary, Toronto and Reformed Theological Seminary, Jackson. Allan has also written a Mentor commentary on Psalms (ISBN 1 85792 1682)

ISBN 1 85792 665X

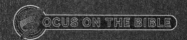

1 Chronicles

God's Faithfulness to the People of Judah

Cyril J. Barber

1st Chronicles
God's Faithfulness to the People of Judah
Cyril J. Barber

The book of Chronicles has had a chequered past.

Neglected for many years under the unfortunate name Paraleipomenon or 'Things Omitted', meant that they occupied a subordinate position in the scriptures until the 4th century AD when the title 'A Chronicle of the whole of Sacred History' was suggested instead. This has since been shortened to Chronicles and the rest is, literally, history.

Probably penned by Ezra, Chronicles is a selective history of the Jews encouraging them to trust that God is intimately involved in their story. Written at a time when the Jews were newly out of captivity and with their capital city in ruins, Chronicles assures them of God's faithfulness.

If they would obey and serve him then his people would still enjoy his blessing.

Cyril Barber has also written the Focus on the Bible commentary on 2nd Chronicles ISBN 1 85792 9365.

CYRIL J. BARBER has authored more than 30 books including 8 on Old Testament books of the Bible. He taught for over 25 years at Trinity Evangelical Divinity School, Talbot Theological Seminary and Trinity International University.

ISBN 1 85792 935 7

2 Chronicles

God's Blessing of
His Faithful People

Cyril J. Barber

2nd Chronicles
God's Blessing of His Faithful People
Cyril J. Barber

The book of Chronicles has had a chequered past.

Neglected for many years under the unfortunate name Paraleipomenon or 'Things Omitted', meant that they occupied a subordinate position in the scriptures until the 4th century AD when the title 'A Chronicle of the whole of Sacred History' was suggested instead. This has since been shortened to Chronicles and the rest is, literally, history.

Probably penned by Ezra, Chronicles is a selective history of the Jews encouraging them to trust that God is intimately involved in their story. Written at a time when the Jews were newly out of captivity and with their capital city in ruins, Chronicles assures them of God's faithfulness.

If they would obey and serve him then his people would still enjoy his blessing.

Cyril Barber has also written the Focus on the Bible commentary on 1st Chronicles ISBN 1 85792 9357.

CYRIL J. BARBER has authored more than 30 books including 8 on Old Testament books of the Bible. He taught for over 25 years at Trinity Evangelical Divinity School, Talbot Theological Seminary and Trinity International University.

ISBN 1 85792 936 5